The Politics of Nuclear Weapons

The Politics of Nuclear Weapons

Andrew Futter

Los Angeles | London | New Delhi
Singapore | Washington DC

Los Angeles | London | New Delhi
Singapore | Washington DC

SAGE Publications Ltd
1 Oliver's Yard
55 City Road
London EC1Y 1SP

SAGE Publications Inc.
2455 Teller Road
Thousand Oaks, California 91320

SAGE Publications India Pvt Ltd
B 1/I 1 Mohan Cooperative Industrial Area
Mathura Road
New Delhi 110 044

SAGE Publications Asia-Pacific Pte Ltd
3 Church Street
#10-04 Samsung Hub
Singapore 049483

Editor: Natalie Aguilera
Assistant editor: James Piper
Production editor: Victoria Nicholas
Copyeditor: Audrey Scriven
Proofreader: Neil Dowden
Indexer: Silvia Benvenuto
Marketing manager: Sally Ransom
Cover design: Jennifer Crisp
Typeset by: C&M Digitals (P) Ltd, Chennai, India
Printed in Great Britain by Henry Ling Limited at
The Dorset Press, Dorchester, DT1 1HD

MIX
Paper from
responsible sources
FSC™ C013985
www.fsc.org

Library of Congress Control Number: 2014945945

British Library Cataloguing in Publication data

A catalogue record for this book is available from
the British Library

ISBN 978-1-4462-9430-7
ISBN 978-1-4462-9431-4 (pbk)

At SAGE we take sustainability seriously. Most of our products are printed in the UK using FSC papers and boards.
When we print overseas we ensure sustainable papers are used as measured by the Egmont grading system.
We undertake an annual audit to monitor our sustainability.

CONTENTS

List of tables   viii
About the author   ix
Acknowledgements   x
Map – States with nuclear weapons   xi

Introduction   1

General introduction to the book   1
Central aims of the book   5
Pedagogical features   6
Key points and guide to further information and resources   10

1 What are nuclear weapons?   13

Uranium, plutonium and nuclear fission   14
Genesis of the bomb: from the Manhattan Project to the
Trinity Test   16
Little Boy and Fat Man: Hiroshima and Nagasaki   19
Atom bombs and hydrogen bombs: assessing destructive capacity   22
Key points and guide to further reading and resources   25

2 Testing, defining and delivering nuclear weapons   30

Nuclear testing   31
Radiation, contamination and fallout   34
Defining nuclear weapons   37
Different ways to deliver nuclear weapons   39
Who has what: current nuclear forces   42
Key points and guide to further reading and resources   44

**3 Nuclear proliferation: why states build or don't build
the bomb**   49

Different reasons for 'going nuclear'   50
Vertical and horizontal proliferation   54

The nuclear proliferation debate in the second nuclear age | 56
Nuclear latency and virtual nuclear arsenals | 60
Key points and guide to future reading and resources | 65

4 Nuclear strategy: understanding the MADness | 70

Nuclear deterrence and the security dilemma | 71
Mutual assured destruction (MAD) | 73
Posture, targeting and extended nuclear deterrence | 76
Escalation and nuclear war | 81
Key points and guide to further reading and resources | 86

5 Vertical proliferation challenges: assessing Article VI of the NPT | 89

Article VI and the commitment to disarmament | 90
The United States and the new triad | 93
Russia and great power status | 96
The United Kingdom and Trident replacement | 98
France and the *force de dissuasion* | 101
China and minimum deterrence | 102
Key points and guide to further reading and resources | 104

6 Horizontal proliferation challenges: the nuclear outliers | 110

Israel and nuclear opacity | 111
Pakistan, India and the challenge to stability in South Asia | 116
Dealing with a nuclear North Korea | 120
Future trajectories in the Iranian nuclear stand-off | 124
Key points and guide to further reading and resources | 128

7 Managing nuclear proliferation challenges: limiting, preventing and defending | 133

Limiting: negotiating nuclear arms control | 134
Preventing: the international non-proliferation regime | 140
Defending: active and passive defences | 146
Key points and guide to further reading and resources | 149

8 Nuclear weapons and new global actors | 154

Illicit nuclear trade and the A.Q. Khan network | 155
Nuclear terrorism | 159
How could terrorists acquire a bomb? How might terrorists use a bomb? | 162
Securing against nuclear terrorism | 164
Key points and guide to further reading resources | 167

CONTENTS

9 Nuclear disarmament   172

Historical attempts at disarmament   173
States that have given up the bomb   178
The spread of nuclear-weapon-free zones   181
The Global Zero agenda   182
Key points and guide to further reading and resources   186

10 Enduring nuclear challenges   191

The growing demand for civilian nuclear power   192
The command and control of nuclear forces   197
The nuclear taboo and the norm of non-use   204
Key points and guide to further reading and resources   208

Conclusion: surviving our nuclear future   211

Appendix 1: Nuclear weapons timeline   216
Appendix 2: Glossary of key terms and acronyms   223
Appendix 3: Countries with civilian nuclear power   234
Appendix 4: Nuclear weapons in fiction, film and TV   236
Bibliography   239
Index   255

TABLES

1 Current estimated global nuclear weapons stockpiles   3
2 Little Boy and Fat Man bombs compared   20
3 Estimated casualties and destruction from a nuclear blast   24
4 Number of nuclear tests by country   33
5 Strategic, non-strategic and battlefield weapons compared   38
6 Advantages and disadvantages of nuclear weapon delivery methods 41
7 Models of nuclear weapons acquisition   53
8 Nuclear proliferation   54
9 Horizontal versus vertical proliferation threats   56
10 The first and second nuclear ages compared   58
11 The proliferation debate   61
12 Different levels of nuclear deterrence   77
13 Counter-force and counter-value targeting   79
14 Possible scenarios for escalation to nuclear use   82
15 The debate over Article VI of the NPT   92
16 The debate over UK nuclear weapons   100
17 Costs and benefits of Israeli nuclear policy   115
18 Assessing the North Korean nuclear threat   124
19 Key Cold War bilateral arms control treaties   137
20 Post-Cold War bilateral arms control agreements   137
21 The Nuclear Non-Proliferation Treaty   142
22 Different views of the nuclear terrorism threat   161
23 Nuclear disarmament groups   177
24 Nuclear-weapons-free zones   182
25 Command and control of nuclear weapons   197
26 Selected nuclear weapons accidents   199
27 Examples of (selective) nuclear non-use   207

ABOUT THE AUTHOR

Andrew Futter is a Senior Lecturer in International Politics at the University of Leicester, UK. He is the author of *Ballistic Missile Defence and US National Security Policy* (2013), and has published widely on nuclear strategy, nuclear proliferation and contemporary nuclear challenges. He is an Honorary Fellow at the Institute for Conflict, Cooperation and Security at the University of Birmingham, a member of the Euro-Atlantic Security Initiative run by the Carnegie Endowment for International Peace and the co-convenor of the BISA Global Nuclear Order working group.

ACKNOWLEDGEMENTS

There are many people to thank in putting this book together, but particular mention must be made of Wyn Bowen, Stephen Cimbala, Oliver Daddow, James Davidson, David Dunn, Stephen Ellis, Tom Fretwell, Nicola Horsburgh, Michael McNally, Jamie Missing, Jonna Nyman, Mark Phythian, Nick Ritchie, Nick Wheeler, Arn Wilkins, Heather Williams and Ben Zala, as well as the useful comments from the various anonymous reviewers, and Natalie Aguilera and James Piper at SAGE. Above all this work would not have been possible without the support and guidance of Jon Moran, and of my mum Alison and brother Jack.

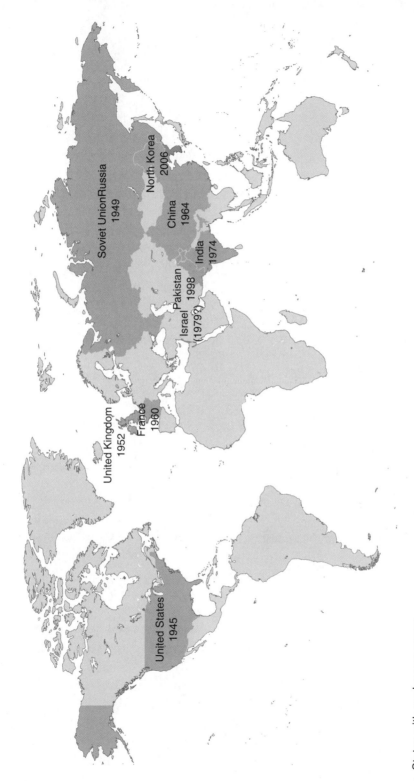

Soviet Union/Russia
1949

North Korea
2006

China
1964

India
1974

Pakistan
1998

Israel
(1979?)

United Kingdom
1952

France
1960

United States
1945

States with nuclear weapons

INTRODUCTION

General introduction to the book

Central aims of the book

Pedagogical features

Outline of the book

Key points and guide to further information and resources

(1) General introduction to the book

Seven decades since their first and only use in war in August 1945, nuclear weapons remain as central to international security in the modern world as they have ever been. The detonation of just one of the approximately 16,300 warheads that exist today[1] would cause considerable destruction to any large modern city, and even a very limited nuclear exchange could risk the destruction of entire societies. Indeed, some scientists suggest that the use of nuclear weapons could lead to a nuclear winter where the world might suffer years of freezing temperatures due to the enormous amount of radioactive fallout released into the atmosphere, and where all life forms would struggle to survive.[2] Others suggest that a nuclear war could cause human society to return to the Stone Age, or even end the human race entirely. In the words of Joseph Nye:

> The prospect of a nuclear war is horrifying. It brings us face to face not only with death, but with destruction of the civilization that makes our life meaningful. It might even destroy our species. There is no precedent for the challenge that nuclear weapons present to our physical and moral lives.[3]

The need to avoid this catastrophic scenario is clear enough for all to see.

While the threat of nuclear war has undoubtedly receded since the darkest days of the bipolar Cold War (1945–1991) between East and West, the potential for devastating nuclear use either accidentally – by one of the nine states that currently possess nuclear weapons – or deliberately – most likely by new emerging global actors such as an international terrorist group, but also possibly by current nuclear armed states – remains. This is particularly significant given the fact that most nuclear warheads today are appreciably more powerful, accurate and sophisticated than the two that were used against Japan in the final days of the Second World War, and because a large number can be launched with just a few minutes notice. Despite advances in nuclear safety and security precautions, air and missile defence technologies and the growth of a nuclear taboo and norm of non-use, it is important to note that no foolproof defence against nuclear attack exists. It is also equally important to note that just because nuclear weapons have only been used twice many decades ago, this does not mean that they will not be used in the future. Indeed, some commentators have suggested that the only way to prevent future nuclear use is to rid the world of these weapons entirely.

Since 1945, eight nations have openly acquired and retained a nuclear weapons capability (the USA, Russia, the UK, France, China, India, Pakistan and North Korea); Israel is widely believed to have nuclear weapons – although does not publicly admit this – while a handful of others have acquired the bomb and given it up or been persuaded or forced to curtail their nuclear weapons programmes through diplomacy or force. The first five states to acquire nuclear weapons are all signatories to the 1968 Treaty on the Non-Proliferation of Nuclear Weapons, or Non-Proliferation Treaty (NPT), which recognises these powers as nuclear-weapon states (NWS) that can legally possess nuclear weapons now but must concurrently take steps towards the goal of global nuclear disarmament, while India, Pakistan, North Korea (which left the NPT in 2003) and Israel, are not legally recognised as such by the treaty (and can never, under its current format, become recognised NWS). This is because they all developed nuclear weapons after the NPT was agreed.

The fact that so few states have chosen to acquire nuclear weapons in the past has been seen by many as a considerable achievement – the majority of states have acceded to the NPT as non-nuclear-weapon states (NNWS), and there are large parts of the globe where there are no nuclear weapons at all (notably in the southern hemisphere). This number includes several states that have had nuclear weapons research programmes but decided to cancel them (Argentina, Brazil, Egypt, Libya, South Korea, Sweden, Switzerland, Taiwan); Iraq and Syria that have been forcibly prevented from pursuing nuclear weapons; the former Soviet Republics of Belarus, Kazakhstan and Ukraine that gave up the nuclear weapons based on their soil after the Soviet Union collapsed in 1991; and the unique case of South Africa, which dismantled its nuclear weapons for internal political reasons in the early 1990s. North Korea, which tested its first nuclear weapon in 2006 after decades spent seeking such a capability, is the only state to have left the treaty, under Article X, in 2003.

At the time of writing Iran does not possess a nuclear weapon, is still a member of the NPT, but *might* be moving into a position where it *could* build a bomb.

Although nine states currently possess nuclear weapons, the vast majority of these (over 90 per cent) are owned and operated by the United States and Russia (see Table 1). This is primarily the result of the Cold War nuclear arms race, which at its nadir saw nuclear weapons stockpiles soar to a total of over 70,000 – many of which were held on hair-trigger alert, and many of which were significantly more powerful than the bombs dropped on Hiroshima and Nagasaki in 1945. As of August 2014, it is estimated that the UK, France and China all have between 200–300 nuclear warheads, India and Pakistan (and Israel) between 80–120 each, and North Korea probably less than 10.[4] In addition to this, approximately 200 free-fall nuclear bombs are currently stationed at US military bases in Europe (in Belgium, Germany, Italy, the Netherlands and Turkey) under the North Atlantic Treaty Organization (NATO) nuclear sharing agreement[5] – no other nation currently deploys nuclear weapons on another state's territory. Current estimated global nuclear stockpiles are shown in Table 1.

The overall total indicated in Table 1 includes nuclear weapons held in reserve and those awaiting decommissioning/dismantlement – therefore the

Table 1 Current estimated global nuclear weapons stockpiles[i]

	Date of First Nuclear Weapons Test	Location of First Test	Estimated Nuclear Warhead Stockpile
United States	16 July 1945	White Sands Proving Ground, New Mexico	7,300
Soviet Union/ Russia	29 August 1949	Semipalatinsk, Kazakhstan	8,000
United Kingdom	3 October 1952	Montebello Islands, Australia	225
France	13 February 1960	Sahara Desert, Algeria	300
China	16 October 1964	Lop Nur Test Base, Xinjiang	250
India	18 May 1974[ii]	Pokhran Test Range, Rajasthan	100
Pakistan	28 May 1998	Ras Koh Hills, Balochistan	120
North Korea	9 October 2006	Punggye-ri Nuclear Test Site, North Hamgyong	Less than 10
(Israel)	(1979?)	(Indian Ocean)	(Estimated 80)
Total			Approximately ~16,300

[i] Based on the Ploughshares Fund, 'World Nuclear Stockpile Report', updated 28 August 2014, available at http://ploughshares.org/world-nuclear-stockpile-report.
[ii] India's 1974 test was labelled as a 'peaceful nuclear test' – its first overt weapons test came in 1998 (see Chapter 6).

actual number of weapons ready to be used at short notice (those currently deployed or that could be deployed quickly in a crisis) is in fact actually far lower. Under the 2010 New Strategic Arms Reduction Treaty (New START), for example, the United States and Russia have agreed to *deploy* no more than 1,550 *strategic nuclear warheads* (long-range and high yield) each by 2018, although this agreement does not directly address the number of weapons held overall by either party.

Producing these stockpiles has involved a substantial amount of nuclear testing, some ostensibly for civilian non-military purposes, but the majority in search of bigger and more powerful bombs. Over 2,000 nuclear devices have been exploded since 1945 (the vast majority by the USA and the Soviet Union/Russia), and these tests have been conducted on land, at sea, underground, above ground, in the atmosphere and even in space. The result is that certain areas of the globe are now uninhabitable, and while we cannot be sure of the exact human and environmental cost of these tests, an enormous amount of radioactive material has been released into the global ecosystem – a large proportion of which will say active for hundreds of years – and many people have become seriously ill or have died as a result. Since 1996, the Comprehensive Test Ban Treaty (CTBT) has sought to ban all nuclear testing, but this has yet to enter force.

In addition to the nine states that possess nuclear weapons, civilian nuclear power plants are operated in more than 30 countries across the globe (see Appendix 3) – which (due to the links in technological requirements and processes) gives many of these states a tacit nuclear weapons capability should they decide to pursue the path towards weaponisation. The right to civilian nuclear power is a central part of the 1968 NPT, and seems set to become increasingly important for future domestic energy requirements as access to fossil fuels becomes more difficult and costly. It is the close links between civilian nuclear energy and a threshold, latent or virtual nuclear weapons capability that has driven the current stand-off between the international community and Iran, and that is a source of possible future concern about some notable others. The spread of civilian nuclear technology has also led to increased fear of nuclear accidents, such as those at Three Mile Island (USA) in 1979, Chernobyl (Ukraine) in 1986 and more recently at Fukushima (Japan) in 2011.

While most states view nuclear weapons as a deterrent (through a condition of mutual assured destruction or MAD) – and something which should only be used to deter aggressive actions by another state and not as a weapon of war – the potential for accidental use remains (particularly by less stable nuclear capable states), and in a worst case scenario the deliberate use by either a state or by a third party. Moreover, while MAD has been credited by many with keeping the peace in the nuclear world since 1945 – essentially because any nuclear use against another nuclear-armed state would be suicidal – the debate is split over just how important MAD has actually been, and whether the lack of nuclear use might better be explained simply by luck. The 1962 Cuban Missile Crisis in particular is just one example of how close the USA and the Soviet Union came to using nuclear weapons during the Cold War, and history is littered with many other troubling examples and near misses – most recently the Indo-Pakistani Kargil War of 1999. Moreover, the spectre of a non-state group acquiring and using nuclear weapons threatens to undermine many of the axioms that have governed our nuclear past entirely. Nevertheless, nuclear deterrence and the threat of nuclear retaliation remain the bedrock of nuclear strategy for all nuclear weapons powers in the twenty-first century.

The result is that nuclear weapons and efforts to prevent their use remain as central to our everyday lives as at any point since 1945. As Rudolph Herzog explains:

> The end of the Cold War brought with it new feelings of disinterested distance. People are beginning to forget the popular fears of nuclear war and total destruction from a bygone epoch. But the new sense of security among many in the West is misleading. The experiments of the Atomic Age continue to affect the world today, and many of the old problems have actually gotten worse.[6]

The fact that nuclear weapons have not been used since 1945 should not be taken as proof that they will not be used again in the future; in fact, the law of averages and the concept of 'normal accidents'[7] suggests that every year that passes may make nuclear use more likely. This book is therefore intended not only as an introductory guide to the subject, but also as a wake-up call.

(2) Central aims of the book

Given the potential for disaster inherent in the acquisition and maintenance of large nuclear stockpiles across the globe, it is essential that we understand the concepts, dynamics and debate that surround nuclear weapons. With this in mind, the book has been designed as an introductory guide – a starting point for those wishing to familiarise themselves with the fundamentals of nuclear weapons and nuclear strategy – and therefore also as both a springboard and conduit towards further and more specialised readings and understanding. It has been written in such a way so as to be of equal use to advanced undergraduate and postgraduate students interested in the subject from an academic perspective, as well as a guide for those involved with nuclear weapons issues in a professional context, and who require a 'way in' to what can often be a highly complex and contested subject. The book therefore has six main aims:

1. to provide a historical background and context to the role of nuclear weapons in international security;
2. to introduce the political, scientific/technological and strategic aspects of nuclear weapons;
3. to highlight the main controversies and debates surrounding nuclear weapons facing policymakers and analysts today;
4. to give readers a solid basis from which to think about and ultimately address the challenges that will shape our nuclear future;
5. to offer a link to further information and resources on specific aspects of nuclear politics and strategy;
6. to produce a guide that can be equally useful to those embarking upon academic study or professional careers in the field of nuclear politics and nuclear strategy.

In order to achieve this, the book has five main objectives: to explain the basic science and principles behind nuclear weaponry; to introduce the conceptual models and thinking which underpin nuclear strategy; to highlight the ever-increasing range of contemporary nuclear threats we face; to consider the relative merits of different options available to control the threat of nuclear weapons; and to begin to think about how we go about securing our global nuclear future.

Finally, it must be noted that the book does not seek to advance a particular agenda – it is neither a defence of current thinking nor a call for radical change; instead, its purpose is to provide the information and skill sets necessary for readers to make these decisions for themselves. In many ways there are no right and wrong answers when it comes to nuclear weapons, only ones that work, but we can certainly increase our future nuclear prospects if we raise the level of knowledge and understanding that informs these decisions and debates. Whether the world can survive the next century without suffering the catastrophic effects of some type of nuclear use may well depend on this.

(3) Pedagogical features

This book has been designed specifically to be of interest and use to those beginning their journey into the murky world of nuclear weapons and nuclear strategy, whether you come from an advanced undergraduate or postgraduate academic background, a professional or political background, or just have a general interest in the subject. It is the intention that those new to the topic will be able to use it as a stepping-stone and launch pad towards the more specialised, specific and complex works that exist, and for those already more familiar with the literature, as a resource that can be referred back to and dipped in and out of as and when required. With this in mind, the book contains a number of features designed to help facilitate learning:

- Each key concept introduced in the text will be explained in more detail in the *Glossary* at the back of the book, providing explanations for the many acronyms and terms that are used in the field.
- In order to highlight key points, each chapter in the book finishes with a summary of the *Key Points* related to that specific topic.
- Each chapter also contains a section *detailing links to further specialised readings* on the subjects covered. These include not only books and articles but also various organisations and professional resources dedicated to these specific aspects of global nuclear politics.
- At the back of the book, a *detailed timeline* has been included referencing the major developments in nuclear weapons and nuclear strategy up to the present day. This is a great way to understand how global nuclear politics has developed.
- Also included at the back of the book are two further appendices providing information on *civilian nuclear power capabilities* worldwide and links to resources relating to *nuclear weapons in fiction, film and TV*.
- The book is accompanied by a *webpage* (https://study.sagepub.com/futter) providing access to journal articles published by SAGE, key online materials and resources, and a selection of questions for class discussion, revision and/ or mock exam practice.

In addition to these pedagogical features, the book also contains numerous tables to help facilitate understanding of key aspects of each topic.

(4) Outline of the book

The book is primarily designed to be thematic – covering different aspects of the politics of nuclear weapons – but it is also implicitly chronological – beginning with the basic science behind the bomb, early nuclear thinking and the development of nuclear strategy, before examining the new nuclear dynamics that characterise the post-Cold War second nuclear age, and outlining the set of key future nuclear challenges. In this way, it can be read either all-in-one-go, or specific chapters can be read individually as and when these are required for preparation, revision, essays or general interest. In this way, you as the reader do not necessarily need to read the whole book in one go, although if you are new to the subject you may find it useful to build your knowledge in the manner set out in the book.

Chapter 1 provides you with a grounding in the basic science of nuclear weapons, how they work, and the damage they are capable of causing both to us as humans and also to the environment. First and foremost, you are given an introduction to the basic science or 'what makes them go bang', including an explanation of nuclear fission, and the importance of uranium and plutonium for a nuclear explosion. Thereafter, the Second World War race to master nuclear technology and the Manhattan Project are covered, as are the only wartime use of nuclear weapons on Hiroshima and Nagasaki in August 1945, and the effect the two nuclear detonations had on these cities. Finally, the chapter looks at the differences between atom bombs and hydrogen bombs and begins to give you an idea of the destructive capacity of these weapons should they ever be used again.

In Chapter 2 the analysis is widened to look at atomic testing, radiation and contamination, the different classifications of nuclear weapons and finally a detailed overview of which states currently have what. The chapter begins by investigating the impact of nuclear tests that have taken place since 1945, and how testing has driven the development of more powerful and more sophisticated nuclear weapons. It then examines the impact of radiation, contamination and nuclear fallout that has resulted from testing, and looks closely at past incidents where humans have been deliberately and accidentally exposed to the effects of a nuclear blast. Following this, the chapter seeks to demystify the often-complex nuclear nomenclature or 'jargon' by addressing the somewhat hazy distinctions between 'strategic', 'non-strategic', 'tactical' and 'theatre' nuclear weapons, and the types of missions these munitions might be used for. Next, the chapter looks at how these diverse nuclear devices can be delivered to their target, and considers the relative strengths and weaknesses of various methods for using nuclear weaponry. Lastly, the chapter provides an approximate overview of the current capabilities of the nine states with nuclear weapons.

Chapter 3 turns its attention to nuclear proliferation and to why some states have chosen to build the bomb while others have not, before introducing the concept of nuclear latency. The first part of this chapter looks at different models to explain nuclear acquisition – in particular the security/politics/culture framework and the idea of technological determinism – and equally, why some states have chosen not to acquire nuclear weapons, or indeed, even given up nascent nuclear weapons programmes before building the bomb. Second, the chapter examines the challenges presented by the vertical and horizontal proliferation of nuclear weapons over the last six decades, and at how the number of weapons and number of actors has changed over this time-period, before explaining the proliferation debate between optimists and pessimists that has become embodied by political scientists Kenneth Waltz and Scott Sagan. Finally, it considers the concept of nuclear latency whereby some states can achieve a position where they could – if desired or required to – transform a civilian nuclear capability into a weaponised one in a relatively short period of time.

Chapter 4 looks at how thinking about nuclear weapons and nuclear strategy developed after 1945, and how we came to embrace notions of MAD and nuclear deterrence as central aspects of global politics. The chapter also looks at the importance of the security dilemma as a driver of the nuclear arms race, from debates over first nuclear use and assured second strike capability, through to the logic of mutual vulnerability to nuclear attack codified in the 1972 Anti-Ballistic Missile (ABM) Treaty between the United States and the Soviet Union. It explains the reasons for different nuclear postures and the nuances of nuclear targeting strategy as well as the development and logic of extended nuclear deterrence. Lastly, it looks at the notions of escalation and nuclear war, and examines four cases where the world appeared to stand on the brink of disaster: the 1962 Cuban Missile Crisis, Able Archer in 1983, and the more recent 1995 Norwegian Rocket Incident and 1999 Kargil War between nuclear-armed India and Pakistan.

In Chapter 5, the current nuclear thinking of the so-called P5 states – those recognised as legally possessing nuclear weapons by the NPT – is analysed. To begin with, the chapter considers the complications inherent in the commitment to nuclear disarmament made by the five declared NWS, before looking at the more recent P5 process, whereby these states have begun to address the issue of nuclear disarmament as a result of increasing international pressure. The chapter then outlines US, Russian, UK, French and Chinese nuclear thinking and doctrine, and the debates and dynamics which continue to underpin their respective nuclear weapons programmes, before considering some of the main hurdles and problems that will have to be addressed for those states to reduce and possibly relinquish entirely their nuclear capabilities in the future as they are required to under Article VI of the NPT.

The main aim of Chapter 6 is to analyse the new (and some would argue, growing) challenges posed by the post-Cold War horizontal proliferation of nuclear weapons to new nation-state actors. First, it turns to Israel and the peculiar case of nuclear opacity, whereby Israel neither confirms nor denies the possession of nuclear weapons. Second, it examines the nuclear rivalry between India and Pakistan and the challenge this is presenting to stability in South Asia. Third, the chapter looks at North Korea and at whether the world's newest nuclear-armed state can be contained and safely managed, before finally analysing the current debate over the latest aspirant nuclear power, Iran.

In Chapter 7 attention is turned to the options available to manage and counter nuclear threats, and to the costs and benefits of these various strategies. First, the chapter considers the relative merits and successes of nuclear arms control as a means to mitigate and moderate nuclear threats, and details key arms control agreements that have been achieved in the past. Next, it examines the role of the NPT and the various means and mechanisms available to enforce the global non-proliferation regime, including the International Atomic Energy Agency (IAEA), economic sanctions, and threat and use of military force. It concludes by considering the role of active and passive defences as a means to ensure against nuclear attack, with particular focus on the role of ballistic missile defence (BMD) and civil defence.

Chapter 8 addresses what many believe to be the most pressing contemporary nuclear challenge – that of new global actors (such as terrorists) and the threat that they may acquire and use nuclear weapons. First, the chapter sets the stage by looking at the threat of illicit nuclear trafficking and at the damage caused by the A.Q. Khan Network, and explains why such organisations remain a serious global concern. It then goes on to examine the concept of nuclear terrorism in detail by outlining the diverse nature of the threat, its seriousness, the groups of most concern, and how terrorists might seek to use a nuclear weapon – before considering some of the active and more passive measures that are and can be taken to reduce this threat, such as the nuclear security agenda, interdiction, enhanced export controls and a Fissile Material Cut-off Treaty (FMCT).

Chapter 9 examines the debates surrounding nuclear abolition and the possibility of achieving a nuclear world that is free of nuclear weapons. First, it explains the three phases of the global nuclear disarmament movement, and how and why nations have denuclearised in the past, or chosen not to take the final step towards acquiring a nuclear weapons capability. Second the chapter focuses on the spread of nuclear-weapon-free zones (NWFZs), and shows how large areas of the world are currently nuclear weapons-free. Finally, the chapter assesses both the feasibility and desirability of a world free of nuclear weapons. Recent developments, such as Barack Obama's Prague and Berlin speeches, the International Campaign to Abolish Nuclear Weapons (ICAN) and the Global Zero movement, are placed in their historical context alongside previous and more established groups seeking nuclear elimination, such as the Campaign for Nuclear Disarmament (CND), the Greenham Common protesters and the Nuclear Freeze.

The penultimate chapter of the book, Chapter 10 considers three key enduring nuclear challenges that will shape our nuclear future: how to safely and securely manage the proliferation of civilian nuclear power generation capabilities – including nuclear security, weapons proliferation and waste management – without undermining international security; how to ensure the safe command and control of military nuclear forces, and in particular, guard against accidents and unauthorised or third party use; and, finally, whether the nuclear taboo and norm of non-nuclear use can continue to hold as we move further into the twenty-first century.

The final chapter, the Conclusion, reflects on some of the lessons learnt from our nuclear past and assesses some of the key challenges that we will face as we go about securing our nuclear future in what has become popularly termed a second nuclear age.

(5) Key points and guide to further information and resources

This chapter has sought to provide you with a basic introduction to the book, but also to outline some fundamentals of the nuclear weapons enterprise. A summary of these key points is as follows:

1. Nuclear weapons are considered as being different from other weapons due to their enormous destructive capacity. Just one bomb could destroy a large modern city. A nuclear exchange could mean the end of life as we know it.
2. According to recent figures, there are approximately 16,300 nuclear warheads in the world, although not all of these are ready to be used, and many are awaiting decommissioning. The majority of these weapons are held by the USA and Russia.
3. Eight countries have officially tested nuclear weapons – the USA, Russia, the UK, France, China, India, Pakistan, North Korea – and Israel is widely believed to have a nuclear weapons capability. Only five of these countries – the USA, Russia, the UK, France and China – are legally recognised as NWS by the 1968 NPT. Iran does not currently have nuclear weapons.
4. Large parts of the globe – notably the southern hemisphere – contain no nuclear weapons, and some areas are part of regional NWFZs.
5. Many more countries have civilian nuclear power plants and associated industry, which at least theoretically gives them the possibility of building a nuclear weapon should they choose to.
6. Despite progress in many different areas, there is no foolproof defence against nuclear weapons.

Discussion and debate about nuclear weapons spans an increasingly wide range of media, institutions and genres, and this is reflected in the enormous – and ever expanding – amount of information available on the subject. While those new to the subject are advised to begin with this introductory book, the potential for broader research and information is vast – as is demonstrated by the tailored research guides at the end of each chapter of the book. A good mix of books, academic journals and periodicals, official documents and work produced by think tanks, combined with the material available from a number of real-time and internet-based news sources, is recommended as a solid basis for understanding. Equally, at the back of the book is an appendix providing details of numerous links to nuclear weapons in popular culture, which can also be a great way to learn.

Notes

1. This is the number given by the Ploughshares Fund in their 2014 'World Nuclear Stockpile Report', updated 28 August 2014, and available at http://ploughshares.org/world-nuclear-stockpile-report.

2. On this see Carl Sagan, 'Nuclear winter and climatic catastrophe: some policy implications', Foreign Affairs, 62:2 (Winter 1983–4) pp.257–292.
3. Joseph Nye, 'Nuclear ethics', (London, Collier Macmillan Publishers: 1988) p.ix.
4. Numbers courtesy of the Ploughshares Fund in their 2014 'World Nuclear Stockpile Report', updated 28 August 2014, available at http://ploughshares.org/world-nuclear-stockpile-report.
5. See Robert Norris and Hans Kristensen, 'US tactical nuclear weapons in Europe, 2011', Bulletin of the Atomic Scientists, 67:1 (2011) pp.64–73.
6. Rudolph Herzog, 'A short history of nuclear folly', (London: Melville House: 2013) pp.4–5.
7. On the concept of normal accidents see Charles Perrow, 'Normal accidents: living with high-risk technologies', (Princeton N.J., Princeton University Press: 1999).

1

WHAT ARE NUCLEAR WEAPONS?

Uranium, plutonium and nuclear fission

Genesis of the bomb: from the Manhattan Project to the Trinity Test

Little Boy and Fat Man: Hiroshima and Nagasaki

Atom bombs and hydrogen bombs: assessing destructive capacity

Key points and guide to further reading and resources

While most people probably have a general understanding of nuclear weapons – primarily that they are highly destructive, and that they were used against Japan at the end of the Second World War – why they are so powerful or, indeed, just how powerful they are, is often far less understood. As a result, and although this book is not intended as a comprehensive scientific and technological analysis, before we can begin to think about many of the political and strategic aspects of nuclear weapons, it is useful to get a better idea of the basic science. Essentially, we must be clear exactly how, why and with what consequences nuclear weapons go bang.

With this in mind, the chapter proceeds in four sections: the first introduces the key ingredients needed for a nuclear bomb, and explains why the elements uranium and plutonium can be used to produce an explosion; the second section chronicles the race to build the first atomic bomb during the 1930s and 1940s, provides an overview of the Manhattan Project and culminates with the Trinity Test conducted by the United States in 1945; the third looks closely at the only time that nuclear weapons have been used in war – by the United States against Hiroshima and Nagasaki in August 1945 – and at the effects that just two atomic bombs had on those Japanese cities; finally, the chapter examines the differences between atom bombs and hydrogen bombs, and begins to give an idea of just how destructive nuclear weapons can be. It then finishes with a summary of key points and a guide to further reading and resources.

(1) Uranium, plutonium and nuclear fission

While nuclear science may appear a daunting place to begin an understanding of the politics of nuclear weapons, it is nevertheless fundamental in order to appreciate the political debates that surround their acquisition, use, management and possible eradication. Therefore, as a scholar of nuclear politics and nuclear strategy, it is essential that you understand a few basics of how and why a nuclear bomb works. Specifically, it is important to know: (1) how a nuclear explosion works; (2) what ingredients you need for a nuclear bomb; (3) how this necessary material can be acquired; and (4) why a nuclear weapon produces so much power.

Everything in the world is made up of tiny atoms; these atoms are made up of a nucleus (containing protons and neutrons) and electrons that surround the nucleus. A nuclear explosion results when the nucleus of an atom of an unstable isotope of a particular chemical element (chemical elements can have different isotopes, with different numbers of neutrons) is bombarded with extra neutrons, causing the atom to split or fission. As a result of this split, the nucleus – which has been destabilised by the extra neutron(s) – is forced to emit neutrons to retain its atomic balance. If enough of these atoms are placed together (known as the critical mass) they can produce a nuclear chain reaction, whereby the neutrons emitted from atom A bombard atom B, thereby causing atom B to fission and emit further neutrons which may bombard atom C and possibly D – with enough material this reaction can become self-sustaining. Most importantly, each individual 'fission' of the atom produces a vast amount of energy, primarily as heat. If this is done in a controlled manner a steady stream of energy can be produced by using the heat to drive steam turbines – such as in a civilian nuclear power station or nuclear-powered submarine – but if it is done rapidly the energy released can be used to produce an enormous explosion. As a result, the first major challenge in making a nuclear bomb is how to control the nuclear reaction taking place within and between the atoms of a particular element, and then maximise the energy produced: if the reaction is too slow, the heat generated will mean that much of the fissile material (the particular chemical isotope) will be burnt/melt/blown apart before it can fission, which will minimise the energy released and therefore the power of the explosion.

There are only two (known) chemical substances that can be used to make a nuclear bomb: the naturally occurring element uranium 235 (U235); and the predominantly man-made element plutonium 239 (PU239) (a tiny amount of plutonium 239 exists naturally in nature, but not enough to build a bomb).

These are referred to as 'fissile materials' due to their ability to fission and sustain a nuclear chain reaction. However, while uranium is a naturally occurring element found in small quantities in certain areas of the world (over a quarter of natural uranium deposits are in Australia), only a very small percentage of this is the isotope U235 (which is fissile), while over 99 per cent of natural uranium consists of the isotope U238 which is not fissile (i.e. it cannot be used to make a bomb). As a result, to create enough U235 to make a bomb, very large quantities of uranium are needed, and the U235 isotope must be separated from the heavier element U238 and then continually refined (this is a process known as uranium enrichment). This cannot be done chemically (due to the similarities of various elements of uranium), so the enrichment must be achieved by other means. The preferred method to achieve this is to use fast-spinning centrifuges, which separate the elements by minute differences in their atomic weight through gravity or diffusion.[1] More recently, however, scientists have begun to experiment with using lasers to separate uranium isotopes.[2] Separating the different isotopes of uranium to purify U235 is an enormous scientific and engineering task – and is arguably the biggest hurdle to any actor seeking to build a nuclear device.

Only minuscule amounts of plutonium 239 exist naturally in the world, and therefore the quantities required to build a bomb have to be created. The only way to produce plutonium is through a nuclear reaction of uranium – plutonium is a by-product of uranium fission – and therefore any plutonium bomb can only be derived from uranium. However, the plutonium must still be separated from the other waste products through various chemical reactions (a process known as plutonium separation).[3] Of course, producing plutonium therefore requires the production/acquisition of enough enriched uranium to fuel a nuclear reactor in the first place, and the uranium used in producing plutonium cannot itself be used in a bomb (although certain other nuclear waste products can be reprocessed for use in a power reactor – see Chapter 10).

These two elements, as well as uranium 233 (U233), can also be used to fuel civilian nuclear reactors for domestic energy requirements. For civilian nuclear power purposes the uranium 235 need only be enriched to around 5 per cent purity (known as low-enriched uranium (LEU)) as opposed to the 80–90 per cent highly enriched uranium (HEU) needed for a bomb – this is due to the relative amount of energy produced by the chain reaction. Uranium can also be enriched to around 20 per cent U235 for certain medical purposes, and between 20 and 50 per cent for use in nuclear-powered submarines and ships. The technology and processes required to produce nuclear energy for peaceful purposes and those required to build a nuclear bomb are broadly the same. As a result, any country with a civilian nuclear power reactor and the right technology could theoretically enrich uranium beyond the level needed for civilian purposes or separate the plutonium produced by a reactor for a bomb (for more on this link see Chapters 3 and 10). Weapons-grade plutonium can be produced at the same time as civilian nuclear energy from a reactor with the right technology, and this is part of the reason why plutonium rather than uranium is often used in nuclear weapons (it also has a much smaller critical mass).

A nuclear bomb draws its immense power from the energy contained in an atom of a particle of a fissile chemical isotope (U235 or PU239), and the basic science of a nuclear bomb is derived from Albert Einstein's famous maxim that energy equals mass multiplied by a constant (the speed of light) – more popularly known as $E = mc^2$.[4] While Einstein did not invent the nuclear bomb, his assertion that large chemical elements with a heavy atomic mass must contain enormous amounts of stored energy paved the way for the generation of scientists that followed to think about how this stored energy could be released and how it could be used, first as a means of generating civilian nuclear power, but also more ominously as a very powerful weapon. Uranium and plutonium are both heavy elements, and feature towards the bottom of the periodic table.

Consequently, and while the advances in physics and mathematics that led to the development of nuclear weapons were revolutionary and ground-breaking, the basic science behind an atomic bomb is relatively straightforward if you have the right materials, know-how and technology. Essentially, you need a certain amount of fissile material (the critical mass), a mechanism to initiate and manage a nuclear reaction (i.e. a way to start the process, and ensure that it happens at the right time), and a means of delivering the weapon to the intended target – such as a ballistic missile, aircraft, or simply a suitable container (for more on this see Chapter 2). Of these components, acquiring the necessary fissile material for a nuclear device is arguably the most challenging aspect as around 40kg of HEU are needed for a single crude uranium-based bomb – a sizeable task given the difficulties of extracting this from the far more prevalent U238. Equally, and while just several kilograms of PU239 are needed for a crude bomb, this must be separated from other waste products following a uranium-based nuclear reaction.[5]

(2) Genesis of the bomb: from the Manhattan Project to the Trinity Test

The nuclear bomb has its genesis in two revolutionary scientific discoveries of the early twentieth century: the first was Albert Einstein's Theory of Special Relativity in 1905 ($E = mc^2$ – explained above); the second was the discovery of the atomic nucleus by Ernest Rutherford in 1911. Put together these discoveries paved the way for the possibility of a bomb with enormous destructive capacity. However, it was not until 1938 that German chemists Otto Hahn and Fritz Strassman observed that when uranium atoms were bombarded with neutrons, fission would often occur in the nucleus, causing more neutrons to be emitted, and a significant amount of energy to be released.[6] This process could be repeated so that a chain reaction was initiated whereby neutrons discharged by one atom would stimulate the next and so on, a process known as transmutation (the conversion of one chemical isotope into another). Each event would release a substantial amount of energy, meaning that a large amount of fissile uranium atoms placed together could produce enormous amounts of energy – potentially many thousands or even millions of times more powerful per atom than conventional dynamite or TNT.[7]

The findings published by Hahn and Strassman in 1938 meant that the theoretical potential of developing a nuclear bomb had now become a real possibility, and with the world seemingly on the brink of war, the race was on to master the challenge of nuclear fission and produce the first atomic weapons. Recognising the possibility that a potentially war-winning weapon could be developed by the Nazis, in August 1939 leading physicists Leo Szilard and Eugene Wigner drafted a letter to US President Franklin Roosevelt – signed and delivered by Albert Einstein – which warned against the possibility of a Nazi atomic bomb, and recommended the immediate establishment of a US atomic programme.[8] This would become known as the Einstein–Szilard letter, and would represent the beginning of the US atomic weapons effort. However, while the Nazi Uranverein Project to develop nuclear weapons began almost immediately (as did a small programme in the United Kingdom, known as Tube Alloys[9]) – in late August 1939 – it would be another two years before President Roosevelt would formally establish the US atomic programme. Evidence would later suggest that by this point Nazi nuclear research had almost ground to a halt – partly as a result of pressure for other war-winning resources, but also as a longer-term result of the mass exodus of leading scientists from Germany during the preceding years. Many of these scientists took refuge in the USA and UK, and many would go on to work on the American nuclear weapons programme both during and after the Second World War. The scientists that remained in Germany were highly sought after prizes for both East and West as the war came to an end in 1945, and the debate continues about just how close the Nazis came to developing a nuclear weapon during the Second World War.[10]

The Manhattan Project – so called because the initial headquarters were in the Manhattan district of New York City[11] – began in 1942 with the sole purpose of creating an atomic bomb before Nazi Germany (Imperial Japan had a nuclear weapons research programme, but was not considered capable of building an atomic bomb in the short term[12]), and that might then be used to end the war. While the project was American-led and conducted in the United States, it was officially a joint effort with the United Kingdom and Canada, and scientists on the project came from a wide variety of countries, especially in continental Europe. The project was led by renowned scientist J. Robert Oppenheimer, and overseen by Major General Leslie Groves – an efficient and combative army engineer. Oppenheimer would lead the team to build the bomb while Groves would oversee the project and manage the security and logistics. Work was spread across numerous sites in the United States, with the main scientific and design effort being conducted at Los Alamos in the New Mexico desert, and the work to produce uranium and plutonium at Oak Ridge, Tennessee and Hanford, Washington. In all, some 129,000 people worked on the Manhattan Project between 1942 and 1945, although due to its compartmentalised structure the overall objectives of the programme remained secret from the US general public and even from many of the scientists involved.[13]

Two main lines of atomic bomb research were conducted as part of the Manhattan Project, and while both had been shown to be theoretically possible, they also presented numerous practical challenges. The first line of research was into a uranium bomb – a concept that had been proven as scientifically viable by Otto Frisch and Rudolf Peierls in 1938[14] – but this required an enormous industrial effort to separate the fissile U235 from the more prevalent isotope U238. Because natural uranium (when it is in ore form in the ground) is over 99 per cent U238, and because both isotopes have almost identical atomic properties, separating U235 presented a colossal task (as indeed it would be for future nuclear aspirants). The second line of research involved plutonium – which had only been first synthesised in 1940 – and this could only be produced through a nuclear reaction of uranium – uranium that therefore could not be used in a bomb. Both methods required vast amounts of uranium ore, and enormous facilities to process it. It is estimated that of the roughly $21 billion (in 1996 dollars) spent on the Manhattan Project, nearly 90 per cent went on producing the necessary fissile material.[15] It was due in part to these challenges that the Manhattan Project would prove to be one of the most expensive military programmes ever undertaken in history.

A second problem – once enough fissile material had been produced and collated – involved how to control the nuclear reaction so that the bomb would not explode prematurely or simply fizzle out. This was relatively straightforward for a uranium bomb whereby two subcritical pieces of U235 could be kept apart and then blasted together when needed, but far more complicated for the less stable plutonium. To make matters more difficult, while a uranium bomb was theoretically easier to control than a plutonium bomb, far more uranium was needed to achieve a critical mass than was required for a plutonium bomb, and the fissile uranium was harder to produce (see above). Eventually, scientists at Los Alamos came up with a spherical implosion-type device that would ensure that the plutonium did not begin a chain reaction until initiated.

The first test of a nuclear device, and the culmination of the Manhattan Project, occurred on 16 July 1945 at the White Sands Proving Ground in the Jornada Del Muerto desert in southern New Mexico. The test was conducted using plutonium, partly because the scientists felt so confident that a crude uranium gun-type device (explained below) would work, and also because they were less confident with regard to the implosion device. The bomb – nicknamed 'the gadget' – was hoisted to the top of a 30 metre-high tower to better reflect how it would behave when dropped from a bomber and exploded above the target (nuclear explosions have different effects if they are detonated above the target or on the ground). The Trinity Test, as it became known, was measured as being the equivalent of 20,000 tons of conventional explosive, or 20 kilotons – an amount roughly ten times the tonnage of conventional bombs dropped on Tokyo by 334 US heavy bombers in March 1945.[16] The shockwaves from the test were felt up to 100 miles away, and the never-before-seen mushroom cloud rose to a height of 7.5 miles.[17] J. Robert Oppenheimer would later memorably reflect on his feelings following the test by quoting an ancient Hindu script: 'Now I am become death, the destroyer of worlds.'[18]

The results of the Trinity Test were immediately sent to US President Harry Truman, who was attending a conference at Potsdam, Germany, with other Allied leaders to decide the fate of a post-war world (Truman had in fact being trying to postpone the conference until the bomb had been tested).[19] Buoyed by the results of the Trinity Test, Truman expedited plans to use the first atomic bombs against Japan in the Pacific if Tokyo did not agree to surrender immediately. As part of the 26 July Potsdam Declaration, Soviet leader Joseph Stalin agreed that the Soviet Union would enter the war against Japan in early August 1945, and some scholars would later suggest the bomb was dropped in part to prevent this.[20]

It would also later emerge that a number of scientists working on the Manhattan Project were passing key information on the nuclear programme back to the Soviet Union. Indeed, the rich material gleaned by these Soviet spies during the 1940s was a fundamental reason why the Soviet Union was able to produce its own atomic bomb so quickly (much to the surprise of the United States) in August 1949. The device, known as Joe 1, looked suspiciously like the Fat Man bomb developed by the United States in 1945. Two of these spies – Julius and Ethel Rosenberg – who were found guilty of coordinating the Soviet espionage network aimed at the US nuclear programme, were later executed in the United States.[21] Richard Rhodes wrote afterwards that 'Russian spies, not scientists, were chiefly responsible for breaking the American nuclear monopoly'.[22] Nuclear espionage would remain a central theme of the atomic age.[23]

(3) Little Boy and Fat Man: Hiroshima and Nagasaki

The Manhattan Project had initially been conceived as a hedge against Nazi Germany, but after Germany surrendered in May 1945, attention shifted towards how atomic weapons might help win the war against Japan in the Pacific. The United States had called for a Japanese surrender at the Potsdam conference of July 1945 (just days after being notified of the success of the Trinity Test), and had threatened 'prompt and utter destruction' if Japan failed to accede to their demands. The Japanese refused, and the first atomic bomb was dropped on Hiroshima on 6 August 1945. A second atomic bomb and was dropped on Nagasaki three days later.

The two devices used in August 1945 were very different. The first bomb, dropped on Hiroshima, and known as Little Boy – which weighed four tonnes and was over 3 metres in length – used 64.1kg of approximately 89 per cent enriched uranium 235.[24] This device had never been tested before, primarily because the scientists involved with its design were so certain that it would work. The initiation mechanism used was known as the 'gun type', whereby a subcritical piece of U235 would be fired at another subcritical piece of U235 to create the critical mass and therefore the explosion. A need to keep both pieces of U235 apart, as well as to generate sufficient speed for the reaction, necessitated a long and thin bomb design. The design was so crude that only a small amount of the fissile material was actually used up in the explosion (approximately 1.4 per cent efficiency[25]). The B-29 Superfortress *Enola Gay*, piloted by Colonel Paul Tibbets, dropped the Little Boy bomb on Hiroshima on 6 August 1945.[26] The Nagasaki bomb – referred to as Fat Man because of its shape – was very similar to the one tested at Alamogordo just a few weeks earlier. This second bomb weighed 4.6 tonnes and was 3 metres long and 1.5 metres in diameter. Unlike the Little Boy uranium bomb, Fat Man required just 6.2kg of plutonium to achieve critical mass.[27] However, because plutonium is less stable than uranium, a different mechanism was required to initiate the bomb – one whereby the reaction could be more carefully controlled. Fat Man was dropped on Nagasaki by the B-29 Superfortress *Bockscar* piloted by Major Charles Sweeney on 9 August 1945, although it was originally intended to be dropped on the city of Kokura (it was not dropped on Kokura due to cloud cover obscuring the target; Nagasaki was a secondary target). While the plutonium nuclear reaction was considerably more efficient than the uranium bomb, it still only used around 17 per cent of its full explosive potential.[28]

Table 2   Little Boy and Fat Man bombs compared

	Little Boy	Fat Man
Target	Hiroshima	Nagasaki (originally, Kokura)
Date	6 August 1945	9 August 1945
Fissile material	64.1kg of enriched Uranium 235	6.2kg of Plutonium 239
Firing mechanism	'Gun type'	'Implosion'
Shape and weight	Long thin bomb, weighing 4 tonnes	Oval-shaped bomb, weighing 4.6 tonnes
Approximate yield	16kt	20kt
Approximate destruction	90–160,000 deaths 60% of all buildings destroyed	60–80,000 deaths

Both bombs were detonated high above each city to maximise damage by spreading the blast outwards, rather than exploding when they hit the ground.

The devastation caused by the two devices shocked everyone: even the scientists involved in the Manhattan Project and who had been present at the Trinity Test a few weeks before were surprised by the extent of the damage. The Little Boy uranium bomb generated the equivalent of 16,000 tonnes of TNT (conventional explosive) and the Fat Man plutonium bomb used just a few days later produced approximately 20,000 tonnes of TNT, or 20 kilotons.[29] While estimates vary, it is thought that 90–160,000 people died because of the single bomb dropped on Hiroshima and approximately 60–80,000 in Nagasaki (numbers might have been higher in Nagasaki if cloud cover hadn't prevented a more accurate detonation). Evidence suggests that around half of all deaths were caused by the initial blast and the firestorm it produced on the first day (both cities contained a large proportion of wooden buildings that caught fire easily), and many more as a result of radiation sickness burns and other illnesses – particularly cancers and leukaemia – thereafter (see Chapter 2). In Hiroshima, it is believed that four square miles (approximately an eighth of New York City) of the city were destroyed, including some 60 per cent of buildings.[30] Before the Japanese announced their surrender on 15 August 1945, plans were afoot for a third US bomb to be dropped on Japan in late August, and potentially several more in September and October 1945.[31]

The decision to drop the two bombs in August 1945 was far from uncontroversial, and continues to this day to split historians and commentators. Traditionalist historiography emphasises the choice between dropping the atomic bombs and launching what was believed to be a very costly military invasion – with perhaps up to one million US solders being killed:

> Sidetracking the plan to use the bomb was probably never on the cards. A convincing argument that Japan was being so badly hurt and depleted that its leaders were ready to surrender might have made a difference. But that argument was not being made convincingly. Instead, the prevailing attitude was that even the terrible fire bombings of the cities were having no apparent effect on Japanese morale and determination to go on fighting.[32]

According to the traditionalist view, therefore, dropping the atomic bombs on Japan was the strategic thing to do. In the words of John Newhouse, ' a decision against using the bomb that was meant to spare hundreds of thousands of American lives was most unlikely'.[33] It also appeared to be justified by the enormous amount of time and money that had gone into the project.

Revisionist accounts, on the other hand, have tended to point to three main arguments against the use of the bomb: if the USA had guaranteed the future of their Emperor, the Japanese would have surrendered, and a diplomatic resolution to the war could have been achieved; the bomb was dropped for deliberate future geopolitical purposes – foremost of which was sending a signal to the

Soviet Union; and the proposed invasion would not have been as costly as US officials claimed (and that the Truman administration knew this). In the words of J. Samuel Walker:

> The historical evidence makes clear that the popular view about the use of nuclear weapons is a mythological construct for the following reasons: (1) there were other options available for ending the war within a reasonably short time without the bomb and without an invasion; (2) Truman and his advisers believed that Japan was so weak that the war could end even before an invasion began, that is, they did not regard an invasion as inevitable; and (3) even in the worst case, if an invasion of Japan proved to be necessary, military planners in the summer of 1945 projected the number of lives lost at far fewer than the hundreds of thousands that Truman and his advisers claimed after the war.[34]

It is unlikely that any definitive answer to these questions can be agreed, and the bombings of Hiroshima and Nagasaki will probably be debated for years to come.[35] The truth is probably somewhere between the two poles of this debate. Either way, the first use of a nuclear weapon represented a game-changing moment in global politics. The world would never be quite the same again.

(4) Atom bombs and hydrogen bombs: assessing destructive capacity

While the majority of atomic weapons research up to 1945 concerned atomic bombs based on nuclear *fission*, scientists were conscious of another vastly more powerful type of nuclear bomb based on nuclear *fusion*, which would become known as the hydrogen bomb (and also as the thermonuclear bomb, the Super, or simply the H-bomb). In fact, scientists had been aware of the possibility of creating a 'superbomb' based on the fusion of hydrogen atoms as early as the 1930s, but it was Edward Teller – later dubbed the 'father of the hydrogen bomb' – who would be the main driving force behind its development in the 1940s.[36] Following the first H-bomb test by the United States in 1952, the new fusion device soon became the weapon of choice for all nuclear bomb designs. Indeed, because the majority of nuclear weapons are now based on fusion rather than fission it is important to understand the difference between the two. Ultimately, fusion bombs can be vastly more powerful than fission bombs.

Essentially while an atomic bomb gets its destructive power through splitting an atom (fission) and initiating a nuclear chain reaction to produce energy, a hydrogen bomb goes a step further and uses the heat generated by fission to forge particular atoms of hydrogen together (in this case deuterium and/or tritium – both heavier isotopes of hydrogen) through the process of fusion to produce energy. Put simply, nuclear fusion is forcing two atoms together to create a new isotope, a process that releases vast amounts of energy – this is similar to the process that gives the sun its heat. It is also a process that requires enormous amounts of heat and energy to initiate it – energy that can only be achieved through a basic nuclear fission reaction. This is why an H-bomb is sometimes referred to as a 'two-stage' nuclear device – with the first stage being the fission reaction. While the power of a fission reaction is limited by size, speed and weight, there are no theoretical limits to the power of a two-stage nuclear fusion device. Both processes produce enormous heat and release vast amounts of stored energy, although far more is produced through fusion. No major scientific obstacle prevents an actor that has the resources to build an A-bomb from acquiring the capability for an H-bomb. It should, however, be noted that while fission reactions can be controlled sufficiently to produce domestic civilian energy, harnessing the power of nuclear fusion for anything other than a bomb remains unfulfilled.[37]

The first test of a thermonuclear bomb was conducted by the United States on 1 November 1952 on Bikini Atoll – a small island in the Pacific Ocean. What became known as the 'Ivy Mike' test was not strictly speaking a weapons test as the bomb was too big and heavy to be deployed by the aircraft available at the time, but it did validate the concept of a thermonuclear explosion, and it would not be long before both the USA and the Soviet Union deployed operational H-bombs that could be delivered by aircraft, and later ballistic missiles. The 62-tonne bomb produced an estimated 10 megatons (10,000,000 million tonnes of TNT) of explosive power and a 3.5 mile-wide fireball.[38] The Soviet Union conducted its first thermonuclear test less than a year later on 12 August 1953 at the Semipalatinsk test site in Kazakhstan. Over the next 15 years, the UK, China and France all tested and deployed hydrogen bombs (for more on the effects of these tests see Chapter 2).

Following the first H-bomb test, the United States and the Soviet Union, and later the other nuclear powers, began amassing enormous stockpiles of nuclear weapons of ever-increasing destructive power (for more on this see Chapter 2). Within 15 years, the devices used against Japan to destroy two medium-sized cities had been dwarfed by arsenals of thermonuclear bombs that could wipe out entire societies. A broad idea of the type of destruction the ever-more powerful bombs could inflict is demonstrated in Table 3. While the destructive capacity of these larger devices almost feels like something from science fiction, most modern nuclear weapons do not far exceed the 1-megaton yield. Nevertheless, it is important to note that modern nuclear weapons are exponentially more powerful than those used in 1945.

In the 1980s, scientists predicted that any large-scale use of nuclear weapons – particularly if directed against big population centres – could result in a phenomenon called nuclear winter. The firestorms caused by such an exchange might potentially release so much smoke, dust and fallout that momentous

Table 3 Estimated casualties and destruction from a nuclear blast[i]

Nuclear Yield	Examples	Estimated Scale of Destruction
500 tons	North Korean nuclear test in 2006 (approx. 0.5kt)	100% fatalities within 200 metre radius. Over 50% mortality rate within 750 metre radius.
15-20 kilotons	Fat Man and Little Boy (16kt & 20kt) detonated over Japan by the USA in 1945	Most buildings collapse and fatalities universal within 1.5 mile radius. Approximately 90,000–160,000 people died in Hiroshima, 60,000–80,000 in Nagasaki.
100 kilotons	W-76 warhead – common on US and UK SLBMs	Universal injuries and almost total destruction within 2 mile radius.
1 megaton	Minuteman I warhead deployed by the USA in 1965	Most buildings collapse, universal injuries, and high causalities within 4.5 mile radius. Third-degree burns to exposed skin up to 7.25 miles from blast.
10 megatons	'Ivy Mike' first US H-bomb (tested 1952), approximately 10.4mt	100% fatalities within 3.5 mile radius. Universal injuries and most buildings collapse within 10 mile radius.
50 megatons	Tsar Bomba (57 megatons) tested by the Soviet Union in 1961	A fireball with 1.5 mile radius; most buildings collapse within a 16 mile radius; third-degree burns up to 36 miles away.

[i] I am grateful to Alex Wellerstein and his 'nukemap' website for this information: http://nuclearsecrecy.com/nukemap

climatic effects would result – most notably much colder weather and reduced sunlight – which in turn would present a considerable challenge to all life on the planet. In fact, it has been argued that there would be more human casualties globally from a nuclear winter than from the initial nuclear exchange.[39] As Carl Sagan warned back in 1983:

> cold, dark, radioactivity, pyrotoxins and ultraviolet light following a nuclear war – including some scenarios involving only a small fraction of the world strategic arsenals – would imperil every survivor on the planet. There is a real danger of the extinction of humanity.[40]

And as Alan Robock et al. point out: 'The indirect effects of nuclear weapons would have devastating consequences for the planet, and continued nuclear arsenal reductions will be needed before the threat of nuclear winter is removed from the Earth.'[41] While the nuclear winter debate referred primarily to the large Cold War era nuclear stockpiles of the United States and the Soviet Union, the logic of climatic and human catastrophe has been re-energised in recent years as part of the Humanitarian Initiative to Prohibit Nuclear Weapons (see Chapter 9).[42]

A combined total of approximately 150,000–240,000 people died as a result of the Little Boy and Fat Man bombs dropped in 1945: a significant percentage almost immediately from the explosion. The destructive capacity of these bombs shocked the world as two bombs inflicted the equivalent damage of several hundred aircraft each dropping thousands of pounds of conventional bombs. However, compared with modern nuclear weapons, these bombs – with yields of between 15 and 20 kilotons – look disturbingly mild. It must be assumed that if a thermonuclear bomb were exploded in or above a large and densely populated modern city, the death rate and destruction would be many times that of Hiroshima and Nagasaki; and if many were used it could mean the destruction of entire countries and even life as we know it.

(5) Key points and guide to further reading and resources

This chapter has sought to provide you with some basics about nuclear weapons, how they work and why they are so powerful. A summary of these key points is provided below:

- The power of an atomic bomb comes from the energy released when an atomic nucleus is bombarded with extra neutrons. If sufficient fissile material can be brought together quickly enough, a chain reaction is initiated which releases enormous power that can be used for a bomb.
- Nuclear weapons must contain fissile material. The only two chemical isotopes that are known to be fissile are uranium 235 and plutonium 239. Both are difficult to acquire. It is harder to make a bomb with uranium given the enrichment process involved and much less plutonium is needed for critical mass; however, a basic uranium bomb is easier to detonate than one made with plutonium.
- The United States was the first country to develop a nuclear weapon (1945), although the Soviet Union (1949) and the United Kingdom (1952) soon followed. The first test of a nuclear weapon was in July 1945 in the New Mexico desert, USA.
- Nuclear weapons have only been used twice – by the United States against Hiroshima and Nagasaki in Japan in August 1945. Several hundred thousand people died because of these two bombs. Modern nuclear weapons are exponentially more powerful.
- The decision to drop the atomic bombs in 1945 is the subject of a fierce ongoing and highly divided debate between those who view it as strategically necessary to win the war against Japan and those who suggest it was a political ploy aimed at the Soviet Union.

(Continued)

(Continued)

- Atom bombs work by splitting the atom to release power through fission. Hydrogen bombs use the heat from a fission reaction to forge atoms together through fusion. Essentially, fission is *splitting the atom* to release energy; fusion is *forcing atoms together* to release energy. H-bombs are much more powerful than A-bombs, and the power of an H-bomb is theoretically limitless. Most modern nuclear weapons are H-bombs.
- While the effects of a large nuclear exchange are difficult to judge, some scholars have warned that a so-called nuclear winter could result, where the earth could suffer a prolonged period of darkness, freezing temperatures and catastrophic loss of life.

Further reading and resources

Arguably, the best introduction to the genesis of the atomic bomb is Richard Rhodes' 'The making of the atomic bomb' (1986). His follow-up book 'Dark sun' (1996) offers a highly readable account of the development of the hydrogen bomb. Frank Barnaby's 'How to make a nuclear bomb' (2003) is also a highly accessible technical introduction to nuclear weapons science, as is Jeremy Bernstein's 'Nuclear weapons' (2008). Some basics of nuclear weapons components can also be found at the Union of Concerned Scientists website: www.ucsusa.org/nuclear_weapons_and_global_security/nuclear_terrorism/technical_issues/fissile-materials-basics.html.

General Leslie Groves' 'Now it can be told' (1983) offers an insightful first-hand account of the Manhattan Project, while Jim Baggot's 'Atomic' (2009) and Cynthia Kelly's 'The Manhattan Project' (2007) both give a highly readable history of the US atomic bomb project during the 1940s. Jeremy Bernstein's 'Hitler's uranium club' (2001) and Mark Walker's 'Nazi science' (2001) are good overviews of the Nazi Uranverein Project, while Robert Wilcox's 'Japan's secret war' (1995) provides an interesting overview of Japanese attempts to build the bomb during the Second World War. The film *Shadowmakers* also addresses the wartime race to build the bomb. An interesting study of the key people involved in the development of US nuclear weapons is provided by Gregg Herken in 'The brotherhood of the bomb' (2003), while Kai Bird and Martin Sherman's 'American Prometheus' (2009) provides a fascinating insight into J. Robert Oppenheimer, as does Jennet Conant's '109 East Palace' (2005).

John Hersey's 'Hiroshima' (2001) is a must-read on the impact of the atomic bomb dropped on that Japanese city, while Craig Collie's 'Nagasaki' (2011) is a good overview of the second nuclear detonation over Japan. Paul Ham's 'Hiroshima Nagasaki' (2013) provides a good overview of both. The

Hiroshima Peace Memorial Museum (www.pcf.city.hiroshima.jp/top_e.html) and the Nagasaki Atomic Bomb Museum (www.city.nagasaki.lg.jp/peace/english/abm/) both have very good websites, and are well worth a visit.

On the debate over the decision to use atomic bombs against Japan in 1945 see Ronald Takaki 'Hiroshima: why America dropped the atomic bomb' (1995); Wilson Miscamble 'The most controversial decision' (2011); and Samuel Walker's 'Prompt and utter destruction' (1997) and 'Recent literature on Truman's atomic bomb decision' (2005). The film *Hiroshima* is also a useful resource on this topic.

On the destructive capacity of nuclear weapons see Samuel Glasstone and Philip Dolan's 'The effects of nuclear weapons' (1977); the Atomic Archive (www.atomicarchive.com/Effects/), and Alex Wellerstein's interactive 'Nuke map' (www.nuclearsecrecy.com/nukemap/).

On the concept of nuclear winter see Carl Sagan 'Nuclear war and climatic catastrophe' (1983/4); Richard Turco et al. 'A path where no man thought' (1991); Carl Sagan et al. 'The nuclear winter debate' (1986); Mark Harwell 'Nuclear winter' (1984); and Owen Greene, Ian Percival and Irene Ridge's 'Nuclear winter' (1985).

Notes

1. Stephen Younger, 'The bomb: a new history', (New York, HarperCollins: 2009) pp.21–22.
2. See, for example, Richard Macey, 'Laser enrichment could cut cost of nuclear power', Sydney Morning Herald, (27 May 2006), www.smh.com.au/news/national/laser-enrichment-could-cut-cost-of-nuclear-power/2006/05/26/1148524888448.html.
3. Stephen Younger, 'The bomb: a new history', (New York, HarperCollins: 2009) p.22.
4. Joseph Siracusa, 'Nuclear weapons: a very short introduction', (Oxford, Oxford University Press: 2008) p.4.
5. See Union of Concerned Scientists, 'Nuclear Weapons Basics' www.ucsusa.org/nuclear_weapons_and_global_security/nuclear_terrorism/technical_issues/fissile-materials-basics.html.
6. See Gerald de Groot, 'The bomb: a life', (London, Jonathan Cape: 2004) pp.14–16.
7. Stephen Younger, 'The bomb: a new history', (New York, HarperCollins: 2009) pp.14–15.
8. Richard Rhodes, 'The making of the atomic bomb', (London, Simon & Schuster: 1986) pp.303–311.
9. On this see Margaret Gowling, 'Britain and atomic energy 1939–1945', (London, Palgrave Macmillan: 1964).
10. On this see Jeremy Bernstein, 'Hitler's uranium club', (New York, American Institute of Physics: 1996).
11. William Broad, 'Why they called it the Manhattan Project', New York Times, (30 October 2007), www.nytimes.com/2007/10/30/science/30manh.html?pagewanted=all&_r=0.

12. For an interesting take on the Japanese atomic programmes during the Second World War see Robert Wilcox, 'Japan's secret war: Japan's race against time to build its own atomic bomb', (Emeryville CA, Marlowe & Co.: 1995).
13. The best source on the Manhattan Project is Richard Rhodes, 'Making of the atomic bomb', (New York, Simon & Schuster: 1986).
14. Jeremy Bernstein, 'Nuclear weapons: what you need to know', (Cambridge, Cambridge University Press: 2008) pp.87–88.
15. Kevin O'Neill, 'Building the bomb', chapter in Stephen Schwartz (ed.), 'Atomic audit: the costs and consequences of US nuclear weapons since 1940', (Washington DC, The Brookings Institution Press: 1998) pp.58–59.
16. Jeremy Bernstein, 'Nuclear weapons: what you need to know', (Cambridge, Cambridge University Press: 2008) pp.4–5.
17. For more on the Trinity Test see Richard Rhodes, 'The making of the atomic bomb', (London, Simon & Schuster: 1986) pp.670–678.
18. A video of the interview with Oppenheimer is available on YouTube, www.youtube.com/watch?v=lb13ynu3Iac.
19. Richard Rhodes, 'The making of the atomic bomb', (London, Simon & Schuster: 1986) p.656.
20. Gerald de Groot, 'The bomb: a life', (London, Jonathan Cape: 2004) pp.78–81.
21. For more on this, see Herbert Romerstein and Eric Breindel, 'The Venona secrets: exposing Soviet espionage and America's traitors', (London, Regnery Publishing Inc: 2001), particularly Chapters 6–8.
22. Richard Rhodes, 'The making of the atomic bomb', (London, Simon & Schuster: 1986) p.656.
23. On nuclear espionage see Jeffrey Richelson, 'Spying on the bomb: American nuclear intelligence from Nazi Germany to Iran and North Korea', (New York, W.W. Norton & Company: 2007).
24. Jeremy Bernstein, 'Nuclear weapons: what you need to know', (Cambridge, Cambridge University Press: 2008) p.xi and p.133; Federation of American Scientists, 'Nuclear bomb design', www.fas.org/nuke/intro/nuke/design.htm.
25. Jeremy Bernstein, 'Nuclear weapons: what you need to know', (Cambridge, Cambridge University Press: 2008) p.xi.
26. The B-29 *Enola Gay* is currently on exhibition at the Smithsonian Air and Space Museum at Washington Dulles Airport, USA.
27. Jeremy Bernstein, 'Nuclear weapons: what you need to know', (Cambridge, Cambridge University Press: 2008) p.xi.
28. Ibid.
29. Ibid.
30. Joseph Siracusa, 'Nuclear weapons: a very short introduction', (Oxford, Oxford University Press: 2008) p.23.
31. On this see Barton J. Bernstein, 'The perils and politics of surrender: ending the war with Japan and avoiding the third atomic bomb', Pacific Historical Review, 46:1 (1977) pp.1–27.
32. John Newhouse, 'The nuclear age: from Hiroshima to Star Wars', (London, Michael Joseph: 1989) p.47.
33. Ibid., p.42.
34. J. Samuel Walker, 'Prompt and utter destruction: Truman and the use of the A-bombs against Japan', (London, University of North Carolina Press: 1997) pp.5–6.
35. For a good overview of the historiography of the decision to drop the bomb see J. Samuel Walker, 'Recent literature on Truman's Atomic Bomb decision: a search for middle ground', Diplomatic History, 29:2 (2005) pp. 311–33.

36. On this see William Broad, 'Tellers' war: the top secret story behind the Star Wars deception', (New York, Simon & Schuster: 1992) pp.33–40.
37. On the quest for nuclear fusion power see Daniel Clery, 'A piece of the sun: the quest for fusion energy', (London, Gerald Duckworth & Co. Ltd: 2013).
38. Gerald de Groot, 'The bomb: a life', (London, Jonathan Cape: 2004) p.179.
39. Richard Turco, Owen Toon, Thomas Ackerman, James Pollack and Carl Sagan, 'Climate and smoke: an appraisal of nuclear winter', Science, 247:4939 (1990) p.174.
40. Carl Sagan, 'Nuclear war and climatic catastrophe: some policy implications', Foreign Affairs, 62:2 (Winter 1983–4) pp.291–292.
41. See Alan Robock, Luke Oman and Georgiy Stenchikov, 'Nuclear winter revisited with a modern climate model and current nuclear arsenals: still catastrophic consequences', Journal of Geophysical Research: Atmospheres, (1984–2012), 112:D13 (2007) p.1.
42. On this see John Borrie and Tim Caughlet (eds), 'Viewing nuclear weapons through a humanitarian lens', (Geneva, Switzerland, United Nations Institute for Disarmament Research: 2013) available at www.unidir.org/files/publications/pdfs/viewing-nuclear-weapons-through-a-humanitarian-lens-en-601.pdf.

2

TESTING, DEFINING AND
DELIVERING NUCLEAR WEAPONS

Nuclear testing

Radiation, contamination and fallout

Defining nuclear weapons

Different ways to deliver nuclear weapons

Who has what: current nuclear forces

Key points and guide to further reading and resources

Although nuclear weapons have only ever been used twice in warfare, global stockpiles of nuclear arms have grown exponentially since 1945 (see Chapter 3), including new devices designed for every imaginable warfare scenario. To facilitate this, over 2,000 nuclear tests have been conducted – many of them in the atmosphere – releasing vast amounts of radioactive material and making certain areas of the world virtually uninhabitable for human, animal and plant life. Indeed, many people have lost their lives as a result of nuclear testing, primarily through radiation poisoning, and not all of these have been through accident or negligence. Although the 1963 Partial Test Ban Treaty (PTBT) (also known as the Limited Test Ban Treaty or LTBT) and the more recent 1996 Comprehensive Test Ban Treaty (CTBT) have sought to curb these deleterious effects, nuclear testing remains a dangerous business. The result is that while understanding what makes a bomb go bang is fundamentally important it is really only half of the story when we think about nuclear weapons. Without adequate testing, actors might never be sure if the bomb would work if and when required, and more powerful and more accurate bombs and increasingly advanced and accurate delivery systems could not have been developed or deployed. Indeed, testing has bequeathed a whole gamut of new bomb types to states eager to consider how 'the bomb' could be used in every aspect of post-Second World War warfare. The result has been the emergence of a new nomenclature of terms and terminology, and a raft of new methods to deliver a nuclear weapon to its target. While in 1945 a single bomb would be delivered by a heavy bomber to hit a medium-sized city, a decade or more later a nuclear warhead could be placed on ballistic missiles on land or at sea, fitted to artillery pieces, gravity bombs or even landmines, and designed for possible use in every conceivable scenario.

With this in mind, the chapter seeks to broaden out the introductory information contained in Chapter 1 and place the bomb in context. The first section focuses on nuclear testing and the negotiation of international agreements initially to restrict testing, and more recently to outlaw it altogether. In the second section, the chapter looks at radiation, contamination and fallout, and at the potential and actual impact of nuclear explosions on humans and our environment. Section three seeks to demystify the murky world of nuclear nomenclature produced primarily by the Cold War nuclear arms race, help provide some definitions of key types of nuclear weaponry and explain what these classifications mean in practice. Finally, section four describes the many ways in which nuclear weapons can be delivered to their specific targets, and the strengths and weaknesses of these delivery methods. The chapter finishes with a summary of key points and a guide to further reading and resources.

(1) Nuclear testing

While nuclear weapons have only ever been used twice in war, there have been (approximately) 2,053 nuclear tests conducted since 1945, with a combined output many thousands of times more than the yield of the bombs dropped on Hiroshima and Nagasaki.[1] For the best part of the first two decades of the nuclear age, the majority of these tests were conducted above ground, releasing vast quantities of radioactive material into the atmosphere, with potentially catastrophic long-term consequences. The result is that certain areas of the globe are now largely uninhabitable, and many of the shocking human costs associated with nuclear testing are only now coming to light (see below). While the 1963 PTBT banned nuclear testing above ground, in the sea and in space, nuclear explosions continued underground throughout the Cold War, and to a lesser extent afterwards, including North Korea's tests in the 2000s and 2010s. The majority of these tests (North Korea notwithstanding) have been far more powerful than the bombs exploded over Hiroshima and Nagasaki. Only France, China and North Korea of the current states with nuclear weapons have not signed the PTBT – although France has subsequently signed the Comprehensive Test Ban Treaty, which bans all types of nuclear weapons testing.

Nuclear testing was and is seen as a fundamental condition for proving the credibility of a nuclear weapons programme, and for the development of ever more powerful nuclear devices. As Dahlman et al. explain:

> testing has provided detailed insight into the physics of nuclear explosions and how to control their various basic parameters, such as yield, radiation etc. Testing was also used to develop specific nuclear warhead designs to fit operational requirements and different nuclear weapons systems. Series of tests were conducted to develop and validate such new weapons.[2]

During the Cold War testing ever more powerful and sophisticated nuclear weapons also became part of a game of brinksmanship between the United States and the Soviet Union, whereby each side sought to demonstrate its potential power to the other.

As a result, after 1945, more and more tests of increasingly powerful weapons were carried out – primarily by the United States and the Soviet Union – and in October 1961 the Soviet Union tested the 'Tsar Bomba', with an estimated yield of 50–58 megatons (50–58,000,000 tonnes of conventional explosive), in the Novaya Zemyla archipelago in the Arctic Ocean. According to Rudolph Herzog, this bomb was approximately 1,400 times more powerful than the two atomic bombs dropped on Japan in 1945 combined.[3] The Tsar Bomba was the largest weapon ever tested, producing a mushroom cloud roughly 40 miles high; the heat generated by the explosion would theoretically have caused third-degree burns to exposed human flesh up to a range of 100km, and the thermal pulse was felt by an observer 250km away from the blast.[4] The bomb was just 8 metres long, weighing approximately 20 tonnes, and was dropped by a specially modified Soviet bomber.[5] The fear that nuclear testing was spiralling out of control – a fear exemplified by the Tsar Bomba test – led to the creation of the 1963 PTBT which banned nuclear testing in the atmosphere, in space and underwater, but importantly, not underground, and in 1974 the Threshold Test Ban Treaty (TTBT), which limited the size of nuclear tests to less than 150kt.

As Table 4 shows, the vast majority of nuclear tests have been carried out by the United States, and to a lesser extent the Soviet Union, while most other powers have appeared content with just a relatively small number of nuclear explosions. Nuclear testing reached its height in the 1960s, with some 140–178 nuclear tests conducted in 1962 (the most in any year of the nuclear age).[6] However, following the signing of the PTBT in 1963, nuclear testing gradually reduced, and only India, Pakistan and North Korea have tested nuclear devices since 1996 (the date of the last Chinese test). In 1996, the CTBT was opened for signature, with the sole purpose of prohibiting all types of nuclear weapons test in any environment, and the CTBT Organisation (CTBTO), based in Vienna, was established to oversee the treaty and verify compliance.[7] However, the CTBT cannot come into force until it is signed by all the nations that currently possess either nuclear weapons or nuclear power capabilities. At the time of writing notable non-signatories or states that haven't ratified the Treaty include China, India, Iran, Israel, North Korea, Pakistan and the United States – although the USA did declare a unilateral moratorium on nuclear testing in October 1992.[8] Russia, the United Kingdom and France are the only nuclear-armed states that have signed and ratified the CTBT. Table 4 provides further details on each country's nuclear testing record.

Geographically – and despite the fact that all states with nuclear weapons are in the northern hemisphere – nuclear testing has taken place across the globe. While China, India, Pakistan and North Korea have all conducted tests exclusively on their own territory, the USA (in the United States, the Atlantic Ocean and in the Pacific Ocean), Russia (in Russia and Kazakhstan), the UK (in Australia, the Indian Ocean and the USA) and France (in Algeria and the Pacific Ocean) have all tested overseas.[9] Israel is widely believed to have conducted a secret nuclear detonation in conjunction with South Africa in September 1979 in the southern Indian Ocean. However, the Vela Incident – as it has become known – has never been confirmed by either Israel or South Africa (more on this in Chapter 6).[10]

While most nuclear testing has been for weapons development, a small number of nuclear experiments have ostensibly been designed to explore the potential use of nuclear explosions for non-military purposes. These detonations are known as peaceful nuclear explosions (PNEs). Operation Plowshare was the name given to the US effort to develop nuclear explosive devices for peaceful purposes – such as mining or large earthworks during

Table 4 Number of nuclear tests by country[i]

Country	Number of Tests/ (Devices Exploded)	Most Recent Test	CTBT
United States	1030 (1054)	September 1992	Signed not ratified
USSR/Russia	715	October 1990	Ratified 2000
United Kingdom	45	November 1991	Ratified 1998
France	210	January 1996	Ratified 1998
China	45	July 1996	Signed not ratified
India	3 (6) Includes PNE	May 1998	No
Pakistan	2 (6)	May 1998	No
North Korea	3	February 2013	No
TOTAL	2053 (2084)[ii]		

[i] Figures adapted from the CTBTO Preparatory Commission website: www.ctbto.org/nuclear-testing/history-of-nuclear-testing/nuclear-testing-1945-today

[ii] The figures for nuclear testing vary depending on counting rules. For example, whether one counts the number of devices detonated or the number of tests conducted (which might contain more than one device).

the 1960s and 1970s – while the Soviet Union conducted over 200 PNE tests during the Cold War. In fact, it was in response to a plan by the United States Atomic Energy Commission to conduct a so-called PNE in Alaska in the late 1960s that the international organisation Greenpeace was established. In a similar vein, India claimed that their 1974 'Smiling Buddha' test was a PNE (not until the tests of 1998 did India declare a nuclear weapons capability), and Australia and Germany have both previously entertained the idea of using a nuclear blast for civilian engineering purposes.[11] While the reasons behind peaceful nuclear testing may have been reputable (in some cases), the fact that the tests clearly had and still have military applications and importance cannot simply be overlooked.

(2) Radiation, fallout and contamination

Radioactivity is the process whereby energy is emitted from an atom of a chemical element due to the instability of the nucleus. This radiation can be released in several different forms, with the most prevalent being alpha, beta and gamma rays. Of these, gamma radiation is considered the most dangerous for humans because it is the most penetrative – high levels of gamma can only be stopped by lead or concrete. While an exact estimation of the amount of radioactive material released into the atmosphere because of nuclear testing is difficult to ascertain, it is undeniable that these tests have had an effect on various living organisms on our planet. Some people blame a rise in certain cancers and leukaemia on radioactive fallout (radioactive particles can enter the body and damage or alter cells) along with other illnesses and diseases to plant life and animals.[12] Indeed, there is a growing list of people and groups seeking to sue governments for the after-effects of nuclear testing, and rumours abound that some individuals may have been deliberately exposed to radiation to test how it affects the human body (see below) – this has certainly happened with animals and plant life. Either way, the huge volume of atomic testing conducted since 1945 means that parts of the globe will remain no-go areas for a very long time.

In addition to the deaths and destruction caused by the heat, shockwave and firestorms created by a nuclear blast (see Chapter 1), by far the most potentially harmful impact of a nuclear device comes from the radiation and radioactive fallout that follow the initial explosion. Radiation is produced directly by the nuclear blast (or from a damaged nuclear power reactor), while radioactive fall-out consists of the irradiated soil and other material that is thrown into the air and dispersed as a result of the nuclear blast (particularly through a ground burst explosion). When humans are exposed to these radioactive particles (either through direct radiation from a blast or through fallout), damage is caused to bodily tissues and organs, which can lead to radiation sickness, cancers and death – this is known as ionising radiation. The most prevalent radionuclides released (the particles that cause the problems) are Caesium-137, Iodine-131 and Strontium-90, all of which can cause various cancers and other unpleasant illnesses.[13] While ionising radiation in small doses can be employed for medical purposes, such as in treating cancer or in x-ray machines, 'When the body is exposed to higher doses of radiation so many cells are damaged that the body's repair mechanisms cannot cope'.[14] The result is often severe illness and a painful death. As Frank Barnaby explains:

> the first symptoms of radiation sickness include nausea, diarrhoea, vomiting and fatigue. These symptoms may be followed by, among others, headache, hair loss, dehydration, breathlessness, haemorrhage, anaemia, permanent darkening of the skin, loss of weight, fever, fatigue and sweating … very high doses of radiation can produce symptoms within minutes. Death may occur from short-term (acute) effects, within about two months. Death from long-term effects, particularly leukaemia, may occur several years later and other cancers may occur after very long times, of thirty or more years.[15]

While it is possible to protect against radiation poisoning – nuclear reactors and other materials are usually shielded to protect workers, or in a far more limited manner, humans can be protected through enhanced civil defence measures (see Chapter 10) – prolonged exposure to nuclear radiation will often prove lethal.

During the Cold War a number of states tested and deployed enhanced radiation weapons (ERWs) more commonly referred to as neutron bombs. The neutron bomb was an H-bomb explicitly designed to maximise the release of radiation from a nuclear blast – and therefore to maximise its lethality against humans rather than buildings and infrastructure.[16] Given the design to maximise radiation, neutron bombs could also be used to produce enormous electromagnetic pulse (EMP) waves capable of widespread damage to electrical equipment. As Clay Wilson explains:

> Electromagnetic Pulse (EMP) is an instantaneous, intense energy field that can overload or disrupt at a distance numerous electrical systems and high technology microcircuits, which are especially sensitive to power surges. A large scale EMP effect can be produced by a single nuclear explosion detonated high in the atmosphere.[17]

The large waves of magnetic and electrical energy created by an EMP attack could therefore be used to disable enemy electrical systems (such as early warning, radar, or command and control facilities) before a full-scale (possibly nuclear) attack was launched. Similarly, the so-called cobalt bomb – which was never actually built – was a nuclear bomb concept that would produce such a large cloud of radiation that it could (theoretically) destroy every living thing on the planet.[18]

Throughout the nuclear age, and particularly during its early years, there have been a number of examples where nuclear testing has directly affected humans, and it is highly likely that there are many more examples that we simply don't know about. Whether by miscalculation, ignorance or perhaps worse, many people have suffered as a result of nuclear testing by contracting horrible illnesses, and in certain cases have died. Examples of these cases are provided below:

- *Harry Daghlian* Daghlian was a scientist on the Manhattan Project and was the first known case of death from radiation poisoning in September 1945 after he accidently irradiated himself during a critical mass experiment at Los Alamos. Another scientist, Louis Slotin, died from a similar accident in May 1946.[19]
- *Soviet human experiments* In September 1954, the Soviet Union deliberately exposed some 45,000 people to a nuclear blast at the Totskoye testing range to measure its impact on humans, and whether soldiers could fight immediately after a nuclear detonation. Thousands of people are believed to have died as a result.[20]
- *US human experiments* From the 1940s to the 1970s, various US governmental and research agencies carried out hundreds of tests and radiation experiments on human beings, a large number without their consent. Experiments ranged from injecting subjects with uranium and plutonium and exposing them to high levels of radiation, to the deliberate release of radionuclides into the atmosphere, and placing radioactive particles in food.[21]
- *Lucky Dragon* A Japanese fishing boat was severely contaminated during a US hydrogen bomb test in March 1954. The crew were unaware of the test and were sailing approximately 100 miles away from 'ground zero' when they saw the flash of the explosion. The radioactive fallout subsequently hit *Lucky Dragon*. All 23 crew members showed symptoms of radiation poisoning, and one member later died.[22]
- *Marshall Islanders* During US nuclear tests (codenamed Castle Bravo) in the South Pacific in 1954, many Marshall Islanders were exposed to heavy nuclear fallout, and later showed signs of radiation poisoning. As Jane Dibblin explains, 'The island of Rongelap was directly in the path of Bravo's fallout. Since then, the Rongelap people have been plagued by ill health – most commonly, thyroid tumours, cataracts and babies so deformed they could not live'.[23] These islands, along with Eniwetok and other atolls in the South Pacific, remain uninhabitable today
- *UK testing in Australia* In 2010, a group of 250 people – including ex-British servicemen and Australian Aborigines – filed a lawsuit against the British government for diseases and disabilities that they claim resulted from atmospheric nuclear testing in the 1950s.[24] The UK Ministry of Defence later admitted that it had exposed British, Australian and New Zealand servicemen to radiation in the 1950s and 1960s.[25]

- *French soldiers* Another report released in 2010 claimed that French soldiers stationed in Algeria were deliberately put in harm's way by a military command keen to know more about the impact of nuclear weapons. French Defence Minister Herve Morin later 'confirmed that about a hundred soldiers had been involved in exercises which aimed to test the effects of fallout on human beings'.[26]

Throughout the early decades of nuclear testing, many animals were also deliberately exposed to radiation.

It is very difficult to measure precisely the effects of nuclear testing, or for that matter to predict the radiological impact of a nuclear detonation or a civilian nuclear accident, but it is clear that many people, animals and the environment have suffered either deliberately or indirectly as a result of nuclear testing. Many of these cases are only now coming to light, and it seems likely that there may be far more incidents that we simply do not know about. However, since the PTBT forced testing underground, exposure to radiation has been reduced considerably, and if the CTBT comes into force, this should help to curtail the issue entirely.

(3) Defining nuclear weapons

When we talk about nuclear weapons, the nuclear warhead that contains the fissile material and the bomb is really only half of the story, for in most circumstances the bomb is relatively useless unless you can 'deliver it' to your intended target. Nuclear bombs can be delivered in a number of ways, especially smaller nuclear bombs designed for smaller targets – often on the battlefield, but traditionally nuclear weapons have been delivered by aircraft, missiles (on land, at sea and on submarines), and even a mixture of all three. These types of delivery system have been somewhat problematically defined as either 'strategic' or 'non-strategic' depending on the objectives, range and yield of the nuclear weapon (this is primarily a result of Cold War-era categorisations). As such, it is essential to understand the typology of nuclear weapons, and what the myriad different classifications actually mean in practice.

There are essentially three ways to classify nuclear weapons: one is by the explosive yield of the warhead; the second is by the means of delivery and the range of targets that can be hit; while the third is by the target or purpose of the device. Traditionally, this has led to a split between 'strategic nuclear weapons' – those with a high warhead yield, that can hit targets anywhere in the world, and that are primarily designed for mass destruction and national deterrence (i.e. destroying major cities and military installations) – and 'sub-strategic', 'tactical' or 'battlefield' nuclear weapons – those with a lower warhead yield, designed primarily for use against enemy military forces in a limited operational area (such as on the battlefield). However, this distinction can sometimes be confusing – and is in many ways a product of the Cold War bipolar stand-off between the United States and the Soviet Union – because some types of nuclear weapons can essentially be both, and a number of delivery systems also straddle the grey divide between these classifications.

To make this easier, it is best to think of strategic nuclear forces as consisting of assets with a global range and large payload that could be used to inflict enormous strategic damage on another state – intercontinental ballistic missiles (ICBMs), submarine-launched ballistic missiles (SLBMs) and long-range strategic bombers are the best examples of this. The specifics of what constitutes a *non-strategic nuclear weapon* (often referred to as a *tactical nuclear weapon* or *TNW*) are less clear, but are perhaps best thought of as either (1) nuclear forces with only a regional capability – such as medium- and intermediate-range ballistic missiles (MRBMs and IRBMs), fighter aircraft, and short-range ballistic missiles and cruise missiles; or (2) nuclear forces which could be used on the battlefield against enemy military targets, such as gravity bombs, artillery, landmines, torpedoes and cruise missiles. Increasingly, non-strategic nuclear weaponry refers to nuclear weapons with a regional capability, as battlefield nuclear forces are seen more and more as a relic of the Cold War by the major nuclear powers (although there were calls in the USA in the wake of September 11 for new 'mini-nukes' that could be used in the War on Terror[27]). In terms of destructive capacity the main limiting factors are size and weight, which means that a weapon with any yield could be used in either a strategic or tactical capacity, although the yield of strategic nuclear weapons – given their objective of causing mass destruction – tends to be higher than for non-strategic/tactical or battlefield nuclear weapons, which normally have more limited objectives. A rough guide to nuclear weapons typology is provided in Table 5.

Table 5 Strategic, non-strategic and battlefield nuclear weapons compared

	Strategic	Non-Strategic/Tactical	
		Regional	Battlefield
Range of yield	100kt upwards	Variable yields	Lower kilotons/tons
Operational range	Global – more than 3,400 miles	Regional – up to 3,000 miles	Battlefield – typically less than 100 miles
Types of delivery vehicle	ICBMs, SLBMs, long-range bombers	MRBMs, IRBMs, fighter jets, cruise missiles	Gravity bombs, cruise missiles, artillery shells, land mines, torpedoes, surface-to-air missiles
Mission	Cause overwhelming destruction to enemy cities and military installations Strategic deterrence	As strategic but smaller range and possibly smaller yield	Use against enemy forces on the battlefield Limited nuclear war? (See Chapter 4)

Of course, given the differences in geography and geopolitics between nuclear-armed states, what constitutes strategic rather than non-strategic nuclear weapons varies by country and by adversary. During the Cold War, for example, the United States, the Soviet Union, the UK, France and China all acquired forces with a global strike capability to ensure their perceived *strategic* objectives, whereas Israel's main strategic objectives, or Pakistan's for example, could be seen as being more regional in nature. Equally, many strategists would argue that there is really no distinction between types of nuclear weapon, and any nuclear use should be classified as strategic given the potential destruction and likelihood that any nuclear use would result in an escalation (more on this in Chapter 4).

(4) Different ways to deliver nuclear weapons

While there is no reason why a nuclear weapon could not be delivered to its target in the back of a truck or in a shipping container, most nuclear weapons are assigned particular delivery vehicles to enable them to strike the desired target. Given the definitions provided above, it makes sense to split these into two broad sections: (1) methods for delivering warheads for strategic and national security purposes; and (2) methods of delivery for other purposes, including use on the battlefield (methods that might be used by non-state actors are covered in Chapter 7). As such, the first part of this section looks at the main ways that nuclear weapons can be delivered to a target for strategic purposes – by bomber or fighter aircraft, by land-based missiles, and by ship or submarine-based missiles – before examining various other battlefield methods to deliver these weapons in the second.

- *The air: strategic bombers and fighter aircraft* Historically, the most common method of delivering a nuclear weapon to its target is by using long-range bomber aircraft. Long-range bombers – such as those that dropped the two bombs on Hiroshima and Nagasaki in 1945 – were the delivery vehicles of choice throughout most of the early part of the atomic age, and remain a central part of most nuclear states' arsenals today. This is because bombers are generally less expensive than other means of long-range nuclear delivery, comparatively easier to build, more flexible in terms of role, can carry very heavy payloads and, perhaps most importantly, they can be called back (unlike missiles). However, bombers are vulnerable to a pre-emptive attack when they are on the ground and susceptible to air-defence and anti-aircraft weapons when they are in the air. Traditionally, bombers have dropped a free-fall or gravity bomb which has meant that the aircraft needs to get very close to the target, but more recently, they have been adapted to carry air-launched cruise missiles (ALCMs) which makes them effective at a slightly longer range. Nuclear capable fighter aircraft have similar dynamics, but a far shorter operational range. They can also be used for battlefield nuclear roles, or deployed on aircraft carriers.

- *The ground: ballistic missiles* A ballistic missile is essentially a guided rocket with a warhead on the top that follows a ballistic flight path (i.e. it goes up into the atmosphere before falling back to earth). Longer-range ballistic missiles exit the atmosphere as part of their flight path, while shorter-range missiles may stay inside the atmosphere – this simply depends on the distance they are required to travel (cruise missiles do not leave the atmosphere and do not follow a ballistic trajectory). The missile is thrust upwards by powerful rocket engines (often built in several stages, of which the actual warhead is by far the smallest), before falling back to earth to hit the intended target. The further the distance to the target and the heavier the warhead(s) the more initial power is required to achieve the necessary height, trajectory and velocity. A powerful ballistic missile can deliver its nuclear payload to the other side of the world within 30 minutes, and reach speeds of up to 15km per second when in orbit – less powerful ballistic missiles are slower because they do not have the same initial boost, and do not reach the high speeds possible in orbit. Broadly speaking, ballistic missiles can be classified by their operational range:

  o Short-range ballistic missiles (SRBMs) can hit targets at less than 1000km.
  o Medium-range ballistic missiles (MRBMs) can hit targets between 1000km and 3500km.
  o Intermediate-range ballistic missiles (IRBMs) can hit targets between 3500km and 5500km.
  o Intercontinental-range ballistic missiles (ICBMs) can hit targets of over 5500km.

Ballistic missiles are seen as more reliable than bombers because they are highly likely to evade any attempt at defence (ballistic missile defence is covered in Chapter 7). However, a ballistic missile cannot be called back when launched, and may be vulnerable to a pre-emptive strike while they are still in the ground waiting to be fired (ballistic missiles are often placed in underground silos, but can also be kept above ground and mobile). Long-range ballistic missile technology (not to mention the challenge of building warheads that can survive re-entry into the atmosphere) is also difficult to master, and only a few states possess intercontinental range missiles.

- *The sea: submarines and ships* The final main method to deliver nuclear weapons is by a missile fired from a submarine, or via a cruise missile or aircraft based on a surface ship. In addition to the points noted above for land-based missiles, missiles launched from a submarine have a number of advantages: submarines are the least vulnerable to any sort of pre-emptive surprise attack because they can be anywhere in the ocean and are very quiet (this is particularly the case with modern nuclear-powered submarines); they can carry many missiles and many warheads (and these can be aimed at different targets); and they can stay submerged for months at a time – only needing to surface for human reasons, such as fresh food. However, this is by far the most costly and most difficult means of delivery – a modern SSBN (which stands for ship submersible ballistic nuclear, because it is armed with ballistic missiles and nuclear powered) can be up to 150m in length and costs enormous sums of money to build. It is also possible to use submarine-launched cruise missiles (SLCMs) armed with nuclear warheads. A submarine armed with nuclear-tipped cruise missiles can be smaller than their SSBN counterparts, but has the relative disadvantage that cruise missiles have a far shorter range than ballistic missiles, and are much slower. In addition to this, nuclear-capable aircraft and both ballistic and cruise missiles can be deployed from a surface ship – this method of delivery provides high flexibility but comes at the cost of considerable vulnerability due to the size and slow speed of surface ships.

An overview of the various advantages and disadvantages of nuclear delivery systems is provided in Table 6.

Table 6 Advantages and disadvantages of nuclear weapon delivery methods

Type	Advantages	Disadvantages
Land-based missile	Quick response/large yield Very hard to defend against	Cannot be called back Vulnerable to surprise attack
Long-range bomber/ fighter aircraft	Can be called back Affordable and flexible	Have to get close to the target Vulnerable to air defence and pre-emptive strike
Submarine-launched missile	Low level of vulnerability Guaranteed second strike Can carry many missiles and warheads	Command and control issues (see Chapter 10) Very expensive and difficult to build
Ship-based missile/ aircraft	Flexibility and dual purpose Visibility of intent – signalling	Highly vulnerable Susceptible to air defence/ missile defence

Given the relative advantages and disadvantages of the different methods of nuclear weapons delivery, some states have opted for a mixture of nuclear forces. This may either be a *dyad* – consisting of two means of delivery – or a *triad* – consisting of three (surface ships are generally used for nuclear-capable aircraft or missiles and therefore don't count as an extra category). The idea behind the triad is to ensure that the use of nuclear weapons can be threatened in any scenario and at any time, and that any possible surprise first strike against a state's forces can never be fully disarming. Equally, having a range of delivery methods ensures against a problem with any one 'leg' of that state's nuclear forces, and allows for modernisation without necessarily undermining its capabilities. The USA, Russia and to a lesser extent China currently operate a triad of forces, while India is believed to be seeking this capability.

In addition to the longer and more powerful methods of nuclear delivery, many different systems have been designed to facilitate the use of nuclear weapons on the battlefield. These have included gravity bombs dropped by aircraft, nuclear artillery shells, nuclear landmines, depth charges and torpedoes, as well as other specially designed munitions. The smallest nuclear weapons ever produced include the 'Davy Crocket' recoilless gun, and the so-called 'suitcase bombs' produced by the United States and the Soviet Union during the Cold War. The types of methods that terrorist groups might use to deliver a nuclear weapon are addressed in Chapter 8.

(5) Who has what: current nuclear forces

When we refer to the total number of nuclear weapons, we normally mean nuclear warheads rather than nuclear delivery systems, and therefore it is necessary to look not just at how many nuclear warheads a state possesses but also at what they have to deliver them. That said, many arms control treaties have focused on delivery vehicles rather than warhead numbers (see Chapter 7), because a warhead that cannot be delivered is not seen as being readily useable. A nuclear warhead that cannot be credibly delivered is very different from one that sits atop a ballistic missile inside a submarine, ready to strike anywhere on the planet in a number of minutes. The aim of this section therefore is to outline the approximate capabilities of current nuclear-armed states:

The *United States* currently deploys its nuclear weapons in three main ways, and operates a triad of nuclear forces to deliver its nuclear warheads. This consists of Minuteman III Intercontinental Ballistic Missiles deployed in the continental United States (in silos in Montana, North Dakota and Wyoming), Submarine Launched Ballistic Missiles deployed on Ohio Class SSBNs, and air-launched cruise missiles and gravity bombs on B-2 and B-52 long-range strategic bombers. In addition to this, the US has several hundred B-61 gravity bombs that can be delivered by aircraft, some of which are currently deployed in Europe under the NATO nuclear-sharing agreement.[28] The USA also has a number of delivery systems that are held in reserve or are waiting decommissioning and dismantlement.

Russia also maintains a strategic triad of nuclear forces: deploying a number of different ICBMs at various bases inside Russia; SLBMs on nuclear-powered submarines; and a variety of nuclear tipped cruise missiles on long-range strategic bombers. Estimates suggest that Russia also maintains a large stockpile of sub-strategic or tactical nuclear weapons for a variety of different roles, ranging from strategic air defence to regional deterrence.[29] Like the USA, Russia has a large inventory of retired delivery vehicles awaiting decommissioning and destruction.

The *United Kingdom* only deploys nuclear weapons on SLBMs on just four submarines – one of which is always at sea and ready to fire under a policy of continuous-at-sea deterrence (or CASD). Each of these submarines is equipped to carry up to 16 SLBMs, each of which can theoretically carry a maximum of 12 warheads, meaning that each submarine can potentially carry up to 192 nuclear warheads. However, in 1998 the UK government announced that each submarine would be armed with a maximum of 48 warheads.[30] The United Kingdom previously operated a nuclear-capable strategic bomber force but this was retired in the early 1990s.

France currently operates a two-legged nuclear force as part of its *force de dissuasion*, consisting of four SSBNs and a number of nuclear-capable fighter and bomber aircraft armed with air-launched cruise missiles, or ALCMs (some of which can be deployed on aircraft carriers). Until 1996, France also deployed a number of land-based nuclear-capable ballistic missiles.[31]

China theoretically operates a triad of nuclear forces consisting of ICBMs and other missiles deployed in mainland China, a handful of nuclear capable SSBNs, and a range of heavy bombers and fighter aircraft. However, China relies primarily on its ICBMs as its main means of delivery, and will continue to do so until a new generation of quieter and more capable SSBNs have been developed.[32]

India has a range of missiles, including the soon-to-be deployed Agni V – the most powerful, with an estimated range of up to 5000km and able to hit targets in any part of China – as well as a large nuclear-capable airforce. India is also developing an SSBN capable of launching SLBMs, and a new ship-launched ballistic missile. At the time of writing India appears on the road to developing a full triad with global reach.[33]

Pakistan has developed a mixture of land, air and naval nuclear delivery systems, all of which are primarily regional in scope. It is believed that Pakistan may seek to develop a nuclear-capable submarine in response to India, but this is unlikely to happen in the short term. Pakistan is also rumoured to be investing in new battlefield nuclear weapons technologies for deployment along its contested boarder region with India.[34]

North Korea possess a number of different types of SRBMs and MRBMs that could be used to deliver nuclear weapons within the Northeast Asian region, and it has been suspected for some time that Pyongyang is trying to build an ICBM able to hit North America (although estimates of their progress towards this capability vary considerably).[35]

While *Israel* neither confirms nor denies the existence of nuclear weapons, it is assumed to possess air-, land- and sea-based options for delivery of its nuclear forces. The main components of this are nuclear-armed cruise missiles that can be launched from Dolphin class submarines, and land-based missiles, including the Jericho III ICBM. Israel also has a highly capable air-force that can deliver nuclear free-fall gravity bombs.[36]

Many other countries possess advanced missile, aircraft and submarine technologies and capabilities that could theoretically be used to deliver nuclear weapons should they choose to do so.[37]

(6) Key points and guide to further reading and resources

This chapter has sought to provide you with information about the impact of nuclear testing and the different types and ways nuclear weapons can be used and delivered to their target, and give you an up-to-date summary of who currently has what. A summary of these key points is provided below:

- There have been over 2,000 nuclear tests since 1945; the majority of these have been conducted by the United States.
- Nuclear testing has had a considerable impact on the environment, and the vast amounts of radiation released into the atmosphere have had severe consequences. Some parts of the globe are now uninhabitable due to this contamination.
- The radiation and fallout produced by nuclear testing (and accidents) have caused considerable damage to the environment, and in some cases led to human fatalities.
- The 1963 Partial Test Ban Treaty bans nuclear testing in the atmosphere, in space and underwater. The 1996 Comprehensive Test Ban Treaty bans all testing, but has not yet come into force.
- Several states have conducted peaceful nuclear explosions for use in civilian engineering and construction programmes – although these are essentially very similar to weapons tests.
- Nuclear weapons can be classified as 'strategic' or 'non-strategic/tactical/battlefield' – this relates primarily to their explosive yield intended target, and operational range, although this distinction can sometimes be blurred.
- There are many different ways by which to deliver nuclear weapons, with the most popular being via a missile (ballistic or cruise), aircraft or submarine. Each of these modes of delivery has advantages and disadvantages.

- Each state with nuclear weapons has at least one of these delivery methods, and some have a mixture of forces to ensure that they can be used if needed (see Chapters 5 and 6).

Further reading and resources

On US nuclear testing, you should consult Richard Miller 'Under the cloud' (1991); Jane Dibblin 'Day of two suns' (1990); David Blades and Joseph Siracusa 'A history of US nuclear testing' (2014); and Howard Ball 'Justice downwind' (1986). Lorna Arnold's 'Britain, Australia and the H-bomb' (2001) provides a fascinating insight into British nuclear testing in the 1950s, as does the film *Blowing Up Paradise* (2005) about French nuclear testing in the South Pacific.

A comprehensive guide to the CTBT is provided by Ola Dahlman et al. in 'Nuclear test ban' (2009); you may also like to take a look at Keith Hansen 'The comprehensive nuclear test ban treaty: an insider's perspective' (2006). Further information and excellent resources related to nuclear testing can be found on the CTBT website (www.ctbto.org) and (www.ctbto.org/nuclear-testing/). A YouTube video detailing chronological nuclear testing is also available at www.youtube.com/watch?v=LLCF7vPanrY.

On peaceful nuclear explosions, see Scott Kaufman 'Operation Plowshare' (2012); or Scott Kirsch 'Proving grounds' (2005). Edward Teller et al. 'The constructive uses of nuclear explosives' (1968) is an interesting historical viewpoint on PNEs.

On radiation, contamination and fallout see Robert Gale 'Radiation: what you need to know' (2013); Eileen Welsome 'The plutonium files', (1999); Kate Brown 'Plutopia: nuclear families, atomic cities, and the great Soviet and American plutonium disasters' (2013); Glenn Alan Cheney 'They never knew' (1996); Dean Kohlhoff 'Amchitka and the bomb' (2003); Philip Fradkin 'Fallout' (2004); and Rudolph Herzog 'A brief history of nuclear folly' (2012). On the *Lucky Dragon* incident see Oishi Matashichi 'The day the sun rose in the west: Bikini, the *Lucky Dragon*, and I' (2011). Carole Gallagher's 'American ground zero' (1993) might also be of interest.

On EMP attack see Clay Wilson 'High altitude electromagnetic pulse' (2008); Glasstone and Dolan 'The effects of nuclear weapons' (1977); and Larry and Cheryl Poole (eds.) 'EMP survival' (2011).

Bernard Brodie's 'Nuclear weapons: strategic or tactical?' (1954) and Paul Nitze's 'The relationship of strategic and theatre nuclear forces' (1977)

(Continued)

(Continued)

provide an interesting discussion of strategic and tactical nuclear weapons, as do Brian Alexander and Alistair Millar's 'Tactical nuclear weapons' (2003), and Amy Woolf's 'Non-strategic nuclear weapons' (2014). On delivery systems, see Polmar Norman and Robert Norris 'The US nuclear arsenal' (2009) and Paul Gibson 'Nuclear weapons of the United States' (1996).

On current nuclear weapons capabilities, readers are encouraged to consult the 'Nuclear notebook' published by the Bulletin of the Atomic Scientists, which provides an excellent up-to-date resource on the nuclear inventories of current nuclear-weapon states (available at http://bos. sagepub.com/cgi/collection/nuclearnotebook), and the Stockholm International Peace Research Research's annual 'SIPRI yearbook'.

Notes

1. Daryl Kimball, 'The nuclear testing tally', Arms Control Association, www.armscontrol. org/factsheets/nucleartesttally and CTBTO Preparatory Commission website: www. ctbto.org/nuclear-testing/history-of-nuclear-testing/nuclear-testing-1945-today/. Others quote 2084, which involves counting nuclear explosions rather than tests – for example the USA has conducted 1,032 tests with 1,054 devices.
2. Ola Dahlman, Svein Mykkwltveit and Hein Haak, 'Nuclear test ban: converting political visions into reality', (New York, Springer: 2009) p.9.
3. Rudolph Herzog, 'A short history of nuclear folly', (New York, Melville House: 2013) p.38.
4. Gerald de Groot, 'The bomb: a life', (London, Jonathan Cape: 2004) pp.253–255.
5. Ibid.
6. Daryl Kimball, 'The nuclear testing tally', Arms Control Association, www.armscontrol. org/factsheets/nucleartesttally; the CTBTO Preparatory Commission website: www.ctbto.org/nuclear-testing/history-of-nuclear-testing/nuclear-testing-1945-today.
7. For more on the CTBT see Ola Dahlman, Svein Mykkwltveit and Hein Haak, 'Nuclear test ban: converting political visions into reality', (New York, Springer: 2009).
8. On this see Tom Collina and Daryl Kimball, 'Going back: 20 years since the last US nuclear test', The Arms Control Association Issue Brief, 3:14 (20 September 2012), www.armscontrol.org/issuebriefs/No-Going-Back-20-Years-Since-the-Last-US-Nuclear-Test%20.
9. For more on this see the Atomic Archive, www.atomicarchive.com/Almanac/Testing. shtml.
10. Jeffrey Richelson, 'Spying on the bomb: American nuclear intelligence from Nazi Germany to Iran and North Korea', (New York, W.W. Norton Co.: 2007) pp.314–316.

11. A good overview of peaceful nuclear testing is provided by Rudolph Herzog, 'A short history of nuclear folly', (London, Melville House: 2013) p.83–111.
12. See Frank Barnaby, 'How to build a nuclear bomb and other weapons of mass destruction', (London, Granta Books: 2003) pp.23–31.
13. Robert Gale, 'Radiation: what it is, and what you need to know', (New York, Vintage Books: 2013) pp.23–25.
14. Frank Barnaby, 'How to build a nuclear bomb and other weapons of mass destruction', (London, Granta Books: 2003) p.29.
15. Ibid, p.31.
16. Gerald de Groot, 'The bomb: a life', (London, Jonathan Cape: 2004) pp.301–302.
17. Clay Wilson, 'High Altitude Electromagnetic Pulse (HEMP) and high power microwave (HPM) devices: threat assessments', Congressional Research Service, (21 July 2008), www.fas.org/sgp/crs/natsec/RL32544.pdf.
18. See Ruldoph Herzog, 'A short history of nuclear folly', (London, Melville House: 2012) pp.115–119.
19. Richard Miller, 'Under the cloud: the decades of nuclear testing', (Texas, Two Sixty Press: 1991) pp.67–69.
20. Marlise Simons, 'Soviet atom test used thousands as guinea pigs, archives show', New York Times (7 November 1993), www.nytimes.com/1993/11/07/world/soviet-atom-test-used-thousands-as-guinea-pigs-archives-show.html?pagewanted=all&src=pm.
21. Arjun Makhijani and Stephen Schwartz, 'Victims of the bomb', chapter in Stephen Schwartz (ed.), 'Atomic audit: the costs and consequences of US nuclear weapons since 1940', (Washington DC, The Brookings Institution Press: 1998) pp.421–428.
22. See Oishi Matashichi, 'The day the sun rose in the west: Bikini, the Lucky Dragon, and I' (Honolulu, HI, University of Hawaii Press: 2011).
23. Jane Dibblin, 'Day of two suns: US nuclear testing and the Pacific Islanders', (New York, New Amsterdam Books: 1990) p.4.
24. Bonnie Malkin, 'Aborigines to sue British government over nuclear tests', Telegraph, (2 March 2010), www.telegraph.co.uk/news/worldnews/australiaandthepacific/australia/7352075/Aborigines-to-sue-British-Government-over-nuclear-tests.html.
25. On this see www.nuclearfiles.org/menu/key-issues/ethics/issues/scientific/human-nuclear-experiments.htm.
26. Lizzy Davies, 'French soldiers "deliberately exposed to radiation" during nuclear tests', Guardian, (16 February 2010), www.theguardian.com/world/2010/feb/16/france-soldiers-exposed-nuclear-radiation.
27. 'America's nuclear weapons: ban the min-bomb', The Economist, (15 May 2003), www.economist.com/node/1781213.
28. Hans Kristensen and Robert Norris, 'US nuclear forces, 2013', Bulletin of the Atomic Scientists, 69:2 (2013) pp.77–86.
29. Hans Kristensen and Robert Norris, 'Russian nuclear forces 2013', Bulletin of the Atomic Scientists, 69:2 (2013) pp.71–81.
30. See Robert Norris and Hans Kristensen, 'The British nuclear stockpile 1953-2013', Bulletin of the Atomic Scientists, 69:4 (2013) pp.69–75.
31. Phillip Schell and Hans Kristensen, 'French nuclear forces', in Stockholm International Peace Research Institute, 'SIPRI yearbook 2013', (Oxford, Oxford University Press: 2013).
32. See China country profile on the Nuclear Threat Initiative website, www.nti.org/country-profiles/china/delivery-systems.
33. Hans Kristensen and Robert Norris, 'Indian nuclear forces, 2012', Bulletin of the Atomic Scientists, 68:4 (2012) pp.96–101.

34. Usman Ansari, 'Pakistan test-fires tactical nuclear missile', Defense News (12 February 2013), www.defensenews.com/article/20130212/DEFREG03/302120029/Pakistan-Test-Fires-Tactical-Nuclear-Missile.
35. See Shannon Kile, 'North Korea's nuclear forces' in Stockholm International Peace Research Institute, 'SIPRI yearbook 2013', (Oxford, Oxford University Press: 2013).
36. For more on this see Phillip Schell and Hans Kristensen, 'Israeli nuclear forces' in Stockholm International Peace Research Institute, 'SIPRI yearbook 2013', (Oxford, Oxford University Press: 2013).
37. The best resource on this can be found in the annual 'SIPRI yearbook' published by the Stockholm International Peace Research Institute in Sweden.

3

NUCLEAR PROLIFERATION: WHY STATES BUILD OR DON'T BUILD THE BOMB

Different reasons for 'going nuclear'

Vertical and horizontal proliferation

The nuclear proliferation debate in the second nuclear age

Nuclear latency and virtual nuclear arsenals

Key points and guide to further reading and resources

Given that the technology and know-how needed to build nuclear weapons has existed since the 1940s, it has come as a surprise to many that only a small number of states have sought to acquire or have acquired the bomb. Indeed, US President John F. Kennedy warned in a March 1963 speech that as early as the 1970s some 25 states might have acquired the bomb,[1] and throughout the nuclear age there have been many dire warnings of rapid proliferation to new actors. The reality is that while the number of states that possess nuclear weapons has increased (gradually), this has generally been much lower than people had dared to hope, and has actually been surprisingly limited (averaging just over one per decade since the 1940s). The reasons why such a relatively small number of states have chosen to acquire the bomb are mixed, as are the reasons why so many states that *might* have chosen to build the bomb – including those with the necessary facilities and expertise – have decided not to. At the same time, the implications of nuclear proliferation remain the subject of considerable debate. Do nuclear weapons help keep the peace, as has been suggested that they did during the Cold War? Or is the spread of nuclear weapons an inherently bad thing that increases the likelihood of accidents and nuclear use, particularly in what has come to be termed the second nuclear age? It is therefore the purpose of this chapter to begin to think about why states have decided to build or not to build the bomb, how the bomb has proliferated, and what this means for international security and stability – and finally, the problem of nuclear latency whereby a number of states are theoretically in a position to build the bomb should they choose to, but have not necessarily contravened any laws or regimes.

This chapter proceeds in four sections: the first introduces the various conceptual models that seek to explain why states decide to build and keep nuclear weapons; the second chronicles the vertical and horizontal proliferation of nuclear weapons since 1945, charting the growth in nuclear actors and the fluctuations in global nuclear stockpiles across this period; the third examines the debate over whether nuclear proliferation stabilises or destabilises international politics and assesses this in the context of a transition to a new 'second' nuclear age; and the fourth considers the phenomenon of nuclear latency, whereby a state can manoeuvre itself into a position whereby it could build nuclear weapons if it decided to, but ultimately (at least for the moment) chooses not to do so. The chapter then finishes with some key points and a guide to further reading and resources.

(1) Different reasons for 'going nuclear'

Conventional wisdom would suggest that states choose to build nuclear weapons because they believe that it is the best way to ensure their national security against an external threat in an inherently anarchical international system. By implication, states not faced with an overwhelming threat to their national security therefore choose not to build nuclear weapons. This model certainly has some validity, and it is difficult to cite any case of nuclear acquisition, or even potential acquisition, that was not driven by some aspect of national security:

- The United States built the bomb to end the Second World War.
- The Soviet Union built the bomb because it felt threatened by the United States.
- The United Kingdom and France did so because they felt threatened by the Soviet Union.
- China built the bomb because it felt threatened by both the United States and the Soviet Union.
- Israel built the bomb because of the threat from its Arab neighbours.

- India did likewise because it felt threatened by China.
- Pakistan built the bomb because it felt threatened by India.
- North Korea followed suit for fear of attack by the United States.
- Iran *might* be building nuclear weapons because it also fears attack from the United States and possibly Israel (see Chapter 6).

However, national security is clearly not the only dynamic shaping nuclear calculations. Indeed, it is equally hard to cite many cases (with perhaps a few exceptions, Israel and North Korea possibly among them) of a state that desperately needs to retain its nuclear weapons for immediate existential national security reasons in today's world. More often than not the threats to national security have either changed since each of these states decided to build the bomb, or those threats have been managed in better and more credible ways than simply through the threat of nuclear use. Indeed, it is also clear that other factors were at play in these decisions to build the bomb.

As such, and in addition to the national security driver of nuclear acquisition (for more on this see Chapter 4), we must also consider other factors that drive and shape a state's approach to nuclear weapons. Instead, or in addition to a perception of immediate or future existential national security threats, such decisions are often taken based on powerful domestic and internal factors that may have relatively little relationship with external factors at all. As Scott Sagan points out:

> Nuclear weapons, like other weapons, are more than just tools of national security; they are political objects of considerable importance in domestic debates and internal bureaucratic struggles and can also serve as international normative symbols of modernity and identity.[2]

Or as Jacques Hymans argues:

> decisions to go or not to go nuclear result not from the international structure, but rather from individual hearts. Simply put, some political leaders hold a conception of their nation's identity that leads them to desire the bomb; and such leaders can be expected to turn that desire into state policy.[3]

In his seminal work on the issue, Scott Sagan suggested that the reasons why states choose to acquire and retain nuclear weapons should be broadened to include factors other than national security. As is explained below, Sagan added two new 'models' for nuclear acquisition in addition to national security. The three models loosely reflect the theoretical divide between realism, liberalism and constructivism in International Relations Theory scholarship.

- The *security model* suggests that states build and retain nuclear weapons primarily for reasons of national security, and in this way it fits squarely within the theoretical tradition of realism. In this scenario, state A would seek to acquire nuclear weapons because of a threat to its national security from state B that could not be met by other means. As long as state B remained a threat, state A would retain nuclear weapons. Conversely, if state B did not represent a threat then state A would theoretically have no need for nuclear weapons.

- The *domestic politics model* suggests that irrespective of threats to national security, states might choose to build or retain the bomb due to certain internal domestic and bureaucratic interests. An example of this may be the use of the nuclear issue by one political party or interest group within a state for popularity or electoral purposes. Another may be the importance placed on a nuclear programme by a particular governmental department, large industrial corporations, the military, or even a specific branch within the military.

- The *norms model* suggests that nuclear weapons may be sought and kept due to the particular value they are seen to have for a state's prestige and national identity. In this scenario, nuclear weapons represent national strength, modernity and vitality, and even provide 'great power' status.

One further reason widely cited for why states build the bomb, but not included in Sagan's framework, is *technological determinism*, whereby a nuclear programme is the result of increases and developments in technology that shape nuclear thinking (driven by supply-side rather than demand-side pressures). In this model, technological developments – irrespective of security, politics and identity – drive the acquisition of nuclear weapons and the development of more and increasingly powerful and capable warheads and delivery systems. In this sense, a nuclear weapons capability becomes almost a natural extension of an advanced military–industrial complex and civilian nuclear capability. However, the fact that a large number of states that could theoretically have built a bomb but have chosen not to provides a powerful counterpoint to the notion of technological determinism. As Jacques Hymans points out, the 'yawning gap between technical potential and military reality should have led to widespread re-thinking of the phenomenon of nuclear weapons proliferation'.[4]

We can think of these 'drivers' of nuclear acquisition and retention as being co-constitutive, but often one driver has proven more important than others for the decisions taken by particular states. This is explained in Table 7. While these models have been analysed as being distinct, the reality is that the reasons that any state builds nuclear weapons – and chooses to keep them – are complicated, and may involve a mixture of all of the drivers described above. Equally, states that have chosen not to build the bomb will have done so for different and differing reasons – threats to national security notwithstanding. Nevertheless, the typology is a useful tool to think beyond a one-dimensional security-based understanding of why states might or might not choose to build nuclear weapons and of course retain them.

Table 7 Models of nuclear weapons acquisition[i]

Model	Explanation	Theoretical Home	Examples
National Security	States build and retain nuclear weapons because their national security is threatened	Realism	The Soviet Union built nuclear weapons in the 1940s primarily due to concerns about the United States
			Israel built nuclear weapons in the 1960s due to the perceived threat from its regional allies
			France built nuclear weapons in the 1960s because it did not trust the United States to protect it against the Soviet Union
			North Korea built nuclear weapons to protect itself from the USA
Domestic/ Bureaucratic Politics	States build and retain nuclear weapons due to domestic parochial and bureaucratic interests	Liberalism	Domestic political influences are a key reason why the United States, United Kingdom, France and Russia have found nuclear reductions very difficult to agree, and stand as a major barrier to disarmament (see Chapter 5)
Norms	States build and retain nuclear weapons because of the prestige the weapons offer	Constructivism	The decision by the United Kingdom to develop and maintain nuclear weapons is seen as being key to 'great power status'
			Pakistan and India both saw nuclear weapons as a means by which to highlight their modernity and development
Technological Determinism	Nuclear weapons are a natural product of technological development	Structuralism	The Manhattan Project in the early 1940s made nuclear weapons acquisition by the United States almost inevitable
			Nuclear latency (see main text)

[i]This table is based on Sagan's three-model typology. See Scott Sagan, 'Why do states build nuclear weapons? Three models in search of the bomb', International Security, 21:3 (1996–1997) pp.54–86.

(2) Vertical and horizontal proliferation

Since 1945 nuclear weapons have proliferated in two ways: first, to a range of new actors – known as *horizontal proliferation*; and second, in the quantities possessed by the nuclear armed states – known as *vertical proliferation*. The aim of this section is to show how these two dynamics have fluctuated over the past seven decades, and demonstrate that while the number of nuclear actors has slowly increased, this has had relatively little impact on overall global nuclear warhead inventories (in fact recent trends have been towards more nuclear actors but less overall nuclear weapons).

Since 1945 it is estimated that approximately 128,000 nuclear warheads have been built by the nuclear armed states – a staggering number, particularly given the fact that until early 1998 only the USA, Russia, the UK, France and China were publicly acknowledged as having the capability to do so.[5] Perhaps even more astonishing is the fact that close to 98 per cent of these bombs were built by either the United States or the Soviet Union between 1945 and 1991.[6] While many of these weapons have since been decommissioned or/and or dismantled (or at least are awaiting dismantlement), large numbers are still theoretically usable or, potentially far worse, vulnerable to theft or misuse, and what to do with all the fissile material and irradiated bomb components produced since 1945 remains a serious global problem. Total global nuclear stockpiles peaked in 1986 at approximately 69,368 warheads, with well over 50 per cent of these in the then Soviet Union.[7] Since this time, we have seen significant reductions in global nuclear stockpiles. Nevertheless the numbers remain alarmingly high, particularly the totals held by the USA and Russia.

Table 8 details how the numbers of weapons and numbers of actors have fluctuated since 1945.

Table 8 Nuclear proliferation[i]

Year	Nuclear Armed States	Estimated Total Global Nuclear Stockpiles	Increment/ Decrease
1945	1 (USA)	2	
1955	3 (USA, Soviet Union, UK)	2,636	+2,632
1965	5 (USA, Soviet Union, UK, France, China)	37,741	+35,105
1975	6 (USA, Soviet Union, UK, France, China, *Israel*[ii])	47,454	+9,713
1985	6 (as above)	63,632	+16,178
1995	6 (as above)	39,123	−24,509
2005	8 (USA, Soviet Union, UK, France, China, *Israel*, India, Pakistan)	26,388	−12,735

Year	Nuclear Armed States	Estimated Total Global Nuclear Stockpiles	Increment/ Decrease
(2015)	9 (USA, Soviet Union, UK, France, China, *Israel*, India, Pakistan, North Korea)	~16,300	−10,088

[i] Data taken from Robert Norris and Hans Kristensen, 'Global nuclear weapons inventories, 1945–2010', Bulletin of the Atomic Scientists, 66:7 (July/August 2010) pp.81–82 and Ploughshares Fund, 'World Nuclear Stockpile Report', updated 28 August 2014, available at http://ploughshares.org/world-nuclear-stockpile-report.

[ii] Israel is believed to have developed nuclear weapons by this time, but did not publicly declare this (see Chapter 6).

The table above shows a number of interesting things about vertical and horizontal nuclear proliferation since 1945:

- The largest increase in global nuclear stockpiles (35,105) occurred between 1955 and 1965.
- Nuclear weapons building dipped noticeably to 9,713 between 1975 and 1985.
- The decade 1985–1995 experienced the biggest drop in global stockpiles – primarily due to the end of the Cold War.
- Cuts in global nuclear stockpiles since 1985 appear to be slowing – and further cuts beyond 2015 are likely to prove increasingly difficult.
- The number of nuclear actors has had relatively little – if any – impact on global nuclear stockpile numbers.

Essentially the table shows that during the early part of the Cold War, nuclear inventories expanded rapidly, particularly between the early 1950s and early 1980s, but that overall, numbers have decreased substantially over the last two and a half decades. It is also interesting to note that the US stockpile peaked much earlier than that of the Soviet Union/Russia (some 19 years beforehand[8]), and that the increase in states with nuclear weapons has made relatively little difference to the overall number of weapons in the world. Many other states have had nuclear programmes and have chosen to abandon them during this period: the most notable are Argentina, Brazil, Libya, South Africa, South Korea, Sweden, Switzerland and Taiwan (see Chapter 9), while Syria and Iraq both had their respective nuclear weapons programmes curtailed by sanctions and force. As will be detailed below, some of these states (as well as notable others) retain a theoretical ability to build nuclear weapons should they choose to do so.

Both the spread of nuclear weapons to new actors and the increase in overall levels of nuclear weapons in the world present particular risks and dangers, and depending upon the view of which is more serious also suggest slightly different remedies. As Table 9 shows, the threat of horizontal proliferation requires enhanced non-proliferation efforts while the threat associated with vertical proliferation demands a greater push for nuclear reductions and disarmament. However, the two are of course linked: vertical proliferation may make nuclear weapons more attractive to non-nuclear armed states, while horizontal proliferation may make nuclear reductions less appealing for those who already have them. This is a central paradox of the nuclear international agenda, and is one of the key problems contained in the 1968 nuclear Non-Proliferation Treaty (this is explained in more detail in Chapters 5 and 7).

Table 9 Horizontal versus vertical proliferation threats

Horizontal Proliferation	Vertical Proliferation
The spread of nuclear weapons to new actors	The acquisition of more nuclear weapons by current nuclear armed states
New nuclear actors may not be as 'rational' or experienced as established nuclear powers	Large nuclear stockpiles make nuclear weapons more attractive to other states
More nuclear actors mean a greater chance of accidents, misuse, or even a deliberate nuclear exchange	More nuclear weapons mean a greater chance of accidents or misuse
	Vertical proliferation can also lead to arms racing and subsequent instability
More nuclear actors represents the greater danger	More nuclear weapons represents the greater danger
Nuclear non-proliferation needs to be prioritised (Articles I and II of the NPT).	Nuclear reductions and disarmament need to be prioritised (Article VI of the NPT)

(3) The nuclear proliferation debate in the second nuclear age

The nuclear proliferation debate centres around one key question in international politics: does the spread of nuclear weapons increase or decrease global security and stability? As is explained below, this is at the heart of a fiercely fought intellectual argument between *proliferation optimists* and *proliferation pessimists*, and is a debate that has grown exponentially in importance as we have entered what has become popularly termed the second nuclear age. This section therefore seeks to address the following broader questions regarding nuclear proliferation:

- Will new nuclear states act with the same restraint as the more established nuclear powers?
- Did nuclear weapons keep the peace during the Cold War, and if so can this remain the case today?
- Does the spread of the bomb make future nuclear use – be it deliberate or accidental – more or less likely?

(i) Nuclear proliferation in the second nuclear age

Rightly or wrongly, it has become popular to conceive of the atomic age as comprising two separate periods: the first nuclear age, which was dominated by the superpower nuclear rivalry between the United States and 'the West' and the Soviet Union and 'the East', and lasted roughly from 1945 to 1991; and a second nuclear age, which emerged after the end of the Cold War (1991–), and involves more nuclear actors in a more fluid strategic context. While this first nuclear age was characterised by stability (at least in hindsight), the prognosis for the second appears far less sanguine. As Paul Bracken explains:

> With a mixture of prudence and luck, the world made it through the first nuclear age without a nuclear disaster. Unless we prepare for the second nuclear age with a far more sober attitude, we may not be so lucky this time.[9]

The nuclear proliferation threat in the second nuclear age is addressed in more detail below.

At its most basic, the notion that we are now living in a second nuclear age is based on the idea that international nuclear politics experienced a comprehensive shift with the end of the Cold War. Rather than a world where nuclear strategy was played out through a bilateral world order (i.e. East versus West), and where only five states publicly deployed nuclear weapons, the second is instead characterised by the spread of the bomb and bomb-related technologies to new actors in a more fluid and nuanced international environment. In the words of Victor Cha:

> The second nuclear age is substantively different from the first. In the first nuclear age, whether this term referred to the United States and the Soviet Union or the next tier of nuclear powers (Britain, France, China), there were fewer agents and, generally speaking, greater uniformity among them. By contrast, the second nuclear age is like comparing apples and oranges. Not only are the levels of proliferation greatly varied, but they differ on a whole range of dimensions.[10]

In the second nuclear age, the greatest nuclear risk no longer appears to be from a large-scale conflict between major powers (although this possibility always remains), but instead from regional instability or even non-state actors (for more on the non-state actor threat see Chapter 8). Again, in the words of Paul Bracken:

> [the] greatest risk of nuclear war is in the regions, not between major powers against one another [South Asia, the Middle East and East Asia] ... how these rivalries play out will be one of the most important questions of the second nuclear age.[11]

This threat has been exacerbated by the spread of weapons of mass destruction (WMD) technology, and particularly the combination of nuclear power and ballistic missile capabilities to new actors across the globe.

Consequently, and while the first nuclear age was dominated by superpower rivalry between the United States and the Soviet Union, and predominantly by vertical proliferation, the second is characterised by horizontal proliferation and a new range of nuclear challenges. Indeed, in the past two decades three states have demonstrated a nuclear weapons capability, and others have either tried, or may be trying to do the same, and it is because of this that the nuclear threat appears to have shifted. These differences between the nuclear ages are contrasted in Table 10.

Table 10 The first and second nuclear ages compared

	First Nuclear Age (1945–1991)	Second Nuclear Age (1991–present)
Actors	The United States, Soviet Union, the United Kingdom, France, China	The USA, Russia, the UK, France, China India, Pakistan, North Korea, Israel Certain non-state actors
Threat	A large-scale nuclear war between the 'West', led by the USA and NATO, and the 'East', led by the Soviet Union and the Warsaw Pact countries	A regional crisis that escalates to the nuclear level Nuclear weapons in the hands of non-state actors
Causes	A crisis/miscalculation between the superpowers – or their proxies - could result in a large-scale nuclear exchange One side would seek a first nuclear strike capability	A small, perhaps unauthorised, regional nuclear exchange A deliberate use of nuclear weapons for war fighting purposes by a state Small-scale nuclear use by a non-state actor
Themes	The theory of mutual assured destruction was key to stability This was based on secure second-strike nuclear capabilities	Questions over whether MAD still remains fully applicable Most new nuclear states do not have a secure second strike capability
Focus	Focus on arms control and nuclear reductions to address the nuclear threat	Focus on non-proliferation, nuclear security and disarmament to address the threat
Features	This period was characterised by vertical nuclear proliferation	This period is characterised by horizontal nuclear proliferation (and vertical nuclear reductions)
Summary	*Nuclear weapons helped keep the peace (or at least prevented major war) during the Cold War stand-off between East and West*	*The spread of nuclear weapons to more actors presents a new set of global challenges, and makes nuclear use more likely*

Ultimately, the central theme of the second nuclear age is that the spread of the bomb to new actors – along with the means to build and deliver nuclear weapons – has changed the game, and consequently we may no longer be able to rely on the nuclear toolkit that helped us survive the first nuclear age. In the words of Fred Ikle:

Half a century after it began, the nuclear drama has reached the conclusion of its first act – a rather happy ending in spite of the gloomy prospects for civilization that darkened the stage at the outset. This respite, though, is not a lasting redemption from the dangers of nuclear warfare.[12]

Fundamentally, the nuclear proliferation challenge in the second nuclear age rests on one central question: do nuclear weapons make international politics more or less stable and peaceful?

(ii) Optimists and pessimists: the Waltz–Sagan debate

Perhaps the most pivotal challenge of the second nuclear age is that presented by horizontal nuclear proliferation to new actors – a challenge quite different from the vertical nuclear proliferation by East and West that characterised much of the first. Consequently, arguably the most fundamental question of the second nuclear age is whether nuclear proliferation to new actors will stabilise or destabilise international politics, and whether nuclear proliferation makes interstate (and possibly nuclear) war more or less likely. This subject is at the centre of a debate between two leading political scientists – Kenneth Waltz and Scott Sagan. That debate can be succinctly explained as follows;

> Kenneth Waltz argues that fear of the spread of nuclear weapons is exaggerated: 'more may be better' since new nuclear states will use their weapons to deter other countries from attacking them. Scott Sagan argues that the spread of nuclear weapons will make the world less stable: 'more will be worse' since some new nuclear states will engage in preventive wars, fail to build survivable forces, or have serious nuclear weapons accidents.[13]

We can think of this split as being between *proliferation optimists* and *proliferation pessimists*. Kenneth Waltz is seen as the champion of the nuclear proliferation optimists, and Scott Sagan of the pessimists. The central tenets of these two positions are explained below.

The proliferation optimists The nuclear proliferation optimists hold that horizontal nuclear proliferation in the second nuclear age should not necessarily been seen as automatically destabilising. As Kenneth Waltz explains:

> Those who dread a world with more nuclear states do little more than assert that more is worse and claim without substantiation that new nuclear states will be less responsible and less capable of self-control than the old ones have been … Such fears have proved unfounded as nuclear weapons have slowly spread. I have found many reasons for believing that with more nuclear states the world will have a promising future.[14]

This is partly because:

> New nuclear states will confront the possibilities and feel the constraints that present nuclear states have experienced. New nuclear states will be more concerned for their safety and more mindful of dangers than some of the old ones have been.[15]

Ultimately, this viewpoint believes that 'Nuclear weapons reasonably used make wars hard to start'.[16] As such, the optimists hold that the spread of nuclear weapons – in certain circumstances – should actually be welcomed, and retaliatory nuclear deterrence does and should remain the bedrock of global nuclear relations.

The proliferation pessimists The pessimistic viewpoint, on the other hand, contends that horizontal nuclear proliferation can only ever lead to an increase in nuclear dangers and the possibility of nuclear use. Pessimists point to a number of factors that make horizontal proliferation potentially dangerous: the growth of nuclear terrorism and illicit networks (see Chapter 8), the possibility of nuclear accidents, problems with ensuring civilian control, and broader command and control of nuclear weapons (see Chapter 10), the spectre of preventive war against aspirant nuclear states (see Chapter 7), and the problem of building survivable second strike forces, amongst other things.[17]

Foremost amongst these, however, is a critique of the misplaced belief that nuclear weapons helped keep the peace during the first nuclear age. In the words of Scott Sagan:

> Deterrence optimism is based on mistaken nostalgia and a faulty analogy. Although deterrence did work with the [United States and] the Soviet Union and China, there were many close calls; maintaining nuclear peace during the Cold War was far more difficult and uncertain than U.S. officials and the American public seem to remember today.[18]

Proliferation pessimists also focus on the problems of organisational culture and the ever-increasing threat of accidents and unauthorised use as the bomb spreads to new nuclear actors, 'because of common biases, inflexible routines, and parochial interests' that make 'deterrence failures and deliberate or accidental nuclear war' more likely.[19] Consequently, pessimists argue that retaliatory nuclear deterrence may not represent the panacea that it is held to be by proliferation optimists. We can compare and contrast these views in Table 11 on the next page.

(4) Nuclear latency and virtual nuclear arsenals

While only a small number of states have taken the decision to build nuclear weapons, and while the vast majority have decided not to build nuclear weapons

Table 11 The proliferation debate

Proliferation Optimists	Proliferation Pessimists
'The more may be better' thesis	'The more will cause instability' thesis
The spread of nuclear weapons will induce greater stability since new nuclear states will use their weapons to deter other states from attacking them	Instability will result from more states acquiring nuclear weapons because of a greater potential for preventative nuclear wars and serious nuclear accidents
	It is optimistic to expect rational deterrence theory to prevail
Nuclear weapons prevented a major war during the first nuclear age	We have avoided nuclear use so far due in large measure to luck rather than judgement
The nuclear terrorism threat is overstated	The nuclear terrorism/threat of unauthorised nuclear use is ever-present and will increase as the bomb proliferates
Actors are essentially rational, therefore more nuclear weapons will increase stability Nuclear deterrence works	More states with nuclear weapons make nuclear use more likely Nuclear deterrence is likely to fail in the future
An Iranian nuclear weapon could stabilise the Middle East	An Iranian nuclear weapon would fundamentally destabilise the Middle East
The likelihood for war decreases as nuclear deterrent capabilities increase *Nuclear weapons make wars hard to start*	*We must reduce the demand for nuclear weapons, strengthen the non-proliferation regime and work towards disarmament*

at all, the peculiarities of nuclear technology mean that there exist a number of states theoretically capable of building nuclear weapons at short notice should they chose to, but which are not currently considered to be nuclear armed. These states possess their own civilian nuclear programmes, often including the ability to produce highly enriched U235 or to separate weapons grade PU239, and have a relatively advanced military infrastructure that could be used to develop a nuclear weapon (for more on this see Chapter 10). While these states may not be able to build a working bomb overnight (or in total secrecy), they could probably do so in a relatively short space of time should they choose to, although estimates of this vary from case to case and amongst experts. These states are known as *virtual nuclear-weapon states* or *threshold nuclear-weapon states* because they adopt a position referred to as nuclear latency. As Avner Cohen and Joseph Pilat explain:

> Virtual weapons are indeed a reality of physics and cannot be ignored, because knowledge, experience, materials and other requirements to make nuclear weapons are widespread. A continuum of virtual capabilities exists, ranging from general technology diffusion and the existence of nuclear energy pro-grammes to conscious decisions to develop or maintain militarily significant nuclear-weapons capabilities.[20]

Nuclear latency remains one of the biggest proliferation challenges facing the international community today.

Why is it a problem? The complication of nuclear latency stems from the fact that the technology needed for a civilian nuclear power programme is very similar to that needed to produce fissile material for a bomb, and because some military hardware designed for non-nuclear weapons systems can be modified to deliver nuclear weapons (by aircraft and missiles for example). The problem is compounded by the central bargain of the 1968 NPT, whereby all states have a right to produce their own civilian nuclear energy (for more on the NPT see Chapter 7). As a result, countries can move fairly close to acquiring a nuclear 'breakout' capability without actually undermining the NPT or breaking international law – this is at the heart of the current controversy over Iran's ostensive civilian nuclear programme and whether or not this is being used as a basis to develop nuclear weapons (see Chapter 6). Because an increasing number of states are opting for civilian nuclear power programmes as the world searches for new sources of energy, the theoretical challenge of nuclear latency is also increasing. According to the then Director of the Atomic Energy Agency Mohammed ElBaradei:

> Some estimates indicate that 40 countries or more now have the know-how to produce nuclear weapons, which means that if they have the required fissile material – high enriched uranium or plutonium – we are relying primarily on the continued good intentions of these countries ...[21]

While ElBaradei's statement should not necessarily be interpreted as meaning that all these states will or could easily build nuclear weapons, it does underline the importance of this challenge. Indeed, despite the recent Fukushima nuclear disaster and the decision taken by Germany in 2011 to phase out civilian nuclear power[22] the global trend is likely to be towards more rather than less nuclear power generation in the future (on the implications of this see Chapter 10).

Who does it involve? In theory any country with an active civilian nuclear industry and a modern hi-tech military infrastructure could build a nuclear bomb, although this would not be a straightforward task for any nation that decided to do so. The best-placed states to do this have full control of the nuclear fuel cycle – that is, they can enrich the fuel for (uranium) and/or separate the by-products of nuclear fission (plutonium). States that have civilian nuclear power reactors but have to buy nuclear fuel from abroad are far less of a proliferation risk – although because plutonium is a by-product of uranium fission (see Chapter 1) these civilian power plants must be closely monitored by the relevant international authorities, such as the International Atomic Energy Agency (IAEA). However, technological capabilities are only one dynamic of proliferation, and must of course be matched with the political will and broader technological expertise required to build a bomb. Developing a nuclear warhead small enough to be placed on a missile and survive the pressures of flight and possibly atmospheric re-entry, for example, is a very difficult task, although by no means insurmountable for a modern state. In general, a nation wishing to move from latency to full nuclear weapons capability would need to meet significant challenges – not least keeping its programme secret from the international community and the IAEA.

Below are a number of examples of states that we might consider as having various degrees of nuclear latency:

- *Japan* is usually held up as the model of a latent nuclear-weapon state because it has an advanced civilian nuclear industry, the ability to produce HEU or plutonium (in addition to the stockpiles it already has), and a modern military. Given the geopolitical tensions in Northeast Asia, the threat that Japan may decide to 'go nuclear' is ever-present, although most observers would suggest that there is little enthusiasm for such a move, and Japan remains a key member of the NPT. However, it could probably build a deliverable nuclear bomb if it chose to do so within a relatively short space of time.[23] In the words of Maria Rost Rublee,

  > Japan's continued non-nuclear status seems rather puzzling. With high levels of economic, scientific, and technological development, and a sophisticated nuclear energy program … and bordered by nuclear-armed neighbors with which it has had armed conflicts, Japan also has the motive to acquire nuclear weapons.[24]

  Should the geostrategic situation in Northeast Asia change, Japan may well consider the nuclear option.
- *South Korea* operates a number of civilian nuclear power plants and has expressed an interest in acquiring the technology necessary to control the nuclear fuel cycle.[25] Like Japan and Taiwan, South Korea sits in a potentially volatile region and future changes could drive the case for a bomb. South Korea previously had a indigenous nuclear weapons programme that was cancelled in the 1970s, and until 1991 hosted US tactical nuclear weapons on its territory.[26] In the words of Jonathan Pollack and Mitchell Reiss, 'The Republic of Korea undoubtedly possesses the individual infrastructure and manufacturing base to underwrite an indigenous nuclear weapons programme'.[27]
- *Taiwan* is not a member of the NPT given its unique status in international society, and established an embryonic nuclear weapons programme in the 1970s. While it is not currently believed to have enrichment capabilities, Taiwan does (like Japan) have specific regional concerns that could lead to arguments for a nuclear weapons capability, but the costs of doing so are probably too high for the time being (US opposition, international condemnation, or even a Chinese pre-emptive strike). Nevertheless, Taiwan probably possesses the necessary infrastructure (although work would be needed to build a suitable missile and warhead) should this intention change in the future.[28] However, as Arthur Ding suggests, 'Despite the fact that strategic

THE POLITICS OF NUCLEAR WEAPONS

logic might dictate the acquisition of a modest nuclear arsenal. Taiwan is unlikely to develop nuclear weapons.'[29]

- *Brazil* possesses all the major elements needed to produce fissile material for a bomb but currently lacks the means to deliver nuclear weapons should it choose to build them – although it is suspected of having a nuclear bomb programme in the past (see Chapter 9). Brazil is also an active member of the NPT, and is therefore seen as an unlikely future nuclear-weapon state.[30]
- *Iran* is a member of the NPT but many suspect that its nuclear programme could be designed for military purposes. It is seeking to achieve full control of the fuel cycle – which would mean an ability to produce HEU and PU239 – and has a large military, including a relatively advanced ballistic missile programme. Iran is perhaps the biggest concern for future proliferation due to its current geopolitical situation[31] (for more on Iran see Chapter 6).
- *Saudi Arabia* Sitting at the heart of a region with ever-changing security requirements – not least the possibility of a nuclear-armed Iran on its doorstep, coupled with a perceived decline in US influence – and with an advanced infrastructure and burgeoning economy, Saudi Arabia represents a serious nuclear proliferation concern. As James Russell points out, 'Saudi Arabia is an important proliferation candidate and is the most likely country to move the Middle East toward an altered nuclear posture'.[32] Saudi Arabia does not currently operate any civilian nuclear facilities, but it is rumoured to have close nuclear ties with Pakistan and other states that do.[33]

A number of other states theoretically have the capability to build a nuclear bomb should they chose to (see Appendix 3), but the likelihood of this happening is deemed slight – and some of the reasons for this are detailed below (for more on the weapons proliferation aspects of civilian nuclear power programmes see Chapter 10).

Challenges involved in moving from latency There are a number of challenges facing any state that decides to move from latency to a full nuclear weapons capability, and the most pressing of these are listed below:

- Perhaps the most difficult and most important is secrecy: the implications of discovery would be severe for any would be proliferator. If discovered, it is likely that international action would be taken to prevent weaponisation – likely through sanctions but also potentially by military force. States must bypass IAEA inspections, satellite imagery and other forms of foreign intelligence in their quest to build the bomb.
- Building a nuclear warhead small enough and reliable enough to use would be another considerable challenge, as would building the missiles or other forces needed to credibly deliver those warheads to their targets.
- Any aspirant nuclear power would probably want to test a device to ensure that it worked, and this would have significant implications – not least

undermining the NPT and other international agreements – but also for secrecy, explained above.

- Diplomatically, a move to build nuclear weapons would probably lead to pariah status within the international community and a wide range of crippling economic sanctions (as we have seen with North Korea and to a lesser extent Iran).

- Above all, a move away from latency would need strong political will and a highly advanced technological and scientific infrastructure.

Nuclear latency is the natural result of the close link between the production of civilian nuclear energy and the technology needed to build a nuclear bomb. While this doesn't mean that every nation with nuclear power reactors, enrichment or reprocessing capabilities and associated technologies could easily build a bomb or will build a bomb, it does give varying degrees of potential (latency) to build one if such a decision was to be made. Nations of most concern are those with control of the nuclear fuel cycle (enrichment and separation capabilities), an advanced scientific and military technological base (particularly ballistic missile technology), and immediate or potential future geopolitical and security concerns. Iran, and to a lesser extent Japan, South Korea, Taiwan and perhaps Saudi Arabia, fit this bill closest at the moment, but it could include others in the future as geopolitics change. As Michael Mazarr explains, 'for most developed and a few developing states the question is not whether they could have nuclear weapons but, rather, how long it would take to deploy them'.[34]

(5) Key points and guide to further reading and resources

This chapter has sought to provide you with an introduction to why states have decided to build or not build nuclear weapons. A summary of these key points is provided below:

- While threats to national security are certainly one reason why some states have chosen to build the bomb, this is not the only model to explain nuclear acquisition and retention. Other key drivers include domestic politics, cultural norms and technological determinism.
- *Vertical proliferation* involves current nuclear states building more nuclear weapons. *Horizontal proliferation* is the acquisition of nuclear weapons by new actors. Both present challenges for global nuclear order.

(Continued)

(Continued)

- During the first four decades of the nuclear age, total global nuclear stockpiles rose exponentially, but overall numbers have reduced considerably since the 1980s. Over the same time period there has been a slow spread of nuclear weapons to new actors. However, an increase in nuclear actors has not meant an increase in nuclear weapons.
- It has become popular to divide the atomic age between a first nuclear age (1945–1991) and a second nuclear age (1991–). The main actors, challenges and dangers are perceived to have changed between these two periods.
- The impact of nuclear proliferation is the subject of intense debate. *Proliferation pessimists* suggest that the spread of nuclear weapons makes accidents, unauthorised use, or even a deliberate nuclear exchange more likely, whereas *proliferation optimists* suggest that such fears are overstated, and that nuclear proliferation can lead to stability through nuclear deterrence. Pessimists suggest that this problem has become worse in the second nuclear age.
- Nuclear latency refers to a situation whereby a state has the potential capability to produce nuclear weapons but has chosen not to do so. A latent nuclear state is likely to have most of the ingredients needed for a bomb, and could build one in a relatively short time if desired, although this varies from state to state. Japan, South Korea and Brazil are often cited as notable latent nuclear states, and Iran may be on the same path.

Further reading and resources

The best resource on why states decide to build nuclear weapons is Scott Sagan's seminal article, 'Why do states build nuclear weapons?' (1996–7). You may also want to consult the special edition of the journal Security Studies (2:3–4) published in 1993. Jacques Hymans' 'The psychology of nuclear proliferation' (2006) provides an interesting insight into why certain states have chosen not to develop nuclear weapons that might have done, as do Mitchell Reiss's 'Bridled ambition' (1995); TV Paul's 'Power versus prudence: why nations forgo nuclear weapons' (2000); and Maria Rost Rublee's 'Nonproliferation norms' (2009). Kurt Campbell et al. (eds.) 'The nuclear tipping point' (2004) and James Wirtz and Peter Lavoy (eds.) 'Over the horizon proliferation threats' (2012) are also useful resources on this topic. While Thomas Reid and Danny Stillman's 'The nuclear express' (2009) provides a solid historical overview of nuclear proliferation in general. More detailed information on why Israel, India, Pakistan and North

Korea 'went nuclear' can be found in Chapter 6. More details on why some states have given up the bomb can be found in Chapter 9.

On the idea of a second nuclear age and the rise of new nuclear proliferation challenges, you should see Paul Bracken 'The second nuclear age' (2013); Colin Gray 'The second nuclear age' (1999); Fred Ikle 'The coming of the second nuclear age' (1996); Toshi Yoshihara and James Holmes 'Strategy in the second nuclear age' (2012); and Keith Payne 'Deterrence in the 2nd nuclear age' (1996).

On the proliferation debate readers should begin with 'The spread of nuclear weapons' (Scott Sagans and Kenneth Waltz 1995) which was updated in 2003, before looking at Tanya Ogilvie-White 'Is there a theory of nuclear proliferation?' (1996); David Karl 'Proliferation pessimism and emerging nuclear powers' (1996); Jeffrey Knopf 'Recasting the proliferation optimism-pessimism debate' (2002); Jacques Hymans 'Theories of nuclear proliferation' (2006); and William Potter and Gaukhar Mukhatzhanova 'Divining nuclear intentions' (2008). See also the special edition of the journal Security Studies (4:4) from 1995.

Scott Sagan's chapter 'Nuclear latency and nuclear proliferation' (2010) is an excellent introduction to the concept of nuclear latency, as is Jacques Hymans' 'When does a state become a nuclear weapon state?' (2010). Michael Mazarr 'Nuclear weapons in a transformed world' (1997) and 'Virtual nuclear arsenals' (1995) are both useful resources. Benjamin Frankel 'Opaque nuclear proliferation' (1991) and Avner Cohen and Joseph Pilat 'Assessing virtual nuclear arsenals' (1998) are also helpful, while Maria Rost Rublee 'The nuclear threshold states' (2010) provides an interesting analysis of the threshold status of Brazil and Japan. The Nuclear Threat Initiative website is a great up-to-date resource on particular countries' nuclear and WMD programmes (www.nti.org/country-profiles/).

Notes

1. John Fitzgerald Kennedy, Presidential News Conference, The American Presidency Project, (21 March 1963), www.presidency.ucsb.edu/ws/?pid=9124.
2. Scott Sagan, 'Why do states build nuclear weapons? Three models in search of the bomb', International Security, 21:3 (1996–7) p.55.
3. Jacques Hymans, 'The psychology of nuclear proliferation: identity, emotions and foreign policy', (Cambridge, Cambridge University Press: 2006) p.1.
4. Ibid, pp.4–5.
5. Robert Norris Hans Kristensen, 'Global nuclear weapons inventories, 1945–2010', Bulletin of the Atomic Scientists, 66:7 (July/August 2010) p.78.
6. Ibid.
7. Ibid.

8. Robert Norris and Hans Kristensen, 'Global nuclear weapons inventories, 1945–2010', Bulletin of the Atomic Scientists, 66:7 (July/August 2010) pp.81–2.
9. Paul Bracken, 'The second nuclear age: strategy, danger and the new power politics', (New York, St. Martin's Press: 2013) p.274.
10. Victor Cha, 'The second nuclear age: proliferation pessimism versus sober optimism in South Asia and East Asia', The Journal of Strategic Studies, 24:2 (2001) p.81.
11. Paul Bracken, 'The second nuclear age: strategy, danger and the new power politics', (New York, St. Martin's Press: 2013) p.95.
12. Fred Ikle, 'The coming of the second nuclear age', Foreign Affairs, 75:1 (1996) p.119.
13. Scott Sagan and Kenneth Waltz, 'The spread of nuclear weapons: a debate' (London, W.W. Norton & Company: 1995) p.viii.
14. Kenneth Waltz, 'The spread of nuclear weapons: more may be better', Adelphi Paper 171, (London, International Institute for Strategic Studies: 1981) pp.29–30.
15. Ibid, p.30.
16. Ibid.
17. Scott Sagan and Kenneth Waltz, 'The spread of nuclear weapons: a debate renewed', (London, W.W. Norton & Co.: 2005) p.158.
18. Scott Sagan, 'How to keep the bomb from Iran', Foreign Affairs, 85:5 (2006) p.46.
19. Scott Sagan and Kenneth Waltz, 'The spread of nuclear weapons: a debate renewed', (London, W.W. Norton & Co.: 2005) p.47.
20. Avner Cohen and Joseph Pilat, 'Assessing virtual nuclear arsenals', Survival, 40:1 (1998) p.130.
21. Quoted in John Mueller, 'Atomic obsession: nuclear alarmism from Hiroshima to Al-Qaeada', (Oxford, Oxford University Press: 2010) p.93.
22. Judy Dempsey and Jack Ewing, 'Germany, in reversal, will close nuclear plants by 2022', New York Times, (20 May 2011), www.nytimes.com/2011/05/31/world/europe/31germany.html?_r=0.
23. See Nuclear Threat Initiative, 'Country Profile – Japan', www.nti.org/country-profiles/japan.
24. Maria Rost Rublee, 'Nonproliferation norms: why states choose nuclear restraint', (London, University of Georgia Press: 2009) p.53.
25. Daniel Horner, 'S Korea, US at odds over nuclear pact', Arms Control Today, (September 2012), www.armscontrol.org/act/2012_09/Sout-Korea-US-at-Odds-Over-Nuclear-Pact.
26. See Mark Hibbs, 'Will South Korea go nuclear?', Foreign Policy, (15 March 2013), www.foreignpolicy.com/articles/2013/03/15/will_south_korea_go_nuclear.
27. Jonathan Pollack and Mitchell Reiss, 'South Korea the tyranny of geography and the tyranny of history', chapter in Kurt Campbell, Robert Einhorn and Mitchell Reiss (eds.), 'The nuclear tipping point: why states reconsider their nuclear choices', (Washington DC, The Brookings Institution Press: 2004) p.258.
28. See the Nuclear Threat Initiative, 'Country Profile – Taiwan' www.nti.org/country-profiles/taiwan.
29. Arthur Ding, 'Will Taiwan go nuclear?', chapter in James Wirtz and Peter Lavoy (eds.), 'Over the horizon proliferation threats', (Stanford, Stanford University Press: 2012) p.34.
30. See Nuclear Threat Initiative, 'Country Profile – Brazil', www.nti.org/country-profiles/brazil.
31. On this see Mark Fitzpatrick, 'Can Iran's nuclear capability be kept latent?', Survival, 49:1 (2007).

32. See James Russell, 'Nuclear proliferation and the Middle East's security dilemma: the case of Saudi Arabia', chapter in James Wirtz and Peter Lavoy (eds.), 'Over the horizon proliferation threats' (Stanford, Stanford University Press: 2012) p.48.

33. Ibid, pp.58–9.

34. Michael Mazarr, 'The notion of virtual nuclear arsenals', in Michael Mazarr (ed.), 'Nuclear weapons in a transformed world: the challenge of virtual nuclear arsenals', (Basingstoke, Macmillan: 1997) p.14.

4

NUCLEAR STRATEGY: UNDERSTANDING THE MADNESS

Nuclear deterrence and the security dilemma

Mutual assured destruction (MAD)

Posture, targeting and extended nuclear deterrence

Escalation and nuclear war

Key points and guide to further reading and resources

A fascinating aspect of the atomic age is that while nuclear-capable states have been keen to build ever-greater numbers of increasingly powerful nuclear weapons – especially the United States and the Soviet Union during the early years of the Cold War – these states have been far less clear about what these huge nuclear stockpiles are actually for, how they might ever be used and how they fit with a broader security strategy. In fact, many of the questions facing policy makers in each of the states that currently possess nuclear weapons today are generally the same as those that faced policy makers several decades ago:

- How many and what types of nuclear weapons are needed to deter another actor?
- How can you create a credible retaliatory nuclear capability without this capability looking like it could be used for a nuclear first strike?
- Should you target large population centres or military facilities, and can a worthwhile distinction be made between the two?
- Is it better to try to defend against nuclear attack or leave yourself vulnerable?

- Do nuclear forces have to be on high alert to be effective?
- Can a nuclear war ever be 'won'? What would constitute victory? And is it possible to have a 'limited nuclear war'?
- How can you ensure that your nuclear forces and threat of retaliation are 'credible'?

It is these types of questions that have puzzled nuclear strategists since the dawn of the atomic age, and it is far from clear that an ultimate and workable set of answers has been achieved. Indeed, the exact mix of nuclear tactics and strategy will probably always be slightly different for each nuclear weapons capable state at different times due to differences in culture, geography, history and strategic requirements. Nevertheless, the aim of this chapter is to examine the concept of nuclear strategy, and in particular to outline the challenges facing any state attempting to incorporate nuclear weapons into broader strategic and military security planning.

The chapter proceeds in four sections: the first introduces the idea of the security dilemma, and explains how mutual distrust and the pursuit of supposed military advantage have led to nuclear arms racing, and the perceived need for ever-greater and more diverse nuclear forces; the second section explains the concept of mutual assured destruction (MAD) and how the notion of vulnerability to nuclear attack has become enshrined as a centre piece of nuclear thinking; section 3 examines the dynamics of nuclear posture, targeting strategy and the concept of extended nuclear deterrence; and in section 4 the chapter moves on to consider the threat of escalation and the prospect of a limited nuclear exchange, as well as four separate occasions when the world stood at the brink of nuclear war, but through a mixture of luck and judgement, a potential Armageddon was avoided. The chapter then finishes with a summary of the key points and a guide to further reading and resources.

(1) Nuclear deterrence and the security dilemma

The attacks on Hiroshima and Nagasaki in 1945 notwithstanding (see Chapter 1), most experts would agree that the main function of nuclear weapons is for nuclear deterrence – that is, states build nuclear weapons in order to deter other states from using nuclear weapons (or other forms of violence) against them. In this scenario, no rational leader would choose to use nuclear weapons as long as they believe that in response their opponent would destroy them in a retaliatory (nuclear) strike. As a result, for nuclear deterrence to work, the nuclear-armed state must be credible in both its *intention* and *ability* to use nuclear weapons as retribution for an attack. Essentially, in order to be deterred, a would-be attacker must be convinced that the nuclear-armed state in question would choose to retaliate in kind (or with overwhelming force), and that sufficient nuclear forces would survive a surprise first strike to do this. Deterring threats through the possession and credible intention to use nuclear weapons is therefore the bedrock of nuclear deterrence. As such, whether by luck or judgement, the overwhelming paradox of the nuclear age is that states primarily (although not always) build nuclear weapons and plan how they would be used with the hope that in doing so they will never actually have to use them.

The perceived necessity to have a credible nuclear deterrent – that is, one that could survive a surprise first strike from an adversary – does not of course occur in a vacuum. Actions taken to increase the credibility of one's own nuclear forces – such as by building more warheads, keeping forces on higher alert, or building different types of delivery systems for example (see Chapter 2) – will necessarily have knock-on effects for the thinking and nuclear deterrence calculations of other states. This phenomenon is known as the *security dilemma*, and can result in highly destabilising strategic scenarios as rival nuclear-armed states vie for superiority and military advantage, and therefore credibility, through nuclear arms racing. Put simply, a decision by state A to build a credible nuclear deterrent force might lead state B to feel it has to do likewise. State A may then feel it has to build more (or more advanced) nuclear weapons to retain its margin of security (or of course for other reasons such as those discussed in Chapter 3), leading to reciprocal decisions by B. This process can then begin to spiral as each state seeks what it perceives is necessary for its own security, and in the realm of nuclear weapons, this may well give rise to a costly and often destabilising nuclear arms race. We can think of this in the following way:

- State A builds nuclear weapons – this could be for any number of reasons, and may have nothing to do with state B.
- Nevertheless, state B sees state A building nuclear weapons and views this as a threat to their security (irrespective of why state A has chosen to build the weapons). As a result, state B chooses to build nuclear weapons too.
- State A sees state B building nuclear weapons and feels it must build more nuclear weapons to ensure its security and regain the strategic balance.
- State B feels it has to follow suit. A spiralling arms race begins, and instability ensues.

Consequently, even when state A is building nuclear weapons for no particular strategic purpose (it could be driven primarily by identity and prestige for example), the perception of this to others – for a nuclear arms race will often necessarily involve more than two states – is that this move *could* be a threat. In the nuclear age, such uncertainty and misperception have been amplified considerably due to the potential – and some would argue existential – stakes involved. As Ken Booth and Nicholas Wheeler put it, 'the security dilemma gets to the very heart of politics among nations: the existential condition of uncertainty in human affairs'.[1]

There is perhaps no better example of this phenomenon than the arms race that developed between the United States and the Soviet Union throughout early years of the Cold War (especially during the 1950s and 1960s). US nuclear weapons (first tested in 1945) were seen as a threat to the Soviet Union, so the Soviet Union decided that it had to build them too, and this in turn led to a greater number of US nuclear weapons, to which the Soviets responded likewise. The result was that as early as the 1960s thousands of nuclear weapons – some of enormous destructive capacity – were built by both sides, with increasingly little idea of how these might be used, but all ostensibly under the banner of 'nuclear deterrence' (on historical proliferation see Chapter 3). More recently, we can see similar dynamics at play in a number of unstable regional rivalries – most notably in South Asia, where tensions run high, and the prospect of instability and a nuclear arms race between India and Pakistan is an ever-present concern,[2] but also in the greater Middle East, where dire predictions of nuclear proliferation abound should Iran decide to build nuclear weapons,[3] or even in Northeast Asia, amongst Japan, South Korea and even Taiwan, as a response to North Korean nuclear weapons development or changes to Chinese nuclear policy[4] (for more on these regional proliferation and deterrence challenges see Chapter 6).

A nuclear arms race is not simply about numbers of nuclear bombs (although this has generally been held as the key measurement); it is also about the types and capabilities of different nuclear systems (and also in coordination with conventional armaments). For example, the US–Soviet nuclear arms race soon expanded to include defensive systems, different types of missiles and bombs, and various deployment plans, all of which were designed to protect against a surprise first strike by an opponent, and ensure a retaliatory nuclear capability following an attack – but all of which simply served to unnerve that opponent. In this sense the Cold War nuclear arms race was driven by a notion that every type of system that could be built should be built, and any new offensive system must be challenged by defensive systems. The result was an ever-increasing number of systems, warheads and war plans, costing enormous sums of money, and it is perfectly feasible that we could see this happen again between other modern adversaries in the regions discussed above.

(2) Mutual assured destruction (MAD)

Mutual assured destruction (more commonly referred to by the acronym MAD) is a theory that posits that stability in a nuclear arms race – and in broader international nuclear relations – can be achieved through mutual vulnerability to a nuclear attack. In such a scenario, it can never be beneficial to launch a first nuclear strike on your nuclear-armed opponent because they will be able to respond with their nuclear weapons in a retaliatory nuclear strike that will annihilate you (or at least make the cost of attacking your adversary in the first place unacceptably high). As a result, under a condition of MAD, it is believed that no rational actor would ever elect to use nuclear weapons first or to initiate a nuclear war. The logic is as follows:

- If a state is vulnerable to a retaliatory nuclear attack it will not launch a nuclear first strike for fear of reprisal.
- If two states (or potentially more than two) are equally vulnerable to a retaliatory strike then neither will seek to start a nuclear exchange.
- States therefore only need enough nuclear weapons to ensure a retaliatory strike for deterrence.
- This can be enhanced by prohibiting or limiting defences to maximise vulnerability.
- The result is that the numbers of nuclear weapons needed for deterrence can be capped or even reduced.

We can think of mutual assured destruction as a condition whereby any move to strike first with nuclear weapons to achieve a debilitating attack on your opponent – and thus a supposed strategic advantage – will be suicidal (even a surprise attack by a modern ballistic missile leaves enough time to order a response in most scenarios, and an attacker can never be 100 per cent sure of disarming an adversary). Consequently, under a condition of MAD (for it is regarded as a condition rather than a policy), deterrence is achieved through the threat of *punishment* (a retaliatory nuclear capability following a surprise first strike – potentially on population centres) rather than through *denial* (disarming an adversary through a first strike on their nuclear facilities, and limiting any response through defences).

Somewhat paradoxically, therefore, the theory of MAD posits that the best way to ensure stability is to make sure both sides are vulnerable to a nuclear attack. The best example of this during the arms race between the United States and the Soviet Union was the 1972 Anti Ballistic Missile Treaty (ABM Treaty) that prohibited the deployment of a range of anti-ballistic missile defences by both sides (for more on ballistic missile defence see Chapter 7), the logic here being that defences complicate any retaliatory strike and could therefore undermine the condition of MAD. As Lawrence Freedman explains:

> The underlying assumptions of the Theory of Mutual Assured Destruction were that, for the foreseeable future, the offence would be able to maintain advantage over the defence. Because of this, all one could do to prevent the other from inflicting crippling devastation was to threaten retaliation … The lesson drawn for arms control was that, as every step in one side's defence provided no extra security but merely a spur to the offence of the other, once both sides ceased making defensive moves forces could stabilize at current levels.[5]

The notion of MAD has been attacked from a moral standpoint – how can it be right, people ask, to rely on a policy that leaves a nation's population entirely vulnerable to nuclear attack? Essentially the answer is part strategic and part practical: vulnerability to attack makes it (theoretically) easier to curb arms races as any extra nuclear weapons have increasingly limited value, and no credible means of defence (currently) exist against a large-scale nuclear strike (for more on this see Chapter 7). Nevertheless, this model has proven more complicated for newer nuclear rivalries.

For nuclear deterrence through MAD to work therefore the threat of nuclear retaliation must be credible – a state must be able to withstand a 'bolt from the blue' first strike from an opponent, and then convince that opponent that it will definitely respond and inflict an unacceptable level of damage. A failure to convince an adversary of either of these things fundamentally undermines nuclear deterrence. As such, a state's nuclear forces must be designed in such a way that it can always respond – this is why some states opt for a number of different nuclear delivery systems, and why SSBNs are a particularly vital part of a nuclear deterrent posture given their relative invulnerability to a first strike (see Chapter 2). In this sense, the logic of nuclear deterrence is that you must make every effort to show that you can and will use nuclear weapons in order that you should never have to, and this is what underpins MAD. As Jeremy Bernstein explains, MAD 'reflected the uncertain times in which decisions were made, the novelty of the weapon, and, quite simply, an inability to come up with anything better'.[6] Nevertheless, it remains central to global nuclear thinking.

While the theory of MAD is arguably the basis for international nuclear relations (although increasingly being challenged by new concepts of deterrence), it is not without its controversies and detractors. It is worth noting three of these challenges in particular:

- *Rationality* Traditional nuclear deterrence and MAD rely on the assumption that all actors are rational – that is, that they would not make a decision to launch a suicidal first strike. However, in reality, it may be that some actors are not rational, or that they may not act in ways considered to be rational in certain circumstances. This is often a claim made against new 'rogue states' and certainly against non-state actors such as terrorists (more on this in Chapters 6 and 8).
- *Accidents* Ensuring a credible second strike means that a certain number of nuclear forces must be kept on high alert (the so-called 'use it or lose it' phenomenon) – this in turn raises the possibility of miscalculation or accidents (as discussed in more detail in Chapter 10). While we have been lucky so far in the nuclear age there is no guarantee that this will continue, especially as nuclear weapons spread to new actors. The safe and secure command and control of nuclear forces remains an ever-present challenge (see Chapter 10).
- *Morality* MAD relies on vulnerability to attack, and for many this is seen as being morally wrong – how can it be right not to try to defend against a

nuclear attack given the large number of casualties that even a small attack would likely involve? While there are strategic reasons for this, it has been much harder to convince the public of the wisdom of vulnerability, particularly given the issues raised above regarding rationality and accidents.

Given the problems inherent in a doctrine of MAD, there has always been strong opposition towards simply relying on retaliation and a policy of vulnerability (deterrence by punishment), and in recent years we have begun to see moves away from policies based purely on retaliatory nuclear deterrence through MAD, particularly by the United States (on this see Chapter 5).

(3) Posture, targeting and extended nuclear deterrence

While a strategic commitment to 'nuclear deterrence' is something of a catch-all term, the particular way in which a state seeks to achieve and design its deterrent force can vary considerably. Decisions must be made about the overall purpose of the nuclear force, the types, numbers and operational doctrine of these weapons to achieve this strategic purpose, the level of readiness and alert that these forces need to be kept at to fulfil these requirements, and who and what need to be deterred with these weapons. Each of these decisions has implications for an overall nuclear strategy, and each is determined by particular factors relating to the perceived strategic requirements at any given time.

(i) Nuclear posture

The concept of nuclear deterrence can be thought of as involving different types of nuclear postures – that is, the thinking and strategy that underpin the utility and role of nuclear weapons for any one state. We can think of these postures as existing along a continuum from minimum deterrence (the smallest force possible to provide deterrence against nuclear attack) through limited deterrence (a small nuclear force that could be used against a variety of threats) to maximum deterrence (a large sophisticated force designed potentially for nuclear supremacy and even war fighting). We can compare deterrence postures in the following way:

- *Minimum nuclear deterrence:* A posture based on deterring a nuclear attack on that country through the threat of retaliation – probably against large civilian targets (counter-value). It may also involve a small nuclear force of warheads and delivery vehicles, a 'no first use' (NFU) commitment and de-alerted nuclear forces. Deterrence is through the threat of punishment after an attack.

- *Limited nuclear deterrence:* Is similar to minimum deterrence except that nuclear weapons might be used against a wider range of threats, and possibly before a nuclear attack – and conceivably in a counter-force role. However, this posture still involves a small stockpile of weapons and delivery vehicles. Deterrence is primarily through the threat of punishment, but also in exceptional circumstances, through denial.
- *Maximum nuclear deterrence:* All options are on the table in this posture – nuclear forces will be sophisticated, diverse, large and possibly deployed globally. Nuclear weapons can be used rapidly, either for punishment or denial purposes, and against any targets deemed necessary, possibly in a massive nuclear attack. The goal of this doctrine is superiority, and could involve extended nuclear deterrence guarantees to other states. The quest for maximum nuclear deterrence can lead to instability and nuclear arms racing.

Table 12 provides a comparison of these different nuclear postures.

Table 12   Different levels of nuclear deterrence

	Minimum Deterrence	**Limited Deterrence**	**Maximum Deterrence**
Doctrine	Deter a nuclear attack on your own country	Deter all types of threats to your national security	Seek a strategic advantage and nuclear superiority
Delivery vehicles/ Stockpile	A small number of survivable delivery vehicles Low-yield weapons/ accuracy desirable but not essential A limited nuclear stockpile	Small warhead stockpile, and a survivable nuclear force A mixture of weapon yields with high accuracy	A nuclear triad and a large number of different delivery vehicles A mixture of tactical and strategic nuclear warheads High-yield weapons with high accuracy and penetration capability
Alert status	Nuclear forces not on trigger alert ready for use, they may be de-targeted, and warheads and delivery vehicles might be de-mated	A small number of forces on alert ready to retaliate quickly if necessary	Forces on trigger alert, deployed globally, able to unleash an overwhelming strike if necessary Could be launched on warning
Declaratory policy	Nuclear weapons only ever used to respond to a nuclear attack A policy of no first nuclear use	Nuclear weapons may be used in certain extreme circumstances	All options are on the table Nuclear weapons might be used pre-emptively if necessary
Targeting	Soft targets and counter-value	Some counter-force, some counter-value	All
Examples	China	The UK, France, India, (Pakistan, Israel)	The United States, Russia

China is the most obvious case of a minimum nuclear deterrence posture because its nuclear weapons are not kept ready to fire, and only a small stockpile of nuclear warheads are operational (at least compared with the USA and Russia).[7] China also has a NFU policy – which means (theoretically[8]) that it will only ever use nuclear weapons following a nuclear attack on its territory. The United Kingdom and France perhaps best represent limited nuclear deterrence postures due to their continuous capability to launch nuclear weapons with only limited warning. Although they do not possess large stockpiles of nuclear weapons (with just a few hundred apiece), neither has ruled out using nuclear weapons first in an emergency. India, Pakistan and Israel are slightly more difficult to classify because although they too have limited nuclear arsenals, their status and overall posture are less clear. However, it is believed (albeit contested) that India currently operates a NFU policy.[9] The United States and to a lesser extent Russia are best considered as maximum nuclear deterrent powers – both have built arsenals far beyond what might be required for purely retaliatory deterrence, and both retain the capability and option to strike first with nuclear weapons. (For more detail on this see Chapters 5 and 6.)

(ii) Targeting strategy

Different types of nuclear posture require different nuclear capabilities and this is reflected in the types of targets that they are intended to hit. Broadly speaking there are two different ways that nuclear weapons can be used to deter another actor: the first is by targeting enemy forces, and the second is by targeting the enemy population. Each requires different capabilities and tactics: *ground burst* detonations tend to be used for attacking hardened military targets to maximise the concentration of the blast on a small area, while an *air burst* (detonated several hundred feet above the target) tends to be used when targeting a city to maximise the spread and impact of the blast, or to create an electromagnetic pulse (EMP) (see Chapter 2). Hiroshima and Nagasaki were both air bursts.

Targeting enemy forces (also known as *hard targets*, because they tend to be well protected) is generally seen as a more aggressive strategy than targeting large population centres (or *soft targets*) because attacking enemy forces could be part of a disarming first strike (i.e. destroy the enemies nuclear forces so they cannot retaliate). Targeting forces rather than population centres does present the theoretical possibility of limiting a nuclear exchange to military targets only (a concept discussed below), while targeting cities and population centres is generally considered as a threat of second-strike punishment in response to any first strike made, because it is easier to hit large and soft targets and hold them vulnerable. As Table 13 shows, both strategies also have different costs and benefits.

Table 13 Counter-force and counter-value targeting

	Counter-force	Counter-value
Type of target	Military forces, military installations, airforce bases, command headquarters, ICBM launch sites, submarine pens	Large population centres, cities, urban areas, civilian infrastructure
Weapon requirements	High accuracy, ability to penetrate defences, possibly high yield, possibly large numbers per target	Basic nuclear weapons, small numbers, not necessarily high yield
	High level of penetration/accuracy	Small percentage of penetration is okay/accuracy is not essential
	Targets may be hardened against attack	Targets are unlikely to be well protected
	Ground-burst explosion	Air-burst explosion
Strengths	Avoids civilian population centres (at least in theory)	Only needs crude weapons to be effective
	Potentially limits war to military forces (see below)	Compatible with a policy of minimum retaliatory nuclear deterrence
Weaknesses	Requires very advanced weaponry	Raises questions about the morality of deliberately targeting civilians
	Such a capability might be seen as a first-strike capability and therefore destabilising	Raises questions of credibility – would anyone order mass civilian slaughter?
	The certainty of destruction of these types of hardened targets is difficult to calculate	

However, while the table above suggests that there are quantifiable differences in targeting strategy, the reality may not be so clear. Military facilities can be located near or within large population centres, as might command headquarters, while in small nuclear states (such as the United Kingdom, Israel or North Korea for example) any nuclear strike on any target is likely to have an enormous impact on the whole country and society. This has considerable implications for theories that suggest nuclear warfare can possibly be limited and not involve escalation (see below).

(iii) Extended nuclear deterrence

Although there are only nine states that possess nuclear weapons, many other states are also covered by these nuclear weapons through a policy of extended nuclear deterrence – in fact, during the Cold War large proportions of the globe were covered by nuclear deterrence assurances. Essentially, extended nuclear deterrence is a policy whereby a nuclear-armed state guarantees the security of other non-nuclear armed states (normally its close allies) in the event of a nuclear attack on that country. As such, if one of these non-nuclear armed states were to be threatened or even attacked by another nuclear actor, its nuclear-armed guarantor would threaten to retaliate, potentially with nuclear weapons on its behalf. The logic is as follows:

- Nuclear-armed state A provides an extended nuclear deterrence guarantee to its ally state B who does not have nuclear weapons.
- State B is threatened with nuclear weapons (or possibly a conventional attack) by a hostile state C.
- State A threatens state C with a nuclear attack if it attacks state B.

For extended deterrence to work, state B and state C must be convinced of the credibility of state A to use nuclear weapons – and suffer the potential consequences – in this scenario, even if the national interests of state A are not necessarily at stake.

The best contemporary example of extended nuclear deterrence is the North Atlantic Treaty Organization (NATO), which guarantees the security of all 28[10] of its members via US and UK nuclear weapons and ostensibly through a small number of non-strategic nuclear weapons stationed in Europe.[11] The USA also maintains a number of bilateral extended nuclear deterrence guarantees in the Asia Pacific to key allies including Australia, Japan, the Philippines and South Korea. During the Cold War, the Soviet Union provided extended nuclear deterrence guarantees to its Warsaw Pact allies in Central and Eastern Europe and to Cuba. These extended deterrence guarantees can be carried out through the deployment of nuclear weapons on the territories of allies – as is currently the case in Europe, and was previously the case in East Asia – or through certain 'offshore' nuclear capabilities such as submarines, ICBMs, or aircraft launched from carriers (see Chapter 2).

Extended nuclear deterrence guarantees have been credited with preventing a number of countries that might have decided to embark upon a nuclear programme from doing so – particularly in Europe and Northeast Asia (and perhaps most notably Germany, Japan and South Korea). Nonetheless, the credibility of a NATO guarantee was not deemed sufficient for the United Kingdom or for France in the early Cold War, with the French in particular doubting whether policy makers in Washington would really be willing to risk a nuclear attack on the USA in order to defend France.[12] As such, the reluctance to place their faith in extended deterrence guarantees was a key reason why both the UK and France developed their own independent nuclear weapons programmes in the early years of the Cold War (see Chapter 5). That said, the extended nuclear deterrence guarantees that the United States provides to a number of countries in Europe and the Asia-Pacific are seen as integral to the past and future of nuclear non-proliferation and national security in those regions. However, providing an extended nuclear deterrence guarantee has obvious effects on doctrine, targeting policy and nuclear stockpiles.

(4) Escalation and nuclear war

The underlying paradox of nuclear deterrence and the theory of MAD is that the intention and ability to use nuclear weapons as a last resort (or in retaliation as punishment) must be credible. This means that while a state may not want to fight a nuclear war, logic suggests that it must nevertheless plan to do so in case such a scenario arises – and at worst convince any opponent that it is willing to do so should it have to. Consequently, a nuclear-armed state must have a credible plan of how it will use nuclear weapons, the types of targets it will attack, and how nuclear forces and a nuclear exchange might be managed. In this sense, a credible plan for nuclear use in conflict is both essential to the underlying rationale of nuclear deterrence and also integral should that deterrence break down.

Consequently, if faced with disaster, or if its deterrence policy should fail, it is at least possible that a state may seek to use nuclear weapons to ensure its security or survival. It may also seek to do this in a 'limited' manner not only to avoid widespread nuclear use and a possible catastrophe, but also to demonstrate resolve. Equally, a crisis could escalate to the nuclear level by accident or unauthorised action, or even through simple miscalculation (see Chapter 10). Once it has entered this level, the potential for further escalation and nuclear use begins to increase, due in part to the pressures of the security dilemma discussed earlier.

(i) Escalation and limited nuclear war

Escalation refers to the possibility that a dispute or minor conflict between nuclear armed adversaries (including those covered by extended nuclear deterrence guarantees) might lead to the use of nuclear weapons, and that a potential conflict could then spiral out of control. In the words of Michael Quinlan:

> escalation refers to the familiar general fact that in situations of competition or conflict actions by one side are apt to induce reactions by the other in order to recover advantage or redress disadvantage, and that in war this process may progressively raise the intensity of fighting.[13]

Escalation might occur in three forms: (1) a deliberate decision taken to use nuclear weapons pre-emptively – either as a means of signalling intent or as a disarming first strike; (2) a nuclear device may accidentally or without authorisation be detonated in the middle of a crisis; and (3) as the result of a miscalculation arising either from the misperception of the enemy intentions or faulty intelligence. These three scenarios are examined in more detail in Table 14.

Table 14 Possible scenarios for escalation to nuclear use

Deliberate	Accidental/ Unauthorised	Miscalculation
A disarming first strike on nuclear facilities	A bomb or warhead is accidentally detonated	Escalation from a skirmish or conventional exchange
Nuclear force is used to signal intent in an escalating conventional crisis	An unauthorised attack by a rogue commander	A belief that the other side is about to use nuclear forces leads to a pre-emptive strike
Nuclear weapons are used as a last resort by a country facing destruction	Failure of command and control systems, such as early warning/intelligence	'Use it or lose it' – the pressure to act before it's too late
Small use of nuclear force targeting enemy military installations or forces (perhaps on the battlefield)	An accidental nuclear launch/ detonation due to human or computer error	An erroneous belief that an attack has been launched and therefore nuclear forces must be used immediately
The use of a nuclear weapon by terrorists	An unauthorised decision taken by a rogue military commander to use nuclear weapons (possibly on the battlefield)	Brinkmanship (testing an adversary) that goes wrong
	The *Dr Strangelove* scenario	

The nuclear taboo and norm of non-use (addressed in Chapter 10) would suggest that the deliberate use of nuclear weapons has become increasingly less likely – but that said, there are still certain scenarios where actors could escalate to the nuclear level: a conflict between India and Pakistan in South Asia, a dispute over Taiwan or the actions of North Korea in Northeast Asia, or a future Israeli–Iranian altercation in the Middle East (see Chapter 6), not to mention a future crisis between the USA/NATO and Russia. Ultimately, as long as nuclear weapons exist, the threat of miscalculation, accident or unauthorised use of nuclear weapons always remains (on accidents see Chapter 10).

Once a crisis has escalated to the nuclear level – that is, one or more of the parties has used nuclear weapons in some form – attention necessarily turns to what happens next. Is it possible to have a limited nuclear war, where only a small number of nuclear forces are used, societies are not destroyed, and a negotiated cease-fire or peace has been achieved? British strategist Colin Gray has suggested that 'a small nuclear war is an oxymoron'[14] because any crisis will necessarily escalate. But others have suggested that a small nuclear exchange, limited to nuclear and strategic forces – and avoiding population centres – could indeed be possible. Desmond Ball, for example, has argued that:

> It does not follow that all limited or selective nuclear operations would necessarily lead to an all out nuclear exchange. Small, carefully conducted attacks designed to demonstrate political resolve could well have a salutary effect. However, it is difficult to envisage the maintenance of control in situations beyond the detonation of several tens of nuclear weapons.[15]

Ideas and theories of limited nuclear use have never disappeared in the atomic age, particularly the so-called battlefield use of tactical nuclear weapons (see Chapter 2). However, whether a large-scale nuclear conflict can be prevented once nuclear weapons have been used is a question that has puzzled strategists and policy makers since the dawn of the nuclear age, and continues to do so to this day. The general consensus is that it is best not to find out, but it is far from certain that this norm will continue to hold in the future (see Chapter 10).

(ii) Surviving and winning a nuclear war

Conventional wisdom suggests that a war involving large-scale use of nuclear weaponry cannot be 'won' in the traditional military sense due to the enormous destructive capacity of these weapons and the likelihood of nuclear escalation. Even a small nuclear exchange is likely to cause crippling and possibly irreversible damage (see Chapter 1), making the idea of a victory seem essentially meaningless. In the words of Michael Howard:

> what is absolutely clear is that to engage in nuclear war, to attempt to use strategic nuclear weapons for 'war-fighting' would be to enter the realm of the unknown and the unknowable, and what little we do know about it is appalling.[16]

Such logic is based on the premise that any attempts to control or limit a nuclear war would be futile – crises would almost inevitably escalate as participants sought to retrieve an (often perceived) strategic advantage from the other. As has been explained in Chapters 1 and 2, even a relatively small nuclear exchange could have catastrophic consequences, and it is not at all clear that a limited nuclear war could be endured by any state, let alone a geographically small one, given the likely destruction, death and disruption that would be caused. Indeed, former Soviet Premier Nikita Khrushchev once famously remarked that in a nuclear war 'the living will envy the dead'.[17]

That said, throughout the nuclear age strategists and officials have constantly revisited the question of nuclear war. There were essentially two reasons for this: first, it has been argued that policy makers must consider how to fight a nuclear war in case deterrence fails; and second, some have argued that it might be possible to devise a theory of victory in a nuclear war. In the words of American strategist Herman Khan:

> Despite a widespread belief to the contrary, objective studies indicate that even though the amount of human tragedy would be greatly increased in the post-war world, the increase would not preclude normal and happy lives for the majority of survivors and their descendants.[18]

Former Chinese leader Mao Tse-tung echoed Khan's thoughts in a rather more chilling manner:

> The atomic bomb is nothing to be afraid of. China has millions of people. It cannot be bombed out of existence. If someone else can drop an atomic bomb, I can too. The death of 10 or 20 million people is nothing to be afraid of ...[19]

In truth, we can only speculate what would happen in a nuclear exchange as we do not have any hard data on which to base our assumptions, other than that many people would probably die and significant destruction would likely result from any nuclear use – limited or otherwise. The spectre of what might happen and what could happen, however, is clear. A limited nuclear exchange could very quickly escalate, and the idea of some type of victory may become a hollow and largely meaningless term. In the words of Ronald Reagan and Mikhail Gorbachev, 'Nuclear war can never be won, and must never be fought'.[20]

(iii) Nuclear near misses

The history of the nuclear age is littered with near misses, many of which are only now coming to light, and it is likely that there are many more that we will never know about. The four cases listed below give you an idea of just how easily miscalculation and misjudgement could potentially lead to catastrophic nuclear outcomes. In three of these scenarios two well-armed nuclear powers (in this case the USA and the Soviet Union/Russia) came perilously close to initiating a nuclear war. That they didn't was perhaps down to the personalities involved, but also equally down to a large amount of luck. In the other scenario two newly nuclear-armed states – India and Pakistan – fought a limited conventional war that might easily have escalated to the nuclear level.

- *The Cuban Missile Crisis (1962)* The Cuban Missile Crisis of October 1962 began when a US U2 spy aircraft discovered that a number of Soviet nuclear ballistic missile sites were under construction in communist Cuba. The crisis continued for 13 days as the United States considered a range of options – including a direct attack on Cuba – which later declassified documents suggest could have resulted in a nuclear exchange between the United States and the Soviet Union. Following a period of incredible tension, President John F. Kennedy ordered a quarantine of the island, and the crisis was resolved diplomatically between Kennedy and the Soviet leader Nikita Khrushchev.
- *Able Archer 83 (1983)* Able Archer was a highly realistic military exercise conducted over ten days by NATO forces in November 1983, simulating the procedures that might prelude a nuclear strike on the Soviet Union. The exercise came at a time of heightened tension in the Cold War

(new nuclear missiles had been deployed to Europe, the Strategic Defense Initiative (SDI) had been announced and US rhetoric had been substantially increased), and was consequently misinterpreted by the Soviet leadership as a diversion tactic by the West in preparation for a nuclear first-strike attack on the Soviet Union. As a result, the Soviets readied their nuclear forces and placed various units deployed in Europe on high alert, while a number of false alarms in Soviet early warning systems heightened tensions ever further. NATO leaders only learnt of how seriously the Soviet Politburo took the exercise, and how close they could have been to nuclear war, years after the event.[21]

- *The Norwegian Rocket Incident (1995)* In January 1995 Norwegian and American scientists launched a four-stage rocket from the north-western coast of Norway to carry scientific equipment into space to study the Aurora Borealis (the Northern Lights) over Svalbard. The flight path of the rocket was very similar to one that might have been used by a nuclear-armed US ballistic missile aimed at Moscow, and displayed similar flight characteristics to a US SLBM launched from the sea – a tactic that might be used for a disabling electromagnetic pulse detonation to disable Russian forces before a full US/NATO strike. Russian nuclear forces were put on high alert and Russian president Boris Yeltsin was given the decision whether to order a nuclear retaliation – in fact he was given the infamous 'nuclear suitcase' containing the launch codes for Russian ICBMs and other weapons. Luckily for all he decided to wait.[22]

- *The Kargil War (1999)* In 1999, just a few months after both nations had conducted overt nuclear weapons tests in mid-1998, India and Pakistan went to war along the Line of Control in the disputed territory of Kashmir (the fourth time since 1947). While the war lasted only a few months (from May to June), there have been allegations that both sides considered escalating this to the nuclear level.[23] Concern remains that any future conflict in South Asia might involve a nuclear exchange. (For more on India–Pakistan nuclear relations see Chapter 6.)

We may never truly know how close the world has come to nuclear war in the past – calm heads or simply luck appear to have spared us so far, but it is not at all clear that we will continue to be so fortunate in the future. Would Israel act with restraint if faced with a possible existential first nuclear strike, perhaps from Iran? Could a balance be kept between India and Pakistan in a similar scenario, or in Northeast Asia if North Korea raises tensions again – as it has in the past? Equally, the nuclear element must always be remembered in any future crisis between the USA/NATO and Russia, such as the recent clash over Ukraine. Miscalculation and misjudgement are natural human traits, but the introduction of nuclear weapons makes the cost of getting this wrong potentially catastrophic.[24] While these are open-ended and difficult questions, they must be considered as we move forward and seek to secure our nuclear future.

(5) Key points and guide to further reading and resources

This chapter has sought to provide you with an introductory guide to nuclear strategy and the different thinking that has underpinned and continues to shape the development and deployment of nuclear weapons. A summary of these key points is provided below:

- Nuclear deterrence is the ability to dissuade or prevent a conventional or nuclear attack through the threat of nuclear retaliation. The desire and ability to use nuclear weapons is a fundamental part of nuclear deterrence.
- Nuclear arms races are driven by the security dilemma – the condition of uncertainty about the actions and intentions of others that defines international politics – irrespective of the original reasons for nuclear acquisition.
- The centrepiece of MAD is ensuring that both sides are vulnerable to nuclear attack and that both can retaliate. In theory, this ensures that no rational actor will ever seek to strike first with nuclear weapons, but in practice it has proved hard for the general public to accept.
- States have different requirements for nuclear weapons and this is reflected in their nuclear postures. These can range from minimum deterrence involving small stockpiles and de-alerted forces, to maximum deterrence involving large sophisticated nuclear weapons and delivery systems and the possibility of pre-emptive use.
- Conventional wisdom suggests that a nuclear war can never be 'won', but this has not stopped states considering options for a limited nuclear exchange during a crisis – which could escalate from a conventional dispute or skirmish. Indeed, the logic of nuclear deterrence means that planning for nuclear use is intrinsic to credibility and therefore stability.
- Miscalculation and misjudgement are natural human traits – but in the nuclear age the costs of getting this wrong are potentially catastrophic.

Guide to further reading and resources

The best book on nuclear strategy and on how nuclear thinking has changed since 1945 is undoubtedly Lawrence Freedman's 'The evolution of nuclear strategy' (2003), but you should also consult Bernard Brodie et al. 'The absolute weapon' (1946) and 'Strategy in the missile age' (2008 [1959]), each of which provide a good introduction to early nuclear thinking in the USA, as well as Thomas Schelling's 'Arms and influence' (1966). Herman Kahn's 'On thermonuclear war' (2007 [1960]) is a good insight into unconventional early Cold War US nuclear thinking. Ken Booth and Nicholas Wheeler's book 'The security dilemma' (2008) and Robert Jervis 'Perception and misperception in international politics' (1976) and 'Cooperation under the security dilemma' (1978) are the best resources on the security dilemma.

On extended deterrence see David Yost 'The US and extended deterrence in Europe' (1999) and 'Extended deterrence in NATO' (2009); Lawrence Freedman 'The evolution and future of extended nuclear deterrence' (1989); and Matthew Fuhrmann and Todd Sechser's more recent 'Signalling alliance commitments' (2014).

On theories of fighting, limiting and winning nuclear war see Henry Kissinger 'Nuclear weapons and foreign policy' (1957); Colin Gray 'Nuclear strategy: the case for victory' (1979); Michael Howard 'On fighting a nuclear war' (1981); Colin Gray and Keith Payne 'Victory is possible' (1980); and Robert Scheer 'With enough shovels: Reagan, Bush and nuclear war' (1983). Ian Clarke's 'Limited nuclear war' (1982) is another useful resource, as are Desmond Ball's 'Can nuclear war be controlled?' (1981), and Bernard Brodie's 'Escalation and the nuclear option' (1966).

On the Cuban Missile Crisis, see Michael Dobbs 'One minute to midnight' (2009); Graham Allison and Phillip Zelikow 'Essence of decision' (1999 [1971]); or Aleksandr Fursenko and Timothy Naftali's 'One hell of a gamble' (2001 [1997]). You may also be interested in the film *13 Days*, which depicts the events surrounding the 1962 Cuban Missile Crisis. On Able Archer 83 see Arnav Manchanda 'When truth is stranger than fiction' (2009) and on the Kargil war see the suggested reading at the end of Chapter 6.

Eric Schlosser's 'Command and control' (2013) provides a excellent overview of accidents and near misses involving US nuclear weapons, as does Shaun Gregory's 'The hidden cost of deterrence' (1990), and Peter Pry's 'War scare' (1999). Nuclear near misses have also been a rich source for Hollywood films, most notably *Fail Safe*, which is based on a novel by Eugene Burdick and Harvey Wheeler, and William Prochnau's *Trinity's Child* (see Appendix 4).

Notes

1. Ken Booth and Nicolas Wheeler, 'The security dilemma: fear, cooperation and trust in world politics', (Basingstoke, Palgrave Macmillan: 2008) p.1.
2. See S. Paul Kapur, 'India and Pakistan's unstable peace: why nuclear South Asia is not like Cold War Europe', International Security, 30:2 (2005) pp.127–152.
3. On this see David Blair, 'Iran's nuclear programme "may spark Middle East" weapons race', Telegraph, (20 May 2008), www.telegraph.co.uk/news/worldnews/middleeast/iran/1994117/Irans-nuclear-programme-may-spark-Middle-East-weapons-race.html.

4. See, for example, James Clay Moltz, 'Future nuclear proliferation scenarios in Northeast Asia', The Nonproliferation Review, 13:3 (2006) pp.591–604.
5. Lawrence Freedman, 'The evolution of nuclear strategy', (Basingstoke, Palgrave Macmillan: 2003) p.245.
6. Stephen Younger, 'The bomb: a new history', (New York, HarperCollins: 2009) p.45.
7. On this see Taylor Fravel and Evan Medeiros, 'China's search for assured retaliation: the evolution of Chinese nuclear strategy and force structure', International Security, 35:2 (2010) pp.48–87.
8. In reality a no-first-use policy is only a declaration. China, or any other nuclear-armed state, could in theory use nuclear weapons first if it chose to do so.
9. For an up-to-date view on this debate see Vipin Narang, 'Five myths about India's nuclear posture', The Washington Quarterly, 36:3 (2013) pp.143–157.
10. Albania, Belgium, Bulgaria, Canada, Croatia, the Czech Republic, Denmark, Estonia, France, Germany, Greece, Hungary, Iceland, Italy, Latvia, Lithuania, Luxembourg, the Netherlands, Norway, Poland, Portugal, Romania, Slovakia, Slovenia, Spain, Turkey, the United Kingdom, the United States.
11. A small number of nuclear gravity bombs (approximately 200) are deployed in Belgium, Germany, Italy, the Netherlands, and Turkey. See Robert Norris and Hans M. Kristensen, 'US tactical nuclear weapons in Europe, 2011', Bulletin of the Atomic Scientists, 67:1 (2011) pp.64–73.
12. Bruno Tertrais, 'The last to disarm? The future of France's nuclear weapons', The Nonproliferation Review, 14:2 (2007) p.251.
13. Michael Quinlan, 'Thinking about nuclear weapons: principles, problems, prospects', (Oxford, Oxford University Press: 2009) p.62.
14. Colin Gray, 'The second nuclear age', (Boulder CO, Lynne Rienner Publishers: 1999) p.94.
15. Desmond Ball, 'Can nuclear war be controlled?' Adelphi Paper 165, (London, The International Institute for Strategic Studies: 1981) p.2.
16. Michael Howard, 'On fighting a nuclear war', International Security, 5:4 (1981) p.14.
17. Fred Shaprio (ed.), 'The Yale book of quotations', (Newhaven CT, Yale University Press: 2007) p.426.
18. Herm an Kahn, 'On thermonuclear war', (London, Transaction Publishers: 2007 [1960]) p.21.
19. Quoted in David Halberstam, 'The coldest winter: America and the Korean War', (London, Pan Macmillan Ltd: 2009) p.355.
20. Ronald Reagan and Mikhail Gorbachev, 'Joint Soviet–United States statement on the summit meeting in Geneva', (21 November 1985), www.reagan.utexas.edu/archives/speeches/1984/112185a.htm.
21. See Arnav Manchanda, 'When truth is stranger than fiction: the Able Archer incident', Cold War History, 9:1 (2009) pp.111–133.
22. For a good overview of this see Peter Pry, 'War scare: Russia and America on the nuclear brink'', (Westport CT, Greenwood Publishing Group: 1999) pp.183–185.
23. See Feroz Hassan Khan, 'Eating grass: the making of the Pakistani bomb', (Stanford, Stanford University Press: 2012) pp.313–315.
24. On this see Robert Jervis, 'Perception and misperception in international politics', (Princeton NY, Princeton University Press: 1976).

5

VERTICAL PROLIFERATION CHALLENGES: ASSESSING ARTICLE VI OF THE NPT

Article VI and the commitment to disarmament

The United States and the new triad

Russia and great power status

The United Kingdom and Trident replacement

France and the *force de dissuasion*

China and minimum deterrence

Key points and guide to further reading and resources

The nuclear Non-Proliferation Treaty (NPT) recognises the right of five states to possess nuclear weapons – the USA, Russia, the UK, France and China – and these states are often referred to as the nuclear-weapon states (NWS) or as the P5 because they are also the five permanent members of the United Nations Security Council (although the UN Security Council was established before most of these states acquired nuclear weapons). In return, under the terms of Article VI of the NPT (see Chapter 7), these five states are committed to the eventual goal of complete nuclear disarmament. However, they have repeatedly been accused by others of not living up to this central bargain, and instead have continually found ways to justify keeping their nuclear arsenals. In the words of Joseph Rotblat:

nuclear disarmament is not just an ardent desire of the people, as expressed in many resolutions of the United Nations. It is a legal commitment by the five official nuclear states, entered into when they signed the Non-Proliferation Treaty.[1]

The result is that while global nuclear order is undoubtedly challenged by new aspirant nuclear states and potentially by non-state actors (see Chapters 6 and 8), the reluctance of the P5 states to fully address their treaty commitments remains a constant thorn in the international non-proliferation agenda. Moreover, those nuclear armed states not recognised by the NPT have described this current condition as one of 'nuclear apartheid' whereby it is legal under the treaty for some states to have nuclear weapons but not for others (i.e. those that developed nuclear weapons after 1968).[2] The aim of this chapter therefore is to give an overview of each of the P5 states' current nuclear thinking, what underpins their nuclear strategy, and what key factors are likely to affect their future commitment to disarmament under Article VI of the NPT.

This chapter proceeds in six sections: it begins by outlining the commitment made by the P5 NWS to the ultimate goal of nuclear disarmament under Article VI of the NPT, and how the recent P5 process has sought to advance this; the second section examines current nuclear thinking in the United States, specifically regarding arms reductions and moves towards a more nuanced deterrence strategy and a new triad of strategic forces; section 3 looks at Russia and analyses the important role that nuclear weapons continue to play for Moscow, both strategically and politically; in section 4 the current nuclear debate in the United Kingdom is addressed, focusing closely on the recent dispute over replacing the Trident nuclear weapons system; section 5 considers the case of France, and French approaches to nuclear weapons and nuclear disarmament; and finally, in section 6, contemporary Chinese nuclear strategy and policy are analysed. The chapter finishes with a summary of the key points and a guide to further reading and resources.

(1) Article VI and the commitment to disarmament

As part of the central bargain of the 1968 NPT, the five states recognised by the treaty as NWS (the USA, Russia, the UK, France and China) – known as the P5 – pledged to work in 'good faith' towards total nuclear disarmament under Article VI of the treaty. In return, the other non-nuclear-weapon states (NNWS) party to the treaty agreed not to seek a nuclear weapons capability for themselves. As a result, and while the treaty recognised and legalised 'the division of the world into nuclear haves and nuclear have-not's' this would 'not be permanent. Eventually the nuclear weapon states would eliminate their arsenals'.[3] As Article VI of the NPT points out:

> Each of the Parties to the Treaty undertakes to pursue negotiations in good faith on effective measures relating to cessation of the nuclear arms race at an early date and to nuclear disarmament, and on a treaty on general and complete disarmament under strict and effective international control.[4]

The legal commitment to work towards total nuclear disarmament was a central part of the agreement, and without this it would have been highly unlikely that any international regime could have been established. Essentially, the commitment to eventual disarmament was also seen as the counterbalance for efforts towards preventing further nuclear proliferation: in the words of Sverre Lodgaard, a disarmament *quid* for the non-proliferation *quo*.[5] However, while a lack of progress towards nuclear disarmament was perhaps reluctantly accepted during the Cold War, pressure has mounted considerably during the past two decades for the NWS to make more of an effort to fulfil their legal commitments under Article VI.

The actual meaning of Article VI has always been a matter of dispute between the NWS and the NNWS, and while this difference played a limited role between 1968 and the conclusion of the first nuclear age in 1991, in the past two decades concerns that the nuclear-armed states recognised by the NPT are not taking their disarmament commitments under Article VI seriously enough have mounted considerably. As Andrea Berger and Malcolm Chalmers explain:

> Non-Nuclear Weapon States (NNWS) party to the Non-Proliferation Treaty (NPT) charge that the five recognised Nuclear-Weapon States (NWS) – China, France, Russia, the UK and the US – are too lackadaisical about their commitments to pursue disarmament in good faith, particularly since the international environment has changed so dramatically since the end of the Cold War. They complain that disarmament-relevant initiatives agreed to by the NWS in NPT meetings since the 1990s have progressed at little more than a snail's pace. The NWS counter that they have substantially reduced their nuclear-weapons stockpiles in the past two decades and have accepted a responsibility to continue to pursue disarmament.[6]

Fundamentally, the NNWS charge is that there is no real commitment to disarm – as is required under Article VI – by the P5, and that the NWS and the NPT regime more broadly have focused too much on non-proliferation and not enough on disarmament. As Steven Miller argues:

> the NWS have clearly perceived Article VI to be ancillary and subordinate to the principle purposes of the NPT – that is, preventing the spread of nuclear weapons to other states.[7]

Moreover, the reluctance of the P5 states to meet their disarmament obligations under the NPT is viewed as one of the key drivers of horizontal nuclear proliferation since 1968.[8]

Part of the problem is the ambiguous nature of Article VI – in fact, the vague wording of the disarmament commitment in the NPT is cited by both the NWS and NNWS as justification for their current nuclear policies. While the P5 NWS focus on the first part of the text that stipulates *negotiating in good faith* as the key clause – and cite recent arms control reductions as evidence of this good faith – the NNWS argue that the clause makes *nuclear disarmament an obligation*, and charge that the NWS are not taking this seriously enough, and have little intention to disarm. Irrespective of which side is correct, this split is becoming increasingly important to the future of the entire NPT regime. The ongoing debate over Article VI is examined in more detail in Table 15.

Table 15 The debate over Article VI of the NPT

P5 Nuclear-Weapon States (NWS)	Non-Nuclear-Weapon States (NNWS)
Article VI commits the P5 NWS to *work towards* disarmament at some point in the future	Article VI is a *formal legal obligation* of the P5 NWS to eliminate their nuclear weapons as soon as possible
The NWS – particularly the USA and Russia – have made significant cuts in their nuclear forces in recent years, and will continue to do so	The NWS are not taking their commitment to disarm under the NPT seriously, and this is undermining the bargain at the heart of the treaty
The nuclear weapons of the NWS help maintain global peace and stability	The failure to meet disarmament is driving nuclear proliferation to new actors
The NWS are increasingly moving towards 'minimum nuclear deterrence' postures	The failure of the NWS to disarm is making it more difficult to deal with nuclear outliers
It is more important to focus on preventing the horizontal spread of nuclear weapons (Articles I & II) rather than on nuclear disarmament	It is more important to focus on nuclear disarmament (Article VI) rather than on preventing horizontal nuclear proliferation
As long as nuclear weapons exist the P5 should retain them	*As long as the P5 keep their nuclear weapons more states will seek the same capabilities*

Pressure to address the requirements of Article VI has grown considerably over previous decades, particularly at the NPT Review Conferences (also known as RevCons) held in New York in 1995, 2000, 2005 and 2010, and particularly from the so-called Non-Aligned Movement (NAM) group of states.[9] Moreover, and although a proposed plan for a Nuclear Weapons Convention (NWC) ultimately failed at the 2010 RevCon, the final agreement did make the centrality of Article VI clear:

> The Conference notes the reaffirmation by the nuclear weapon states of their unequivocal undertaking to accomplish, in accordance with the principle of irreversibility, the total elimination of their nuclear arsenals leading to nuclear disarmament, to which all States parties are committed under article VI of the Treaty.[10]

It also committed the P5 states to report on their disarmament activities at the 2014 NPT preparatory committee meeting, prior to the main conference in 2015.[11]

A direct result of the increasing pressure on the P5 states was the announcement in 2009 of the so-called P5 process, which would begin with an inaugural meeting of the P5 in London to discuss ways of working towards eventual disarmament. Andrea Berger and Malcolm Chalmers explain this in more detail:

> In 2009, in a further effort to assuage NNWS concerns, the NWS took the unprecedented step of commencing a process of multilateral consultations and cooperation on disarmament-related issues. Although the NPT had already been in force for almost forty years, no previous attempt had been made to create a forum in which all five NWS would discuss collectively, and on a regular basis, how they would fulfil their unique responsibilities under the treaty. The very establishment of this 'P5 process', therefore, was an important step forward.[12]

Subsequent P5 meetings have been held in Paris in 2011, Washington in 2012, and Geneva in 2013,[13] but progress has been slow, and discussions have not moved far beyond attempting to agree a nuclear terminology, increase the transparency of nuclear arsenals and work towards a fissile material production ban. According to Nick Ritchie:

> The P-5 process has raised hopes of meaningful outcomes at the 2015 NPT Review Conference for non-nuclear weapon states. Failure to generate such outcomes will likely compound the regime's current malaise and risk disengagement from the treaty review process by disaffected NNWS.[14]

As the following sections show, the P5 process – not to mention the ultimate goal of nuclear disarmament – remains a long way off for most of the P5 states, and this has important broader implications. Essentially, as long as the P5 NWS fail to meet their obligations under Article VI (or at least are viewed as not working in 'good faith' towards this goal), it will be difficult if not impossible to stop the proliferation of nuclear weapons to other actors. Or as Sverre Lodgaard puts it, 'as long as *some* states possess nuclear weapons, *others* will seek them too'.[15]

(2) The United States and the new triad

As the first nation to develop nuclear weapons, and the only country ever to have used them, the United States is viewed as bearing a special responsibility in the global nuclear order, and this is something that President Barack Obama appears to be particularly cognizant of. Since he took office in 2009, the Obama administration has striven to place the issue of nuclear disarmament and Article

VI of the NPT back at the centre of the US political debate – rhetorically through high-level speeches in Prague and Berlin, and more concretely as part of the 2010 New START nuclear reductions agreement with Russia (see Chapter 7). However, and while President Obama has certainly rejuvenated the idea of nuclear disarmament in American and global politics, he has nevertheless made it clear that nuclear weapons remain central to US national security thinking:

> I have made it clear that America will not disarm unilaterally. Indeed, as long as states retain nuclear weapons, the United States will maintain a nuclear deterrent that is strong, safe, secure, and reliable.[16]

Equally, recent US moves to diversify national security capabilities away from nuclear weapons and towards advanced conventional weaponry – in which the USA enjoys a significant global qualitative advantage – may well be making nuclear cuts by other powers far more difficult.

While the Obama administration has sought to re-engage with the international non-proliferation regime, and in particular to address the growing concern about US commitments under Article VI of the NPT, there is relatively little mainstream political enthusiasm in the United States for total nuclear disarmament any time soon. Moreover, the USA still retains a large and diverse nuclear weapons capability, continues to view nuclear weapons as key to fulfilling US national and global security commitments, has yet to ratify the CTBT, and appears set to remain the foremost global nuclear power for some time to come. That said, over the past two decades it has taken steps to reduce its nuclear stockpile (both unilaterally, and bilaterally with Russia), and has also sought to reduce the reliance it places on nuclear weapons for US national security. Indeed, as part of what has become known as the new triad of strategic forces (nuclear and non-nuclear strike options, active and passive defences, and an advanced infrastructure), there has been a gradual move towards a greater reliance on advanced conventional military forces to augment and even replace the missions and roles assigned to nuclear weapons. According to the 2010 US Nuclear Posture Review:

> With the advent of U.S. conventional military preeminence and continued improvements in U.S. missile defenses and capabilities to counter and mitigate the effects of CBW, the role of U.S. nuclear weapons in deterring non-nuclear attacks – conventional, biological, or chemical – has declined significantly. The United States will continue to reduce the role of nuclear weapons in deterring non-nuclear attacks.[17]

Essentially, this broader spectrum of military forces has been designed to provide more flexibility when dealing with nuclear issues. These new capabilities provide extra assurance (and insurance) in case deterrence should fail – especially through the deployment of ballistic missile defences – and they also offer ways to get around the problems inherent in threatening to use nuclear weapons – exemplified by the so-called nuclear taboo (see Chapter 10) – because technological progress allows conventional weapons to be used for roles previously reserved solely for nuclear weapons. As David McDonough explains:

> The new triad represents a complex and potentially contradictory effort to reduce American self-deterrence by de-emphasising the role of nuclear weapons through an expansion of non-nuclear components in US deterrence calculus, while simultaneously attempting to modify American nuclear forces to play a more tailored deterrent role against potential adversaries.[18]

That said, and at least to some extent, the United States – and especially the Obama administration – have adopted these developments as part of a concerted effort to re-engage with its obligations under the NPT.

However, a move in this direction is not without its complications, and it may be that a greater reliance on conventional forces (particularly missile defence and conventional global and precision strike programmes) by the United States makes nuclear weapons even more valuable for the national security of others, and thereby could well undermine the broader commitment to work towards disarmament.[19] As I have pointed out elsewhere in a piece with Benjamin Zala:

> The net result is that if reducing the role of nuclear weapons in US defense and security thinking cannot be delinked from qualitative and quantitative advances in programs such as BMD and PGS [Prompt Global Strike], the Obama approach may actually make the goal of nuclear disarmament more difficult.[20]

As is discussed below, advances and qualitative advantages in US conventional forces – particularly BMD – are a major reason for the Russian and Chinese reluctance to contemplate reducing their own nuclear forces. In this sense, and while a greater reliance on conventional forces might well help to facilitate reductions in US nuclear weapons, it will do little to create the conditions for broader multilateral nuclear cuts.

There is perhaps no better example of this than in the relationship with Russia. While significant progress on nuclear arms reductions has been made over the past two decades, this has come about because nuclear forces could be reduced without any significant implications for national security (see Chapter 3) – cuts beyond the levels agreed under the current 2010 New START agreement will, however, begin to have far greater implications. There are two important components to this: (1) further cuts in US nuclear weapons numbers will require reciprocal moves from Russia, but for this to be politically acceptable in the USA, any deal will almost certainly have to exclude limits of US ballistic missile defence systems; and (2) Russia appears unwilling to discuss further arms control/reductions without a legal commitment to limit the deployment of ballistic missile defences. The net result is that the prospect of further cuts beyond the current status quo – and therefore moves towards involving the other NWS, who have far smaller nuclear stockpiles – appear bleak.

The United States is arguably the pivotal player in the quest to work 'in good faith' towards the legal requirements of Article VI of the NPT: US actions are intrinsic to Russian and particularly Chinese nuclear policy; central to any notion that the nuclear arms control/reductions agenda can be truly multilateralised, and that eventual nuclear disarmament can ever be achieved. However, and while the commitment to disarmament has been rhetorically adopted by the Obama administration, the USA appears to remain committed to retaining a nuclear capability as long as others do, and its current actions may actually be making wider nuclear cuts by other P5 states more rather than less complicated.

(3) Russia and great power status

Although the Cold War is now well behind us, nuclear weapons remain just as vital to Russian security today as they did in 1949 when the first Soviet atomic bomb test took place. Indeed, there is a wide range of evidence to suggest that nuclear weapons are becoming more important to Russian national security thinking rather than less. In addition to deterring a nuclear (or conventional) attack on the Russian homeland, nuclear weapons play an increasingly crucial role for Russia in other ways too, not least as compensation for the weakness of its conventional military forces, but also for national status and prestige.[21] As Stephen Blank explains:

> Russia's nuclear capability ensures Russia's strategic independence as an international actor, but even more to the point, its identity as a truly sovereign state, i.e., one that makes policy strictly on the basis of its own calculation of national interest, not the actions of other states.[22]

As a result, the current prospects for Russian nuclear disarmament are weak, and achieving further nuclear arms reductions will remain a considerable challenge.

A fundamental driver of Russian nuclear thinking is its perception of itself as a 'great power', and the view that nuclear weapons are 'a symbol and a guarantee of Russia's influence, independence, and security – the ultimate unbeatable card in global power politics'.[23] Russian policy makers also remain nostalgic for the strategic balance based on nuclear weapons and nuclear deterrence that characterised the Cold War relationship with the USA and NATO.[24] As Vladimir Dvokin points out:

The growing importance of this factor has, first and foremost, got to do with the fact that of all the main characteristics of the USSR as a superpower; compared to the US; that is to say the military strength, influence on world development, a developed military industrial complex and other characteristics, the only one that is left is the nuclear parity (in addition to the size of the country).[25]

The desire for an international system based around the concept of MAD also reflects another key driver of current Russian nuclear thinking; that is the growing weaknesses of Russian conventional forces and at the same time the growth in advanced US/NATO conventional forces and in particular ballistic missile defence. While once it was US and NATO nuclear weapons programmes being driven by an overwhelming Soviet superiority in conventional military forces, the roles have now been reversed, not just in Europe, but also in Asia. As Nikolai Sokov explains:

The profile of nuclear weapons is further increased by the wide (and perhaps even unbridgeable) gap between Russia and the United States/NATO in modern technology. This gap prevents Moscow from shifting emphasis from nuclear to conventional assets and further strengthens long-term reliance on nuclear weapons in national security policy.[26]

Equally, this means that Russia is unlikely to agree to any further US-Russian nuclear cuts without some type of agreement on BMD and conventional US/NATO–Russia military force balances. As Alexei Arbatov explains:

Russia is reluctant to commit itself to much deeper reductions after the New START in view of US/NATO advantages in BMD technology and conventional weapon systems and forces, the potential threat from other nuclear weapon states (all eight of which have weapons that can reach Russian territory) and American space support and potential strike capabilities, as embodied in the Prompt Global Strike concept and systems.[27]

More broadly, without further US–Russian nuclear cuts, it is difficult to see how other nuclear powers – but in particular China – can be brought into the disarmament process.

In fact, in recent years the central trend in Russian nuclear thinking has been to modernise its nuclear forces, and to expand the roles that they might play in Russian national security policy. In 1993, for example, Russia dropped its no first use pledge, and announced that it would consider using nuclear weapons first in a crisis, while in 1998 it was announced that all three legs of the Russian nuclear triad would be modernised, and that the missions for nuclear forces would be expanded – although the exact details of this remain vague.[28] As the 2010 Russian Military Doctrine makes clear:

The Russian Federation will reserve the right to use nuclear weapons in a situation when nuclear weapons and other kinds of weapons of mass-destruction are being used against it and (or) its allies, and also against a large scale aggression with conventional weapons in a crisis situation where the national security of The Russian Federation is at stake.[29]

In this regard – and notwithstanding the fact that Russian nuclear forces are 'likely to decay in an uncontrolled and unpredictable fashion'[30] in the future – nuclear weapons are becoming more not less important to Moscow. Andrei Shoumikhin explains this current position well:

Nuclear weapons retain a high profile in Russian national security strategy and will keep it in the foreseeable future. Contrary to official statements, there is no reason to believe that Russia could agree to a very significant reduction, much less elimination, of its nuclear arsenal.[31]

As a result, it seems unlikely that Russia will be making any significant steps towards its obligations under Article VI in the near future.

(4) The United Kingdom and Trident replacement

The United Kingdom was the third nation to join the nuclear club after it tested its first device in 1952, and since this time the UK has remained committed to deploying only a limited or minimum nuclear deterrent capability. Since 1958 the UK has relied on the United States for part of its nuclear forces – under the Mutual Defence Agreement (MDA) – and since 1997, after the WE177 free-fall nuclear bomb was retired, has only deployed nuclear weapons on a single bal- listic missile submarine. With less than 200 useable nuclear warheads, and with an ongoing debate about whether to replace this capability needing to be made in the near future, the UK is often seen as being the closest of the P5 states towards nuclear disarmament. In the words of Nick Ritchie:

The UK's determination to acquire a nuclear capability was born out of the strategic context of the Cold War and post-war pretensions to great power status … but the context has changed, and changed dramatically. Today, there is deep disquiet within Westminster and amongst the general public about the necessity and wisdom of investing heavily in reproducing a strategic nuclear weapons capability.[32]

That said, it is likely – although not certain – that the UK will chose to replace its current Trident nuclear deterrent system and therefore remain a nuclear-capable state well into the middle of this century. As Ian Anthony notes, there is also considerable evidence for the view that political, technical, and industrial issues create a very large inertia that would have to be overcome before the current decision to maintain a national deterrent could be reversed.[33]

The United Kingdom is due to make the final decision whether to replace its current submarine-based nuclear deterrent force in 2016, after the next general election.

UK nuclear policy rests on several central pillars. The first is the commitment to a minimum nuclear deterrent capability – in this case ballistic missiles fired by a single undetectable submarine, and the maintenance of a minimum credible stockpile of nuclear warheads. In 1998, for example, the Strategic Defence Review (SDR) reduced operationally deployable warheads to no more than 200: this was reduced to 160 in 2006, and is due to be reduced further to 120 by the mid-2020s.[34] Second is the policy of continuous-at-sea deterrence (CASD) whereby one nuclear-armed submarine (the UK currently has a fleet of four SSBNs) will always be on patrol under the sea and ready to fire if and when it is required to do so. Third, the UK maintains a strong link with the United States to provide the Trident ballistic missiles required for the deterrent, although the UK remains in complete control of its strategic nuclear forces, and builds and maintains the submarines and warheads itself.[35] Fourth, UK nuclear forces are formally obligated to NATO for the common defence of the Alliance. Fifth, the UK is publicly committed to the goal of nuclear disarmament, and has ratified the CTBT and ceased production of fissile material.[36] The combined result is what the United Kingdom perceives to be the minimum credible force structure for deterrence purposes. As Chief Secretary to the UK Treasury Danny Alexander pointed out in July 2013:

Britain has the smallest nuclear arsenal of any of the declared nuclear powers. Some would argue that Britain has done its bit for disarmament and we have reached the minimum level possible for nuclear deterrence to be credible before stepping off the ladder altogether.

That said, Alexander went on to point out that:

This argument has been deployed at every point we've scaled down over the last 20 years – but each time it has proven not to be true. The same argument will be made for maintaining continuous nuclear deterrence. But we seem to find we have the ability to step down the nuclear ladder when we find the political will to do so.[37]

However, and while Britain is seen as the model of minimum nuclear deterrence by many, the UK does retain a policy of first nuclear use should the British state ever face an existential threat.

The UK has recently undertaken a thorough review of its nuclear deterrence posture and capability, and this has involved two linked debates. The first is whether or not it should retain nuclear weapons or unilaterally disarm; the second – assuming it wishes to retain nuclear weapons – is what type of force structure is required. However, in reality, it is widely believed that anything less than four SLBM-armed SSBNs operating CASD would not be compatible with a credible nuclear deterrent. The result of the highly contested Trident Alternative's Review released in 2013 suggests that a like-for-like replacement of the current nuclear deterrent system will go ahead, but that the next UK government will take a final decision in 2016.[38] A summary of this debate can be found in Table 16.

Table 16 The debate over UK nuclear weapons

Keep Nuclear Weapons	Unilateral Disarmament
Nuclear weapons provide the UK with insurance against an uncertain future	It is not clear who exactly the UK is trying to deter with these weapons, or who the UK might use them against
The ultimate security offered by nuclear weapons is worth the cost	UK nuclear weapons cost huge sums of money that could be spent on other things
A UK decision to disarm would have little impact on others, and might even encourage nuclear acquisition	Disarmament would provide a much-needed boost to the NPT regime, and fulfil British obligations under Article VI
Nuclear weapons are central to the British identity and world role	Nuclear weapons are not central to the British world role – finance, IT, culture and education are more important assets globally
Nuclear weapons provide a lot of high-skilled jobs and add to the hi-tech knowledge infrastructure. The UK would never be able to reconstitute this capability in the future	Other conventional military options to fulfil deterrence requirements are available to the UK
Why give up what the UK already has, and might need in the future?	*Why keep something that costs lots of money and doesn't appear to address current security requirements?*

Should the UK decide to go ahead with the replacement of its current submarine-based nuclear deterrent in 2016, this will ensure that Britain retains a nuclear weapons capability well into the second half of the twenty-first century.

However, the debate over Trident renewal and Britain's continued status as a NWS was thrown into question in September 2014 by the referendum on Scottish independence. Had Scotland voted 'yes' for independence, the Scottish National Party (SNP) had made it clear that it would have ordered the removal of all UK nuclear weapons and associated facilities – the submarines and war-heads are currently based at Faslane, near Glasgow – from Scottish territory.[39] Given the particular requirements for a submarine base and the enormous sums of money that would be required to relocate (if indeed this proved possible) such a move would have significantly complicated the Trident renewal debate, and could have sounded the death knell for the UK's nuclear weapons.[40]

(5) France and the *force de dissuasion*

In 1960, France became the fourth nation to test a nuclear device, and since this time French nuclear thinking has encompassed a very specific view of the so-called *force de dissuasion* (previously known as the *force de frappe*). France essentially built nuclear weapons because they offered three important perceived benefits: (1) it provided the ultimate national security guarantee against the threat from the Soviet Union; (2) it allowed independence from the United States, both politically, and militarily in case of a crisis (i.e. France would not have to rely on the USA to come to its aid); and (3) an indigenous nuclear weapons programme offered equality with the United Kingdom, and was a source of broader national prestige.[41] Over 50 years later, and despite seismic changes in the international system, France continues to believe that nuclear weapons are essential to its security and defence policies in today's world. In the words of French President François Hollande in 2013:

> global security threats have made nuclear weapons essential for France, which is the only country in continental Europe to have them … it's a deterrent force that allows us protection against all threats and allows us to play a strong role on the world stage.[42]

In particular, nuclear weapons are seen as essential insurance should a new major threat to Europe emerge, or to prevent blackmail or coercion by another state armed with WMD.[43] According to Bruno Tertrais:

> the original rationales for the French nuclear program are still considered valid. From the French point of view, potential strategic threats to European security have not disappeared, and the U.S. guarantee through NATO is not seen as more credible than in the past.[44]

Equally, and although less publicly admitted, nuclear weapons remain central to French prestige and the conception and status of France as a great or world power. As Matthew Moran and Matthew Cottee point out, 'France's position as a nuclear weapon state fulfilled the desire for prestige and status that is deeply ingrained in the French national narrative'.[45]

While France has embarked upon a dual policy of modernisation and rationalisation over the past two decades – in January 1996, all land-based nuclear missiles were deactivated and the submarine force was reduced from 5 to 4 boats,[46] and in 2008 President Nicolas Sarkozy announced reductions to the number of nuclear weapons that could be delivered by aircraft – it still retains a dyad of nuclear delivery systems (submarines and aircraft) and a stockpile of around 300 deployable warheads.[47] In addition to this, there is very little internal political debate about nuclear abolition in France. Indeed, unlike in the UK, the nuclear issue remains almost taboo, and is rarely discussed openly.[48] French officials have also been notably silent about the Global Zero agenda, and perhaps unsurprisingly the then government of Nicolas Sarkozy reacted very cautiously to President Obama's Prague speech on nuclear abolition in 2009.[49] As Venance Journe points out:

> The French authorities response to the push for nuclear zero is that the nuclear deterrent is the best way to respond to nuclear proliferation and it will remain at the core of France's security for the foreseeable future.[50]

Consequently, it appears that any recent French moves to reduce nuclear force levels have been designed to increase efficiency and financial savings rather than to move closer to abolition.[51] In the longer term therefore, as Bruno Tertrais has suggested, 'French nuclear policy is most likely to remain on a path of prudence, conservatism, and restraint for the next 20–25 years'.[52]

The apparent internal French political consensus on the nuclear issue and general scepticism over nuclear disarmament has led analysts to portray the country as 'the most conservative of the three Western nuclear weapon states'.[53] As a result, it is difficult to envision a set of circumstances in the short term that might lead France towards nuclear disarmament – if anything nuclear weapons remain as central to French thinking as they did in 1960, and this seems unlikely to change any time soon.

(6) China and minimum deterrence

In 1964 China became the fifth state to join the nuclear club, and the last to do so before the 1968 NPT was agreed. Since that time, it has appeared content with maintaining a small but effective nuclear arsenal and a political commitment never to use nuclear weapons first, and at the same time general support for the goal of total nuclear disarmament contained in Article VI.[54] The result is that Chinese nuclear force levels have not risen to the heights of those of the United States and Russia, and have remained fairly consistent over time. That said, China is modernising its nuclear capability, primarily as a response to moves being made by the United States – above all the deployment of ballistic missile defences – and such moves are making the Chinese increasingly reluctant to make reductions in their nuclear forces. Moreover, Chinese officials believe that further and deeper nuclear arms reductions need to be made by the United States and Russia before China will become involved in any credible multilateral nuclear disarmament discussions.

China has adopted a rather different nuclear philosophy to the other P5 states, and has never – at least not publicly – seen nuclear weapons as weapons of war. Through a no first use declaration and the de-alerted status of its nuclear forces, it has maintained what it perceives to be the absolute minimum force levels required for nuclear deterrence. As a 2010 Ministry of Defense White Paper explains, 'By giving up the first use option, China has limited nuclear weapons to retaliatory strikes only ... pre-emptive nuclear use has never been a possibility'.[55] Ultimately, China's nuclear force composition has and continues to be determined predominantly by what is required to ensure a retaliatory second nuclear strike should it ever be attacked:

> China's minimum deterrence policy is that, after absorbing a first nuclear strike, at least some nuclear warheads should survive that can retaliate against the enemy's soft targets, such as cities.[56]

Consequently, it is committed to keeping its nuclear forces at the lowest levels possible to ensure national security.

China has been publicly committed to the ultimate goal of nuclear disarmament since its first nuclear test in 1964.[57] However, Chinese views on nuclear abolition are increasingly being clouded by international developments. The first main challenge is that fact that China's two main rivals – the United States and Russia – retain significantly bigger nuclear forces than it does. Consequently, officials in Beijing believe that considerable further nuclear cuts must be made before China can credibly enter any nuclear disarmament dialogue. As Hui Zhang explains:

> Given the huge qualitative and quantitative gap between the Chinese arsenal and those of the United States and Russia ... Beijing cannot be expected to involve itself directly in the reduction of its nuclear weapons until the United States and Russia have made deeper cuts in their arsenals.[58]

In addition to the much large nuclear capabilities of its strategic competitors, China is also concerned about developments in conventional weaponry (primarily by the United States), and particularly the growing deployment of US ballistic missile defences (BMD). In the words of Taylor Fravel and Evan Medeiros:

> the PLA's main concerns about maintaining a credible second strike [nuclear] force are driven by the U.S. military's development of a trifecta of nonnuclear strategic capabilities: (1) missile defenses, (2) long-range conventional strike, and (3) sophisticated command, control, communications, computers, intelligence, surveillance, and reconnaissance (C4 ISR) assets to locate and target China's nuclear forces. The combination of these three capabilities, in the eyes of the Chinese, provides the United States with the ability to eliminate China's deterrent in a crisis without crossing the nuclear threshold, reopening the door to U.S. coercion of China.[59]

Essentially, 'the Chinese fear that during a crisis, US monitoring technologies could be used to locate Chinese nuclear assets; the PGS system could then be used to destroy them, while missile defences would soak up any subsequent retaliation'.[60] The result is that the apparent utility of a US conventional first-strike capability is leading to a perceived requirement for an enhanced Chinese second-strike nuclear capability. Consequently, China has responded by both qualitatively and quantitatively modernising its strategic nuclear forces.[61]

These dynamics have two broader implications for global nuclear order and the prospects for disarmament. The first is that as long as it feels threatened by the United States – or at least open to coercion – and while the USA and Russia retain much larger nuclear forces, China will not entertain the idea of nuclear disarmament. The second is that Chinese reactions to these current security dynamics, in particular Chinese nuclear modernisation, will have significant implications for other states – most notably India, but also potentially for Japan, South Korea and Taiwan, and by implication Pakistan, the USA and Russia. As Lora Saalman explains:

> In terms of delivery vehicles and modernization, China's nuclear capabilities remain largely focussed on increasingly survivability vis-à-vis one potential adversary, namely the United States. However, many of these systems have implications for other powers with which China has unresolved disputes or tense relations, including India.[62]

Consequently, and while China remains publicly committed to its obligations under Article VI of the NPT, any prospects for a near-term movement towards nuclear disarmament appear bleak.

(7) Key points and guide to further reading and resources

This chapter has sought to provide you with an overview and assessment of the current nuclear thinking – and the subsequent prospects for disarmament – of the P5 group of NWS. A summary of these points is provided below:

- Under Article VI of the NPT the five recognised NWS are committed to work in good faith towards nuclear disarmament. However, there is a growing feeling that two decades after the Cold War the USA, Russia, the UK, France and China are not living up to this obligation. The P5 process is a recent diplomatic initiative to explore this.
- The United States is moving towards a more diverse deterrence strategy contained in the 'new triad'. While this will reduce some reliance on nuclear weapons for the USA – and possibly allow for deeper nuclear

cuts – such a move is likely to be a concern for US strategic competitors and potential rivals.

- Nuclear weapons remain central to Russian strategic and security thinking, and this is unlikely to change any time soon. In fact, a number of dynamics – but particularly US missile defence plans, weakening Russian conventional forces, national prestige and the 'rise of China' – are probably making nuclear weapons more attractive to Moscow rather than less.

- The United Kingdom is perhaps the closest of the P5 powers to disarming, and at the time of writing still hasn't completely decided to replace the Trident-based nuclear weapon system. That said, and while a final decision on trident replacement will not be made until 2016, a number of domestic and cultural dynamics will make it very difficult for Britain to disarm unilaterally.

- France remains staunchly committed to possessing nuclear weapons for security and prestige, and is arguably the most conservative of the three Western nuclear-armed states. Indeed, unlike in the USA and UK, nuclear weapons remain a taboo subject in France and are rarely publicly debated.

- China has a complicated relationship with nuclear weapons involving a commitment to a small nuclear force and disarmament, but at the same time a set of genuine security concerns that are driving modernisation. Chinese nuclear thinking is highly contingent on US and Russian actions regarding nuclear and conventional military forces, and on security developments in Northeast Asia.

Further reading and resources

On the commitment for the P5 to disarm see Sverre Lodgaard 'Nuclear disarmament and non-proliferation' (2011); Jeffrey Knopf 'Nuclear disarmament and nonproliferation' (2012); Christopher Ford 'Debating disarmament' (2007); and Jan Ruzicka 'Reflections on the 2010 NPT review conference' (2010). On the P5 process see Andrea Berger and Malcolm Chalmers 'Great expectations' (2013) and Nick Ritchie 'Pathways and purposes for P-5 nuclear dialogue' (2013).

On the United States, see Aidan Warren 'The Obama administration's nuclear weapons strategy' (2014); David McDonough 'Nuclear superiority' (2006); Scott Sagan and Jane Vaynman 'Introduction: reviewing the nuclear posture review' (2011) and 'Conclusion: lessons learned from the 2010 Nuclear Posture Review' (2011); Steven Pifer and Michael O'Hanlon 'The opportunity' (2012); Harald Muller 'A nuclear proliferation test' (2011);

(Continued)

(Continued)

and Andrew Futter and Benjamin Zala 'Advanced US conventional weapons and nuclear disarmament' (2013).

On Russia, see Stephen Blank (ed.) 'Russian nuclear weapons' (2012); Pavel Podvig 'Russian strategic nuclear forces' (2004); Steven Zaloga 'The Kremlin's nuclear sword' (2002); Mark Schneider 'The nuclear forces and doctrine of the Russian Federation' (2008); and Nikolai Sokov 'The origins of and prospects for Russian nuclear doctrine' (2007).

On the United Kingdom, readers should see Nick Ritchie 'A nuclear weapons free world' (2012); Malcolm Chalmers and William Walker 'Unchartered waters' (2001) and 'Will Scotland sink the United Kingdom's nuclear deterrent?' (2013); Robert Paterson 'Britain's strategic nuclear deterrent' (1997); Frank Barnaby and Douglas Holdstock 'The British nuclear weapons programme, 1952–2002' (2003); Jeremy Stocker 'The United Kingdom and nuclear deterrence' (2007); and Malcolm Chalmers 'Towards the UK's nuclear century' (2013). On US–UK nuclear cooperation see Jenifer Mackby and Paul Cornish 'US–UK nuclear cooperation after 50 years' (2008).

On France, see Bruno Tertrais 'The last to disarm' (2007); David Yost 'France's new nuclear doctrine' (2006) and 'France's evolving nuclear strategy' (2005); Pierre Billaud and Venance Journé 'The real story behind the making of the French hydrogen bomb' (2008); Matthew Moran and Matthew Cottee 'Bound by history' (2011) and Jean-Loup Samaan and David Gompert 'French nuclear weapons, Euro-deterrence, and NATO' (2009).

On China, see Jeffrey Lewis 'The minimum means of reprisal' (2007); Paul Bolt and Albert Willner 'China's nuclear future' (2005); Taylor Fravel and Evan Medeiros 'China's search for assured retaliation' (2010); Hui Zhang 'China's perspective on a nuclear-free world' (2010); Brad Roberts et al. 'China: the forgotten nuclear power' (2000); Mark Schneider 'The nuclear doctrine of the People's Republic of China' (2008); Lora Saalman (ed.) 'The China–India nuclear crossroads' (2012); Paul Bolt and Albert Willner (eds.) 'China's nuclear future' (2005); and Baohui Zhang 'US missile defence and China's nuclear posture' (2011).

Notes

1. Joseph Rotblat, 'Nobel lecture 1995', www.nobelprize.org/nobel_prizes/peace/laureates/1995/rotblat-lecture.html?print=1.
2. On this see Jaswant Singh, 'Against nuclear apartheid', Foreign Affairs, 77:5 (1998) pp.41-53 and Shane Maddock, 'Nuclear apartheid: the quest for American atomic supremacy from World War II to the present', (Chapel Hill, NC, University of North Carolina Press: 2010).

3. Steven Miller, 'Proliferation, disarmament and the future of the Non-Proliferation Treaty', chapter in Morten Bremer Maerli and Sverre Lodgaard (eds.), 'Nuclear proliferation and international security', (Abingdon, Routledge: 2007) pp.50–51.
4. See 'Treaty on the Non-Proliferation of Nuclear Weapons', www.un.org/en/conf/npt/2005/npttreaty.html.
5. Sverre Lodgaard, 'Nuclear disarmament and nonproliferation: towards a nuclear free world?', (Abingdon, Routledge: 2011) p.85.
6. Andrea Berger and Malcolm Chalmers, 'Great expectations: the P5 process and the Non-Proliferation Treaty', RUSI Whitehall Report, (August 2013) p.1, www.rusi.org/downloads/assets/WHR_3-13_Web.pdf.
7. Steven Miller, 'Proliferation, disarmament and the future of the Non-Proliferation Treaty', chapter in Morten Bremer Maerli and Sverre Lodgaard (eds.), 'Nuclear proliferation and international security', (Abingdon, Routledge: 2007) p.53.
8. On this see Jeffrey Knopf, 'Nuclear disarmament and nonproliferation: examining the linkage argument', International Security, 37:3 (2012) pp.92-132.
9. On this see William Potter and Gaukhar Mukhatzhanova, 'Nuclear politics and the Non-Aligned Movement: principles vs. pragmatism', Adelphi Paper 427, (London, Routledge for the International Institute for Strategic Studies: 2012).
10. '2010 Review Conference of the Parties to the Treaty on the Non-Proliferation of Nuclear Weapons', Final Document, (New York, 2010), section 79, p.12, www.un.org/ga/search/view_doc.asp?symbol=NPT/CONF.2010/50%20(VOL.%20II).
11. See Harald Müller, 'The 2010 NPT review conference: some breathing space gained, but no breakthrough', The International Spectator 45:3 (2010) pp.5–18.
12. Andrea Berger and Malcolm Chalmers, 'Great expectations: the P5 process and the Non-Proliferation Treaty', RUSI Whitehall Report, (August 2013) p.1, www.rusi.org/downloads/assets/WHR_3-13_Web.pdf.
13. 'Fourth P5 Conference: on the way to the 2015 NPT Review Conference', (19 April 2013), www.state.gov/r/pa/prs/ps/2013/04/207768.htm.
14. Nick Ritchie, 'Pathways and purposes for P-5 nuclear dialogue', European Leadership Network Policy Brief, (September 2013) p.9, www.europeanleadershipnetwork.org/medialibrary/2013/09/03/ca6e5ece/Nick%20Ritchie%20Pathways%20and%20Purposes%20for%20P%205%20Nuclear%20Dialogue%20ELN%20Policy%20Brief%20September%202013.pdf.
15. Sverre Lodgaard, 'Nuclear disarmament and nonproliferation: towards a nuclear free world?', (Abingdon, Routledge: 2011) p.85.
16. Barack Obama, 'Presidential Q & A: President-elect Barack Obama', Arms Control Today, (December 2008), www.armscontrol.org/print/3360.
17. See 'Nuclear Posture Review', United States Department of Defense, (April 2010), www.defense.gov/npr/docs/2010%20nuclear%20posture%20review%20report.pdf.
18. On this see David McDonough, 'Nuclear superiority: the "new triad" and the evolution of nuclear strategy', Adelphi Paper 383, (Abingdon, Routledge for IISS: 2006) p.11.
19. On this see Andrew Futter and Benjamin Zala, 'Advanced conventional weapons and nuclear disarmament: why the Obama plan won't work', The Nonproliferation Review, 20:1 (2013) pp.107–122.
20. Ibid, p.119.
21. Richard Weitz, 'Russian tactical nuclear weapons: current policies and future trends', chapter in Stephen Blank (ed.), 'Russia nuclear weapons: past, present and future', (Carlisle PA, US Army War College: 2011) pp.365–366.
22. Stephen Blank, 'Russia and nuclear weapons', chapter in Stephen Blank (ed.), 'Russia nuclear weapons: past, present and future', (Carlisle PA, US Army War College: 2011) p.307.

23. Nikolai Sokov, 'Nuclear weapons in Russian national security strategy', chapter in Stephen Blank (ed.), 'Russia nuclear weapons: past, present and future', (Carlisle PA, US Army War College: 2011) p.187.
24. Andrei Shoumikhin, 'Nuclear weapons in Russian strategy and doctrine', chapter in Stephen Blank (ed.), 'Russia nuclear weapons: past, present and future', (Carlisle PA, US Army War College: 2011) p.138.
25. Vladimir Dvokin, 'The nuclear policy of Russia and the perspective for nuclear disarmament', chapter in Olav Njolstad (ed.), 'Nuclear proliferation and international order: challenges to the Non-Proliferation Treaty', (Abingdon, Routledge: 2011) p.169.
26. Nikolai Sokov, 'Nuclear weapons in Russian national security strategy', chapter in Stephen Blank (ed.), 'Russia nuclear weapons: past, present and future', (Carlisle PA, US Army War College: 2011) p.188.
27. Alexei Arbatov, 'Nuclear deterrence, disarmament, and nonproliferation', chapter in Catherine McArdle Kelleher and Judith Reppy (eds.), '"Getting to zero" the path to nuclear disarmament'", (Stanford, Stanford University Press: 2011) pp.100–101.
28. Pavel Podvig, 'Russia's strategic nuclear forces', (Cambridge MA, The MIT Press: 2001) pp.574–579.
29. 'The Military Doctrine of the Russian Federation', (5 February 2010), http://carnegieendowment.org/files/2010russia_military_doctrine.pdf.
30. Steven Zaloga, 'The Kremlin's nuclear sword: the rise and fall of Russia's strategic nuclear forces, 1945–2000', (Washington DC, The Smithsonian Institution Press: 2002) p.229.
31. Andrei Shoumikhin, 'Nuclear weapons in Russian strategy and doctrine', chapter in Stephen Blank (ed.), 'Russia nuclear weapons: past, present and future', (Carlisle PA, US Army War College: 2011) p.249.
32. Nick Ritchie, 'A nuclear weapons-free world? Britain, Trident and the challenges ahead', (Basingstoke, Palgrave Macmillan: 2012) p.2.
33. Ian Anthony, 'British thinking on nuclear weapons', chapter in Catherine McArdle Kelleher and Judith Reppy (eds.), '"Getting to zero" the path to nuclear disarmament', (Stanford, Stanford University Press: 2011) pp.119–120.
34. Nick Ritchie, 'A nuclear weapons-free world? Britain, Trident and the challenges ahead', (Basingstoke, Palgrave Macmillan: 2012) p.2.
35. John Simpson and Jenify Mackby, 'The special nuclear relationship: a historical chronology', chapter in Jenifer Mackby and Paul Cornish (eds.), 'US–UK nuclear cooperation after 50 years', (Washington DC, CSIS Press: 2008) p.12.
36. Nick Ritchie, 'A nuclear weapons-free world? Britain, Trident and the challenges ahead', (Basingstoke, Palgrave Macmillan: 2012) p.20.
37. Malcolm Chalmers, 'Towards the UK's nuclear century', The RUSI Journal, 158:6 (2013) p.25.
38. HM Government, 'Trident Alternatives Review', (16 July 2013), www.gov.uk/government/uploads/system/uploads/attachment_data/file/212745/20130716_Trident_Alternatives_Study.pdf.
39. See Malcolm Chalmers and William Walker, 'Will Scotland sink the United Kingdom's nuclear deterrent?', The Washington Quarterly, 36:3 (2013) pp.107–122.
40. On this see Malcolm Chalmers and William Walker, 'Unchartered waters: the UK, nuclear weapons and the Scottish question', (East Lothian, Tuckwell Press: 2001).
41. Jean-Loup Samaan and David Gompert, 'French nuclear weapons, Euro-deterrence and NATO', Contemporary Security Policy, 30:3 (2009) p.488.
42. Jamey Keaten, 'France affirms nuclear arms despite military cuts', Associated Press, (9 January 2013), http://news.yahoo.com/france-affirms-nuclear-arms-despite-military-cuts-161816266.html.

43. Bruno Tertrais, 'The last to disarm? The future of France's nuclear weapons', The Nonproliferation Review, 14:2 (2007) p.253.
44. Ibid, p.251.
45. Matthew Moran and Matthew Cottee, 'Bound by history? Exploring challenges to French nuclear disarmament', Defense & Security Analysis, 27:4 (2011) p.354.
46. See Declan Butler, 'France seeks to clean up nuclear image', Nature, 380:6569 (1996).
47. Molly Moore, 'Sarkozy announces cuts in nuclear arsenal', The Washington Post, (22 March 2008), www.washingtonpost.com/wpdyn/content/article/2008/03/21/AR200 8032102979.html.
48. Venance Journe, 'France's nuclear stance: independence, unilateralism, and adaptation', chapter in Catherine McArdle Kelleher and Judith Reppy (eds.), 'Getting to zero': the path to nuclear disarmament', (Stanford, Stanford University Press: 2011) p.140.
49. Jean-Loup Samaan and David Gompert, 'French nuclear weapons, Euro-deterrence and NATO', Contemporary Security Policy, 30:3 (2009) p.486.
50. Venance Journe, 'France's nuclear stance: independence, unilateralism, and adaptation', chapter in Catherine McArdle Kelleher and Judith Reppy (eds.), '"Getting to zero": the path to nuclear disarmament', (Stanford, Stanford University Press: 2011) p.124.
51. Ibid, p.133.
52. Bruno Tertrais, 'The last to disarm? The future of France's nuclear weapons', The Nonprolifcration Review, 14:2 (2007) p. 270.
53. Jean-Loup Samaan and David Gompert, 'French nuclear weapons, Euro-deterrence and NATO', Contemporary Security Policy, 30:3 (2009) p.486.
54. Nie Hongyi, 'Comparing nuclear pledges and practice: the view from China', chapter in Lora Saalman (ed.), 'The China–India nuclear crossroads', (Washington DC, The Carnegie Endowment for International Peace: 2012) p.39.
55. Yao Yunzhu, 'China's policy on nuclear weapons and disarmament', chapter in Olav Njolstad (ed.), 'Nuclear weapons and international order: challenges to the Nonproliferation Treaty', (Abingdon, Routledge: 2011) p.250.
56. Hui Zhang, 'China's perspective on a nuclear-free world', The Washington Quarterly, 33:2 (2010) p.141.
57. Ibid, p.139.
58. Ibid, p.143.
59. Taylor Fravel and Evan Medeiros, 'China's search for assured retaliation: the evolution of Chinese nuclear strategy and force structure', International Security, 35:2 (2010) p.83.
60. Andrew Futter and Benjamin Zala, 'Advanced conventional weapons and nuclear disarmament: why the Obama plan won't work', The Nonproliferation Review, 20:1 (2013) p.113.
61. Mark Schneider, 'The nuclear doctrine and forces of the People's Republic of China', Comparative Strategy, 28:3 (2009) p.244.
62. Lora Saalman, 'Introduction', chapter in Lora Saalman (ed.), 'The China–India nuclear crossroads', (Washington DC, The Carnegie Endowment for International Peace: 2012) p.2.

6

HORIZONTAL PROLIFERATION CHALLENGES: THE NUCLEAR OUTLIERS

Israel and nuclear opacity

Pakistan, India and the challenge to stability in South Asia

Dealing with a nuclear North Korea

Future trajectories in the Iranian nuclear stand-off

Key points and guide to further reading and resources

While the end of the Cold War ushered in a period of vertical nuclear arms reductions (predominantly between the United States and Russia – see Chapters 5 and 7), many observers feared that a greater nuclear challenge would come from the horizontal spread of these weapons to a cohort of new states (and potentially non-state actors) seeking to join the exclusive nuclear club. In this sense, while the total number of nuclear weapons has reduced considerably over the past two decades, this period has nevertheless seen the emergence of new nuclear aspirants and growth in the number of states seeking to access and possess nuclear weapons; and some of these states are considered not to be as responsible, rational, or in some cases even as stable as those of the first nuclear generation. The result is that many feel that the danger of nuclear use is now considerably higher than during the Cold War, essentially because the same 'rules' and 'conventions' may no longer apply in a vastly different post-Cold War nuclear environment (see Chapter 3). In the words of the then nominee for Director of the US Central Intelligence Agency (CIA), James Woolsey:

We have slain a large dragon, but we live now in a jungle filled with a bewildering variety of poisonous snakes. And in many ways, the dragon was easier to keep track of.[1]

In addition to the threat of nuclear use by non-state actors (covered in Chapter 8), four challenges in particular stand out: Israel; Pakistan and India in South Asia; North Korea; and Iran – recent nuclear challenges from Iraq, Libya, Syria and Burma all appear to have been averted (at least for the time being). Of these four states, only Iran is currently a member of the NPT. Collectively, we can think of these as residing outside the formal global international nuclear order, and therefore more colloquially as 'nuclear outliers'.

   This chapter proceeds in four sections: the first looks in detail at the peculiar case of Israel and the policy of nuclear opacity, whereby the possession of nuclear weapons is neither confirmed nor denied; section 2 examines the delicate nuclear balance between India and Pakistan, looking at why both states decided to conduct overt nuclear tests in 1998, before considering the future prospects for stability in South Asia; in section 3 the nuclear challenge presented by North Korea is analysed, as is the debate over whether the Democratic People's Republic of Korea (DPRK) can be considered a 'rational' nuclear actor; section 4 outlines the current nuclear stand-off between the international community and Iran that has gathered pace over the past decade. The chapter finishes with a summary of the key points and a guide to further reading and resources.

(1) Israel and nuclear opacity

While Israel neither confirms nor denies whether it possesses nuclear weapons, it is widely accepted that it has been part of the nuclear club since the late 1960s, and currently has a sophisticated nuclear weapons infrastructure and capability. The policy of nuclear opacity means that Israel is the only one of the nine nuclear-armed states that doesn't publicly admit to having nuclear weapons and, despite rumours of an incident in 1979 (see below), has never conducted an overt test to verify this capability. Israel has also never signed the NPT despite considerable international pressure – stating that doing so would undermine its vital national security interests – but has made it clear that it will not be the first to introduce nuclear weapons into the Middle East region.

(i) How and why Israel got the bomb

The reasons why Israel chose to develop the bomb are fairly clear: the leaders of the Jewish state simply could not risk the threat of another Holocaust such as that perpetrated by Nazi Germany during the Second World War, especially given that the newly established state of Israel found itself surrounded by hostile and larger powers after declaring independence in 1948. That said, Israel began work on nuclear energy in the late 1940s without an explicit commitment to build nuclear weapons, but geopolitical regional realities – such as the two wars fought against its Arab neighbours in 1948 and 1956 – soon provided a compelling case for Israeli leaders to build the bomb. Nevertheless, and despite achieving a nuclear capability in the 1960s, Israel would fight further wars against its neighbours in 1967 and 1973, challenging the idea that a nuclear weapons capability would make the state invulnerable to attack.

The Israeli Atomic Energy Commission (IAEC) was established in the spring of 1952, and work began (with the help of France) on the Dimona nuclear reactor in the Negev Desert in 1958. By the time of the Six-Day War in 1967, Israel is believed to have possessed two or three nuclear devices, and the infrastructure to produce more.[2] After the Six-Day War Israel began a full-scale nuclear weapons development programme, and during the Yom Kippur War of 1973 it is rumoured that it considered deploying nuclear weapons as a show of strength against its Arab adversaries and due to a very real fear of military defeat.[3] As a result, by the 1980s, the Israeli nuclear weapons programme was common knowledge, if not commonly acknowledged.

All of this changed in October 1986, after a former technician from the Negev Nuclear Research Centre at Dimona – Mordachai Vanunu – revealed to the London *Sunday Times* the existence of the Israeli nuclear programme – including detailed photographic evidence.[4] Although Vanunu's photos and information were verified by outside experts, the Israeli government continued to deny the existence of a nuclear weapons programme. Vanunu was later kidnapped by the Israeli secret intelligence organisation Mossad, in Rome, and sentenced to 18 years in prison for treason – under the terms of his release in 2004, he is not allowed to leave the country or speak with foreigners. Vanunu's revelations heightened the pressure on the Israeli government to 'come clean' about their nuclear programme, but this was either avoided or simply denied by officials.[5] Since that time it is believed that Israel has steadily increased its nuclear inventory and nuclear delivery vehicle capabilities, and may currently have around 60–80 nuclear weapons (although possibly more), which are deliverable by aircraft, sea-based and ground-based missiles (see Chapter 2).

It is highly unlikely that Israel could have developed the bomb without the substantial assistance of the United States (although it was France that helped initially by providing the necessary nuclear technology). At almost every stage of Israel's nuclear development, it has been protected diplomatically by the USA, and this continues to be the case under the Obama administration.[6] The basis of this can be traced back to an agreement between US President Richard Nixon and Israeli Prime Minister Golda Meir in 1969, whereby Israel would be allowed to develop nuclear weapons as long as this was never publicly revealed:

According to the Nixon–Meir pact, as long as Israel did not advertise its possession of nuclear weapons by publicly declaring or testing them, the United States would tolerate and shield Israel's nuclear program.[7]

This bargain has remained in place to the present day (although it has never been openly acknowledged) despite mounting international pressure, and the link between the United States and Israel has become increasingly significant as the threat of a possible nuclear Iran has continued to grow.

While it has never publicly undertaken an overt nuclear weapons test – unlike all the other states currently deploying nuclear weapons – on 22 September 1979 Israel is rumoured to have conducted a small clandestine nuclear test in the southern Indian Ocean with the help of South Africa. A US Vela spy satellite orbiting above Southern Africa spotted what experts believed to be a nuclear detonation, and consequently the event would become known as the 'Vela Incident'. The test – which was estimated in the 2–4 kiloton range – has never been confirmed by either Israel or South Africa.[8]

(ii) Nuclear policy: opacity and prevention

At the centre of Israeli nuclear strategy is a commitment to a policy of *nuclear ambiguity* or *nuclear opacity*, whereby Israel does not admit to possessing nuclear weapons. Despite the fact that it is widely acknowledged that it does possess nuclear weapons (particularly following the Vanunu revelations in 1986), this policy of neither confirming or denying their existence has allowed Israel to avoid international condemnation while at the same time increase its (perceived) national security. In the words of Avner Cohen:

> Over time and through a great deal of restraint, Israel has created and maintained a nearly impossible and uniquely creative response to its nuclear dilemma. Its solution contains a sleight of hand that allows Israel to live in the best of all possible worlds by having the bomb but without having to deal with many of the negative consequences that such possession entails.[9]

As well as a commitment neither to confirm nor deny the possession of nuclear weapons, nuclear ambiguity involves an Israeli pledge not to be the first to 'introduce nuclear weapons into the Middle East' – a policy that can be traced back to the Eshkol–Comer Memorandum of Understanding agreed in 1965.[10] That said, Israel is believed to have adopted a policy of nuclear use known colloquially as the Samson Option – the deterrence strategy of massive (nuclear) relation should the existence of the Jewish state ever be under threat.

In addition to the dual policy of neither confirming nor denying its possession of nuclear weapons, or to be the first to 'introduce' nuclear weapons into the Middle East, Israeli nuclear strategy also involves a commitment not to allow – and indeed, forcibly prevent – regional adversaries to acquire a nuclear weapons capability. This is driven by genuine security concerns, but has also caused problems internationally as Israel has sought to act pre-emptively and unilaterally against what it perceives to be potential threats. These have taken many forms, from assassination and stealthy aerial bombing, to attacking facilities with computer viruses:

- In August 1962, Israeli Mossad agents assassinated German rocket scientists believed to be helping Egypt to build ballistic missiles able to accommodate radiological or nuclear warheads.[11]
- In June 1981, the Israeli airforce bombed and destroyed the Osirak nuclear reactor under construction outside Baghdad, Iraq.[12]
- In September 2007, the Israeli airforce attacked and destroyed a facility suspected of being linked to a nuclear weapons programme in Syria.[13]
- In June 2010, Iranian officials discovered the Stuxnet computer virus designed to attack Iranian enrichment centrifuges believed to have been developed by Israel and the USA.[14]

Since this time, Mossad agents have also been accused of assassinating technicians involved with the Iranian nuclear programme.

Israel remains committed to preventing any other actor in the Middle East region from acquiring a nuclear capability, and has certainly not ruled out the use of force against Iran should international diplomatic measures fail to curtail the suspected nuclear programme (see below). That said, Israel supports a Middle East free of all weapons of mass destruction but only following the attainment of a comprehensive regional peace agreement.[15] In recent years it has therefore refused to join diplomatic talks on a Middle East WMD free zone (see Chapter 9).

(iii) The current policy debate

There has perhaps never before been as much pressure on Israel (particularly from the major world powers) to reconsider the central tenets of its nuclear policy, and to abandon the policies that have appeared to serve them so well in the past. In fact, many of the key aspects of Israeli nuclear policy – opacity, pre-emption, secrecy – which were previously seen as virtues, are increasingly being viewed as flaws, and even detrimental to wider Israeli security and geopolitical interests. This has been driven partly by domestic pressures – a greater desire for transparency and accountability from the Israeli government and from the Israeli people – but also externally, as pressure continues to mount for a nuclear-weapon-free zone in the Middle East (see Chapter 9), and for Israel to 'come clean' about its capabilities. Indeed, Avner Cohen and Marvin Miller have argued that:

> Israel could increase its credibility as a responsible nuclear state in various ways, but almost all of them would require relaxing the policy of opacity ... This policy made strategic and political sense 40 years ago, but in today's regional and international climate, it has more vices than virtues.[16]

However, this debate is multifaceted, and is explained in Table 17.

Table 17 Costs and benefits of Israeli nuclear policy

Costs	Benefits
Israeli nuclear weapons have driven WMD acquisition by other states in the region – this was part of the reason behind Iraqi, Iranian, Egyptian, Libyan and Syrian nuclear and WMD programmes	Nuclear weapons give Israel self-reliance for its security – unlike in the past, it does not have to rely on any other actors to ensure national survival
Nuclear opacity stands in the way of achieving a Middle East nuclear-free zone – a productive arms control process is unlikely to begin until Israel 'comes clean' about its nuclear arsenal	Nuclear opacity means that Israeli facilities are not subject to inspections from the IAEA, and because it isn't a signatory of the NPT, this technically isn't illegal either
Nuclear weapons offer little protection against terrorist attacks – arguably the main current threat to Israel	Nuclear weapons have helped to deter conventional and WMD on Israel attacks from regional adversaries – at least since 1973
Israeli nuclear weapons policy places a strain on relations with the United States – it is unclear how long the USA will continue to back Israeli nuclear policy unconditionally	Nuclear opacity has prevented Israel from suffering sanctions for its nuclear programme unlike many other would-be nuclear states or states that have built the bomb
Pre-emptive military attacks (and assassinations) on other states' suspected nuclear facilities have international diplomatic and legal costs, and undermine Israeli legitimacy	Pre-emptive strikes and targeted assassinations have prevented regional WMD proliferation. Egypt, Iraq, Syria and more recently Iran have all had their nuclear ambitions stymied by Israel
Current policy prevents Israel from becoming a major stakeholder in the contemporary global nuclear order	Israel has not been asked officially by the international community to give up its nuclear capability
Nuclear weapons have undermined and complicated Israeli security and fail to address the most pressing threats	*Nuclear weapons have increased Israeli security in a hostile and uncertain regional environment*

The key to the debate over the Israeli nuclear option has always been the history of the Jewish people (particularly the Holocaust) and the turbulent early years following independence. Because of this, Israel maintains that it has special reasons for its actions and position, but whether this can continue indefinitely remains to be seen.

(2) India, Pakistan and the challenge to stability in South Asia

Ever since the turbulent partition in 1947 of what was then British India, which created the independent states of India and Pakistan, the subcontinent has seen four wars and many more military skirmishes. The vast majority of these conflicts – 1962 and 1971 notwithstanding – have been fought over the disputed territory of Kashmir and Jammu, and since 1998 these crises have erupted despite both states possessing nuclear weapons. Neither India nor Pakistan has joined the NPT, and South Asia remains one of the top potential regional nuclear flashpoints, with extensive global non-proliferation implications. As Paul Bracken warns, 'Beneath a veneer of nuclear deterrence and a façade command and control system, some very dangerous dynamics are building up in South Asia'.[17]

(i) How and why South Asia went nuclear

Like other nuclear-armed states, India and Pakistan built the bomb for a mixture of reasons, but the key factors were security and prestige. India decided to build nuclear weapons in part due to a perceived external threat from China (but also due to apparent failures of the global non-proliferation regime), while Pakistan decided to build the bomb principally due to concerns about India. Both saw the bomb as a pathway to modernisation and international status, but both also built the bomb for traditional security reasons. That said, while India and Pakistan probably had a tacit military nuclear capability by the late 1980s, both would wait until 1998 before conducting explicit nuclear weapons tests.

India and Pakistan began civilian nuclear programmes very soon after partition, but neither made a decision to build the bomb right away. In fact, India probably did not decide to develop nuclear weapons until the early 1960s after they lost a small border war with China in 1962, and after China detonated its first nuclear device in 1964.[18] The 1965 war between India and Pakistan (who were strongly supported by China) merely served to drive the programme forward. Nevertheless, while development continued in India, official policy was for a 'peaceful nuclear option' – leaving the door ambiguously open for broader nuclear weapons development should it be desired or required in the future. In Pakistan, and although Foreign Minister (later Prime Minister) Zulfikar Ali Bhutto famously declared in 1965 that 'If India makes an atom bomb, then even if we have to feed on grass and leaves – or even if we have to starve – we shall produce an atom bomb ...',[19] it was not until the Indo-Pakistani war of 1971 (when the then East Pakistan seceded and became Bangladesh) that a decision was made to build nuclear weapons. Subsequently, in January 1972 the decision was taken at the so-called Multan Meeting for Pakistan to build a nuclear force. This decision was compounded by the Indian 'peaceful nuclear test' of 1974 (known colloquially as 'Smiling Buddha'). Indeed, the 1971 war and the 1974 test were the catalysts for scientist A.Q. Khan to return to Pakistan from Europe to help the ailing Pakistani bomb programme (for more on A.Q. Khan see Chapter 8).

Tensions increased during the 1980s as both India and Pakistan continued clandestine work on their nuclear weapons programmes (ostensibly under the guise of peaceful nuclear energy capabilities and research). India very nearly conducted overt tests in May 1982 (Prime Minister Indira Gandhi called them off), while between 1983 and 1990 the Pakistan Atomic Energy Committee (PAEC) conducted 24 different underground cold tests (also known as subcritical tests because there is no explosive yield) in the Kirana Hills in Pakistan's Punjab Province (the tests would later be know as Kirana I).[20] In 1984, India considered a pre-emptive attack on Pakistani nuclear facilities, but was deterred by threats from Pakistan that 'they would respond to such an attack by ordering their own air strikes against India's nuclear facilities'.[21] Both states had a nascent nuclear weapons capability by the late 1980s; indeed, in 1987 Pakistani President Mohammad Zia-ul-Haq declared that 'Pakistan is capable of building the bomb whenever it wishes'.[22] Despite a burgeoning opaque nuclear capability, in both 1987 (the so-called Brasstacks crisis) and again in 1990, India and Pakistan came close to going to war – indeed, one CIA intelligence officer later described the 1990 conflict as 'far more frightening than the Cuban missile crisis'.[23] Pakistan and India both refused to sign the CTBT in 1996, despite India playing a key role in the earlier test ban negotiations in the 1950s (see Chapter 9).

(ii) The 1998 nuclear weapons tests

In May 1998, India and Pakistan became the six and seventh declared members of the nuclear club – and the first two officially outside the NPT – after they both conducted overt nuclear weapons tests. While both were suspected of having a nuclear weapons capability already, the tests significantly changed the security dynamics of the region, especially as India and Pakistan went to war barely a year later in Kargil. Since then the nuclear balance in South Asia has remained delicate, and conflict – perhaps even escalating to the nuclear level – remains an ever-present possibility.

- *The tests* In May 1998, India became the sixth state to conduct a nuclear weapons test (notwithstanding the 'peaceful test' of 1974), as it exploded three nuclear devices (including one alleged boosted-fission device designed to give up to a 1mt yield) on the 11th, and two more (low yield devices) on the 13th, at the Pokhran Test Range in the Thar Desert of Rajasthan. The tests became known as Pokhran II (Pokhran I was the name given to the Smiling Buddha test in 1974).[24] In a direct response, and just two weeks later,

Pakistan tested five nuclear devices on 28 May and one more on 30 May at the Ras Koh Hills in Chagai in the province of Baluchistan. These tests would become known as Chagai I and II.[25]

- *The Kargil War* A year later, between May and June 1999, Pakistan and India fought the Kargil War over the long-term issue of Kashmir and Jammu – the only time that two nuclear armed states have engaged directly in conventional conflict. The war was caused by the infiltration of Pakistani solders and Kashmiri militants into Indian-administered territory, and India responded with a major military offensive to drive out the Pakistan forces. Both sides made vague declarations that any and all types of weapon (including nuclear) could be used in the conflict.[26]

- *Subsequent military skirmishes* Since Kargil, relations have remained strained on the subcontinent, and opposing military forces have continued to clash – primarily due to the Indian belief that the Pakistani Inter-Service Intelligence (ISI) agency has been supporting terrorist attacks in India. In 2001–2002, both sides were rumoured to have prepared nuclear weapons and missile forces for use following terrorist attacks on the Indian parliament, and in 2008 Indian and Pakistani forces clashed again following the Mumbai terror attacks.[27] Kashmir and other territorial disputes also remain unresolved and likely to cause increases in tension in the future.

Since the overt nuclear tests conducted in 1998, and despite establishing a nuclear hotline in 2004, India and Pakistan have fought one war, had many skirmishes and engaged in other hostile border incidents. As Feroz Hassan Khan points out, since the nuclear tests 'the region has witnessed increased regional tensions, a rise in religious extremism, a growing arms race, tense stand-offs, and even armed conflict'.[28]

(iii) Future nuclear challenges in South Asia

South Asia remains one of the biggest challenges in contemporary global nuclear order, and little that has happened since 1998 suggests that these dangers are reducing. Indeed, we can think of three main challenges to nuclear order in South Asia; (1) whether regional stability and deterrence can be upheld; (2) whether nuclear facilities and stockpiles can remain secure and command and control of deployed forces successfully maintained; (3) the wider non-proliferation implications of the US–India civilian nuclear cooperation agreement signed in 2005; and (4) the knock-on impact that events in South Asia will have on the wider region and on the global non-proliferation regime more broadly.

- *Regional stability* The greatest fear in South Asia is that a regional nuclear arms race could lead to miscalculation and even nuclear use. At the heart of this problem is the fact that Indian nuclear weapons are designed to deter Pakistan and China, while Pakistan's nuclear weapons are primarily designed to compensate for Indian conventional military superiority.[29] This is exacerbated by India's Cold Start doctrine, which is designed for a rapid conventional attack to neuter Pakistani nuclear forces before they can be used. This means that any conventional war or even skirmish might potentially escalate to the nuclear level.[30] Moreover, concerns abound about the command and control of Pakistani nuclear weapons – particularly as they are not under civilian control – and given that they are placed on high alert (due in part to the Indian Cold Start doctrine). The introduction of battlefield nuclear weapons by either side is unlikely to make this balance any more stable.[31]

- *Regional nuclear security* A second set of challenges involves the security and safety of nuclear weapons in South Asia – but primarily in Pakistan – and the possibility of either unauthorised nuclear use or that these weapons might fall into the hands of non-state actors. This appears especially problematic given Indian concerns that the Pakistani government and/or the Pakistani ISI is helping facilitate terrorist attacks in Kashmir and in India, not to mention Pakistani links with the A.Q. Khan nuclear smuggling network (see Chapter 7). With regard to the A.Q. Khan network, Gordon Corera points out that 'Either they [Pakistan] knew nothing and their most sensitive national security programs were essentially out of their control, or they knew of Khan's actions and failed to stop them'.[32] All of these factors serve to increase insecurity in India, and across South Asia.

- *US–India nuclear deal* South Asian nuclear politics has been further complicated by the civilian nuclear deal signed by the USA and India in 2005, whereby India agreed to place its civilian nuclear facilities (but not its military ones) under IAEA safeguards and inspection, in return for full civil nuclear cooperation with the United States. The deal, known as the 123 Agreement (and also as the Indo-US nuclear deal), appears to tacitly accept India's current position outside the NPT, while at the same time providing India with the benefits of NPT membership – especially after the Nuclear Suppliers Group granted it a waiver in 2008 allowing it access to international nuclear markets.[33] The deal has been met with a mixed reception – particularly in Pakistan – and it is feared that this is likely to send a strong signal to other would-be proliferators.[34]

- *Wider geopolitical impact* Finally, what happens on the subcontinent has considerable wider political impact and security implications. The most immediate impact of the South Asian nuclear balance is on China. Given strained relations between India and China, any Indian moves to counter the perceived threat from Pakistan will also be felt in Beijing.[35] The knock-on effect of any Chinese response will necessarily have implications for Northeast Asian security dynamics. Likewise, Pakistani nuclear policy in light of India is likely to have knock-on effects for security thinking in the Middle East. More broadly, developments in South Asia are intrinsic to the future of the NPT and international non-proliferation regime – as long as India and Pakistan remain outside of this framework, the harder it will undoubtedly prove to achieve its ultimate goals (see Chapter 7).

The South Asian continent remains fundamentally split, and the introduction of nuclear weapons appears to have done little to aid this. In fact, Indian and Pakistani nuclear weapons raise the potential cost of any future conflict or even miscalculation exponentially. The trend in the region appears to be towards more nuclear weapons rather than less, and it is difficult to see how these two states – which remain outside of the NPT – can be brought into global nuclear regimes in the near future.

(3) Dealing with a nuclear North Korea

The Democratic People's Republic of Korea (DPRK) – better known as North Korea – has presented the third key proliferation challenge of the second nuclear age, and in many ways typifies the difficulties in preventing a determined country from building nuclear weapons. In the words of Jonathan Pollack:

> For a quarter of a century, the Democratic Republic of North Korea (DPRK) has defied, stymied, deferred or circumvented repeated efforts by allies, adversaries and the International Atomic Energy Agency (IAEA) to inhibit its pursuit of nuclear weapons and ensure Pyongyang's compliance with its declared non-proliferation obligations.[36]

Ultimately, however, international efforts to this end have failed. In 2003 the DPRK left the NPT (under Article X), and in 2006 conducted its first nuclear weapons test. Geopolitical relations in the Northeast Asian region have remained tense ever since.

(i) How and why North Korea went nuclear

North Korean leaders have always cited external threats (primarily from the USA) as the main reason for their pursuit of nuclear weapons, and this can probably be traced back to the Korean War of the early 1950s. However, and while the Yongbyong nuclear reactor became operational in 1965, a coherent nuclear weapons programme did not begin until the 1970s. Since this time we can think of the evolution of the North Korean programme in terms of three periods: the first, roughly between 1970 and 1991 – as the DPRK established a nascent nuclear weapons programme; the second, between 1991 and 2006 – as the international community wrestled to prevent North Korea leaving the NPT; and the third between 2006 and 2013 – as North Korea went ahead with overt nuclear weapons testing and regional tensions mounted.

The North Korean nuclear weapons programme began under the state's founder Kim Il-sung in the early 1970s, primarily as a response to the worsening regional geopolitical environment in which the regime found itself at this time, but also as a result of growing domestic discontent. While North Korea signed up to the NPT in 1985 (although safeguards were not agreed until 1992), increasing evidence of a nuclear weapons programme would emerge during the 1980s, and by the early 1990s, North Korean nuclear advancement, and a renewed focus on the Korean peninsular following the end of the Cold War, brought the matter to international attention. The result was that in December 1991 – under significant pressure from the United States – the DPRK signed an agreement with the Republic of South Korea (ROK) banning nuclear weapons from the Korean peninsular:

Under the Joint Declaration, the Democratic People's Republic of Korea (DPRK) and the Republic of Korea (ROK) agree not to test, manufacture, produce, receive, possess, store, deploy, or use nuclear weapons; to use nuclear energy solely for peaceful purposes; and not to possess facilities for nuclear reprocessing and uranium enrichment.[37]

Following this announcement the North Koreans submitted seven sites for inspection by the IAEA. As a result, it appeared that the DPRK's pursuit of nuclear weapons had halted. However, hopes of a peaceful future were soon shattered as North Korea and the international community entered into nearly two decades of 'crisis' over the DPRK's nuclear intentions.

The first North Korean nuclear crisis (1993–1994) In April 1993, weapons inspectors from the IAEA reported North Korea to the UN Security Council for being in breach of its commitments under the NPT, and in particular for the failure to disclose all of its nuclear-related facilities, some of which could be related to a secret nuclear weapons programme. In response, Kim Il-sung announced that North Korea would be leaving the NPT. While withdrawal was suspended in June 1993, the next few months were spent frantically trying to find a diplomatic solution to the crisis and prevent the DPRK from weaponising. In early 1994 US President Bill Clinton brokered a deal – known as the Agreed Framework – whereby the DPRK agreed to freeze its nuclear programme in return for Western help and finance for its civilian nuclear programme – including two light water nuclear reactors – and the return of IAEA inspectors. A few months later, Kim Il-sung was replaced by his son Kim Jung-il, and things remained relatively calm until 1998, when the DPRK test fired a ballistic missile over Japan.

The second North Korean nuclear crisis (2002–2006) In late 2002, concerns were again raised that the DPRK was pursuing weaponisation of its nuclear programme, and in January 2003, in response to international pressure, the DPRK announced that it would expel weapons inspectors, and that it would leave the NPT (this time for good). In August 2003, the multilateral six-party talks[38] began, marking the beginning of several years of largely unproductive negotiations over the DPRK's nuclear programme. The crisis reached its culmination on 9 October 2006, as North Korea conducted its first nuclear weapons test (using plutonium) at the Punggye-ri nuclear test site in North Hamgyong near the Chinese border, with an estimated yield of 500t–1kt.[39]

On 14 August 2007, in response to UN condemnation of an attempted (failed) satellite launch, North Korea pulled out of the six-party talks, and two years later, on 25 May 2009, conducted its second nuclear test. The test, with an estimated yield of 2–7kt was notably more powerful than the first – indeed, it is believed that the first test may have been relatively unsuccessful. In the words of Jonathan Pollack, 'The DPRK may have crossed the nuclear threshold in 2006, but the first test did not achieve its anticipated results'.[40] More recently, on 11 February 2013, it conducted its third nuclear test, with an estimated yield of 6–9kt, putting it well on the path to an operational nuclear bomb.[41]

(ii) Rising tensions

Since the early 1990s, and particularly since the nuclear test of 2006, tensions have continued to rise in Northeast Asia, and concerns have mounted about the rationality and stability of the North Korean regime. These tensions began to manifest under Kim Jong-il and have intensified under his successor Kim Jong-un. Indeed, in recent years, there have been a number of direct clashes between North and South Korea – resulting in a number of deaths – as well as an escalation of military threats, and increasingly aggressive rhetoric from the DPRK. Three episodes in particular stand out:

- In November 2009, North Korean and South Korean naval vessels exchanged fire in the Yellow Sea. Both sides blamed each other for initiating the skirmish.[42]
- In March 2010, a North Korean torpedo sunk the South Korean naval vessel *Cheonan* in the Yellow Sea, causing 46 South Korean sailors to lose their lives. While North Korea has never officially admitted being behind the attack, it is generally regarded as being responsible.[43]
- In November 2010, North Korean forces bombarded the South Korean island of Yeonpyeong in the Yellow Sea with heavy artillery. South Korean forces

returned fire. Four South Koreans lost their lives and considerable damage was done to property on the island.[44]

These actions notwithstanding, tensions have appeared to increase considerably following the death of Kim Jong-il and the transition of power to his eldest son, Kim Jong-un. In fact, since taking power in December 2011, the new leader has embarked on a variety of military provocations, greatly increasing concerns in the region. As *The Economist* details:

> his regime launched a satellite into space ... [and] tested a nuclear device ... It promised to restart the plutonium reactor in Yongbyon, and it prevented South Korean workers crossing the border to their jobs at the Kaesong industrial complex, the only surviving joint economic initiative between the two countries. In March cyber-attacks, possibly from the north, debilitated the computer networks of three South Korean banks and three television stations. That was followed by histrionic threats to attack Guam, Okinawa, Hawaii and the American mainland itself.[45]

While much of this has been attributed to domestic political dynamics – primarily the perceived need for Kim Jong-un to consolidate his hold on power – these actions have raised concerns about the intentions and rationality of the DPRK regime.

As of 2014, most estimates suggest that North Korea possess up to ten nuclear weapons, is working on an ICBM capability, and is continuing to augment its uranium enrichment and plutonium separation capabilities. The debate over what this might mean for the security of the region and the wider world is analysed in more detail in the section below.

(iii) Debating the nuclear threat

While the addition of North Korea to the nuclear club is not something widely welcomed, opinions differ significantly on how serious the threat from its nascent nuclear weapons capability actually is. Pessimists suggest that there is little evidence that the DPRK will act as a responsible nuclear actor – that the regime may not be 'rational', and that nuclear miscalculation and disaster are therefore likely. Optimists, on the other hand, suggest that regime survival is key for the DPRK and that the leadership wouldn't do anything that might jeopardise the future of the state. The inherent uncertainty about the North Korean regime is summed up well by Denny Roy:

> The first theory is that the leaders of North Korea are irrational or desperate, and their actions are strategically senseless. If this is the case, other Asia-Pacific

governments will be unable to surmount their disagreements with Pyongyang through agreements and cooperation. They must also expect and prepare for hyper-aggressive and even suicidal North Korean policies. A second common view holds that North Korean leaders believe they need an external enemy for domestic political purposes. They therefore engage in self-alienation to ensure continual tensions with the outside world. According to this view Pyongyang will never give up its nuclear weapons or reconcile with its adversaries. A third theory is that fomenting crises serves two basic North Korean objectives: security and extracting concessions. Pyongyang believes the risks of a tension-raising policy are acceptable given the potential rewards and the lack of other options.[46]

We can examine the debate in more detail in Table 18.

Table 18   Assessing the North Korean nuclear threat

North Korea is a rational nuclear actor	North Korea is not a rational nuclear actor
Regime survival is the central aim for North Korea, and they know that nuclear use would mean overwhelming retaliation and very likely destruction	Power in North Korea is highly centralised, meaning that an irrational leader could order nuclear use
North Korea has acquired nuclear weapons for deterrence purposes, primarily against the threat of military action by the United States	Recent hostile actions increase the perception that North Korean leaders may be unstable. Equally, this raises the prospect of miscalculation
North Korea will accept the logic of MAD that has prevailed since 1945	The collapse of the North Korean state – which is a very real possibility – raises uncomfortable questions about what would happen to nuclear forces
Aggressive posturing by North Korea is primarily about domestic politics, bargaining and seeking concessions	North Korea might proliferate nuclear technology and weapons to other actors or even terrorists – they are suspected of having done this in the past
North Korea needs China, South Korea and the United States to survive	Every effort is being made by North Korea to acquire long-range nuclear delivery capabilities

Ultimately, at the heart of the North Korean challenge is a lack of understanding regarding the regime. This is the reason for what often appears to be worst-case scenario thinking, but equally the key reason why these worst-case scenarios are widely believed.

(4) Future trajectories in the Iranian nuclear stand-off

There is perhaps no better example of the type of challenge that typifies the second nuclear age than the stand-off that has developed with Iran over its suspected nuclear weapons programme during the last decade. While the Iranian leadership has consistently maintained that it is exercising its right to develop civilian nuclear power capabilities and peaceful research programmes under the NPT, the international community – led by the P5+1[47] – contends that this is merely a cover for a nuclear weapons programme. Despite recent diplomatic progress it remains unclear what future Iranian ambitions are, and it is for this reason that Iran presents a serious and perhaps fundamental challenge for addressing nuclear proliferation in the second nuclear age.

(i) How did we get here?

Iran's interest in nuclear energy began as far back as the 1950s after the then pro-Western Shah took advantage of the US-led Atoms for Peace proposal to begin establishing a nuclear programme, and the Tehran Research Reactor was declared operational as far back as 1967. Support for the development of civilian nuclear technology in Iran from the United States and Western Europe continued until the revolution of 1979 when the new Islamic Republic replaced the Western-friendly Shah. It is believed that for the next two decades Iran pursued research on the full spectrum of nuclear capabilities, including possible weaponisation. Nevertheless, while concerns about Iranian nuclear intentions never went away during the 1980s and 1990s,[48] it was not until 2002 that the international community woke up to the very real possibility of a nuclear-armed Iran after dissident Alireza Jafarzadeh revealed to the world the existence of an uranium enrichment facility at Natanz and a heavy-water production plant at Arak.[49] Since then tensions have increased as Iran has moved slowly along the nuclear trajectory: in 2003 the IAEA reported that Iran had not declared sensitive information related to reprocessing and enrichment activities; in 2006 President Mahmoud Ahmadinejad declared that Iran had successfully enriched uranium; and in 2009 the secret uranium enrichment facility at Fordow was finally made public. Throughout this time, various officials have strongly refuted the accusation that Iran is trying to produce a nuclear weapon – arguing instead that the nuclear programme is for domestic civilian purposes – which it is entitled to under the NPT.[50]

In November 2013, a deal was reached between Iran and the P5+1 to temporarily suspend uranium enrichment in return for much needed sanctions relief. Under the so-called Geneva Interim Agreement, Iran agreed to limit levels of uranium enrichment (to a maximum of 5 per cent U235), cease building any new enrichment or reprocessing facilities, and open up its nuclear infrastructure to inspection by the IAEA.[51] Nevertheless, the future trajectory of negotiations and of the Iranian nuclear programme remains unsure. As Wyn Bowen and Jonathan Brewer point out:

it remains far from clear what, if any, timelines the regime has in mind for future possible options such as crossing additional technical thresholds, including enriching uranium to higher levels and developing or even testing a nuclear weapon, or additional diplomatic manoeuvring such as breaking out of the NPT.[52]

(ii) What is Iran trying to achieve?

At the centre of the debate over Iran is the question of what it is trying to achieve with its nuclear programme. The Iranian leadership have consistently maintained that the programme is for peaceful purposes, as Ayatollah Ali Khamenei declared in 2006:

> The West knows very well that we are not seeking to build nuclear weapons. Nuclear weapons are against our political and economic interests and our Islamic beliefs. Therefore, the Islamic Republic will not fear the uproar and will continue the path of scientific progress relying on its principles and the world cannot influence the will of our people.[53]

However, opinion remains split on exactly what Iran is trying to achieve. There are essentially four things that it could be trying to do, and each varies in terms of the challenge it presents. These are explained in more detail below:

1. *Iran is genuinely seeking a civilian nuclear capability* Iran is pursuing a civilian nuclear capability as a sign of modernity and for research and power generation reasons – it has a right to nuclear energy and research under the NPT. However, Iran has enormous reserves of gas and oil that make nuclear power generation somewhat superfluous and it has kept many parts of the programme secret.
2. *Iran is seeking to acquire a breakout or latent nuclear weapons capability* Iran wants to get to a point where it could if it chose to build a nuclear weapon fairly rapidly – this could be anything from a number of years to a number of weeks. This is probably the most likely scenario, and is at the heart of current negotiations.
3. *Iran hasn't decided the future of the programme* The Iranian leadership is keeping its options open. As Kenneth Pollack explains:

> The evidence suggests that the Iranian program is intended for military purposes ... Nevertheless, while the evidence indicates that Iran intends to acquire the capability to build nuclear weapons, it does not definitively indicate that Iran has made the decision to build those weapons and field a nuclear arsenal, and this is where the debate within the international community is currently focussed.[54]

As a result, the future of the programme could depend on a number of internal and external dynamics.

4. *Iran is seeking full weaponisation of its programme* Iran is seeking to build a nuclear bomb under the cover of the NPT under the guise of a civilian nuclear programme.

(iii) What are the possible implications of an Iranian nuclear bomb?

The vast majority of opinion suggests that Iran with nuclear weapons – or even a latent nuclear-armed Iran with the ability to build the bomb – would lead to a wide variety of negative consequences. We can think of six possible negative implications of the Iranian quest for a bomb:

- *Regional proliferation* A major concern about a nuclear Iran is that this would cause other nations in the region to develop their own nuclear weapons capability (primarily for security purposes, but also for regional prestige). The most likely candidates for this would be Saudi Arabia and the Gulf Emirates, but might also include Turkey and Egypt.
- *Damage to the non-proliferation regime* Linked to the point above is the possibility that if Iran is allowed to acquire nuclear weapons it will fundamentally undermine the international nuclear non-proliferation regime, and provide a green light to others thinking of developing nuclear weapons. It may also possibly signal the death knoll for the NPT (see Chapter 7).
- *An emboldened Iran and regional instability* There is a fear that a nuclear-armed Iran would be much bolder and active in the Middle Eastern region, acting to destabilise and undermine its adversaries, and extend its (military) support to various Shia groups outside Iran. A nuclear Iran would also likely make any outside efforts to address such instability more difficult.
- *A concerned Israel* Iran has previously threatened Israel – President Mahmoud Ahmadinejad was quoted as saying that the state should be 'wiped off the map'[55] – and a nuclear-armed Iran may therefore not be tolerable to Israeli leaders. Heightened tension between the two seems likely, and a direct military confrontation cannot be discounted. As Eric Edelman et al. explain, 'The greatest concern in the near term would be that an unstable Iranian–Israeli nuclear contest would emerge, with a significant risk that either side would launch a first strike on the other despite the enormous risks and costs involved'.[56]
- *The link with terrorism* Finally, there is concern that a nuclear-armed Iran could potentially supply (deliberately or otherwise) terrorists with nuclear material or even a nuclear bomb – perhaps through its proxy Hezbollah. While this is the subject of much debate, it is probably unlikely that Iran would give Hezbollah a bomb, although material could be stolen (for more on this see Chapter 8).

However, a small group of scholars – most notably Kenneth Waltz – have argued that a nuclear Iran should not necessarily be feared:

Once Iran crosses the nuclear threshold, deterrence will apply, even if the Iranian arsenal is relatively small. No other country in the region will have an incentive to acquire its own nuclear capability, and the current crisis will finally dissipate, leading to a Middle East that is more stable than it is today.[57]

The options for dealing with Iran depend very much on what one believes that the Iranian regime is trying to do: if the goal of the regime is genuinely a civilian programme then a negotiated diplomatic solution should be reachable; if it is latency then perhaps the regime can be contained; or in a worst-case scenario, if it is full weaponisation, then difficult policy choices will have to be made.

(5) Key points and guide to further reading and resources

This chapter has sought to provide you with an overview of the debate surrounding, and background to, the most pressing horizontal nuclear proliferation challenges. A summary of these points is provided below:

- Since the end of the Cold War, India, Pakistan and North Korea have all tested nuclear devices. Along with Israel, these states are not recognised by the NPT as NWS and are often thought of as nuclear outliers. In recent years concern has mounted that Iran is attempting to build a nuclear weapon, although it remains a NNWS signatory of the NPT.
- Israel is widely believed to possess nuclear weapons but this has never been publicly confirmed – this is known as nuclear opacity or nuclear ambiguity. This position – along with a commitment to prevent other regional powers from acquiring nuclear weapons (through military force if required) – is coming under increasing scrutiny from the international community.
- India and Pakistan both tested nuclear weapons in 1998, and since this time tensions have remained high in South Asia, and a small war was fought in 1999 (the only time two nuclear-armed states have fought a direct conventional war). The risk of escalation to the nuclear level in a future crisis remains ever present.
- North Korea tested its first nuclear device in 2006, after leaving the NPT in 2003. It conducted further tests in 2009 and 2013, and is believed to possess a small usable nuclear stockpile. Concerns have mounted in recent years over whether the DPRK will act 'rationally' with its new leader and nascent nuclear arsenal.

- The Iranian nuclear weapons programme was revealed in 2003, but it remains unclear whether the ultimate goal is to build nuclear weapons or to achieve a breakout or latent nuclear capability. However, Iran remains a signatory of the NPT and has consistently rejected accusations that it is trying to build the bomb.

Further reading and resources

On Israel see Michael Karpin 'The bomb in the basement' (2006), Avner Cohen 'The worst kept secret' (2012) and 'Israel and the bomb' (1999); Seymour Hersh 'The Samson option' (1991); Avner Cohen and Marvin Miller 'Bringing Israel's bomb out of the basement' (2010); and on Mordachai Vanunu see Yoel Cohen 'Whistleblowers and the bomb' (2005). For a more critical view see Zeev Maoz 'The mixed blessing of Israel's nuclear policy' (2003).

On South Asia see Bhumitra Chakma 'The politics of nuclear weapons in South Asia' (2011); Scott Sagan (ed.), 'Inside nuclear South Asia' (2009); Feroz Hassan Khan 'Eating grass' (2012); Samina Ahmed 'Pakistan's nuclear weapons' (1999); Samit Ganguly and Paul Kapur 'Nuclear proliferation in South Asia' (2010) and 'India, Pakistan and the bomb' (2012); Mario Carranza 'An impossible game' (1999); Harsh Pant 'The US–India nuclear pact' (2011); A. Vinod Kumar 'India and the nuclear non-proliferation regime' (2014); and Jaswant Singh 'Against nuclear apartheid' (1998).

On North Korea see Jonathan Pollack 'No exit' (2011); Mike Chinoy 'Meltdown' (2009); Joel Wit et al. 'Going critical' (2004); Charles Pritchard 'Failed diplomacy' (2007); Christopher Hill 'The elusive vision of a non-nuclear North Korea' (2013); James Clay Moltz and Alexander Mansourov (eds.) 'The North Korean nuclear program' (2012); and Denny Roy 'Parsing Pyongyang's strategy' (2010). A detailed timeline of US–DPRK negotiations can be found on the Arms Control Association's website: https://www.armscontrol.org/factsheets/dprkchron. Another good resource on North Korea is www.nknews.org.

On Iran see Alireza Jafarzadeh 'The Iran threat' (2007); Colin Kahl and Kenneth Waltz 'Iran and the bomb' (2012); James Lindsay and Ray Takeyh, 'After Iran gets the bomb (2010); Scott Sagan 'How to keep the bomb from Iran' (2006); Dore Gold 'The rise of a nuclear Iran' (2009); Shashank Joshi 'The permanent crisis' (2012); Kenneth Pollack 'Unthinkable' (2013); Christopher Hobbs and Matthew Moran 'Nuclear dominoes' (2013); Saria Khan, 'Iran and nuclear weapons' (2010); and Wyn Bowen and Jonathan Brewer 'Iran's nuclear challenge' (2011).

Notes

1. See Douglas Jehl, 'CIA nominee wary of budget cuts', New York Times, (3 February 1993), www.nytimes.com/1993/02/03/us/cia-nominee-wary-of-budget-cuts.html.
2. For a detailed historical overview of Israel's nuclear weapons programme see Seymour Hersh, 'The Samson option: Israel, America and the bomb', (New York, Random House: 1991).
3. See Seymour Hersh, 'The Samson option: Israel, America and the bomb', (New York, Random House: 1991) pp.225–240.
4. See ibid, pp.307–316.
5. For more on the Vanunu affair see Yoel Cohen, 'Whistleblowers and the bomb: Vanunu, Israel and nuclear secrecy', (London, Pluto Press: 2005).
6. Avner Cohen, 'The worst kept secret: Israel's bargain with the bomb', (New York, Columbia University Press: 2010) p.xxx.
7. Avner Cohen and Marvin Miller, 'Bringing Israel's bomb out of the basement: has nuclear ambiguity outlived its shelf life?', Foreign Affairs, 89:5 (2010) p.31.
8. See Jeffrey Richelson, 'Spying on the bomb: American nuclear intelligence from Nazi Germany to Iran and North Korea', (New York, W.W. Norton & Co.: 2007) pp.282–316.
9. Avner Cohen, 'The worst kept secret: Israel's bargain with the bomb', (New York, Columbia University Press: 2010) p.xxxiii.
10. Ami Gluska, 'The Israeli military and the origins of the 1967 war: government, armed forces and defence policy 1963–67', (Abingdon, Routledge: 2006) p.30.
11. On this see Roger Howard, 'Operation Damocles: Israel's secret war against Hitler's scientists, 1951–1967', (New York, Pegasus Books: 2013).
12. On this see Rodger Claire, 'Raid on the sun: inside Israel's secret campaign that denied Saddam the bomb', (Random House Digital Inc.: 2004).
13. See Leonard Spector and Avner Cohen, 'Israel's airstrike on Syria's reactor: implications for the nonproliferation regime', Arms Control Today 38:6 (2008), www.armscontrol.org/act/2008_07-08/SpectorCohen.
14. See William Broad, John Markoff and David Sanger, 'Israeli test on worm called crucial in Iran nuclear delay', New York Times, (15 January 2011), www.nytimes.com/2011/01/16/world/middleeast/16stuxnet.html?pagewanted=all&_r=0.
15. Marvin Miller and Lawrence Scheinman, 'Israel and a nuclear weapons free zone in the Middle East', chapter in Morten Bremer Maerli and Sverre Lodgaard (eds.), 'Nuclear proliferation and international security', (Abingdon, Routledge: 2007) p.137.
16. Avner Cohen and Marvin Miller, 'Bringing Israel's bomb out of the basement: has nuclear ambiguity outlived its shelf life?', Foreign Affairs, 89:5 (2010) p.32.
17. Paul Bracken, 'The second nuclear age: strategy, danger and the new power politics', (New York, St. Martin's Press: 2013) p.187.
18. S. Paul Kappur, 'The Indian nuclear programme: motivations, effects and future trajectories', chapter in Olav Njolstad (ed.), 'Nuclear proliferation and international order: challenges to the Non-Proliferation Treaty', (Abingdon, Routledge: 2011) p.13.
19. Feroz Hassan Khan, 'Eating grass: the making of the Pakistani bomb', (Stanford CA, Stanford University Press: 2012) p.7.
20. Ibid, pp.182–186.
21. Sumit Ganguly and Devin Hagerty, 'Fearful symmetry: India–Pakistan crises in the shadow of nuclear weapons', (Seattle WA, University of Washington Press: 2005) p.6.
22. Jeffrey Richelson, 'Spying on the bomb: American nuclear intelligence from Nazi Germany to Iran and North Korea', (New York, W.W. Norton & Co.: 2007) p.331.

23. See Seymour Hersh, 'A reporter at large: on the nuclear edge', The New Yorker, (29 March 1993), www.newyorker.com/magazine/1993/03/29/on-the-nuclear-edge.
24. On this see George Perkovich, 'India's nuclear bomb: the impact on global proliferation', (London, University of California Press: 2002) pp.161–189.
25. Feroz Hassan Khan, 'Eating grass: the making of the Pakistani bomb', (Stanford CA, Stanford University Press: 2012) pp.278–283.
26. See Sumit Ganguly and S. Paul Kapur (eds.), 'Nuclear proliferation in South Asia: crisis behaviour and the bomb', (Abingdon, Routledge: 2010), particularly Chapters 6 and 7.
27. For a good overview of this see Sumit Ganguly and S. Paul Kapur (eds.), 'Nuclear proliferation in South Asia: crisis behaviour and the bomb', (Abingdon, Routledge: 2010).
28. Feroz Hassan Khan, 'Challenges to nuclear stability in South Asia', The Nonproliferation Review, 10:1 (2003) p.62.
29. Raja Menon, 'A mismatch of nuclear doctrines', The Hindu, (22 January 2014), www.thehindu.com/opinion/op-ed/a-mismatch-of-nucleardoctrines/article5602609.ece.
30. See Mario Carranza, 'An impossible game: stable nuclear deterrence after the Indian and Pakistani tests', The Nonproliferation Review, 6:3 (1999). On Cold Start see Zafar Khan, 'Cold start doctrine: the conventional challenge to South Asian stability', Contemporary Security Policy, 33.3 (2012) pp.577–594.
31. See Shashank Joshi, 'Pakistan's tactical nuclear nightmare: déjà vu?', The Washington Quarterly, 36:3 (2013) pp.159–172.
32. Gordon Corera, 'Shopping for bombs: proliferation, global insecurity, and the rise and fall of the A.Q. Khan network', (London, C. Hurst & Co.: 2006) p.xv.
33. For a good overview of this deal see Harsh Pant, 'The US–India nuclear pact: policy, process, and great power politics', (New Dehli, Oxford University Press, 2011).
34. On this see Mario Carranza, 'From non-proliferation to post-proliferation: explaining the US–India nuclear deal', Contemporary Security Policy, 28.3 (2007) pp.464–493.
35. On this see, for example, Lora Saalman (ed.), 'The China–India nuclear crossroads: China, India and the new paradigm', (Washington DC, Carnegie Endowment: 2012).
36. Jonathan Pollack, 'No exit: North Korea, nuclear weapons and international security', Adelphi Papers 418–419, (Abingdon, Routledge for the International Institute for Strategic Studies: 2011) p.13.
37. 'Joint Declaration of South and North Korea on the Denuclearization of the Korean Peninsula', (20 January 1992), www.nti.org/treaties-and-regimes/joint-declaration-south-and-north-korea-denuclearization-korean-peninsula.
38. The six-party talks included: Democratic People's Republic of Korea (North Korea), Republic of Korea (South Korea), Japan, the United States, Russia and China.
39. Richard Garwin and Frank von Hippel, 'A technical analysis: deconstructing North Korea's October nuclear test', Arms Control Today, (November 2006), www.armscontrol.org/act/2006_11/tech.
40. Jonathan Pollack, 'No exit: North Korea, nuclear weapons and international security', Adelphi Paper 418–419, (Abingdon, Routledge for the International Institute for Strategic Studies: 2011) p.163.
41. Kelsey Davenport, 'North Korea conducts nuclear test', Arms Control Today, (March 2013), www.armscontrol.org/act/2013_03/North-Korea-Conducts-Nuclear-Test.
42. Tania Branigan, 'North and South Korean navies exchange fire', Guardian, (10 November 2009), www.theguardian.com/world/2009/nov/10/north-korea-south-navy-ships-exchange-fire.

43. Choe Sang-Hun, 'South Korea publicly blames the North for ship's sinking', New York Times, (19 May 2010), www.nytimes.com/2010/05/20/world/asia/20korea.html?ref=global-home&_r=0.

44. On this and the broader regional impact, see Scott Snyder and See-Won Byun, 'Cheonan and Yeonpyeong: the Northeast Asian response to North Korea's provocations', The RUSI Journal, 156:2 (2011) pp.74–81.

45. 'North Korea: bad or mad? Kim Jong Un is likely to realise his nuclear ambitions, but the two sides already face military stalemate', The Economist, (26 October 2013), www.economist.com/news/special-report/21588196-kim-jong-un-likely-realise-his-nuclear-ambitions-two-sides-already-face.

46. Denny Roy, 'Parsing Pyongyang's strategy', Survival, 52:1 (2010) p.111–112.

47. The United States, Russia, the UK, France, China and Germany.

48. See for example Shahram Chubin, 'Does Iran want nuclear weapons?', Survival, 37:1 (1995) pp.86–104.

49. See Alireza Jafarzadeh, 'The Iran threat: President Ahmadinejad and the coming nuclear crisis', (Basingstoke, Palgrave Macmillan: 2008).

50. See, for example, Iranian President Hassan Rouhani's statement to the United Nations General Assembly, (24 September 2013), http://gadebate.un.org/sites/default/files/gastatements/68/IR_en.pdf.

51. Anne Gearan and Joby Warrick, 'Iran, world powers reach historic nuclear deal', The Washington Post, (23 November 2013), www.washingtonpost.com/world/national-security/kerry-in-geneva-raising-hopes-for-historic-nuclear-deal-with-iran/2013/11/23/53e7bfe6-5430-11e3-9fe0-fd2ca728e67c_story.html.

52. Wyn Bowen and Jonathan Brewer, 'Iran's nuclear challenge: nine years and counting', International Affairs, 87:4 (2011) p.923.

53. Nazila Fathi, 'Iran's Ayatollah affirms peaceful nuclear plans', New York Times, (19 January 2006), www.nytimes.com/2006/01/19/international/middleeast/19iran.html?_r=0.

54. Kenneth Pollack, 'Unthinkable: Iran, the bomb, and American strategy', (New York, Simon & Schuster: 2013) p.39.

55. Ewen MacAskill and Chris McGreal, 'Israel should be wiped off map, says Iran's president', Guardian, (27 October 2005), www.theguardian.com/world/2005/oct/27/israel.iran.

56. Eric Edelman, Andrew Krepinevich and Evan Braden Montgomery, 'The dangers of a nuclear Iran', Foreign Affairs, (2011) p.67.

57. Kenneth Waltz, 'Why Iran should get the bomb: nuclear balancing would mean stability', Foreign Affairs, 91:4 (2012) p.5.

7

MANAGING NUCLEAR PROLIFERATION CHALLENGES: LIMITING, PREVENTING AND DEFENDING

Limiting: negotiating nuclear arms control

Preventing: the international non-proliferation regime

Defending: active and passive defences

Key points and guide to further reading and resources

As the previous two chapters make clear, contemporary global nuclear order is being shaped by two separate but nevertheless interlinked dynamics: the apparent reluctance of the P5 group of recognised nuclear-weapon states (NWS) to make credible efforts to disarm (see Chapter 5); and the problems presented by the horizontal proliferation of nuclear weapons to a new group of 'outlier' states (see Chapter 6). Taken together – and notwithstanding the prospect of nuclear terrorism addressed in Chapter 8 – these two challenges strike at the heart of the complicated nature of international nuclear politics in the twenty-first century. While nuclear deterrence and mutual assured destruction (MAD) (see Chapter 4) might be credited with maintaining a certain level of stability throughout the nuclear age, these mechanisms represent an acceptance of the status quo rather than a conscious attempt to moderate or reduce the myriad different threats posed by nuclear weapons and they do little to address the problems inherent in the condition of MAD, or prevent further complications presented by the existence and spread of nuclear expertise. In trying to move beyond this basic

THE POLITICS OF NUCLEAR WEAPONS

framework, we can think of three other main ways that the dangers of nuclear weapons have been and can be managed:

1. Through diplomatic negotiation between nuclear-armed powers – although sometimes unilaterally – to curb, reduce and even eliminate types of nuclear weapons via nuclear arms control.
2. Through measures to prevent and minimise nuclear risks via international regimes, agreements and widespread norms, such as the NPT – backed up if necessary by the threat and use of economic sanctions and/or military force.
3. By attempts to mitigate against deliberate and accidental nuclear threats – primarily an attack by nuclear-armed ballistic missiles – using active (missile defences and air defences) and passive defences (civil defence measures, hardened facilities and fallout shelters).

All of these measures have their different strengths and weaknesses, and each is naturally more suitable to certain types of nuclear threat than others – as is explained below. That said, none of these measures are foolproof, even when pursued in concert, and a final (arguably more complex) option – global nuclear disarmament – is addressed in Chapter 9.

This chapter proceeds in three sections: section 1 looks at the importance of nuclear arms control as a mechanism for addressing nuclear dangers, with a particular focus on US–Russian bilateral cuts, but also on the challenges to successful nuclear arms control that we will face in the future; in section 2 the importance of the NPT is examined in detail, as are the methods available for ensuring and if necessary enforcing compliance with the international non-proliferation regime; and finally, in section 3 the various means of defence against nuclear attack are analysed along with problems that the notion of defence in the nuclear age has traditionally caused. The chapter then finishes with a summary of key points and a guide to further reading and resources.

(1) Limiting: negotiating nuclear arms control

The first option available for managing contemporary nuclear proliferation challenges is through negotiated arms control agreements to limit, regulate and reduce the threat from global nuclear forces. Nuclear arms control has played a key role in facilitating reductions in US and Russian nuclear stockpiles and in stabilising and reversing the Cold War nuclear arms race (due to the enormous nuclear forces developed during this period), but it has arguably had relatively little impact on wider nuclear challenges – at least until now. Indeed, some have blamed the arms control process for obscuring the ultimate goal of nuclear disarmament rather than helping to move towards it (see Chapter 5). Either way, nuclear arms control agreements remain essential as we seek to manage our contemporary global nuclear environment.

(i) What is nuclear arms control?

Nuclear arms control is the process whereby states have sought and continue to seek stability and security through negotiation and agreement to reduce nuclear dangers. In the words of Thomas Schelling and Morton Halperin:

> Arms control can be thought of as an effort, by some kind of reciprocity or cooperation with our potential enemies, to minimize, to offset, to compensate or to deflate some of these characteristics of modern weapons and military expectations.[1]

Or as Jeffrey Larson and James Smith put it, arms control 'includes measures intended to reduce the likelihood of war, to limit the costs of preparing for war, and should war occur, to reduce the consequences'.[2] Accordingly, rather than focusing on nuclear disarmament (which is covered in Chapter 9) arms control agreements and frameworks were and are designed to *regulate* the development and spread of nuclear weapons and help towards *controlling* their use and effects. While the two things are not mutually exclusive, nuclear arms control is therefore not the same thing as nuclear disarmament – arms control seeks to manage nuclear relations and enhance nuclear deterrence rather than replace it.[3] As Hedley Bull points out:

> disarmament is the reduction or abolition of armaments, while arms control is restraint internationally exercised upon armaments policy – not only the number of weapons, but also their character, development and use.[4]

While it is widely believed that arms control agreements can help us move towards a position whereby nuclear abolition becomes more feasible, the process is nevertheless the source of much debate. Opponents accuse the arms control process as only serving to bolster the role of nuclear weapons rather than seeking to reduce them (particularly for the P5), while proponents of arms control argue that these agreements and limits have helped to stabilise and moderate the nuclear arms race and therefore enhance international stability.

Nuclear arms control has traditionally focused on three main things: limiting the testing of nuclear weapons; limiting the development and deployment of nuclear weapons; and limiting the scope for their use. While arms control agreements can come in many guises, it is perhaps easiest to codify them along three lines – unilateral, bilateral and multilateral:

- *Unilateral* These are arms control measures taken independently by one nation, where no reciprocal moves by another state are necessarily required. Good examples of this are the 1991 US Presidential Nuclear Initiatives (PNIs), the South African decision to disarm in the early 1990s and the decision taken by the UK government to reduce its nuclear stockpile in 1998.
- *Bilateral* These are agreements between two nations – primarily throughout the nuclear age this has meant between the United States and the Soviet Union/Russia. Bilateral agreements necessitate reciprocal measures and are often bolstered by inspection and verification regimes to ensure compliance. Details of key bilateral arms control agreements can be found in Table 19 and Table 20.
- *Multilateral* These are agreements between more than two nations, and potentially have regional or even global implications. They are also bolstered through inspections and monitoring – normally through the United Nations, but also by specialist institutions such as the International Atomic Energy Agency.

As is detailed below, bilateral agreements are by far the most prevalent and have proven to be the most successful. Many multilateral arms control agreements – such as the Comprehensive Test Ban Treaty (CTBT), Fissile Material Cut-off Treaty (FMCT) and the Nuclear Weapons Convention (NWC) – have proved very difficult to negotiate and implement.

Arguably the biggest obstacle inherent in any type of prospective arms control deal is how to verify that the other party is complying with the agreement and not seeking an advantage through cheating. The concern about cheating and the inherent distrust between states goes right back to the security dilemma discussed in Chapter 4, which is often cited as a key driver of nuclear arms racing in the first place. There are a number of options open to states to ensure compliance, ranging from the use of national technical means – such as satellite technology – through regular inspections carried out by the relevant personnel and international bodies, up to clandestine means such as espionage.[5] Agreeing on measures of transparency and verification has always been a complex part of nuclear arms control negotiations, and is likely to become even more important as US and Russian nuclear forces are reduced, and especially if and when other smaller nuclear armed states are brought into the arms control process.

(ii) Notable nuclear arms control agreements

Historically, the majority of nuclear arms control agreements have been bilateral in nature, and have involved the United States and the Soviet Union/Russia. This is because these two nations had acquired enormous nuclear stockpiles over the preceding decades, and between them accounted for the vast majority of nuclear weapons in existence (see Chapter 3). As a result, before the other nuclear powers could or indeed can be brought into arms control discussions it is broadly accepted that significant (further) reductions have to be made in US and Russian forces first.

We can think of two main periods of bilateral nuclear arms control: the first during the second half of the Cold War between the USA and the Soviet Union (1969–1987), which primarily focused on ways to *limit* the nuclear arms race; and the second during the years after the Cold War where agreements were made between the USA and Russia to *reduce* these large nuclear stockpiles (1991–present). Tables 19 and 20 detail the key arms control treaties and agreements reached since 1945.

Table 19   Key Cold War bilateral arms control treaties

Treaty	Date signed	Details
Strategic Arms Limitation Treaty (SALT)	1972	The result of the Strategic Arms Limitations Talks between the USA and Russia from November 1969 to May 1972. The agreement froze the number of strategic ballistic missile launchers deployed by either side.
Anti-Ballistic Missile (ABM) Treaty	1972	Prohibited the deployment of more than two defensive systems in each country designed to intercept ballistic missiles. The treaty enshrined the principle of vulnerability inherent in the condition of MAD. In 1974 an additional protocol reduced the number of permitted sites to one each, and the number of interceptors to 100. US President George W. Bush abrogated in the treaty in 2002.
Strategic Arms Limitation Treaty (SALT II)	1979	The result of talks held between the USA and the Soviet Union from November 1972 to June 1979. The treaty limited ballistic missiles and prohibited space-based nuclear weapons. However, due to political events, it was never ratified and did not come into force.[i]
Intermediate-Range Nuclear Forces (INF) Treaty	1987	Eliminated all ground-launched intermediate and short-range nuclear missiles held by the USA and the Soviet Union over a three-year period, and included a rigorous inspection regime. Some 2,500 weapons were destroyed as part of this deal.[ii]

[i] See Strobe Talbott, 'Endgame: the inside story of SALT II', (New York: Harper & Row: 1979)
[ii] See Lynn Davis, 'Lessons of the INF Treaty', Foreign Affairs, 56:4 (1988) pp.720–734

Table 20   Post-Cold War bilateral arms control agreements[i]

Treaty	Date signed	Details
Strategic Arms Reduction Treaty (START) I	1991	Reduced the number of strategic offensive nuclear weapons (delivery vehicles) held by each side to 1,600 and the accompanying warheads to a maximum of 6,000. The treaty included an extensive range of on-site inspections to verify these numbers. START I came into force on 5 December 1995 and expired in December 2009.

(Continued)

Table 20 (Continued)

Treaty	Date signed	Details
Strategic Arms Reduction Treaty (START) II	1993	Called for operational warheads possessed by each side to be reduced to 3,000–3,500 and eliminated ICBMs with Multiple Independently Targetable Re-entry Vehicles (MIRVs). The treaty was only in effect between 14 April 2000 and 14 June 2002 (after Russia left).
Strategic Offensive Reductions Treaty (SORT/Moscow Treaty)[ii]	2002	Committed the USA and Russia to reduce deployed strategic warheads to 1,700–2,200 apiece by 2012. It was the shortest bilateral arms control treaty ever signed, and contained no provisions for verifications, inspections or compliance. Neither did it require the destruction of excess warheads.[iii]
New Strategic Arms Reductions Treaty (New START)[iv]	2010	The agreement – designed to replace START I and SORT – calls for both sides to reduce deployed strategic nuclear warheads to 1,550 each, and deployed strategic delivery vehicles to 700 (with a further 100 held in reserve). A new verification and inspection regime was agreed to replace earlier agreements. The treaty expires in 2021, although it can be extended to 2026.

[i] Access to all arms control treaties signed by the USA can be found on the State Department's website: www.state.gov/www/global/arms/bureau_ac/treaties_ac.html

[ii] www.nti.org/treaties-and-regimes/strategic-offensive-reductions-treaty-sort/

[iii] Amy Woolf, 'Nuclear arms control: the Strategic Offensive Reductions Treaty', Congressional Research Service, (7 February 2011), www.fas.org/sgp/crs/nuke/RL31448.pdf

[iv] See 'The Treaty between the United States of America and the Russian Federation on Measures for the Further Reduction and Limitation of Strategic Offensive Arms', United States Department of State, www.state.gov/t/avc/newstart

It is important to note that all post-Cold War bilateral arms control treaties between the United States and Russia have been limited purely to deployed strategic nuclear weapons. Sub-strategic nuclear weapons, nuclear weapons held in reserve or those waiting to be decommissioned are not part of these agreements.

That said, some notable arms control measures have been taken independent of these more formal treaties. Perhaps the most noteworthy are those that took place between September 1991 and January 1992, as US President George H.W. Bush announced a number of unilateral nuclear arms reductions are part of his PNIs, shortly followed by reciprocal moves from Soviet Premier Mikhail Gorbachev. This involved the following:

- the removal of all US tactical nuclear weapons from surface ships, attack submarines and land-based naval aircraft worldwide;
- cancelling plans to develop a new short-range nuclear attack missile (SRAM II) and the Peacekeeper ICBM;
- proposals eliminating all ICBMs with Multiple Independently Targetable Re-entry Vehicles (MIRVs) (later codified in START II).

In response, both Gorbachev and Boris Yeltsin (who replaced Gorbachev in late 1991) committed the Soviet Union and then Russia to a similar range of extensive nuclear cuts.[6] The initiatives paved the way for and bolstered the more formal START I that was signed in 1991. Since this time, both the United Kingdom and France have also scaled back their nuclear forces unilaterally (for more on this see Chapter 5).

(iii) The future of nuclear arms control

It seems highly likely that nuclear arms control will remain at the centre of international efforts to manage nuclear proliferation and the broader threats relating to nuclear weapons. While arms control agreements have undoubtedly proved successful in the past (as is detailed above), as nuclear weapons numbers come down, negotiations become not just far more complicated but also increasingly contingent on a much broader array of factors. Essentially, while the USA and Russia were able to cut their nuclear forces substantially over the past two decades, they could do this without any real impact on their security. If global nuclear stockpiles begin to equalise, however (if the USA and Russia get closer to the stockpile numbers of the other nuclear powers – i.e. in the low hundreds), qualitative differences and cultural variables will become far more important.

While further successful nuclear arms control agreements should certainly not be ruled out, we can think of two principal challenges that stand in the way of any future progress: how to achieve further in cuts in US–Russian nuclear weapons, and how to bring the other nuclear powers into the arms control process.

- *Challenge 1: Further cuts to US–Russian nuclear stockpiles* The next step in nuclear arms control will involve the USA and Russia reducing their current nuclear forces to levels closer to those of the other nuclear armed states. This may take the form of a further joint reduction in strategic arms, an agreement on tactical nuclear weapons or reserve forces, or all of the above. It also seems likely to have to include some type of provision on US conventional forces, such as BMD. As Anatoli Diakov et al. point out, 'Ballistic missile defenses are the key issue. On one hand, reducing the gap in the two sides' attitudes toward missile defense would promote resolution of the two other issues. On the other hand, a lack of progress on missile defense will block dialogue on tactical weapons and conventional strategic arms as well as on further reductions of strategic nuclear arms.'[7] If the USA and Russia cannot agree further reductions, then the future of multilateral nuclear arms control appears bleak (for more on this see Chapter 5).
- *Challenge 2: Multilateralise the nuclear arms control process* Assuming that further cuts can be made in US and Russian nuclear stockpiles, attention will then need to turn to how the arms control process can be expanded to other nuclear states. This must be done in such a way that it does not disadvantage any participants in these discussions. Stephen Pifer and Michael O'Hanlon express this question pithily:

at what point must other countries be brought into the arms control process so as not to create the potential for new arms races between one or more medium powers and the traditional nuclear superpowers, as the latter reduce their nuclear weapons holdings?[8]

In addition to the general problem of how to multilateralise the nuclear arms control process, two further inherent challenges will need to be addressed: (1) the first is how to engage the P5 NPT signatory states in arms control dialogue when Britain, France and China all currently maintain that they are operating at a minimum nuclear force structure already (see Chapter 5); and (2) the second arguably more complicated challenge is how to involve the non-NPT signatory nuclear states in these discussions, when India, Pakistan, North Korea and Israel have shown precious little interest in disarming (see Chapter 6).

Perhaps, above all, the biggest task confronting the arms control agenda will be preventing the further vertical and horizontal spread of nuclear weapons. Vertical proliferation – most likely by Russia or China in relation to advances in US conventional capabilities such as BMD – but also possibly by others, is a key aspect of this, as are the significant problems that the further spread of nuclear weapons to new actors will likely cause. Moreover, the more that the current nuclear-armed states – particularly the P5 – appear reluctant to meet their disarmament commitments or at least to reduce their nuclear forces, the more attractive these weapons will become to others, and the harder it will be to enforce non-proliferation.

(2) Preventing: the international non-proliferation regime

The bedrock of the international nuclear non-proliferation regime is the NPT agreed in 1968. The treaty recognises the United States, Russia, the United Kingdom, France and China as the five states legally allowed to possess nuclear weapons: these are known as nuclear-weapon-states (NWS) and all the other signatories (those who do not possess nuclear weapons) to the treaty are known as non-nuclear-weapon states (NNWS). Any states acquiring nuclear weapons after 1968 cannot become legally recognised NWS under the treaty in its current format. The treaty also establishes the principle that these five states must work towards nuclear disarmament in good faith (see Chapter 5), and that *all states* have a right to access the benefits of nuclear energy (see Chapter 10). To enforce these norms, the international non-proliferation regime relies on a variety of mechanisms to ensure compliance, ranging from inspections carried out by the International Atomic Energy Agency (IAEA), through to the use of economic sanctions and military force.

(i) The nuclear Non-Proliferation Treaty

The nuclear Non-Proliferation Treaty (NPT), or more formally the Treaty on the Non-Proliferation of Nuclear Weapons, was signed on 1 July 1968 and came into force on 5 March 1970. It came about both as a result of the growing fear of the bipolar nuclear arms race between East and West and also due to the concerns that nuclear weapons would spread to more and more countries – making the world less safe, and some type of nuclear use more likely. The NPT obligates states that are party to the treaty to three main principles:

1. The NWS are prohibited from transferring nuclear weapons or control over such weapons to any recipient, directly or indirectly, or to assist the NNWS to manufacture or otherwise acquire such weapons, or seek control over them.
2. The NWS are required to assist the NNWS in the use of nuclear energy for peaceful purposes.
3. The NWS must actively work towards complete nuclear disarmament.

In this way, the NPT is viewed as being based upon a *central bargain* – that NNWS agree never to acquire nuclear weapons, and in exchange the NWS agree to share the benefits of peaceful nuclear technology and pursue nuclear disarmament aimed at the ultimate elimination of their nuclear arsenals.

A detailed list of all the articles of the NPT can be found in Table 21.

As of 2014, 190 states are signatories of the NPT, with notable exceptions being India, Israel, Pakistan and North Korea (which left in 2003) who are known (or believed) to possess nuclear weapons, but can never be recognised as such under the provisions of the treaty. In 1995 it was agreed at a review conference in New York to extended the NPT indefinitely (its original mandate had been for 25 years). Further review conferences were held in New York in 2000, 2005 and 2010, and the next is scheduled for 2015.

(ii) Debate about the NPT

While the NPT has perhaps been the central mechanism for controlling global nuclear order since the 1970s, its past record and future relevance remain the subject of debate. Proponents point to a number of key successes: that more countries have signed the NPT than any other international arms control and disarmament agreement; that only one state has ever left the treaty (North Korea); that only three countries (India, Pakistan and North Korea) have acquired a nuclear weapons capability outside of the treaty (four if we include Israel); that a number of states have given up nuclear weapons programmes, and

Table 21 The Nuclear Non-Proliferation Treaty[i]

I	Each nuclear-weapon State Party to the Treaty undertakes not to transfer to any recipient whatsoever nuclear weapons or other nuclear explosive devices or control over such weapons or explosive devices directly, or indirectly; and not in any way to assist, encourage, or induce any non-nuclear-weapon State to manufacture or otherwise acquire nuclear weapons or other nuclear explosive devices, or control over such weapons or explosive devices.
II	Each non-nuclear-weapon State Party to the Treaty undertakes not to receive the transfer from any transferor whatsoever of nuclear weapons or other nuclear explosive devices or of control over such weapons or explosive devices directly, or indirectly; not to manufacture or otherwise acquire nuclear weapons or other nuclear explosive devices; and not to seek or receive any assistance in the manufacture of nuclear weapons or other nuclear explosive devices.
III	Each non-nuclear-weapon State Party to the Treaty undertakes to accept safeguards, as set forth in an agreement to be negotiated and concluded with the International Atomic Energy Agency in accordance with the Statute of the International Atomic Energy Agency and the Agency's safeguards system, for the exclusive purpose of verification of the fulfilment of its obligations assumed under this Treaty with a view to preventing diversion of nuclear energy from peaceful uses to nuclear weapons or other nuclear explosive devices.
IV	Nothing in this Treaty shall be interpreted as affecting the inalienable right of all the Parties to the Treaty to develop research, production and use of nuclear energy for peaceful purposes without discrimination and in conformity with Articles I and II of this Treaty.
V	Each Party to the Treaty undertakes to take appropriate measures to ensure that, in accordance with this Treaty, under appropriate international observation and through appropriate international procedures, potential benefits from any peaceful applications of nuclear explosions will be made available to non-nuclear-weapon States Party to the Treaty on a non-discriminatory basis and that the charge to such Parties for the explosive devices used will be as low as possible and exclude any charge for research and development.
VI	Each of the Parties to the Treaty undertakes to pursue negotiations in good faith on effective measures relating to cessation of the nuclear arms race at an early date and to nuclear disarmament, and on a treaty on general and complete disarmament under strict and effective international control.
VII	Nothing in this Treaty affects the right of any group of States to conclude regional treaties in order to assure the total absence of nuclear weapons in their respective territories.
VIII	Any Party to the Treaty may propose amendments to this Treaty.
IX	This Treaty shall be open to all States for signature.
X	Each Party shall in exercising its national sovereignty have the right to withdraw from the Treaty if it decides that extraordinary events, related to the subject matter of this Treaty, have jeopardized the supreme interests of its country.

[i] Adapted from www.un.org/disarmament/WMD/Nuclear/NPT.shtml

in the case of South Africa, Belarus, Kazakhstan and Ukraine have given up nuclear weapons in order to join the treaty (see Chapter 9).

However, and while the NPT is recognised by many as an outstanding achievement, it is not without its problems. Indeed, critics of the NPT point to three main inherent issues:

1. *That it enshrines the status quo because there is no real intention to disarm* The main criticism of the NPT is that it has allowed the recognised NWS to continue deploying nuclear weapons without any real mechanism to move towards disarmament. Critics also argue that there has been a greater focus

on non-proliferation and counter-proliferation than there has been on genuine nuclear disarmament. As Daniel Joyner points out, 'The treaty has been distorted ... in favour of a disproportionate prioritization of non-proliferation principles, and an unwarranted under-prioritization of peaceful use and disarmament principles'.[9]

2. *That it allows states to go to the brink of achieving nuclear weapons* The intrinsic relationship between a legal right to civilian nuclear power and the ability to establish a nuclear weapons programme means that states can achieve a position of nuclear latency under the treaty, whereby they could theoretically build nuclear weapons in a relatively short period of time (see Chapters 3 and 10). The current stand-off between the international community and Iran is a direct manifestation of this.

3. *That it does not address states with nuclear weapons outside the NPT* States with nuclear weapons that exist outside the NPT (India, Pakistan, North Korea and Israel) are not legally committed to the treaty's principles, and what is more these states can never become legally recognised NWS under the treaty (as it stands). How to engage these non-NPT states in arms control, disarmament and nuclear security talks remains a significant challenge for the international community and the NPT in particular.

In recent times, these criticisms have gained momentum – particularly with the end of the Cold War – and this has resulted in calls for the treaty either to be reformed or even to be scrapped entirely. As Michael Westley has argued:

> the horizontal proliferation of nuclear weapons will probably continue at the rate of one or two additional nuclear weapons states per decade, whether or not the NPT is retained. Persisting with the NPT will make this proliferation much more dangerous than if the NPT is replaced with a more practical regime ... the NPT is a major cause of opaque proliferation, which is both highly destabilising and makes use of transnational smuggling networks which are much more likely than states to pass nuclear components to terrorists.[10]

However, there are no easy answers to the supposed paradox of the NPT, as Marianne Hanson has pointed out:

> Throwing out the NPT would require either a replacement regime, which in the absence of substantial change and political will among key states is merely bound to replicate the existing anomalies and grievances, or allowing and accepting further proliferation ... in the hope that this can be 'managed'. Neither option is appealing.[11]

Ultimately, much will rest on the enduring balance between the P5 NWS, states with nuclear weapons outside of the NPT (addressed in more detail in Chapters 5 and 6) and their NNWS counterparts.

(iii) Enforcing the international non-proliferation regime

There are a number of different options available to enforce the global non-proliferation regime, each involving different mechanisms and bodies, and each with their own inherent problems and difficulties. We can think of these options ranging from the work of the IAEA in overseeing global nuclear facilities and seeking to uncover any malpractice, through the use of sanctions against any state suspected of violating international nuclear norms, right up to the threat of and actual use of military force to ensure compliance. While the IAEA and sanctions have been a central part of the non-proliferation regime since its inception, and particularly in the past two decades, the use of military force remains contentious – and particularly after the 2003 invasion of Iraq.[12]

The NPT does not have a permanent secretariat or administrative body, and therefore relies on other international institutions – principally the United Nations – for its day-to-day administration. The IAEA, based in Vienna, is the body charged with monitoring compliance with the treaty and the implementation of its central articles. Essentially, this makes the main function of the IAEA to prevent peaceful nuclear programmes from being used to produce nuclear weapons by monitoring declared nuclear facilities across the globe. As Article Two of the Agency's statute declares:

> The Agency shall seek to accelerate and enlarge the contribution of atomic energy to peace, health and prosperity throughout the world. It shall ensure, so far as it is able, that assistance provided by it or at its request or under its supervision or control is not used in such a way as to further any military purpose.[13]

The chief mechanism through which the IAEA monitors proliferation concerns is via its Comprehensive Safeguards Agreement which all states party to the NPT must sign up to. In addition to this, the IAEA also has an Additional Protocol that allows for more intrusive inspections of any facilities of proliferation concern – but this must be agreed bilaterally with the host state.[14] Both mechanisms are carried out by IAEA personnel and augmented by national intelligence agencies and coordinated through the UN Security Council.

Should the IAEA or any other body (such as national intelligence agencies) discover illicit facilities with potential nuclear weapons implications, then measures can be taken to increase pressure on the party in question to conform to international non-proliferation requirements. A key means for doing this is through economic (or other types of) sanctions. Sanctions can be comprehensive or targeted, imposed through the United Nations or on a more ad hoc basis, and can involve a range of tools. In the words of Etel Solingen:

> A working definition of sanctions (which might also be labelled negative inducements) refers to international instruments of statecraft that punish or deny

benefits to leaders, rulers, coalitions, or broader constituencies in a given state, in an effort to dissuade those targets from pursuing or supporting the acquisition of nuclear weapons.[15]

However, while sanctions represent a useful tool for enforcing global non-proliferation norms, the approach is not without its critics. We can think of three main problems with sanctions. First, they worsen public opinion and often impinge on the general public most – indeed according to John and Karl Mueller, 'economic sanctions … may have contributed to more deaths during the post-Cold War era than all weapons of mass destruction throughout history'.[16] Second, sanctions only work if the country in question is willing to give up its nuclear programme, as Alireza Nader points out:

> US and multilateral sanctions against Iran may have damaged its economy over the years, but it is not clear if they have changed Iran's resolve to pursue a potentially military nuclear program.[17]

Third, sanctions require widespread international support to be credible – in particular they demand the backing of the major industrial economies. As a result, sanctions have had a mixed record in nuclear non-proliferation.[18]

The final set of options open to ensure compliance with the international non-proliferation regime is the threat and use of military force. Again, this might be limited and targeted – such as through coercive diplomacy, or can involve more comprehensive military and strategic objectives. The use of military force to bolster the non-proliferation regime is highly problematic, and until relatively recently has only had a limited impact in the nuclear realm. We can think of three significant complications with coercive diplomacy and the use of force: that successful coercive diplomacy must threaten and reassure at the same time, and assumes that actions can be changed; that using military force either pre-emptively or preventively raises significant questions as regards legality, legitimacy and proof; and that any credible threat of military force by the international community will almost certainly need to involve the United States and other major powers. There is no better example of this than the debate over Iraq and WMD that led to the US-led invasion in 2003. As George Quester points out:

> The dangerous world of proliferation of weapons of mass destruction may indeed require some pre-emptive or preventive war attacks. But it will always thereafter be difficult to pin down the evidence that such attacks were indeed necessary.[19]

Whether the international community considers the use of force or even preventive war against nuclear aspirants as a viable, effective and legitimate way to bolster the NPT remains the subject of considerable debate. Nevertheless, and irrespective of these problems and challenges, the NPT remains the central pillar of the global non-proliferation apparatus.

(3) Defending: active and passive defences

As soon as nuclear weapons were invented the race was on to find ways to defend against these new heightened threats, but it quickly became clear that defence in the nuclear age would be different from that which had gone before. The advent of ballistic missiles, stealth aircraft and silent submarines made preventing a nuclear attack almost impossible, while the enormous destructive power of nuclear bombs and the speed at which they could be delivered made any type of credible civil defence an equally unmanageable task. It was partly for these reasons that MAD was – and continues to be – seen as the best means of managing the threat of nuclear attack (see Chapter 4). Nevertheless, the idea of defence has never disappeared during the atomic age, and we can best think of these defensive measures as split between active defence – which includes measures to prevent an attack from succeeding (such as air and missile defences, anti-submarine and anti-satellite weapons) – and passive defence – which involves measures to minimise the impact of an attack once it has taken place (such as hardened missile silos, civilian defence, nuclear bunkers and emergency response). These are examined in more detail below.

(i) Active defence

Active defence refers to military systems designed to impede and possibly neuter a nuclear attack by intercepting bombs/warheads before they can hit their intended targets. Active defence refers predominantly to ballistic missile defence (BMD), but it also includes air defence and anti-submarine and anti-satellite weapons, as well as any other capability designed to interdict and intercept a nuclear attack before it reaches its target. Such defences, but particularly BMD, have often been considered as destabilising because they complicate the credibility of a retaliatory second-strike response – which is key to deterrence (see Chapter 4). Nevertheless, as Soviet statesman Alexei Kosygin pointed out in 1967, it has always been hard to escape the view that 'Defense is moral. Offense is amoral.'[20]

A BMD system is designed to track, locate and shoot down enemy nuclear (or conventional) armed ballistic missiles when they are in flight. The system compromises of different radar and satellites (on the ground, at sea and in space) to locate and track the target, a sophisticated command and control infrastructure to process all the information, and finally interceptor missiles to shoot down the incoming warheads (again these might be placed in the ground, at sea or in the air). Ballistic missiles follow a *ballistic* trajectory – that is, they fly up into the atmosphere (and sometimes outside of it) before falling back to earth to hit their intended targets (see more on ballistic missiles in Chapter 2). Enemy missiles can be intercepted at any stage of their flight; boost phase (immediately after launch), mid-course phase (while they are travelling through the atmosphere/ space), or during the terminal phase (as the warhead falls back towards its target on earth). Successful interception during any of these phases is highly complicated – during the mid-course phase for example, a warhead can be travelling at up to 15,000kph, making interception seem the equivalent of 'hitting a bullet with a bullet'.[21]

Missile defences can be designed and configured in different ways and for different purposes. The first key distinction is between tactical/battlefield/theatre missile defence (TMD) (that used for limited defensive purposes, such as protecting troops on the battlefield) and national/strategic missile defence (NMD) (that designed to protect an entire country). This distinction can also be thought of as between *point defence* (defence of a particular military installation such as a missile silo or airfield) and *population defence* (defending cities and urban population centres). Battlefield and point defences are not seen as being inherently destabilising because they do not undermine strategic nuclear deterrents – national and population defences, on the other hand, do because they seek to mitigate the effects of nuclear retaliation. It was because of this that strategic/national/population missile defences were prohibited under the 1972 Anti-Ballistic Missile (ABM) Treaty signed by the USA and the Soviet Union, and part of the reason why the 1983 Strategic Defense Initiative (SDI) proposal by the United States was the source of so much contention.[22] Essentially, large-scale population defences – which may seem moral, given the inherent problems of deterrence – fundamentally complicate MAD because they undermine the credibility of any retaliatory strike (thus potentially making a first nuclear strike with nuclear weapons more attractive), whereas point defences – protecting intercontinental ballistic missile (ICBM) silos for example – enhance deterrence by protecting a retaliatory second-strike capability. However, doubts have always been cast over the efficacy of BMD, and the feeling is that this will always be overwhelmed by a large number of warheads or more sophisticated warhead technology.

In recent years we have seen a strong revival of the idea of missile defence – primarily as a response to the perceived new nuclear challenges of the second nuclear age, but also because the technology has continued to mature. The United States in particular has forged ahead with a limited national missile defence system, ostensibly to protect against the 'rogue state' missile threat, and has also started deploying a range of theatre and battlefield missile defences across the globe.[23] This move has, however, caused a number of problems in traditional nuclear relations between the established nuclear states, particularly between the United States and Russia, but also to a lesser extent with China. This is because any defences deployed against one threat (in the US case North Korea/Iran) will likely have some capability against the nuclear forces of others (Russia/China).[24] As a result, further expansion of active missile defences has the potential to complicate any moves towards nuclear stability, not to mention nuclear reductions and disarmament (this is addressed in more detail in Chapter 5).

Active defences against nuclear attack also include air defences – these are particularly important in protecting against nuclear-armed states without a long-range ballistic missile capability (either land- or submarine-based). Air defence systems might consist of a mixture of radar and early warning facilities, anti-aircraft missiles and interceptor fighter planes. Anti-submarine, anti-satellite and even cyber weapons can also be considered active defence systems, but may also be viewed as possible first-strike capabilities too, because they can be used before an enemy attack is launched.

(ii) Passive defence

Passive defence refers to the various measures taken to minimise the impact of a nuclear strike on a society/country should active defences fail to intercept and neuter an incoming attack. In this way, passive defences are primarily methods designed to be of use *after* an attack has happened (whether deliberate or accidental), although a sophisticated civil defence infrastructure might act as a deterrent to an attack by minimising the perceived gains from a first nuclear strike.

Passive defence can be thought of in two ways: measures to protect particular military assets through hardening (e.g. of missile silos, national command centres, or airfields) or measures to protect the broader civilian population from the effects of a nuclear attack. As is explained in more detail below, the main role of passive military defences is to protect nuclear retaliatory forces and command and control structures, while civilian passive defences are designed to reduce human casualties. Unlike active defences, hardening of missile silos is not seen as destabilising because it increases the survivability of nuclear forces and thus a second-strike capability rather than providing any obvious first-strike advantage. Hardening a missile silo might involve burying the bunker under lots of concrete, or even making the missile launcher mobile (and thus far harder to target). A good example of this is the plan entertained in the 1980s by the United States to build an enormous underground network of tunnels, all of which would be connected by underground railways to house the mobile MX ICBM.[25]

Civilian defensive measures are those designed specifically to mitigate against and limit the impact of a nuclear strike. These include building nuclear bomb shelters and nuclear bunkers for the general population and having a credible plan for responding to any emergency (including the provision of medicines and food and ensuring power generation), as well as plans for the continuity of government after a strike. However, unlike passive military defences, widespread civil defences do have the potential to complicate deterrence, as Dee Garrison points out:

Any really serious attempt to defend one's population from certain destruction sends a dangerous message that the country with a massive civil defense program might even be planning a first strike.[26]

That said, a widespread and credible civil defence system has always proven to be beyond the capabilities of state planners, and has been largely abandoned by most. Nevertheless, civil defence measures and emergency response capabilities have been re-energised in the face of a possible – and theoretically much more limited – terrorist strike with nuclear weapons (see Chapter 8).

(iii) The defence dilemma

Notwithstanding the strategic and political difficulties it causes, defence against nuclear attack has perhaps unsurprisingly always been a popular choice since 1945, and this has increased in the second nuclear age. Active defences in particular are now viewed as essential components of a more nuanced deterrence strategy to deal with new types of nuclear threats, while passive civil defence has become subsumed within the broader institutions of emergency response and homeland security. Ultimately defence will always strike a chord with the general public because it seems such an inherently good idea. As Ronald Reagan famously said in 1983:

> What if free people could live secure in the knowledge that their security did not rest upon the threat of instant US retaliation to deter a Soviet attack, that we could intercept and destroy strategic ballistic missiles before they reached our own soil or that of our allies?"[27]

However, the incorporation of active nuclear defence in the contemporary global nuclear order remains problematic given its intrinsic relationship with the balance of offensive nuclear forces required for deterrence purposes.

(4) Key points and guide to further reading and resources

This chapter has sought to provide you with an overview of the key mechanisms available to combat and manage nuclear threats, and an explanation of their various strengths and weaknesses. A summary of these key points is provided below:

(Continued)

(Continued)

- We can think of three main ways to address the threats posed by nuclear proliferation: diplomacy and arms control; international regimes and norms; active and passive defences. Each of these has relative strengths and weaknesses, and none represent a comprehensive remedy for current nuclear challenges.
- Arms control is the process by which nuclear threats can be managed, reduced or mitigated through diplomacy and legally binding agreements. The majority of these agreements have been between the United States and the Soviet Union/Russia due to their large nuclear stockpiles. The next step in arms control is likely to involve the other states that possess nuclear weapons, and it is therefore likely to become more complex and challenging.
- The centrepiece of the international non-proliferation regime is the NPT, but this is increasingly being challenged. The IAEA is the central mechanism for ensuring compliance with the NPT.
- Sanctions and the use of military force to dissuade or disarm an adversary remain important options for combatting nuclear threats, but these can prove complicated, and even counter-productive.
- Defending against a nuclear attack can be split between active defences – aimed at countering the threat before it strikes – and passive defences – aimed at minimising the damage once a strike has been conducted. Neither of these represents a foolproof defensive option against nuclear weapons, and the pursuit of active defences has traditionally been seen as destabilising.

Further reading and resources

The seminal works on arms control in the nuclear age are Hedley Bull 'The control of the arms race' (1961) and Thomas Schelling and Morton Halperin 'Strategy and arms control' (1961). See also Harald Muller and Carmen Wunderlich 'Norm dynamics in multilateral arms control' (2013), while Jeffrey Larsen and James Smith 'Historical dictionary of arms control and disarmament' (2005) is a useful contemporary resource. A good overview of Cold War bilateral US–Soviet arms control can be found in Michael Sheehan 'Arms control' (1988). Michael Levi and Michael O'Hanlon 'The future of arms control' (2005) is also a useful resource.

On Cold War US–Russia bilateral arms control see John Newhouse 'Cold dawn' (1973) and Strobe Talbott 'Endgame' (1979). On post-Cold War bilateral arms control between the USA and Russia see Ronald Powaski

'Return to Armageddon' (2000) or Kerry Kartchner 'Negotiating START' (1992). On the New START see Alisa Rebane 'The new START Treaty between the US and Russia' (2011); Amy Woolf 'The New START Treaty' (2014), or Stephen Cimbala 'New START or not?' (2010). The text of the New START Treaty can be found on the US State Department website: www.state.gov/t/avc/newstart/. On future arms control challenges see Steven Pifer and Michael O'Hanlon 'The opportunity' (2012) and the guides to further reading in Chapters 5 and 6 of this book.

On the NPT see Olav Njolstad (ed.) 'Nuclear proliferation and international order' (2011); Daniel Joyner 'Interpreting the Non-Proliferation Treaty' (2011); Michael Fry and Patrick Keating 'Nuclear non-proliferation and the Non-Proliferation Treaty' (2011); Michael Wesley 'It's time to scrap the NPT' (2005); Marianne Hanson 'The future of the NPT 1' (2005); Bradley Thayer 'The causes of nuclear proliferation and the utility of the non-proliferation regime' (1995); and Joseph Pilat and Robert Pendley 'A new beginning for the NPT' (1995). The full text of the Non-Proliferation Treaty can be found on the United Nations website: www.un.org/disarmament/WMD/Nuclear/NPT.shtml.

On the IAEA see Mohammed ElBaradei 'The age of deception' (2012); Chen Kane 'Detecting nuclear weapons' (2015); Christine Wing and Fiona Simpson 'Detect, dismantle, disarm' (2013); Theodore Hirsch 'The IAEA additional protocol' (2004); and the IAEA website at www.iaea.org.

On sanctions, coercive diplomacy and the use of force see Thomas Schelling 'Arms and influence' (1966); Etel Solingen 'Sanctions, statecraft and nuclear proliferation' (2012); John Mueller and Karl Mueller 'Sanctions of mass destruction' (1999); George Lopez and David Cortright 'Containing Iraq' (2004); Bruce Jentlesen and Christopher Whytock 'Who "won" Libya?' (2005/6); Susan Allen Hannah 'The determinants of economic sanctions success and failure' (2005); Lawrence Freedman 'Prevention, not preemption' (2003); Sarah Kreps and Matthew Fuhrmann 'Attacking the atom' (2011); and George Quester 'Preemption, prevention and proliferation' (2009).

On active and passive defences, you should consult Richard Burns and Lester Brune 'The quest for ballistic missile defences' (2003); Andrew Futter 'Ballistic missile defence and US national security policy' (2013); Stephen Cimbala 'Shield of dreams' (2008); Dean Wilkening 'Ballistic-missile defence and strategic stability' (2000); and Igor Ivanov 'The missile-defense mistake' (2000). On civil defence see Dee Garrison 'Bracing for Armageddon' (2006); Tracy Davies 'Stages of emergency' (2007); Peter

(Continued)

(Continued)

Hennessey 'The secret state' (2010); and Matthew Grant 'After the bomb' (2010). The animated film *When the Wind Blows* by Raymond Briggs is a fascinating depiction of Cold War civil defence thinking, as is the DVD *Protect and Survive*.

Notes

1. Thomas Schelling and Morton Halperin, 'Strategy and arms control', (New York, Twentieth Century Fund: 1961) p.3.
2. Jaffrey Larsen and James Smith, 'Historical dictionary of arms control and disarmament', (Oxford, Scarecrow Press: 2005) p.23.
3. See Michael Sheehan, 'Arms control: theory and practice', (Oxford, Basil Blackwell Ltd: 1988), p.1–7.
4. Hedley Bull, 'The control of the arms race: disarmament and arms control in the missile age', (New York, Frederick Praeger: 1961).
5. Michael Sheehan, 'Arms control: theory and practice', (Oxford, Basil Blackwell Ltd: 1988) p.123.
6. Matthew Fuhrmann and Bryan Early, 'Following START: risk acceptance and the 1991–1992 presidential nuclear initiatives', Foreign Policy Analysis, 4:1 (2008) pp.21–43.
7. Anatoli Diakov, Eugene Miasnikov and Timur Kadyshev, 'Nuclear reductions after New START: obstacles and opportunities', Arms Control Today, 41:4 (2011) p.15.
8. Steven Pifer and Michael O'Hanlon, 'The opportunity: the next steps in reducing nuclear arms', (Washington DC, The Brooking Institution Press: 2012) p.6.
9. Daniel Joyner, 'Interpreting the Non-Proliferation Treaty', (Oxford, Oxford University Press) p.2.
10. Michael Westley, 'It's time to scrap the NPT', Australian Journal of International Studies, 59:3 (2005) pp.283–284.
11. Marianne Hanson, 'The future of the NPT 1', Australian Journal of International Affairs, 59:3 (2005) p.301.
12. See Robert Litwak, 'Non-proliferation and the dilemmas of regime change', Survival 45:4 (2003) pp.7–32.
13. www.iaea.org/About/statute.html.
14. On this see Theodore Hirsch, 'The IAEA Additional Protocol: what it is and why it matters', The Nonproliferation Review 11:3 (2004) pp.140–166.
15. Etel Solingen, 'Introduction: the domestic distributional effects of sanctions and positive inducements', chapter in Etel Solingen (ed.), 'Sanctions, statecraft, and nuclear proliferation', (Cambridge, Cambridge University Press: 2012) p.5.
16. John Mueller and Karl Mueller, 'Sanctions of mass destruction', Foreign Affairs, 78:3 (1999) p.43.
17. Alireza Nader, 'Influencing Iran's decisions on the nuclear program', chapter in Etel Solingen (ed.), 'Sanctions, statecraft, and nuclear proliferation', (Cambridge, Cambridge University Press: 2012) p.213.
18. On this see Susan Allen Hannah, 'The determinants of economic sanctions success and failure', International Interactions, 31:2 (2005) pp.117–138.

19. George Quester, 'Preemption, prevention and proliferation: the threat and use of weapons in history', (London, Transaction Publishers: 2009) p.183.
20. Richard Dean Burns and Joseph Siracusa, 'A global history of the nuclear arms race: weapons, strategy, and politics', (Santa Barbara CA, Praeger Security International: 2013) p.198.
21. For more detail see 'Missile defense basics', www.nuclearfiles.org/menu/key-issues/missile-defense/basics/general_principles.htm.
22. Harold Brown, 'The strategic defense initiative: defensive systems and the strategic debate', Survival, 27:2 (1985) pp.55–64.
23. On this see Andrew Futter, 'Ballistic missile defence and US national security policy: normalisation and acceptance after the Cold War', (London, Routledge: 2013).
24. On this see Andrew Futter, 'Getting the balance right: US ballistic missile defense and nuclear nonproliferation', Comparative Strategy, 30:3 (2011) pp.254–267.
25. On this see Desmond Ball, 'The MX basing decision', Survival, 22:2 (1980) pp.58–65.
26. Dee Garrison, 'Bracing for Armageddon: why civil defense never worked', (New York, Oxford University Press: 2006) p.7.
27. Ronald Reagan, 'Address to the nation on defense and national security', (23 March 1983), www.atomicarchive.com/Docs/Missile/Starwars.shtml.

8

NUCLEAR WEAPONS AND NEW GLOBAL ACTORS

Illicit nuclear trade and the A.Q. Khan network

Nuclear terrorism

How could terrorists acquire a bomb? How might terrorists use a bomb?

Securing against nuclear terrorism

Key points and guide to further reading and resources

The possibility that a non-state actor or terrorist group could acquire a working nuclear weapon or the fissile material required for a crude nuclear device is one of the most pressing problems for contemporary global nuclear order. Just one small nuclear bomb could cause enormous devastation, disruption and damage to a modern city, and even a conventional dirty bomb could release significant amounts of radioactive material and cause mass panic. While manufacturing fissile material and building a nuclear bomb from scratch are probably beyond the ability of a terrorist organisation (given the engineering and industrial complexities as well as the enormous costs), the possibility that the necessary materials could be either stolen, acquired on the nuclear black market or, in a worse-case scenario, covertly given to a terrorist group by a state – combined with the vulnerability of modern societies to a well-planned terrorist attack – makes the risk of nuclear terrorism a very real possibility. Unlike a nation state – which can (theoretically) be deterred through the threat of retaliation (on MAD see Chapter 4) – terrorist groups often have no 'return address', and terrorists willing to sacrifice their lives – such as those involved with Al-Qaeda – cannot be deterred through the threat of punishment. Consequently, and especially in the wake of the 9/11 terrorist attacks in the United States and the exposure of the A.Q. Khan network, securing nuclear weapons and the relevant fissile materials (uranium and plutonium) has become a top priority for the international community. Nevertheless, as this chapter explains, the threat of nuclear terrorism is more nuanced and complex than is often portrayed.

This chapter proceeds in four sections: the first section explains the threat of illicit nuclear trade and nuclear trafficking before focusing specifically on the A.Q. Khan nuclear smuggling network – showing how nuclear material has been illegally and secretly traded in the past, and why this remains a key challenge today; section 2 looks at the nature, key dynamics and severity of the nuclear terrorist threat; in section 3 the key questions of how terrorists could acquire a nuclear device and how they might use such as device are addressed; and finally, in section 4, the various methods and means of securing against nuclear terrorism are analysed. The chapter finishes with a summary of key points and a guide to further reading and resources.

(1) Illicit nuclear trade and the AQ Khan nuclear network

While nuclear politics often seems principally concerned with 'macro' nuclear issues such as disarmament, arms control and proliferation, it is equally important to understand the 'micro' drivers of current nuclear challenges too. Foremost among these is the continued threat of illicit nuclear trade, and the possibility that certain states or even terrorist groups might be able to acquire nuclear weapons-related designs, material and technology – and theoretically a working bomb – on the black market. Illicit nuclear smuggling networks, such as that run by Pakistani scientist A.Q. Khan during the 1990s and early 2000s, have been directly responsible for the acquisition of nuclear capabilities by certain states, and indirectly for the nuclear weapons programmes of many others. Combatting these illicit nuclear smuggling networks is of intrinsic importance to the global nuclear agenda, and to the prevention of nuclear terrorism in particular.

(i) Illicit nuclear trade

Illicit nuclear trade involves the smuggling and trafficking of the technical information, material, equipment and know-how needed to build a nuclear weapon or a radiological device. This is not a new phenomenon – indeed, most states that have acquired nuclear weapons in the past have relied to some degree on illicit or at best secretive trade deals – but recently the possibility of 'rogue states' or non-state actors acquiring these capabilities has forced the international community to place the illegal trafficking of nuclear-related items at the forefront of the security agenda. According to David Albright et al.:

> That countries build nuclear weapons largely on their own is a common misperception. In fact, most states have depended heavily on overseas acquisition of vital equipment, materials, and know-how to create the industrial infrastructure to build nuclear weapons, a trend that continues today. Over the next few years, several states in dangerous parts of the world, along with terrorist organizations, are expected to seek these weapons. For most of these countries and certainly for terrorists, the pathway to obtaining or improving nuclear weapons remains through illicit nuclear trade.[1]

Illegal nuclear trafficking and smuggling networks could be tacitly state-sponsored, they may involve certain rogue elements within a state or organisation, or they could rely on theft and deception. Trafficking usually involves one of three things: designs and technical know-how; fissile or radioactive material; or the equipment needed for enrichment or reprocessing. It is theoretically conceivable that a complete working bomb could be smuggled into another country, although this is deemed unlikely. It is more likely that the know-how and components necessary for a bomb programme could be acquired through numerous separate illicit deals.

- *Who is involved?* Illicit nuclear trafficking can involve a number of different actors and elements. At the top level it can involve nation states – either deliberately, inadvertently or by certain personnel acting without authority – seeking to buy or sell particular nuclear-related products (North Korea and Pakistan being good examples); internally it could involve hi-tech companies, scientists or technicians involved in precision engineering, metallurgy or other nuclear-related work (again either deliberately or through espionage); finally, it is likely to involve a highly organised network of smugglers and front companies to coordinate the trafficking (such as the A.Q. Khan network described below). Various terrorist groups might also seek access to nuclear materials via these types of network.
- *How is it done?* Nuclear-related material, designs and technology can either be obtained legally through the purchase of dual-use goods – i.e. those that might also be used for non-military purposes – and by exploiting various export law loopholes around the world, or illegally by establishing fake front companies, stealing information or technology, and by deliberately misleading authorities. Buying or acquiring small nuclear-related components from different suppliers through different companies in different countries can make this very hard to track and interdict. In the words of one commentator, 'The barrier to becoming a nuclear power today is not nuclear material but cash'.[2]

- *What is being traded?* A wide range of designs, blueprints, material, technology and components needed for both civilian and military nuclear programmes can be acquired on the nuclear black market. Weapons and warhead designs might be acquired illicitly (these could be put on a CD, or even acquired through hacking) along with uranium ore powder (known as yellowcake) or even fissile material, and the necessary know-how and components required for nuclear enrichment, reprocessing, and separation might be also be traded. In theory it could be possible to put together a fully-fledged nuclear weapons programme from black-market sources – as was nearly the case with Libya in the 1990s (see below).

Illicit networks trading in nuclear goods and knowledge represent a major challenge for the international community and for international nuclear security, and perhaps one that sometimes has not been given the same level of attention as headline issues like disarmament and non-proliferation. However, as the rest of this chapter makes clear, illicit nuclear networks represent the most likely pathway to nuclearisation by any group – be they terrorists or nation states. As David Albright argues, 'governments and businesses have too frequently overlooked or downplayed this pathway to the bomb'.[3] Ways in which this threat can be tackled are addressed later in the chapter.

(ii) The A.Q. Khan network

The most serious manifestation of the trade in illicit nuclear goods was a highly organised network run by Pakistani scientist Abdul Qadeer (A.Q.) Khan from the 1980s until his arrest in 2003. The A.Q. Khan network traded all manner of nuclear-related materials, designs and technology for over two decades, striking deals across the globe, and involving enormous sums of money. In addition to playing a central role in the Pakistani nuclear weapons effort (A.Q. Khan's network was integral to Pakistan achieving the bomb), it is highly likely that the network was directly involved with the North Korean, Syrian, Libyan, Iraqi and Iranian nuclear weapons programmes.

The evolution of the A.Q. Khan nuclear network can be thought of in two phases: (1) seeking the know-how and material to build the Pakistani bomb; and (2) the proliferation of bomb-making information and technology to other countries. These stages are addressed in detail below:

- *Phase 1: building the Pakistani bomb* In 1972 A.Q. Khan joined URENCO – a nuclear fuel supply company based in the Netherlands – as a metallurgist, where he had increasing access to highly sensitive information. Angered by the result of the 1971 Indo-Pakistan war, and extremely concerned by the 1974 'peaceful' Indian nuclear test, Khan offered his services to the Pakistani government – then struggling with its nascent nuclear weapons programme. Following long discussions with the then Pakistani Prime Minister Zulfikar Ali Bhutto, Khan left Europe for Pakistan on 15 December 1975, taking with him considerable amounts of sensitive information and blueprints for uranium-enrichment plants. In 1976, he set up Khan Research Laboratories (KRL) to run the Pakistani uranium-enrichment effort at Kahuta, based on the designs acquired from URENCO, and formed front companies in North America, Japan and Europe to acquire the necessary components for the Pakistani nuclear weapons programme. By the late 1970s Pakistan was well on its way to achieving a nuclear weapons capability thanks to Khan's stolen information and ever-expanding networks of suppliers. Although Khan was convicted in absentia of espionage in the Netherlands in 1983, he was protected by the Pakistani government, and continued his work relatively unhindered.[4] (For more on the Pakistani nuclear programme see Chapter 6.)

- *Phase 2: proliferation* At the same time as using his international networks to build and further the Pakistani nuclear weapons programme, Khan also began to export nuclear designs, technology and components to other potential customers around the world, using his front companies and contacts to get around export controls. In 1981, as part of a deal struck by the Pakistani government with China, Khan received nuclear warhead designs to augment his ever-growing portfolio of enrichment technologies. Shortly afterwards, he brokered a deal with the new Islamic government in Iran for centrifuge blueprints and materials – a so-called 'starter kit', and in 1990 Iran's erstwhile enemy Iraq was offered weapons blueprints and designs as part of Saddam Hussein's crash nuclear weapons programme. Starting in the late 1980s, Khan also struck deals with Libya to supply centrifuge components and designs, and later in the 1990s for weapon and warhead designs, and possibly also advanced missile technologies. This was to be the biggest deal done by the network, and could have involved the sale of some 10,000 centrifuges. Khan also supplied centrifuge technology to North Korea in exchange for missile technology, technology that North Korea then subsequently sought to sell to Syria and Myanmar.[5]

By the early 2000s the Khan nuclear smuggling network was a truly international organisation, involving agents, companies and even governments all across the globe, and seemed to be at the heart of almost every new nuclear proliferation concern. It was not until 31 January 2004 that the network would finally be unravelled as the Pakistani authorities arrested Khan following the receipt of damning evidence from the United States.[6] However, Khan was released from house arrest in 2007, and it has to be assumed that some of the components of the network still remain in place.

(2) Nuclear terrorism

The threat that a terrorist group might somehow acquire a nuclear weapon is arguably one of the most pressing challenges facing the international community today. Unlike nation states, it is believed that terrorist groups would not be deterred through the threat of retaliation, and could strike anywhere and at any time should they be able to acquire the necessary material and/or know-how. As US President Barack Obama has pointed out:

> we must ensure that terrorists never acquire a nuclear weapon. This is the most immediate and extreme threat to global security. One terrorist with one nuclear weapon could unleash massive destruction. Al Qaeda has said it seeks a bomb and that it would have no problem with using it. And we know that there is unsecured nuclear material across the globe. To protect our people, we must act with a sense of purpose without delay.[7]

With this in mind, this section seeks to address three key questions about nuclear terrorism: first, what do we mean by the term nuclear terrorism; second, who is involved and who represents a threat; and third, how serious is this threat?

What is nuclear terrorism? Nuclear terrorism is the threat of a non-state actor using either a nuclear weapon or dirty bomb, or attacking a civilian or military nuclear installation to further their particular cause (political, religious, ethnic, ideological, etc.). Terrorism is a tactic, and can therefore be used by any type of group for any particular purpose, although a nuclear terrorist attack would probably be designed to cause mass panic, make a political statement, and possibly kill lots of civilians. Conventional wisdom suggests that terrorist groups are 'undeterrable' because unlike nation states they have no return address – that is, there can be no credible threat of punishment after an attack. This is particularly the case with terrorists prepared to sacrifice their lives for their cause. However, as is discussed in more detail below, this depends on the type of terrorist group and its objectives.

It is highly unlikely that a terrorist group would choose to deliver a nuclear device in the same way as a nation state, such as by ballistic missile or aircraft (although this not impossible), since access to these types of capability would also probably require considerable help from a nation state (although a missile or aeroplane could theoretically be stolen or hijacked). Instead, it is more likely that a nuclear device would be hidden in a shipping container or a truck (a small nuclear bomb would be incredibly difficult to detect entering a port or a city) or via a direct attack on a civilian or military nuclear installation. As a result, if a terrorist group bent on mass destruction were to acquire a nuclear device or dirty bomb (which spreads radiation but does not involve a nuclear yield), it would probably be impossible to defend against its use irrespective of intelligence, border security and other means of detection and prevention.

Which terrorist groups represent the biggest threat? Nuclear terrorism refers to a broad range of groups and entities with different intentions, and that might use a nuclear device in different ways. According to Charles Ferguson and William Potter,[8] there are four types of terrorist groups that might seek to acquire a nuclear weapon:

- *Apocalyptic groups* Groups that believe the end of the world is approaching and should be brought about through violence – these groups are often small ultra-religious sects. The Japanese Aum Shinrikyo cult is a good example of an apocalyptic group – indeed, Aum is rumoured to have sought nuclear weapons from Russia in the early 1990s, and killed 19 people and injured hundreds more on the Tokyo subways with sarin gas in 1995. These groups are arguably the most likely nuclear threat, although they are small and peripheral.[9]
- *Politico-religious groups* These groups dominate the current debate about nuclear terrorism. They have both political and religious motivations, and can be either transnational or geographically focused. Al-Qaeda is a good example of a politico-religious group, as are Hezbollah in the Lebanon, Jamaat al Islamiya in Indonesia, or certain neo-Nazi parties in Europe and Latin America. Al-Qaeda under Osama bin Laden is believed to have been seeking a nuclear device and/or fissile material since the early 1990s, and may still be trying to do so.[10] However, whether these groups are prepared to conduct a nuclear attack remains the subject of debate (see below).
- *Nationalist/separatist groups* Groups seeking political objectives – such as national territorial independence or greater representation – for a particular ethnic, tribal, or sometimes religious entity. Examples include the Irish Republican Army (IRA) in the United Kingdom, the Tamil Tigers in Sri Lanka, Chechen rebels in Russia, Maoist guerrillas in India and ETA in Spain. These groups are unlikely to see nuclear terrorism as an attractive option due to the impact on their own people and territory. That said, rumours abound that the Chechen separatists have sought a nuclear device (and possibly acquired some material),[11] and it is highly likely that factions within other groups may also have entertained the idea.
- *Single-issue terrorists* The militarised factions of campaign groups that seek to change policies or behaviour regarding a narrow or discrete political or social issue. Environmental, anti-abortion and animal rights groups as well as anti-nuclear protesters fall under this category. These groups are unlikely to engage in nuclear terrorism although small militant cliques within these groups could represent a threat. Anti-nuclear protestors might seek to sabotage a nuclear power plant or military installation to draw attention to their cause, but are unlikely to seek a nuclear device or dirty bomb.

How serious is the threat? The seriousness of the nuclear terrorist threat is very difficult to estimate and it therefore remains the source of much heated debate. John Mueller for one has been highly sceptical of the nuclear terrorism 'hype':

it is not at all clear that any terrorist groups really want the weapons or are remotely capable of obtaining them should the desire to do so take hold of them. If they try, there are a host of practical and organisational difficulties that make their likelihood of success vanishingly small.[12]

Nevertheless, governments around the globe have been obliged to treat the threat with serious consideration. Table 22 gives an overview of the differing views of the threat of nuclear terrorism.

Table 22   Different views of the nuclear terrorism threat

Severe	Manageable	Overhyped
A nuclear attack by terrorists is inevitable	A nuclear attack by terrorists is a significant threat but can be managed	A nuclear attack by terrorists is unlikely and has been overhyped
There is so much loose fissile material that terrorists will eventually get enough for a bomb	Terrorists could acquire fissile material, but action can be taken to minimise this threat	It would be very difficult for a terrorist group to build or otherwise acquire a nuclear weapon
Protecting against nuclear terrorism is virtually impossible – a device could be smuggled into a country in a truck or shipping container	Measures can be taken to reduce the threat – stronger export controls, international cooperation, stronger non-proliferation norms	It is not clear that terrorists would want to use a nuclear weapon
Terrorists could buy or steal nuclear material from a 'rogue state' or via an illicit network	Well-funded, multinational terrorist groups could buy components from an illicit nuclear network, or steal from a state	Acquiring a nuclear weapon would be incredibly expensive and difficult
A dirty bomb or a crude nuclear device detonated in a large city is perfectly possible	Nuclear materials are becoming more secure and interdiction capabilities are advancing	States will not give terrorists the bomb, and have considerable interest in keeping nuclear material secure

According to David Albright, Osama bin Laden approached A.Q. Khan several times in the 1990s seeking nuclear-related material, but was rebuffed.[13] However, it is believed that a rival of Khan's within the Pakistani nuclear hierarchy, Sultan Bashiruddin Mahmood, did meet several times with bin Laden and other leading members of Al-Qaeda, and may have promised nuclear-related technologies through his Ummah Tameer-e-Nau (UTN) network.[14] Indeed, in 1998 bin Laden declared:

Acquiring [nuclear and chemical] weapons for the defense of Muslims is a religious duty. If I have indeed acquired these weapons, then I thank God for enabling me to do so. And if I seek to acquire these weapons, I am carrying out a duty. It would be a sin for Muslims not to try to possess the weapons that would prevent the infidels from inflicting harm on Muslims.[15]

However, the possibility of a safe haven in Afghanistan for a possible Al-Qaeda nuclear bomb project ended when the Taliban regime was toppled in 2001 by coalition forces as part of Operation Enduring Freedom. Nevertheless, and while US Special Forces assassinated Osama bin Laden at a compound in Abbottabad, Pakistan, on 2 May 2011,[16] the spectre and possibility of a nuclear threat from Al-Qaeda or a similar group remains.

(3) How could terrorists acquire a bomb? How might terrorists use a bomb?

There are a number of ways that a terrorist group might seek to acquire and use a nuclear bomb. The hardest and least likely method would be for a terrorist group to build a bomb from scratch without any outside help and in complete secrecy. This is not impossible – but deemed very unlikely. Slightly more plausible is that terrorists could steal or somehow acquire a working bomb or the fissile material and know-how that could then be used in a very crude nuclear device. It is possible that a nation state might provide a terrorist group with a working nuclear bomb, but this state would then face the risk of retaliation if discovered. Finally, terrorists might choose to attack a civilian nuclear power plant or military nuclear facility or use more easily accessible radioactive material in a radiological dirty bomb. The relative challenges of each of these methods are examined below:

1. *Building a bomb* It is highly unlikely that any terrorist group could build a nuclear weapon from scratch without any outside help (e.g. from a nation state – see below). Each stage of the process would be incredibly difficult to master: producing the necessary fissile material would be an enormous challenge and would require access to vast modern facilities; producing a working dirty bomb would be easier, but still require significant expertise, time and money. Even if a terrorist group were to acquire all the necessary material and technology for a nuclear bomb (for example through an illicit source similar to the A.Q. Khan network), they would still need a place to build and possibly test it – which would almost certainly require state support. Finally, terrorists must seek to produce such a weapon in complete secrecy, which would be very difficult, if not impossible.
2. *Acquiring a bomb/fissile material from a state* In theory while there is no reason why a state could not provide a terrorist organisation with either a working nuclear bomb or the fissile material needed for a weapon, a bigger threat is that terrorists could acquire the necessary know-how, technology and material illicitly to produce their own. This illicit acquisition of fissile material is perhaps a greater threat than a state providing terrorists with a

working bomb, although such a move would still have significant ramifications for the state or organisations involved should the transfer be revealed. However, if terrorists did acquire sufficient fissile material and know-how, they could potentially build a crude nuclear device and/or a radiological weapon such as a dirty bomb (see below). While debate remains about whether a 'rogue state' might provide terrorists with nuclear weapons,[17] it is generally accepted that both Pakistani and North Korean authorities were complicit to varying degrees in the A.Q. Khan network.[18]

3. *Stealing a bomb or fissile material* The possibility that a terrorist group might steal a bomb or the necessary fissile material is a very real one, although this is arguably becoming more difficult as concerted efforts are made to secure nuclear weapons and materials (see below). The threat of terrorists stealing a bomb was particularly prominent in the early 1990s after the break-up of the Soviet Union left significant amounts of nuclear-related material and technology (often labelled 'loose nukes') scattered across parts of Eastern Europe and Central Asia,[19] and more recently concerns have been raised about the security of nuclear weapons and materials inside Pakistan (particularly in the wake of the A.Q. Khan network).[20] It is generally believed that newer nuclear powers have less rigid nuclear security controls and are therefore theoretically more vulnerable to theft.[21]

4. *Targeting a nuclear power plant or military installation* While there is no possibility of a full-scale nuclear detonation at a nuclear civilian power plant (because the fuel used is not weapons grade), an attack could lead to the release of enormous amounts of radiation and cause widespread contamination and disruption. The intention would be to either create a radioactive leak in the reactor and/or to make the reactor overheat and go into meltdown. A serious attack on one of these plants could lead to significant casualties from the radiation – similar to the nuclear accidents at Three Mile Island, Chernobyl and Fukushima (for more on this see Chapter 10). Equally, a terrorist group might try to attack a military nuclear installation, such as an air base containing nuclear bombs, where a full-scale nuclear explosion could be a possible worse-case scenario.

5. *Dirty bombs* A dirty bomb is a normal conventional bomb that is used to spread radioactive material as part of the explosion. It is also known as a radiological dispersal device (RDD). A dirty bomb would be relatively easy to build (this is a basic bomb surrounded by radioactive material) and any form of radioactive material (not just fissile material) could be used to produce the widespread dispersal of hazardous radiation. Such radioactive material is fairly widely available, and could probably be acquired on the nuclear black market or stolen from an industrial source. The biggest impact of a dirty bomb is psychological, although widespread radiological contamination may take years to clear up and cause long-term health problems to those exposed (see Chapter 2).

(4) Securing against nuclear terrorism

Addressing the global threat of nuclear terrorism is a multifaceted task and requires different tools and ideas to address the various risks outlined above. That said, if terrorists cannot acquire the necessary fissile material (highly enriched uranium (HEU) or separated plutonium), then they would be unable to detonate a nuclear device. Consequently, the biggest task in securing against nuclear terrorism is preventing the loss, theft or deliberate transfer of fissile material from states that possess nuclear weapons and/or stockpiles of fissile material to terrorists. As Graham Allison has noted:

> The centrepiece of a strategy to prevent nuclear terrorism must be to deny terrorists the access to nuclear weapons or materials. To do this, we must shape a new international security order according to a doctrine of 'Three No's': no loose nukes, no new nascent nukes, no new nuclear weapons states.[22]

We can therefore think of mechanisms for securing against nuclear terrorism in two main ways: through nuclear security measures and through active counter-proliferation efforts and a strengthened global nuclear non-proliferation regime. These are discussed below.

(i) Nuclear security

Nuclear security essentially refers to all the measures, precautions and active defences used to prevent fissile material or nuclear weapons components from falling into the wrong hands. At its most basic, this involves making nuclear facilities as secure as possible against any sort of attack or attempted theft, but also includes measures to prevent the production of new fissile material, and to secure and/or destroy the stockpiles of fissile materials that currently exist across the globe.

While the scientific and technical community has been cognizant of the importance of nuclear security since the Manhattan Project, the issue has only really come to international prominence since the end of the Cold War. In particular, it was the threat of large quantities of nuclear-related technologies and material scattered across the vast former Soviet Union following its collapse in 1991 that really drew attention to the potential problems of nuclear security. To address this threat of so-called 'loose nukes', US senators Sam Nunn and Richard Lugar helped establish the Cooperative Threat Reduction (CTR) programme in the United States in the early 1990s (also known as the Nunn–Lugar programme). The main aim of the CTR was to provide assistance to reduce or eliminate the threat posed by loose nukes and their associated infrastructure (such as the weapons themselves, sensitive material, technology, equipment, and particularly human expertise in the form of scientists and technicians), and other existing weapons of mass destruction (WMD).[23] The CTR regime has been viewed as one of the most successful nuclear security efforts in history. As Micah Zenko and Michael Cohen explain:

> the threat of a nuclear device ending up in the hands of a terrorist group has diminished markedly since the early 1990s, when the Soviet Union's nuclear arsenal was dispersed across all of Russia's 11 time zones, all 15 former Soviet republics, and much of eastern Europe. Since then, cooperative U.S.–Russian efforts have resulted in the substantial consolidation of those weapons at far fewer sites and in comprehensive security upgrades at almost all the facilities that still possess nuclear material or warheads, making the possibility of theft or diversion unlikely.[24]

In fact, so much nuclear material was shipped back to the United States from the former Soviet Republics under the Nunn–Lugar programme, that it is estimated that one in ten light bulbs in the United States are powered by the reprocessed fissile material from former Soviet nuclear weapons under the Nunn–Lugar programme.[25]

The logic of the CTR programme has spurred other efforts to protect against loose or vulnerable nuclear material, most notably UN Security Council Resolution 1540, agreed in April 2004, which commits states to greater nuclear security measures and more active non-proliferation,[26] and the Convention on Physical Protection of Nuclear Material and Nuclear Facilities deposited at the IAEA, which was updated in 2005.[27] More recently, the Nuclear Security Summits initiated by US President Barack Obama in 2010 have also sought to draw attention to the need to secure nuclear materials against the threat of nuclear terrorism. These summits were designed primarily to highlight the significant threat caused by unsecured nuclear weapons materials and insufficient nuclear security, and also to establish a workable global regime and benchmark for the control and security of nuclear materials. Three summits have been held so far in 2010, 2012 and 2014:

- *Washington DC, 2010* Representatives from 47 states attended the first Nuclear Security Summit in Washington with the express purpose of discussing the risks involved with nuclear security and of making political agreements to shore up the protection of material and facilities globally. The result was the Washington Work Plan which (1) affirmed the seriousness and urgency of the threat posed by nuclear terrorism; (2) recognised the need for all parties to work to secure all vulnerable nuclear material worldwide; (3) established the principle that participating countries would shoulder the responsibility for securing nuclear material within their own borders; and (4) committed the parties to work together as an international community to improve nuclear security.[28]
- *Seoul, South Korea, 2012* Representatives from 53 states attended the second Nuclear Security Summit in Seoul, where officials met to discuss progress on

implementing the Washington Work Plan agreed two years earlier. Issues discussed included cooperative measures to combat the threat of nuclear terrorism, the protection of nuclear materials and related facilities, and the prevention of illicit trafficking of nuclear materials. In addition to this, the summit added new clauses to the Washington Work Plan – in particular, the participants recognised the need to increase synergy between nuclear safety and security and to better protect radiological sources from theft and misuse.[29]

* *The Hague, Netherlands, 2014* Approximately 5,000 representatives from 58 states attended the third Nuclear Security Summit in March 2014. The main aim of the meeting was to revisit the objectives and plans discussed and agreed in 2010 and 2012.[30]

A final summit is due to be held in the United States in 2016.

Lastly, the nuclear security agenda seeks an end to the production of fissile materials across the globe. As such, the Fissile Material Cut-off Treaty (FMCT) that opened for negotiation at the United Nations Conference on Disarmament in 1994 (although the idea has been around since the 1950s) is another key aspect of this nuclear security apparatus. The FMCT proposes a worldwide ban on the production of new fissile material for nuclear weapons (both HEU and PU); there are already enormous stockpiles of fissile material around the world – theoretically enough for hundreds of thousands of bombs.[31] However, there is disagreement as to whether the ban should include all fissile material or simply new fissile material as newer and smaller nuclear powers feel that such an agreement is biased against them. As a result, the negotiating committee for the FMCT at the UN Conference on Disarmament has been locked in stalemate since May 2009 – primarily due to the concerns of Pakistan.[32]

(ii) Counter-proliferation and non-proliferation

The second half of the agenda to combat the threat of nuclear terrorism involves a mixture of active counter-proliferation (interdiction based on intelligence, and if necessary the use of force) and non-proliferation (strengthening global frameworks against the proliferation of weapons to new actors and by current nuclear armed states). These strands must be pursued in tandem, and at the same time as efforts are maximised to ensure global nuclear security through the measures described above. Taken together these different components lay the basis for a rigorous and robust global nuclear security apparatus.

Perhaps the most obvious and most basic counter-proliferation measures involve tighter scrutiny of export controls and better mechanisms to target illicit trade through interdiction. Enhanced export controls are a key part of any nuclear security agenda, and the loopholes and problems that have been exploited in the past must be addressed. As Ian Anthony et al. point out:

Export controls can help prevent the acquisition of nuclear weapons by countries that do not already possess them. Export controls can help create an environment where international trade and cooperation in nuclear items and nuclear dual-use items can take place more safely from a non-proliferation perspective.[33]

One way to aid this is through an expansion of the Nuclear Suppliers Group (NSG) – an organisation established in 1978 committed to a set of stringent rules regarding the sale of nuclear-related technologies and material – in addition to greater corporate vigilance and responsibility.

A more active role can also be played through enhanced detection and interdiction capabilities. At the forefront of this is the Proliferation Security Initiative (PSI) established in 2003[34] to interdict suspected shipments of weapons of mass destruction, ballistic missiles and related materials to states and non-state actors of proliferation concern, to streamline related intelligence sharing, to strengthen relevant national and international law, and to take other specific steps to facilitate interdiction of proliferation-related cargoes.[35] Likewise the Global Initiative to Combat Nuclear Terrorism (GICNT) – which was established in July 2006 by US President George W. Bush and Russian Prime Minister Vladimir Putin to develop and improve methods to deal with nuclear security, illicit nuclear trade, possible terrorist safe havens and nuclear disaster response – might also be expanded.

Finally, the nuclear security agenda must be matched by a credible and active nuclear non-proliferation programme, which addresses both the proliferation of weapons technology to new states, and seeks to reduce the nuclear arsenals currently in existence (see Chapters 5 and 6); essentially, the fewer nuclear weapons there are in the world, the less chance there is of those weapons or related material being misplaced or stolen. The centrepiece of this effort must be the Non-Proliferation Treaty (NPT), but it will require other global non-proliferation strategies too (these are discussed also in more detail in Chapter 7). Ultimately, ensuring the security of nuclear material and nuclear technology – but particularly fissile material – is a key challenge for the international community, and the main focus in the quest to protect against the threat of nuclear terrorism.

(5) Key points and guide to further reading and resources

This chapter has sought to provide you with an overview of the nuclear threat posed by new global actors – most notably terrorist groups – and what might be done to address this. A summary of the key points is provided below:

(Continued)

(Continued)

- While attention tends to focus on non-proliferation and disarmament, illicit nuclear trade and smuggling networks remain a key challenge in today's nuclear world, particularly with regard to the threat of nuclear terrorism.

- In the 1980s and 1990s Pakistani scientist A.Q. Khan established a global smuggling network for nuclear-related materials and blueprints and sold nuclear-related technologies to a number of different states across the globe – most notably North Korea and Libya. Illicit nuclear trade remains a considerable threat today.

- The threat of a terrorist group gaining access to nuclear material or a nuclear weapon is ever present, and is perhaps the greatest nuclear risk we face. The seriousness of this threat is, however, the subject of much debate. There are different types of terrorist groups and some of them are more likely than others to seek or use nuclear weapons or a nuclear/ radiological device.

- Terrorists could acquire a nuclear bomb or nuclear material directly from a state (viewed as unlikely), they could steal or otherwise acquire a bomb or bomb-making materials (possibly via a nuclear smuggling network), or they may try to attack a military or civilian nuclear installation.

- Terrorists are unlikely to use missiles or aircraft to deliver a nuclear weapon – instead, they are more likely to hide the bomb in a shipping container or a truck.

- Terrorists might choose to detonate a non-nuclear dirty bomb to cause mass panic and psychological disruption; however, this is not technically a WMD.

- Securing nuclear materials against theft or misappropriation is arguably the most pressing contemporary nuclear challenge facing the international community. Consequently, there are many global initiatives designed to combat the threat posed by nuclear terrorism, and these include the PSI, CIGNT, UNSC 1540, the Nuclear Security Summits held in 2010, 2012 and 2014, the FMCT negotiations, and previously the Nunn–Lugar CTR programme to secure loose nuclear material in the former Soviet Union.

Further reading and resources

On illicit nuclear trade see David Albright 'Peddling peril' (2010) and William Langewiesche 'The atomic bazaar' (2007). The best overview of the A.Q. Khan network is provided in Gordon Corera 'Shopping for bombs'

(2006), while David Albright and Corey Hinderstein 'Unravelling AQ Khan and future proliferation networks' (2005) and David Albright et al. 'Detecting and disrupting illicit nuclear trade after AQ Khan' (2010) are also useful resources. See also David Armstrong and Joseph Trento 'America and the Islamic bomb' (2007).

On nuclear terrorism see Graham Allison 'Nuclear terrorism' (2009 [2004]); Charles Ferguson and William Potter 'The four faces of nuclear terrorism' (2005), Michael Levi 'On nuclear terrorism' (2007); Wyn Bowen et al. 'Multilateral cooperation and the prevention of nuclear terrorism' (2012); and Keir Lieber and Daryl Press 'Why states won't give nuclear weapons to terrorists' (2013). Micah Zenko and Michael Cohen 'Clear and present safety' (2012); Robin Frost, 'Nuclear terrorism after 9-11' (2005); and Anna Pluta and Peter Zimmerman 'Nuclear terrorism' (2006) offer strong opposing views on the subject. On Al-Qaeda, Osama bin Laden and nuclear weapons see David Albright et al. 'Bin Laden and the bomb' (2002). On the Iran–Hezbollah link see Daniel Byman 'Iran, terrorism and weapons of mass destruction' (2008). John Mueller's 'Atomic obsession' (2010) provides a strong critique of the threat of nuclear terrorism.

On Russian 'loose nukes' and suitcase bombs see Graham Allison et al. 'Avoiding nuclear anarchy' (1996); Andrew Cockburn and Leslie Cockburn 'One point safe' (1997); and Kenneth Luongo 'Loose nukes in new neighbourhoods' (2009).

On the Nunn–Lugar CTR programme see John Shields and William Potter 'Dismantling the Cold War' (1997) and Amy Woolf 'Nunn–Lugar cooperative threat reduction programs' (2001); and on the PSI see Andrew Winner 'The Proliferation Security Initiative' (2005) and Thomas Lehrman 'Rethinking interdiction' (2004). On the FMCT see Frans Berkhout et al. 'A cutoff in the production of fissile material' (1994–1995) and Victor Bragin et al. 'Verifying a fissile material production cut-off treaty' (1998). On UNSC 1540 see Olivia Bosch and Peter Van Ham (eds.) 'Global non-proliferation and counter-terrorism' (2007) and Peter Crail 'Implementing UN Security Council resolution 1540' (2006).

Joseph Clyde's novel 'A state of fear' (2013) provides an interesting fictional examination of what a dirty bomb might do to London, while Tom Clancy's novel 'Sum of all fears' describes a terrorist plot to detonate a nuclear device at a baseball game in the United States. The DVD documentary *Countdown to Zero* – which focuses on the threat of nuclear terrorism – may also be of interest.

Further information on the Nuclear Security Summits can be found at www.nss2014.com/en; on GICNT at www.gicnt.org; and on the PSI at www.psi-online.info.

Notes

1. David Albright, Paul Brannan and Andrea Schell-Stricker, 'Detecting and disrupting nuclear trade after A.Q. Khan', The Washington Quarterly, 33:3 (2010) p.85.
2. Ibid, p.93.
3. David Albright, 'Peddling peril: how the secret nuclear arms trade arms America's enemies', (London, Free Press: 2010) p.9.
4. Ibid, pp.13–51.
5. See Gordon Corera, 'Shopping for bombs: nuclear proliferation and the rise and fall of the A.Q. Khan network', (London, Hurst & Company: 2006).
6. See David Albright and Corey Hinderstein, 'Unraveling the A.Q. Khan and future proliferation networks', The Washington Quarterly, 28:2 (2005) pp.111–128.
7. 'Remarks by President Barack Obama, Hradcany Square, Prague, Czech Republic', White House Office of the Press Secretary, (5 April 2009), www.whitehouse.gov/the_press_office/Remarks-By-President-Barack-Obama-In-Prague-As-Delivered.
8. Charles Ferguson and William Potter, 'The four faces of nuclear terrorism', (London, Routledge: 2005) pp.18–20.
9. See Robert Lifton, 'Destroying the world to save it: Aum Shinrikyo, apocalyptic violence and the new global terrorism', (New York, Henry Holt & Company Inc.: 2000).
10. David Albright, Kathryn Buehler and Holly Higgins, 'Bin Laden and the bomb', Bulletin of the Atomic Scientists, 58:1 (Jan/Feb 2002) p.21.
11. On this see, for example, Nick Paton Walsh, 'Russian nuclear theft alarms US', Guardian, (19 July 2002), http://www.theguardian.com/world/2002/jul/19/chechnya.nickpatonwalsh.
12. John Mueller, 'Atomic obsession: nuclear alarmism for Hiroshima to Al Qaeda', (Oxford, Oxford University Press: 2010) p.xiii.
13. David Albright, 'Peddling peril: how the secret nuclear trade arms America's enemies', (London, The Free Press; 2010) p.169.
14. Ibid.
15. Osama bin Laden, interview with TIME magazine, (11 January 1999), http://content.time.com/time/world/article/0,8599,2054517,00.html.
16. See Barack Obama, 'Press Briefing by Senior Administration Officials on the Killing of Osama bin Laden', The White House Office of the Press Secretary, (2 May 2011), www.whitehouse.gov/the-press-office/2011/05/02/press-briefing-senior-administration-officials-killing-osama-bin-laden.
17. See, for example, Daniel Byman, 'Iran, terrorism and weapons of mass destruction', Studies in Conflict & Terrorism, 31 (2008) pp.169–181.
18. See Siegfried Hecker and William Liou, 'Dangerous dealings: North Korea's nuclear capabilities and the threat of export to Iran', Arms Control Today, 37:2 (March 2007), http://www.armscontrol.org/act/2007_03/heckerliou.
19. A good overview of this is provided in Graham Allison, Owen Coté, Steven Miller and Richard Falkenrath, 'Avoiding nuclear anarchy: containing the threat of loose Russian nuclear weapons and fissile material', (Cambridge MA, The MIT Press: 1996).
20. See, for example, Shaun Gregory, 'The terrorist threat to nuclear weapons in Pakistan', European Leadership Network, (4 June 2013), www.europeanleadership-network.org/the-terrorist-threat-to-nuclear-weapons-in-pakistan_613.html.
21. See Peter Feaver, 'Command and control in emerging nuclear nations', International Security 17:3 (1992) pp.160–187.
22. Graham Allison, 'Nuclear terrorism: the ultimate preventable catastrophe', (New York, Henry Holt & Co.: 2004) p.141.

23. William Potter and John Shields, 'Introduction: assessing the dismantlement process', in William Potter and John Shields (eds.), 'Dismantling the Cold War: US and NIS perspectives on the Nunn–Lugar Cooperative Threat Reduction Program', (London, The MIT Press: 1997) pp.3–4.

24. Michad Zenko and Michael Cohen, 'Clear and present safety: the United States is safer than Washington thinks', Foreign Affairs, 91:2 (2012) pp.79–93.

25. Testimony of Sam Nunn before the Commission on the Prevention of Weapons of Mass Destruction Proliferation and Terrorism, New York City, New York, (10 September 2008), www.nti.org/analysis/testimonies/senator-nunn-testifies-commission-prevention-weapons-mass-destruction-proliferation-and-terrorism.

26. On this see Peter Crail, 'Implementing UN Security Council resolution 1540: a risk-based approach', Nonproliferation Review, 13:2 (2006) pp.355–399.

27. See www.iaea.org/Publications/Documents/Conventions/cppnm.html.

28. For the full communiqué see 'Work Plan of the Washington Nuclear Security Summit', The White House Office of the Press Secretary, (13 April 2010), www.white-house.gov/the-press-office/work-plan-washington-nuclear-security-summit.

29. See 'Seoul Communiqué: 2012 Seoul Nuclear Security Summit', www.nss2014.com/sites/default/files/documents/seoul_communique_final.pdf.

30. See 'Hague Nuclear Security Summit Communiqué', www.nss2014.com/sites/default/files/documents/the_hague_nuclear_security_summit_communique_final.pdf.

31. See Frans Berkhout, Oleg Bukharin, Harold Feiveson and Marvin Miller, 'A cutoff in the production of fissile material', International Security, 19:3 (1994) pp.167–202.

32. Zia Mian and A.H. Nayar, 'Playing the nuclear game: Pakistan and the Fissile Material Cutoff Treaty', Arms Control Today, (April 2010), http://www.armscontrol.org/act/2010_04/Mian.

33. Ian Anthony, Christer Ahlstrom and Vitaly Fedchenko, 'Reforming nuclear export controls: the future of the Nuclear Suppliers Group', (Oxford, Oxford University Press for the Stockholm International Peace Research Institute (SIPRI): 2007) p.112.

34. The PSI was established by the United States (alongside Australia, France, Germany, Italy, Japan, the Netherlands, Poland, Portugal, Spain and the UK).

35. Mark Valencia, 'The Proliferation Security Initiative: making waves in Asia', Adelphi Paper 298, (Oxford, Routledge for the International Institute for Strategic Studies: 2005) pp.25–38.

9

NUCLEAR DISARMAMENT

Historical attempts at disarmament

States that have given up the bomb

The spread of nuclear-weapon-free zones

The Global Zero agenda

Key points and guide to further reading and resources

For many people the only way we can realistically hope to secure our nuclear future is by ridding the world of nuclear weapons in their entirety. This is not a new phenomenon – indeed, even before the first atomic bombs were dropped in 1945 scientists and other leading figures had called for a ban on these new weapons with unimaginable destructive power – and since this time a global conscience for total nuclear elimination has steadily retained its place internationally, and has been reinvigorated in the last decade. The global disarmament record is mixed: clearly nuclear weapons have not been abolished – there remain over 16,000 in the world (see Chapter 1) – but, equally, large areas of the globe are now part of nuclear-weapon-free zones (NWFZs), several states have given up the bomb and global pressure for serious moves towards nuclear disarmament is at its highest since the 1950s or the 1980s. The Global Zero agenda – a well-coordinated international coalition to move the nuclear disarmament debate forward which has been championed by, among others, US President Barack Obama – embodies the latest incarnation of the disarmament movement that has never really gone away since 1945. While the Global Zero agenda faces significant hurdles in its application, and nuclear disarmament may not be something we see any time soon, it does seem that for the first time since the end of the Second World War the idea is being seriously considered and thought through at the highest levels. Ultimately, the chapter seeks to examine the viability, desirability and possibility of a world free from nuclear weapons.

This chapter proceeds in four sections: the first looks at the many different attempts to push for nuclear disarmament since 1945, including the notable waves in the 1950s and 1980s, and at some of the key groups that have been behind this agenda; the second examines the small number of cases where states have chosen to give up advanced nuclear weapons development programmes or, in the case of South Africa and three former Soviet Republics, decided to give up a nuclear weapons capability entirely; the third looks at the concept of a NWFZ and shows how large parts of the globe – mostly in the southern hemisphere – are now covered by such agreements; and the fourth outlines the contemporary push for nuclear abolition and assesses the prospects of the Global Zero agenda. The chapter finishes with a summary of the key points and a guide to further reading and resources.

(1) Historical attempts at nuclear disarmament

The movement to 'ban the bomb' and achieve nuclear disarmament did not start with Barack Obama in 2009, the so-called 'Four horsemen of the nuclear apocalypse' in 2007, or even with Ronald Reagan and Mikhail Gorbachev at Reykjavik in 1986. In fact, even as far back as 1914 – when nuclear weapons were still just a theoretical possibility – the author H.G. Wells had suggested in *The World Set Free* that only world government would be sufficient to overcome the enormous potential destructive power of nuclear energy.[1] That said, as Lawrence Wittner explains, a public demand for nuclear disarmament only really came to the fore after the first atomic bombs were dropped in 1945:

> Following the atomic bombing of Hiroshima and Nagasaki, a movement against the bomb rapidly took shape in dozens of countries across the world. Alerted to the existence of nuclear weapons and to their catastrophic effects, hundreds of thousands of people rallied behind a loose, popular crusade to save humanity from nuclear destruction.[2]

However, it was perhaps not until the first H-bomb tests in the 1950s that the nuclear disarmament movement would become fully ingrained in the global conscience.

(i) The first wave (1940s–1960s)

The first wave of the nuclear disarmament movement – which began in the 1940s and continued up until the early 1960s – saw the creation of a variety of new groups aligned against the bomb, the first protests, and the gradual impact of pressure from global civil society on the nuclear arms race between the United States and the Soviet Union. As the Cold War between East and West intensified so did the level of international concern about nuclear weapons, nuclear weapons testing and the ever-increasing possibility of nuclear war.

The nuclear disarmament movement evolved out of the early twentieth-century 'peace movements' and came to embody a wide range of people – notably many leading scientists – aligned against the bomb, and pushing for nuclear abolition. The first notable manifestation was the establishment of the *Bulletin of the Atomic Scientists of Chicago* (later just the *Bulletin of the Atomic Scientists*) in 1945 by former physicists from the Manhattan Project in order to educate the general public about nuclear energy and push for the elimination of nuclear weapons. Since 1947, the Bulletin has published its 'Doomsday Clock', which is a recognised barometer of how close the world is at any point to (nuclear) disaster – the closer the clock is 'to midnight', the closer the world is to catastrophe.[3] A year later, former Manhattan Project members also formed the Federation of American Scientists (FAS) to spread information about nuclear power and campaign to free the world from nuclear weapons.

In June 1946 the United States proposed the creation of an International Atomic Development Authority (IADA), responsible directly to the United Nations, to establish international oversight of the use of atomic energy and to eliminate all nuclear weapons. Under the proposal, which would become known as the Baruch Plan[4] after its author, Bernard Baruch (although it was based on a report by Dean Acheson and David Lilienthal), the United States – at that time the only state with nuclear weapons – would agree to turn over all of its nuclear weapons to the newly established UN on the condition that other states would never produce them, and as long as a rigorous international system of inspection and safeguards could be established.[5] The IADA would be solely responsible for the production and distribution of fissile material for civilian power generation and research purposes, and would monitor its non-military use. However, the plan was rejected by the Soviet Union, and disappeared entirely after the first Soviet atomic bomb was tested in 1949.[6] Although in 1952 the United Nations established the Office of Disarmament Affairs (UNODA), this remained a largely peripheral body until the 1980s.

The first wave of the nuclear disarmament movement attracted many notable personalities, including distinguished scientists and public figures concerned about the development of nuclear weapons. In 1954, for example, Indian Prime Minister Jawaharlal Nehru outlined a proposal for nuclear disarmament – known as the 'standstill agreement' – and warned of the inherent dangers that the spread of nuclear weapons would bring.[7] Nehru's call strongly influenced British philosopher Bertrand Russell and eminent scientist Albert Einstein, and on 9 July 1955 Russell and Einstein released a manifesto calling for global nuclear disarmament, which declared:

> In view of the fact that in any future world war nuclear weapons will certainly be employed, and that such weapons threaten the continued existence of mankind, we urge the Governments of the world to realize, and to acknowledge publicly, that their purpose cannot be furthered by a world war, and we urge them, consequently, to find peaceful means for the settlement of all matters of dispute between them.[8]

The so-called Russell–Einstein Manifesto would become the centrepiece for the Pugwash Conferences on Science and World Affairs established in Nova Scotia, Canada, in 1957. Pugwash remains a leading body for global nuclear disarmament to this day.[9]

Also in 1957 two other key international organisations were formed. The first of these was the Campaign for Nuclear Disarmament (CND), primarily established to protest against British and French nuclear weapons testing, but which by 1958 had expanded its agenda to include campaigning for nuclear disarmament across the globe. During Easter 1958 CND organised a huge march at the British Atomic Weapons Establishment (AWE) at Aldermaston, Berkshire, to protest against the development of British nuclear weapons, and this would become an annual event. The second was the National Committee for a Sane Nuclear Policy (SANE), established in the United States, which would later rebrand itself as Peace Action with a commitment to eliminate the threat posed to humanity by nuclear weapons. Another significant disarmament group, Greenpeace, would be established in 1971 in response to US plans for a series of so-called peaceful nuclear explosions (PNEs) (see Chapter 2) at the Amchitka Islands in Alaska.

In 1961 US President John F. Kennedy appeared to capture the essence of the disarmament movement in a speech given at the United Nations General Assembly on 25 September, in which he declared:

> Today, every inhabitant of this planet must contemplate the day when this planet may no longer be habitable. Every man, woman and child lives under a nuclear sword of Damocles hanging by the slenderest of threads, capable of being cut at any moment by accident or miscalculation or by madness. The weapons of war must be abolished before they abolish us.[10]

Just a few weeks after this speech, the United States, the Soviet Union and the United Kingdom began discussing the Partial Test Ban Treaty (PTBT), which would place significant limits on nuclear testing (for more see Chapter 2). The signing of the PTBT in 1963 owed much to the pressure from nuclear disarmament groups across the globe, and was warmly received by CND and SANE. Nevertheless, in 1962 concern about nuclear war reached its pinnacle as the United States and the Soviet Union began the Cuban Missile Crisis (see Chapter 4).

(ii) The second wave (the 1980s)

The nuclear disarmament movement gained momentum again in the 1980s as the USA and Soviet Union entered what has become popularly known as the 'second Cold War' following the collapse of an era of détente during the 1970s. This period was characterised by a renewed nuclear arms race between East and West and a significant ramping up of tension and rhetoric. It also led directly to renewed peace demonstrations across the world and to the formation of new globally active groups dedicated to nuclear disarmament. The most prominent of these were the International Physicians for the Prevention of Nuclear War (IPPNW) and the European Nuclear Disarmament (END) group, both formed in 1980. The IPPNW was a collection of medical professionals from across the world – notably from NATO member states and the Soviet Union – that sought to avoid nuclear war. The END was a forum for a large nuclear disarmament conference that would be held annually throughout the 1980s.

The worsening of the Cold War also led to a resurgence in active public protests against nuclear weapons across the world, although particularly in the United States and Europe. Perhaps the most notable was the nuclear freeze movement that developed in the early 1980s in the USA (partly through the work of SANE), which sought to freeze testing and the development and deployment of nuclear weapons by the USA and USSR. The nuclear freeze was driven by the increased threat of nuclear war between East and West, and in 1982 over one million people gathered in New York's Central Park to protest against the nuclear arms race.[11] In the UK, CND organised two enormous anti-nuclear demonstrations in London in October 1981 and October 1983 where several hundred thousand protesters joined the marches.[12] Another notable protest occurred in September 1981 at Greenham Common in Berkshire, England, where a group of women protesting against the deployment of NATO cruise missiles in Europe began a demonstration at an RAF airbase, and later established a 'peace camp' that would run for nearly two decades. In December 1982 over 30,000 women joined the protest against nuclear weapons deployment at the base.[13]

While the first half of the 1980s saw a substantial increase in Cold War nuclear tensions, the second half saw a renewed political embrace of the notion of nuclear disarmament. US President Ronald Reagan – who many had viewed as pursuing a dangerous and overly bellicose stance towards the Soviet Union just a few years before – became the unlikely champion of the nuclear disarmament agenda. In October 1986 Reagan met with Soviet leader Mikhail Gorbachev in Reykjavik, Iceland, to address the issue of nuclear arms reductions in what would become known as the Reykjavik Summit. At that summit Reagan proposed the elimination of all offensive ballistic missiles within ten years, and Gorbachev responded by proposing to eliminate all strategic nuclear weapons – this was perhaps the closest we have ever been to a political agreement on nuclear abolition.[14] In the words of John Newhouse:

What occurred at Reykjavik defied comprehension. There can have been no stranger meeting between leaders of big powers – whether allied or adversary – in modern memory. During fifteen hours of conversation, Reagan and Gorbachev came very close to agreement on eliminating most, if not all, of their nuclear weapons. Two high rollers were matching idealized visions and raising each other. They reached a higher and more rarefied place than anyone had been, and then fell off a cliff.[15]

While agreement was not reached on nuclear elimination – primarily because Reagan would not sacrifice the Strategic Defense Initiative (SDI) ballistic missile defence plan – the talks did set the stage for a number of more limited nuclear and conventional arms control treaties that would follow during the next few years (see Chapter 7).[16] The SDI would become a rallying point for anti-nuclear groups for the next two decades, particularly in the United States.[17]

Table 23 Nuclear disarmament groups

	Formed	Description
Campaign for Nuclear Disarmament (CND)[i]	1957–	CND campaigns for a nuclear-free Britain (both weapons and power generation), and the broader abolition of weapons of mass destruction (WMD) worldwide
Pugwash	1957–	An international organisation that holds annual conferences around the world to address global security threats including nuclear disarmament, Pugwash was awarded the Nobel Peace Prize in 1995
National Committee for a Sane Nuclear Policy (SANE)[ii]	1957–	Established in the USA to push for nuclear disarmament. In 1993 SANE joined with the nuclear freeze movement and was rebranded as Peace Action
Greenpeace[iii]	1969/1971	Formed after the USA announced plans to conduct 'peaceful' nuclear tests in Amchita Island, Alaska Works on a number of global issues including nuclear disarmament
European Nuclear Disarmament (END)	1980–1993	Annual European nuclear disarmament conventions
International Physicians for the Prevention of Nuclear War (IPPNW)[iv]	1980–	A federation of non-partisan national medical groups founded in 1980 by physicians from the US and Russia In 2007, IPPNW launched the International Campaign to Abolish Nuclear Weapons (ICAN)

[i] See www.cnduk.org

[ii] See www.peace-action.org

[iii] See www.greenpeace.org.uk

[iv] See www.ippnw.org

Despite significant cuts to US and Russian nuclear forces following the end of the Cold War, the push for global nuclear disarmament gradually lost momentum during the 1990s, particularly after India and Pakistan tested nuclear weapons in 1998 (see Chapter 6), and the United States Congress refused to ratify the Comprehensive Test Ban Treaty (CTBT) in 1999 – and many of the organisations that had been so influential in the 1980s slowly declined. However, by the mid-2000s a third wave of the international nuclear disarmament movement began to emerge, driven partly by a growing concern about nuclear accidents and the risk of nuclear weapons falling into the hands of terrorists or 'rogue states' (see Chapters 8 and 10) – a perception heightened by the terrorist attacks of 11 September 2001, and the North Korean nuclear test in 2006.

Three events would mark the beginning of the third wave of the disarmament movement. On 1 May 2005 some 40,000 protesters demonstrated outside the United Nations building in New York to mark the beginning of the third nuclear Non-Proliferation Treaty (NPT) review conference and the sixtieth anniversary of the bombings of Hiroshima and Nagasaki (the largest public demonstration against nuclear weapons for several decades).[18] Then, in 2007, the IPPNW launched the International Campaign to Abolish Nuclear Weapons (ICAN), bringing together a wide range of anti-nuclear groups that had been active in the past, including CND. Third, the so-called 'four horsemen of the nuclear apocalypse' released their first op-ed in *The Wall Street Journal* calling for global nuclear disarmament (more on this below). This would mark the beginning of the most recent and perhaps most extensive expression of the nuclear disarmament movement, and the one we are living through today.

(2) States that have given up the bomb

While the nuclear disarmament movement has perhaps not been as successful as many of its philosophical architects and ardent supporters might have hoped, it has not been without its successes: a number of countries have pursued a nuclear weapons capability since 1945, before choosing not to go ahead and build the bomb; three countries acquired considerable nuclear arsenals from the former Soviet Union as the Cold War came to an end, which they then agreed to give up; and one country unilaterally decided to destroy its small nuclear weapons stockpile and production facilities in the early 1990s. These cases suggest that the norm for disarmament and non-proliferation remains strong in large parts of the world – and challenges the notion that states cannot or will not give up their nuclear weapons programmes. Key examples of states giving up the bomb and/or advanced nuclear weapons programmes are detailed below:

- *South Africa* In the 1980s, the apartheid government in South Africa constructed six nuclear bombs (based on the uranium gun-type) at the Pelindaba and Adventa nuclear research centres near Pretoria. The programme was driven by the worsening state of South Africa's international position due to its domestic policies and the threat of major war in southern Africa throughout the 1970s and 1980s.[19] While South Africa never conducted an overt nuclear weapons test, it is suspected of collaborating with Israel when a nuclear test was carried out in the southern Indian Ocean in September 1979 – known as the Vela Incident. However, in 1993, with the end of the Cold War, and shortly before the collapse of the apartheid regime, President F.W. de Klerk declared that South Africa had voluntarily destroyed the six nuclear weapons that had been built several years earlier, and had closed the facilities needed to build them.[20] It acceded to the NPT on 10 July 1991 as a non-nuclear-weapon state (NNWS).

- *Former Soviet Republics* After the dissolution of the Soviet Union in 1991, a large number of nuclear weapons remained based in the former Soviet Republics of Belarus, Kazakhstan and Ukraine. Effectively, Ukraine became the third largest nuclear-weapon state (NWS) with some 5,000 warheads stationed on its territory (as well as a number of intercontinental ballistic missile (ICBM) launching facilities), while Kazakhstan, with approximately 1,400 warheads, became the fourth largest, almost overnight (Belarus acquired around 50 warheads).[21] While negotiations were not straightforward, these three states showed little desire to become members of the 'nuclear club' and by the mid-1990s all of these weapons had been transferred back to Russia, and all three countries have now acceded to the NPT as NNWS.[22]

- *Argentina/Brazil* Both Argentina and Brazil began research into nuclear energy in the 1950s, and both appeared to be moving towards establishing full weaponisation programmes in the late 1970s and early 1980s. International suspicions were raised about Argentina in the 1970s after new enrichment and reprocessing facilities with little connection with civilian power production were unveiled, while the Brazilian military even built a supposed nuclear test site at Cachimbo in the Amazon Forest as part of the the Solimoes Project, and pushed hard for a test before the transition to civilian government in 1985.[23] The nuclear rivalry cooled in the 1990s after the establishment of civilian governments in both states: in 1991 a bilateral inspection agreement was signed; in 1994 both states acceded to the Latin American NWFZ Treaty; and in 1995 Argentina signed the NPT (Brazil joined the NPT in 1998).

- *Iraq* Iraqi president Saddam Hussein pursued nuclear weapons in the 1980s and early 1990s – a project codenamed Petrochemical-3 – and had it not been for the Gulf War of 1990–1991 and the subsequent work by inspection teams from the International Atomic Energy Agency (IAEA) and UN to remove all nuclear material and destroy nuclear-related facilities in the country, Iraq may

179

well have been able to build a bomb by the mid-1990s.[24] Nevertheless, by the early 2000s concern was mounting that Saddam was secretly rebuilding the programme, which led in part to the Second Gulf War of 2003. Evidence later emerged that Saddam had not sought to reconstitute the nuclear programme, and his removal from power and subsequent execution ensured that he never would. Iraq signed the CTBT in 2008, and remains a signatory of the NPT.

- *Libya* It is estimated that Libya began its pursuit of nuclear weapons in the 1970s, primarily as a response to the defeats suffered by the Arab states in the wars against Israel in 1967 and 1973. Over the next few decades, Libyan leader Muammar Gaddafi sought to purchase nuclear weapons-related materials from a variety of different sources (despite being a member of the NPT since 1975). In the 1990s, Libya received nuclear weapons-related material from Pakistani scientist A.Q. Khan (see Chapter 7), and in the early 2000s is believed to have acquired a blueprint for a basic atomic bomb.[25] However, in the wake of the 9/11 terrorist attacks and the beginning of the US-led Global War on Terrorism, in December 2003, Libya agreed to eliminate all materials, equipment and programmes related to the production of nuclear weapons, and Gaddafi admitted publicly to the pursuit of a nuclear weapons programme.[26] Interestingly, Libya is the only known case where the same person made the decision to acquire and then abandon a nuclear weapons programme.[27]

- *Others* A number of other states have also started but then abandoned nuclear weapons programmes, these include: Sweden[28] (in the 1950s and 1960s), Switzerland[29] (1950s–1980s), South Korea[30] and Taiwan[31] (1970s), and Algeria[32] (in the 1980s), while West Germany seriously considered a nuclear weapons programme in the mid-1950s.[33] Syria has also entertained the idea of building nuclear weapons in the past,[34] and there are suspicions that Burma/Myanmar may have done so to.[35]

Since 1945 there have also been a number of instances where nuclear weapons have been based on other states' territories, often through a policy of extended nuclear deterrence (see Chapter 4). The United States deployed nuclear weapons in some 27 different countries across the globe at various times between 1945 and 1991, notably in Europe but also in parts of Asia and the Pacific.[36] Similarly, and during the same period, the Soviet Union also deployed nuclear weapons outside of its territory in Eastern Europe and Central Asia (and temporarily in Cuba in 1962). However, as of 2013, only the USA deploys nuclear weapons outside its borders, and these are at US bases on the territory of five NATO allies in Europe (Belgium, Germany, Italy, the Netherlands and Turkey) – although these weapons are increasingly being seen as anachronistic, and as such may soon be removed.[37]

It is therefore important to consider the nuclear disarmament agenda in context, for while it is certainly true that 13 states have built/acquired the bomb since 1945, that nuclear weapons were deployed in over 30 different countries at the height of the Cold War, and many more states entertained the idea of building the ultimate weapon, four states have publicly chosen to give up a working nuclear stockpile, most nuclear weapons are not now deployed outside the nuclear armed states' territory, and a large number of nations have decided against, or have been forcibly prevented from, weaponising their nuclear programmes.

(3) The spread of nuclear-weapon-free zones (NWFZs)

One of the great success stories of the nuclear disarmament agenda is the amount of our planet that is now legally 'nuclear weapons free' – in fact, the majority of the southern hemisphere is now a nuclear-weapon-free zone (NWFZ), along with some parts of Central Asia and North Africa, and as well as in space, under the sea and the entire Antarctic continent. No nuclear weapons may be tested, developed or deployed in these areas by any nation that is a signatory to a NWFZ treaty agreement – and no other state may test or deploy nuclear weapons in these areas. Since the first agreement was signed in 1961, there have been a further seven NWFZ treaties signed across the globe, and negotiations remain outstanding regarding several more (notably in the Middle East). Table 24 provides an overview of the NWFZ agreements that have been signed since 1945 and that remain in force today.

While in some circumstances the establishment of NWFZs essentially codifies the status quo (the vast majority of these states clearly have little intention of building nuclear weapons), the particular stipulations of these agreements mean that in several ways they also fundamentally enhance and go beyond the other key international nuclear agreements. As Jozef Goldblat explains:

> The zones that have been established to date meet other postulates as well. Besides prohibiting the acquisition of nuclear weapons by zonal states, they proscribe (unlike the NPT) the stationing of these weapons in the territories of non-nuclear weapon states. Zonal procedures to verify compliance with the nonproliferation obligations are even stricter than the procedures prescribed by the NPT. Moreover, zonal states benefit from some legally binding security assurances of the great powers.[38]

As a result, the NWFZ agreements that have been achieved since 1945 show that it is possible to find ways to prohibit the development and deployment of nuclear weapons between states.

In 1995 the Non-Proliferation Treaty Review Conference in New York passed a resolution for the establishment of a Middle East nuclear-weapon-free zone (MENWFZ), formalising proposals that had been around since the 1960s and 1970s. However, the realisation of the Middle East NWFZ continues to be hamstrung by the divisive politics of the region – not least Israel's undeclared nuclear weapons capability and concerns about Iran (see Chapter 6), but also

Table 24   Nuclear-weapon-free zones[i]

Treaty	Date established	Details
Antarctic Treaty	1961	Article V of the Treaty prohibits nuclear explosions or disposal of radioactive waste in the Antarctic
Outer Space Treaty	1967	Article VI prohibits placing in orbit around the Earth any objects carrying nuclear weapons, installing such weapons on celestial bodies, or stationing such weapons in outer space in any other manner
Treaty of Tlatelolco	1969	Established a NWFZ in Latin America and the Caribbean
Seabed Treaty	1972	Prohibits the placement of nuclear weapons on the seabed and the ocean floor and in the subsoil.
Treaty of Rarotonga	1986	Established a NWFZ in the South Pacific
Treaty of Bangkok	1997	Established a NWFZ in Southeast Asia
Mongolian nuclear-weapon-free zone	1992	Established Mongolia as a NWFZ
Treaty of Semei	2009	Established a NWFZ in Central Asia (Kazakhstan, Kyrgyzstan, Tajikistan, Turkmenistan and Uzbekistan).
Treaty of Pelindaba	2009	Established a NWFZ in Africa (only the newly created state of South Sudan has not signed)

[i] For more details see www.atomicarchive.com/Treaties

the different conceptions between the parties about how a NWFZ can be agreed. Israel believes a NWFZ can only follow a general Middle East peace treaty, while the Arab states believe Israel (and Iran) must renounce their pursuit/arsenal of nuclear weapons before a peace treaty can be signed.[39] The 2010 NPT Review Conference called for a meeting on the Middle East NWFZ to be held in 2012, but this has so far been postponed. North America, Europe, South Asia, Northeast Asia and the Arctic are the other regions not covered by NWFZ agreements.

(4) The Global Zero agenda

In recent years the nuclear disarmament movement has been re-energised and is now firmly back at the centre of international politics and the global intellectual debate. The springboard for this was an op-ed newspaper article written by four former high-level US officials – Henry Kissinger, Sam Nunn, William

Perry and George Shultz – in *The Wall Street Journal* in January 2007, calling for 'a world free from nuclear weapons'. The authors, who would become known as the 'four horsemen of the nuclear apocalypse', warned in their op-ed that the risk of nuclear use had grown since the end of the Cold War, and that the only way to prevent a future catastrophe was now to work towards the elimination of these weapons:

> Apart from the terrorist threat, unless urgent new actions are taken, the U.S. soon will be compelled to enter a new nuclear era that will be more precarious, psychologically disorienting, and economically even more costly than was Cold War deterrence. It is far from certain that we can successfully replicate the old Soviet-American 'mutually assured destruction' with an increasing number of potential nuclear enemies worldwide without dramatically increasing the risk that nuclear weapons will be used. New nuclear states do not have the benefit of years of step-by-step safeguards put in effect during the Cold War to prevent nuclear accidents, misjudgments or unauthorized launches. The United States and the Soviet Union learned from mistakes that were less than fatal. Both countries were diligent to ensure that no nuclear weapon was used during the Cold War by design or by accident. Will new nuclear nations and the world be as fortunate in the next 50 years as we were during the Cold War?[40]

Coming as it did from four statesmen that had been heavily involved in building up the US nuclear arsenal over previous decades, the piece served to reinvigorate the global nuclear disarmament campaign. In the words of Philip Taubman:

> Here like a bolt from the blue, was a bipartisan group of eminent Cold Warriors eager to upend the atomic applecart. The article couldn't be dismissed as the work of pacifists or antinuclear campaigners. It was the hardheaded vision of men who had played central roles in building, managing, and widening America's nuclear arsenal during the Cold War.[41]

The group wrote a further op-ed piece a year later in January 2008, which stated their encouragement by the progress achieved since the previous year, but warned that more needed to be done.[42]

While the start of the third nuclear disarmament wave can probably be traced back to the early years of the 2000s and even the late 1990s, the intervention by the 'four horsemen' served to strengthen the issue in international civil society. In particular, it led to four key developments: (1) the establishment of the International Campaign Against Nuclear Weapons (ICAN); (2) the formation of the Global Zero group and agenda; (3) a very public embracing of the nuclear disarmament agenda by US President Barack Obama and other leading officials; and (4) most recently the establishment of the Humanitarian Initiative on Nuclear Disarmament.

The first direct result of the renewed enthusiasm and appeal for nuclear abolition was the establishment in 2007 of ICAN – a global initiative to re-invigorate the anti-nuclear civil society movement. According to the organisation's website:

> ICAN is a global campaign coalition working to mobilize people in all countries to inspire, persuade and pressure their governments to initiate and support negotiations for a treaty banning nuclear weapons.[43]

In addition to seeking the establishment of a Nuclear Weapons Convention (in a similar mould to the Biological and Chemical Weapons Conventions), ICAN seeks to organise regular civil society forums on nuclear abolition, and is the organiser of 'Nuclear Abolition Day'.

Another direct offshoot of the renewed international interest in nuclear disarmament was the creation of the 'Global Zero' campaign in Paris in December 2008 – an international movement also aimed at achieving global nuclear abolition. In the first instance the campaign called for a renewed push for US–Russian bilateral nuclear arms reductions, and in the longer term outlined a four-phase plan for total nuclear disarmament:

- Phase 1 (2010–2013) calls for the USA and Russia to conclude a new treaty reducing their nuclear forces to 500 warheads apiece.
- Phase 2 (2014–2018) calls for the USA and Russia to reduce to 500 nuclear weapons each and for all other nuclear-armed states to freeze their stockpiles.
- Phase 3 (2019–2023) would see the negotiation of a multilateral global zero treaty and the institutions required to enforce it.
- Phase 4 (2024–2030) would see the complete and verifiable elimination of all nuclear weapons by 2030.

While the four-phase plan is seen as being highly optimistic (and the proposed dates have already begun to slip), the global zero agenda now has over 300 leading international political figures pledging their support.[44]

The third key development stemming from the appeal made by the four horsemen – and which has added considerable impetus to the global zero agenda – was the very public support for nuclear abolition provided by US President Barack Obama. In a speech in Prague in April 2009, Obama declared:

> So today, I state clearly and with conviction America's commitment to seek the peace and security of a world without nuclear weapons. I'm not naive. This goal will not be reached quickly – perhaps not in my lifetime. It will take patience and persistence. But now we, too, must ignore the voices who tell us that the world cannot change. We have to insist, 'Yes, we can.'[45]

President Obama reiterated this commitment to reducing and possibly eliminating global nuclear arsenals at a speech at in Berlin, Germany, in June 2013:

Peace with justice means pursuing the security of a world without nuclear weapons – no matter how distant that dream may be. And so, as President, I've strengthened our efforts to stop the spread of nuclear weapons, and reduced the number and role of America's nuclear weapons. Because of the New START Treaty, we're on track to cut American and Russian deployed nuclear warheads to their lowest levels since the 1950s.[46]

Finally, the most recent addition to this agenda has been the establishment of the Humanitarian Initiative on Nuclear Disarmament following a conference on the humanitarian impacts of nuclear weapons held in Oslo, Norway, in March 2013. The Humanitarian Initiative aims to bring together national governments, international organisations and other stakeholders in global civil society to address the likely impact of any nuclear use, push for a nuclear weapons ban and pressure the NWS to uphold their commitment to disarmament under Article VI of the NPT (see Chapter 5).[47] A second international meeting was held in Nayarit, Mexico, in February 2014.

Taken together, the various components of this third wave of nuclear disarmament have forced the issue back into high-level policy debate, with more people involved now than at any time in the past three decades. However, the Global Zero and nuclear disarmament agenda is not without its detractors and critics. A selection of these problems and criticisms are explained below:

1. *The who goes first problem* Perhaps the biggest challenge facing nuclear disarmament is the who goes first problem – this is intrinsically linked with the security dilemma discussed in Chapter 4. The central problem is how to convince states to give up their nuclear weapons while others – possibly current or future adversaries – retain theirs.
2. *The we cannot uninvent them problem* Critics of nuclear disarmament are always quick to point out that the knowledge and the science behind nuclear weapons can never be 'un-invented', and therefore we can never truly rid the world of the possibility of nuclear weapons being developed by someone at some point in the future.
3. *The verification and trust problem* A third problem is related to the first and second – namely, how can any state trust another not to seek the advantage of quickly deploying nuclear weapons or failing to live up to agreements to disarm? While there are tested methods of verification and ways to monitor compliance these are far from foolproof (see Chapter 7).
4. *The tacit nuclear capability problem* Any country that has a civilian nuclear power capability and an advanced military–industrial base could theoretically build nuclear weapons (although the timelines and difficulty would vary considerably between cases). The right to civilian nuclear power and control of the fuel cycle is a key part of the NPT, and therefore it would be very difficult to eradicate the possibility of weaponisation entirely (for more on this see Chapters 3 and 10).

5. *The we don't want to get rid of them problem* Perhaps one of the biggest problems is that it is not entirely clear that all current states with nuclear weapons want to get rid of them – and as has been mentioned earlier, nuclear weapons serve different purposes for different states (see Chapters 5 and 6). What is more, it is only those states that are signatories to the NPT (and not Israel, India, Pakistan and North Korea) that actually have a *legal* obligation towards this goal.

6. *The world would be less safe without nuclear weapons problem* The final criticism of the nuclear abolition movement is that a world without nuclear weapons might be a world more likely to experience conventional warfare. In this reading, nuclear weapons have helped keep the peace since 1945 because they significantly increased the likely costs of any war and thus their removal could see a return to pre-1945 inter-state conflict.

Individually, each of these problems represents a considerable hurdle in the push towards nuclear disarmament. Taken together they make for a formidable undertaking. That said, the movement can point to certain achievements in the last few years – the New START Treaty signed by the US and Russia in 2010, and the Nuclear Security Summits held in 2010, 2012 and 2014, not to mention the high level of public support that the goal of nuclear disarmament now draws.

(5) Key points and guide to further reading and resources

This chapter has sought to provide you with an understanding of the history, development and current issues involved with nuclear disarmament. A summary of these key points is provided below:

- Almost as soon as the nuclear bomb was invented there has been pressure to disarm entirely. The 1946 Baruch Plan was the first of several unsuccessful attempts at total nuclear disarmament.
- There have been three main 'waves' of the nuclear disarmament movement: from 1945–1963; during the 1980s; and since the mid–2000s to today.
- A small number of states have given up the bomb and several more have cancelled advanced nuclear weapons programmes. South Africa is the most notable of these states after declaring and then eliminating its small nuclear stockpile in the early 1990s.
- Large parts of the world (and space) are covered by NWFZ – most notably significant parts of the southern hemisphere. No possession, testing or manufacture of nuclear materials can take place in these areas.

- The nuclear disarmament movement has been revived in recent years – most notably by the 'four horsemen' and by US President Barack Obama – but the hurdles to nuclear elimination remain substantial.
- In particular we can think of six main stumbling blocks on the road to nuclear disarmament: the who goes first problem; the we cannot uninvent them problem; the verification and trust problem; the tacit nuclear capability problem; the we don't want to get rid of them problem; and the world would be less safe without nuclear weapons problem.

Further reading and resources

Lawrence Wittner 'Confronting the bomb' (2009) provides an excellent history of the world nuclear disarmament movement, and for greater detail, you should consult Wittner's more in-depth trilogy, 'The struggle against the bomb: one world or none' (1995); 'The struggle against the bomb: resisting the bomb' (1998)'; and 'Towards nuclear abolition" (2003). On SANE see Milton Katz 'Ban the bomb' (1986); on CND see Kate Hudson 'CND – now more than ever' (2005) and their website at www.cnduk.org. On the Greenham Common protests see David Fairhall 'Common ground' (2006); and on the nuclear freeze see David Meyer 'A winter of discontent' (1990). See also Jonathan Schell 'The fate of the earth' (1982), and E.P. Thompson and Dan Smith 'Protest and survive' (1980). On Ronald Reagan, Mikhail Gorbachev and the Reykjavik summit see Paul Lettow 'Ronald Reagan and his quest to abolish nuclear weapons' (2006).

On NWFZs see Ramesh Thakur 'Nuclear-weapons free zones' (1998); Jozef Goldblat 'Nuclear free zones' (1997); Michael Hamel-Green 'Nuclear weapon-free zone initiatives' (2009); and on the Middle East NWFZ in particular see Patricia Lewis 'A Middle East free of nuclear weapons?' (2013) and Claudia Baumgart and Harald Müller 'A nuclear weapons free zone in the Middle East' (2004).

On why states constrain their nuclear capabilities see Mitchell Reiss 'Bridled ambition' (1995) and Kurt Campbell et al. (eds.) 'The nuclear tipping point' (2004). On the South African decision to disarm, consult Hannes Steyn et al. 'Nuclear armament and disarmament' (2007); J.W. de Villiers et al. 'Why South Africa gave up the bomb' (1993); Peter Liberman 'The rise and fall of the South African bomb' (2006); and Helen Purkitt and Stephen Burgess 'South Africa's weapons of mass destruction' (2005). On the Argentinean and Brazilian nuclear programmes see Paul Leventhal and Sharon Tanzer (eds.) 'Averting a Latin American nuclear arms race' (1992)

(Continued)

(Continued)

and John Redick et al. 'Nuclear rapprochement' (1995). On Iraq see Mohammed Obeidi and Kurt Ptizer 'The bomb in my garden' (2004); Hans Blix 'Verification of nuclear proliferation' (1992); George Lopez and David Cortright 'Containing Iraq' (2004); and on Libya see Wyn Bowen 'Libya and nuclear proliferation' (2006).

Michael O'Hanlon 'A skeptic's case for nuclear disarmament' (2010); David Cortright and Raimo Vayrynen 'Towards nuclear zero' (2010); George Perkovich and James Acton 'Abolishing nuclear weapons' (2008); and Lawrence Freedman 'Disarmament and other nuclear norms' (2013) are all good resources on nuclear disarmament, as is Ivo Daalder and Jan Lodal 'The logic of zero' (2008). For a more sceptical view of the 'global zero debate' see Bruno Tertrais 'The illogic of zero' (2010). See also former IAEA head Hans Blix 'Why nuclear disarmament matters' (2008); H.G. Wells 'A world set free' (2010 [1914]) and Bertrand Russell 'Common sense and nuclear weapons' (2001).

For the original article by the 'four horsemen' see 'A world without nuclear weapons', Wall Street Journal (4 January 2007), and for background information on this see Phillip Taubman 'The partnership' (2012). For more on ICAN, see www.icanw.org. For the full text of Barack Obama's Prague speech see www.whitehouse.gov/the_press_office/Remarks-By-President-Barack-Obama-In-Prague-As-Delivered. For more on the Global Zero agenda see the group's website at www.globalzero.org. On the Humanitarian Initiative see John Borrie and Tim Caughlet (eds.) 'Viewing nuclear weapons through a humanitarian lens' (2013) and John Borrie 'Humanitarian reframing of nuclear weapons and the logic of a ban' (2014).

The documentary film *Countdown to Zero* (http://countdowntozerofilm. com) and the anti-nuclear film based on Nevil Shute's novel *On the Beach* (1957) might also be of interest.

Notes

1 H.G. Wells, 'The world set free', (Las Vegas NV, IAP: 2010 [1914]).
2 Lawrence Wittner, 'Confronting the bomb: a short history of the nuclear disarmament movement', (Stanford CA, Stanford University Press: 2009) p.9.
3 More information on the 'Doomsday Clock' can be found at http://thebulletin.org/overview.
4 For more on this see Campbell Craig and Sergey S. Radchenko, 'The atomic bomb and the origins of the Cold War', (New Haven CT, Yale University Press: 2008), particularly chapter 5.
5 See Randy Rydell, 'Looking back: going for Baruch: the nuclear plan that refused to go away', Arms Control Today, (June 2006), http://www.armscontrol.org/print/2064.

6 Richard Rhodes, 'Dark sun: the making of the hydrogen bomb', (London, Simon & Schuster: 2005) pp.229–233 & 238–240.

7 Ola Dahlman, Svein Mykkeltveit and Hein Haak, 'Nuclear test ban: converting political visions into reality', (New York, Springer: 2009) p.60.

8 Available at www.pugwash.org/about/manifesto.htm.

9 See www.pugwash.org.

10 'JFK on nuclear weapons and non-proliferation', Proliferation Analysis, Carnegie Endowment for International Peace, (17 November 2003), http://carnegieendowment. org/2003/11/17/jfk-on-nuclear-weapons-and-non-proliferation/3zcu?reloadFlag=1.

11 See Jonathan Schell, 'The spirit of June 12', The Nation, (2 July 2007), www.thenation. com/article/spirit-june-12#.

12 Lawrence Wittner, 'Confronting the bomb: a short history of the world nuclear disarmament movement', (Stanford, Stanford University Press: 2009) p.144.

13 Ibid, pp.144–145.

14 For a good overview of the Reykjavik summit see Paul Lettow, 'Ronald Reagan and his quest to abolish nuclear weapons', (New York, Random House: 2005) pp.217–229.

15 John Newhouse, 'The nuclear age: from Hiroshima to Star Wars', (London, Michael Joseph Ltd: 1989) pp.394–395.

16 See Michael Mandelbaum and Strobe Talbott, 'Reykjavik and beyond', Foreign Affairs, 65:2 (1986) pp.215–235.

17 On this see Andrew Futter, 'Ballistic missile defence and US national security: normalisation and acceptance after the Cold War', (New York, Routledge: 2013).

18 Lawrence Wittner, 'Confronting the bomb: a short history of the world nuclear disarmament movement', (Stanford, Stanford University Press: 2009) p.219.

19 See Gideon de Wet, 'Forward' in Hannes Stein, Richard Van Der Walt and Jan Van Loggerenberg, 'Nuclear armament and disarmament: South Africa's nuclear experience', (London, iUniverse, Inc: 2007) p.xiv.

20 See J.W. de Villiers, Roger Jardine and Mitchell Reiss, 'Why South Africa gave up the bomb", Foreign Affairs, 72:5 (1993) pp.98-109 and Hannes Stein, Richard Van Der Walt and Jan Van Loggerenberg, 'Nuclear armament and disarmament', (London, iUniverse Inc: 2007).

21 See William Walker, 'Nuclear weapons and the former Soviet Republics', International Affairs, 68:2 (1992) pp.255–277.

22 See Mitchell Reiss, 'Bridled ambition: why countries constrain their nuclear capabilities', (Washington DC, The Woodrow Wilson Centre Press: 2005) pp.89–182.

23 See Julio Carasales, John Redick and Paulo Wrobel, 'Nuclear rapprochement: Argentina, Brazil, and the nonproliferation regime', The Washington Quarterly, 18:1 (1995) pp.107–122 and Mitchell Reiss, 'Bridled ambition: why countries constrain their nuclear capabilities', (Washington DC, The Woodrow Wilson Centre Press: 2005) pp.45–88.

24 Direct General International Atomic Energy Agency, 'The implementation of United Nations security council resolutions relating to Iraq', IAEA General Conference, GC(40)13, (12 August 1996), www.fas.org/news/un/iraq/iaea/gc40-13.html.

25 David Albright, 'Peddling peril: how the secret nuclear trade arms America's enemies', (London, The Free Press: 2010) pp.116–153.

26 See Wyn Bowen, 'Libya and nuclear proliferation: stepping back from the brink', Adelphi Paper 380, (London, Routledge for the International Institute for Strategic Studies: 2006).

27 Maria Rost Rublee, 'Nonproliferation norms: why states choose nuclear restraint', (London, The University of Georgia Press: 2009) p.150.

28 See Jan Parawitz, 'Nuclear option to non-nuclear promotion: the Sweden case', (Stockholm, Swedish Institute for International Affairs: 1995).

29 See Rob Edwards, 'Swiss planned nuclear bomb', New Scientist, 2031, (25 May 1996).

30 Jonathan Pollack and Mitchell Reiss, 'South Korea: the tyranny of geography and the vexations of history', chapter in Kurt Campbell, Robert Einhorn and Mitchell Reiss

(eds.), 'Nuclear tipping point: why states reconsider their nuclear choices', (Washington DC, The Brookings Institution Press: 2004) pp.261–265.

31 Derek Mitchell, 'Taiwan's Hsin Chu program: deterrence, abandonment, and honor', chapter in Kurt Campbell, Robert Einhorn and Mitchell Reiss (eds.), 'Nuclear tipping point: why states reconsider their nuclear choices', (Washington DC, The Brookings Institution Press: 2004) pp.296–301.

32 See David Albright and Corey Hinderstein, 'Algeria: a big deal in the desert?', Bulletin of the Atomic Scientists, 57:3 (2001) pp.45–52.

33 Maria Rost Rublee, 'Nonproliferation norms: why states choose nuclear restraint', (London, The University of Georgia Press: 2009) p.185.

34 Ellen Laipson, 'Syria: can the myth be maintained without nukes?', chapter in Kurt Campbell, Robert Einhorn and Mitchell Reiss (eds.), 'Nuclear tipping point: why states reconsider their nuclear choices', (Washington DC, The Brookings Institution Press: 2004).

35 See Andrew Selth, 'Myanmar's nuclear ambitions', Survival, 52:5 (2010) pp.5–12.

36 See Robert Norris, William Arkin and William Burr, 'Where they were', Bulletin of the Atomic Scientists, 55:6 (1999) pp.26–35.

37 See, for example, Tom Sauer and Bob Van Der Zwaan, 'US tactical nuclear weapons in Europe after NATO's Lisbon Summit: why their withdrawal is desirable and feasible', International Relations, 26:1 (2012) pp.78–100.

38 Jozef Goldblat, 'Nuclear-weapon-free zones: A history and assessment', The Nonproliferation Review, 4:3 (1997) pp.30–31.

39 Patricia Lewis, 'A Middle East free of nuclear weapons: possible, probable or pipe dream?', International Affairs, 89:2 (2013) p.436.

40 Henry Kissinger, Sam Nunn, William Perry and George Shultz, 'A world free from nuclear weapons', The Wall Street Journal, (4 January 2007).

41 Philip Taubman, 'The partnership: five cold warriors and their quest to ban the bomb', (New York, HarperCollins Publishers: 2012) pp.x–xi.

42 Henry Kissinger, Sam Nunn, William Perry and George Shultz, 'Toward a nuclear free world', The Wall Street Journal, (1 January 2008).

43 See www.icanw.org/campaign.

44 See www.globalzero.org/our-movement.

45 'Remarks by President Barack Obama, Hradcany Square, Prague, Czech Republic', The White House Office of the Press Secretary, (5 April 2009), www.whitehouse.gov/the_press_office/Remarks-By-President-Barack-Obama-In-Prague-As-Delivered.

46 'Remarks by President Obama at the Brandenburg Gate, Berlin, Germany', The White House Office of the Press Secretary, (19 June 2013), www.whitehouse.gov/the-press-office/2013/06/19/remarks-president-obama-brandenburg-gate-berlin-germany.

47 On this see John Borrie, 'Humanitarian reframing of nuclear weapons and the logic of a ban', International Affairs, 90:3 (2014) pp.625–646.

10

ENDURING NUCLEAR CHALLENGES

The growing demand for civilian nuclear power

The command and control of nuclear forces

The nuclear taboo and the norm of non-use

Key points and guide to further reading and resources

If we are to continue to avoid the catastrophic possibility of nuclear use, then we must be fully cognizant of the key challenges that lie ahead. Evidence suggests that our nuclear past is characterised at least as much by luck as by solid judgement, and it is far from clear that our luck will continue to hold indefinitely. Indeed, the considerable number of past nuclear weapons accidents that are really only now beginning to come to light, as well as the new challenges presented by new actors and new geopolitical pressures, mean that we must seriously consider how best to secure our nuclear future. As a result, and in addition to many of the themes addressed earlier in the book, this chapter looks at three specific challenges that will have to be met as we go forward; these challenges are by no means unconquerable, but they do require concerted (arguably international) efforts to ensure they can be managed. The dynamics that must be addressed range from securing nuclear materials, preventing accidents and dealing with radioactive waste in a world that appears likely to require more and not less civilian nuclear energy generation, through maintaining safe and secure command and control of nuclear forces and dealing with the new military realities presented by the advent of cyber weapons and the evolution of warfare more generally.

This chapter proceeds in three sections: the first explains the challenges associated with the proliferation of civilian nuclear power generation facilities – namely the safety and security of the reactors, the link with weaponisation and proliferation, and the problem of nuclear waste; the second section looks at the issue of military nuclear accidents and some of the problems involved in the command and control of nuclear forces, including the recent challenge presented by cyber weapons; the third looks at the establishment of the so-called nuclear taboo, and at whether the norm of nuclear non-use is sustainable. The chapter then finishes with a summary of the key points and a guide to further reading and resources.

(1) The growing demand for civilian nuclear power

A central nuclear challenge facing the international community as we move forward is how to continue to safely manage the growing demand for civilian nuclear power generation. There are currently over 30 nations with nuclear power reactors and capabilities, and this seems set to grow in the next few decades – both vertically, as more reactors are built in states that already have nuclear power facilities, and horizontally, as other countries seek to build nuclear power plants and acquire the necessary components and expertise to assure their future energy security. While a civilian nuclear power programme by no means directly equals a nuclear weapons programme, it does create three significant nuclear challenges: (1) how to ensure the safety and physical security of existing and new nuclear power plants; (2) how to safeguard against weapons proliferation from the spread of nuclear know-how and technology as a result of these programmes; and (3) how to manage the ever increasing amounts of spent fuel and nuclear waste in a safe, proliferation resistant and environmentally friendly manner.

(i) Safety and physical security

The most basic challenges presented by civilian nuclear power plants are the safety of the reactor and the security of the complex. There have been a number of serious incidents at nuclear power plants since these were first built in the 1950s, and the threat of an accidental meltdown, fire and/or the release of significant amounts of radioactive material remains an ever-present concern for nuclear security. The most notable civilian nuclear disaster occurred in Ukraine at the Chernobyl nuclear power plant in 1986 – where many people are thought to have lost their lives (either directly or indirectly) – and accidents have occurred regularly throughout the nuclear age. A selection of the most serious are detailed below, but this list is by no means exhaustive:

- *Windscale* In October 1957, the Windscale nuclear reactor near Sellafield in the northwest of England caught fire, leading to the release of large amounts of radioactive material across the UK and parts of Europe.[1]
- *Three Mile Island* On 28 March 1979, one of the two reactors at the Three Mile Island nuclear power plant near Harrisburg, Pennsylvania, in the USA,

suffered a partial meltdown after the flow of coolant was interrupted. A small amount of radioactive material was released into the atmosphere, but the incident was brought under control relatively quickly. There were no direct injuries or deaths, although a large number of people were evacuated from the surrounding area.[2]

- *Chernobyl* On 26 April 1986, one of the reactors at the Chernobyl nuclear power plant in western Ukraine (then part of the USSR), suffered a catastrophic meltdown and explosion. At least 40 deaths were caused directly by the meltdown, and huge amounts of radiation spread across Europe, which some believe has led to many more deaths from cancers and other illnesses. Thousands of people were evacuated and large areas around the plant remain uninhabitable today.[3]

- *Fukushima* On 11 March 2011, a large earthquake and tsunami initiated a reactor meltdown at the Fukushima Daiichi nuclear plant in Japan. While the reactors shut down correctly, floodwater from the tsunami destroyed the emergency diesel generators needed to cool the plant. With no coolant the reactors began to overheat, leading to a meltdown and the release of substantial amounts of radioactive material.[4]

According to the International Nuclear Event Scale that is used to monitor the severity of nuclear accidents, and which runs from 1 (an anomaly) to 7 (a major accident), both Chernobyl and Fukushima have been rated as 7 (i.e. major accidents).

The main risk of an accident at a nuclear plant normally involves a meltdown of the reactor core – essentially the inability to contain the heat of the nuclear reaction – as this can lead to conventional explosions, fires, the release of highly dangerous radioactive particles and widespread contamination. However, it is important to note that it is highly unlikely that a nuclear explosion could occur at a civilian nuclear facility due to the relatively low levels of fissile material used, as well as other safety measures and precautions.[5] In addition to nuclear accidents, civilian power plants must also be protected against a deliberate attack, and it is important that all nuclear-related infrastructure and especially stockpiles of fissile material be closely protected. There is a wide range of potential ways and reasons why a nuclear power reactor might be targeted, the most likely scenario being an attack on the plant or the theft of fissile material by a terrorist group (for more on this see Chapter 8) in order to cause mass panic, disruption and possibly widespread casualties. Any would-be attacker would probably seek to cause a meltdown of the nuclear core in order to release radiation and contamination – much the same as in an accident. For more on radiation and contamination see Chapter 2.

(ii) Weapons proliferation

Arguably a greater fear than an accident or deliberate attack on a nuclear power plant is that a civilian nuclear capability will be used to produce nuclear weapons. France, Israel, India, South Africa, Pakistan and North Korea have all essentially 'gone nuclear' in this way, and this is at the heart of the current proliferation concern regarding Iran. The move towards weaponisation can be made in two ways: by enriching uranium beyond the level needed for civilian reactors to weapons grade, or by reprocessing nuclear waste from the reactor in order to extract plutonium (see Chapter 1). Enriching uranium to weapons grade is considered an easier task because it uses the same techniques that are required to enrich for civilian purposes. Extracting plutonium from other nuclear waste products, on the other hand, requires specialised reprocessing facilities. Any nation that has enrichment and/or reprocessing capabilities can theoretically produce the fissile material needed for a nuclear bomb – these are often known as latent or virtual nuclear-weapon states (see Chapter 3).

This problem is compounded by the central bargain at the heart of the nuclear Non-Proliferation Treaty (addressed in Chapter 7), whereby all states party to the treaty have a legal right to nuclear power and the means to achieve it. Further, there is an obligation for the five recognised nuclear-weapon states (NWS) to provide assistance to the non-nuclear-weapon states (NNWS) seeking a civilian nuclear capability, including access to nuclear fuel. Nothing in the treaty therefore prohibits a state from acquiring the ability to enrich uranium and/or separate plutonium – indeed, many signatories of the treaty have developed one or, in some cases, both methods. Although International Atomic Energy Agency (IAEA) safeguards apply to declared nuclear facilities, the IAEA is not required to make formal assessments of whether a state has undeclared facilities, and cannot inspect these even if it did. However, under the Additional Protocol – which was agreed by the IAEA in 1997 – inspection teams can seek access to undeclared facilities or facilities that may be of proliferation concern. That said, the Additional Protocol is not mandatory and must be agreed individually with each state (more on the IAEA in Chapter 7).

Consequently, a key part of the challenge is how to manage peaceful nuclear cooperation agreements, which have formed a central part of global nuclear trade since US President Dwight Eisenhower's 'Atoms for Peace' speech to the United Nations General Assembly on 8 December 1953. Under the Atoms for Peace proposal, nuclear powers would provide fissile material for civilian nuclear purposes to help the spread of nuclear power but also curtail the threat of weapons proliferation. The logic of this proposal became ingrained in article V of the NPT and is now controlled largely through the international Nuclear Suppliers Group (NSG). However, and while this has allowed the spread of nuclear technology for non-military purposes to dozens of states, it has also unquestionably led to a number of states building or attempting to build nuclear weapons. In fact:

> The United States ... provided research reactors and enriched Uranium to countries such as Iran, Pakistan and Japan in the 1950s and 1960s. France, Brazil, and Italy supplied Iraq with nuclear facilities and materials in the 1970s. And the Soviet Union helped Argentina, Cuba and Libya get their civilian nuclear programs off the ground in the 1980s.[6]

While nuclear cooperation and assistance is one of the central pillars of the NPT, as Matthew Fuhrmann argues 'civilian cooperation provides technology and materials necessary for a nuclear weapons program and helps to establish expertise in matters relevant to building the bomb'.[7] This is one of the central paradoxes of the international nuclear regime.

Ultimately, as is discussed in greater detail in Chapter 3, the decision to build a nuclear bomb is primarily political, and requires a huge amount of political will. However, any country that operates enrichment and/or reprocessing facilities – ostensibly for civilian power production purposes – could make the jump towards weaponisation relatively swiftly. It is because of this that the international community has been so keen to 'close the nuclear fuel' cycle, find ways to supply nuclear energy fairly without the intrinsic proliferation problems, and prevent the production of new fissile material through, for example, a Fissile Material Cut-off Treaty (FMCT) (addressed in Chapter 7).

(iii) Nuclear waste

The third significant challenge arising from the proliferation of civilian nuclear power capabilities concerns the waste products produced in nuclear reactors, some of which can eventually be used for nuclear weapons. Nuclear fuel is removed from a reactor after a certain amount has undergone fission; this is known as *spent, irradiated* or *used fuel,* and typically consists of a large amount of uranium (95 per cent) and a small amount of plutonium (0.9 per cent), as well as other minor actinides and fission products.[8] According to Charles Ferguson, approximately 270,000 metric tonnes of spent nuclear fuel are currently in storage worldwide.[9] This fuel is stored and cooled in deep pools of water, sometimes for several years, before it can be placed into dry storage casks, and finally be buried deep underground..

In addition to storing nuclear waste in deep pools of water and then underground, it is also possible to reprocess it to extract either new fuel for a nuclear reactor or basic fissile material for a bomb. It is theoretically possible to reprocess all spent nuclear fuel – known as closing the fuel cycle – but this is a difficult and costly task. Partial reprocessing of spent fuel can be used to produce mixed oxide fuel (MOX) – which is a combination of uranium and plutonium fissile material – that has similar properties to low-enriched uranium (LEU) and can be used in a reactor. Or, the nuclear waste can be reprocessed in order to separate plutonium for a nuclear bomb – because plutonium is produced when uranium undergoes fission (see Chapter 1). The ability to reprocess spent fuel for a bomb is another challenge associated with the spread of civilian nuclear power technology. Nevertheless, both of these processes require advanced technology and considerable scientific know-how.[10]

The nuclear fuel cycle has five phases: being able to enrich uranium and reprocess spent fuel to produce MOX and separate the plutonium for a bomb means that a state has full control of the fuel cycle. The fuel cycle is explained below:[11]

1. *Mining uranium ore* This involves extracting uranium compounds from the earth and transforming them into a gas (uranium hexafluoride) that can be used in a centrifuge.
2. *Enriching uranium* This involves gradually separating the fissile Uranium 235 from the other isotopes found in natural uranium in a centrifuge. Low-enriched uranium can then be used in a reactor; high-enriched uranium can be used in a bomb.
3. *Use in a nuclear reactor* Low-enriched uranium is used in a nuclear reactor to produce energy for civilian purposes.
4. *Disposal of waste* The spent nuclear fuel is then sent to temporary storage to cool down, and from there to a conditioning plant to be prepared for long-term storage.

    OR

    Reprocessing MOX fuel Uranium and plutonium are separated from the waste products and reprocessed into mixed oxide fuel that can be put back into a specialised nuclear reactor. The rest of the spent fuel is then prepared for long-term disposal and storage.

    OR

    Plutonium separation Plutonium is separated from the spent nuclear fuel for use in a nuclear bomb.
5. *Long-term storage of radioactive waste* Spent fuel is vitrified and placed deep underground in solid containers to decay.

Some states may simply buy the fissile material they require for their domestic reactors from international suppliers – such as member states of the Nuclear Suppliers Group – and they therefore do not have total control of the nuclear full cycle. Consequently, these states present only a limited proliferation risk, and this is the model preferred by the international community for new nuclear powers. Indeed, the idea of establishing an international fuel bank that would control the production and sale of fissile material remains a popular way to ease this tension, but has so far proved difficult to pursue in practice.

It is very likely that the global demand for civilian nuclear power will increase rather than decrease in future generations as societies look for more reliable and cost-effective means of ensuring their energy security. This proliferation of nuclear power – which is a right for any nation under the NPT – will bring with it a number of security challenges – challenges that will have a direct and significant effect on future nuclear security. Securing and safeguarding plants and fissile material, preventing weaponisation and dealing with increasing amounts of radioactive waste will all require a considerable and concerted global effort. As of 2014 no country has opened a permanent nuclear waste facility, although several states have plans to begin long-term storage by the 2020s. The lack of permanent waste facilities is likely to continue to erode confidence in nuclear power.[12]

(2) The command and control of nuclear forces

While there has never been an accidental nuclear explosion (that we know of), there have been a significant number of accidents involving nuclear weapons since 1945, and many people have been killed either directly or indirectly as a result. Accidents can be the outcome of human error, a technical failure or a mixture of both, and while measures have been taken to secure nuclear weapons and minimise the chance of this happening, the requirements for bombs to be usable and reliable (for credible deterrence) has made this task increasingly difficult. Equally, there is an ever-present danger of deliberate and/or unauthorised use of nuclear weapons, or that these could be stolen – perhaps by terrorist groups or other third parties. Indeed, as more weapons have been built, and as more nations have acquired the bomb, the challenge of *command and control* of these forces has increased, and the possibility of an accidental nuclear war – perhaps initiated by a miscalculation – is an ever-present danger as long as nuclear forces exist, and particularly if they remain on high alert.

We can think of the central paradox of command and control of nuclear forces as the tension between the safety and security of nuclear weapons (guarding against the threat of unwarranted use) and the reliability, usability and credibility of these forces in a crisis (the threat that nuclear weapons could be decapitated or destroyed before they can be used). The considerable challenges for nuclear command and control created by these antagonistic demands are outlined in Table 25.

Table 25 Command and control of nuclear weapons

Unwarranted use – ensuring safety and security		Decapitation – ensuring usability
Unauthorised	**Accidental**	
Nuclear forces should be as secure and well protected as possible	Nuclear forces should be as safe as possible	Nuclear forces must not be vulnerable to a surprise first strike
Delegating authority over nuclear forces increases the risk of an unauthorised use	Keeping weapons on high alert increases the chance that accidents will happen	Forces therefore need to be kept on high alert, and potentially delegated to military commanders
Nuclear use must always be kept under strict (civilian) control and contain advanced safety measures	Nuclear weapons should only be usable following a positive command from the relevant authority	Nuclear use may have to be automated to some degree to be credible

Ashton Carter et al. have suggested that 'in devising weapons that concentrate destructive power to an unprecedented degree, governments have also created managerial problems more demanding than any previously encountered'.[13] The inherent trade-offs between the demands of nuclear command and control are examined in more detail in the sections below.

(i) Unwarranted use: accidental and authorised

Unwarranted nuclear use could take several different forms: it could result from an accident caused by either human error or a technical failure; it could result from the unauthorised use of nuclear weapons by a 'rogue commander' or from a computer malfunction; or it may stem from the use of nuclear devices by other actors following their loss or theft. In some circumstances it might also be the result of several of these combined, such as human error, deliberate sabotage and a technical failure.[14] The result can involve anything from the destruction or loss of nuclear bombs right up to an accidental nuclear detonation. In the past, the main danger has been from the detonation of the conventional high explosives used to initiate the bomb and the radioactive material subsequently released in the explosion, rather than from a full nuclear detonation (although we have come close to a full nuclear detonation on more than one occasion – see below).

We can think of three types of nuclear weapons accidents: (1) those involving nuclear weapons that are armed and could lead to an accidental nuclear detonation; (2) those involving nuclear weapons that are unarmed but which could damage or destroy nuclear weapons and/or lead to radioactive dispersal through a conventional explosion; and (3) those causing an unarmed weapon to become armed without the officials responsible realising.[15] There have been over 30 reported nuclear weapons-related accidents in the USA alone, and while none of these accidents has produced a nuclear detonation so far, there have been a number of conventional explosions, leading to the release of radioactive material and causing contamination, considerable physical damage has been caused and a number of nuclear bombs have been lost. Table 26 gives examples of just some of the military accidents that have taken place since 1945.

While the majority of the accidents detailed in Table 26 involve the United States, this is a reflection of the available data rather than a damning indictment on one particular country. Indeed, it is highly likely that other nuclear powers have also had problems in the past, although very little is known about Russian, Chinese, Indian, Pakistani, North Korean or Israeli nuclear weapons safety records. As Eric Schlosser explains:

> I have no doubt that America's nuclear weapons are among the safest, most advanced, most secure against unauthorized use that have ever been built. And yet, the United States has narrowly avoided a long series of nuclear disasters. Other countries, with less hard-earned experience in the field, may not be as fortunate.[16]

Equally, throughout the nuclear age there has always been the possibility that military personnel might use nuclear weapons deliberately and without authorisation. This is particularly the case in scenarios where weapons are kept at a high status of alert, and/or the authority over these weapons has been delegated to particular commanders, or has been mechanised and computerised. This is a possibility that has been explored by a number of Hollywood films, and perhaps most notably in

Table 26 Selected nuclear weapons accidents

When	Where	Description
10 March 1956	Mediterranean Sea	A US B-47 bomber disappeared with its two nuclear weapons and was never found.
23 January 1956	Goldsboro, North Carolina, USA	A US B-52 bomber broke apart in the air releasing two thermonuclear warheads. One of these warheads began the four-stage detonation process – only one small safety mechanism prevented the bomb from exploding.[i]
13 January 1964	Maryland, USA	A US B-52 bomber carrying two thermonuclear bombs broke apart in mid-air. The bombs were recovered intact from the crash site.
17 January 1966	Palomares, Spain	A US B-52 bomber collided with a tanker during in-flight refuelling over southern Spain. Four hydrogen bombs fell from the plane, crashing into a nearby village. Two bombs hit the ground hard enough for the conventional explosives to detonate – scattering Plutonium into the air. Three of the bombs were recovered within a few days; the fourth bomb was only recovered three months later.[ii]
21 January 1968	Thule, Greenland	A US B-52 bomber caught fire over Greenland; its four thermonuclear bombs were either lost or destroyed when the bomber crashed short of the runway at the Air Base at Thule. Large amounts of radioactive material were scattered from the ensuing blast, leading to a huge clean-up operation.[iii]
19 September 1980	Damascus, Arkansas, USA	A Titan II nuclear-armed ICBM exploded in its silo, after it was accidentally punctured by a falling wrench. The 9-megaton warhead flew 600 feet into the air before hitting the ground but did not detonate. Radioactive material and toxic missile fuel were widely dispersed.[iv]
October 1986	Caribbean coast	An explosion in the nuclear missile tube of a Soviet K-19 nuclear submarine caused it to sink off the Caribbean coast.
29–30 August 2007	USA	A US B-52 bomber accidentally took off from Minot Air Force base with six nuclear-armed Air Launched Cruise Missiles on board and flew across mainland USA.[v]
February 2009	Atlantic Ocean	The UK's *Vanguard* and the French *Le Triomphant* nuclear-armed SSBNs collided while on patrol in the Atlantic Ocean.[vi]

[i] See Joel Dobson, 'The Goldsboro broken arrow: the B52 crash of January 24, 1961, and its potential as a tipping point for nuclear war', (lulu.com: 2013)

[ii] See Barbara Moran, 'The day we lost the H-bomb: Cold War, hot nukes and the worst nuclear weapons disaster in history', (New York, Random House: 2009)

[iii] This is covered in depth in Scott Sagan, 'The limits of safety: organizations, accidents and nuclear weapons', (Princeton NJ, Princeton University Press: 1993) pp.156–203

[iv] The story of this accident is covered in detail in Eric Schlosser, 'Command and control', (London, Penguin Books, Ltd: 2013)

[v] Josh White, 'In error, B-52 flew over US with nuclear armed missiles', The Washington Post, (6 September 2007), www.washingtonpost.com/wp-dyn/content/article/2007/09/05/AR2007090500762.html

[vi] Aislinn Simpson, 'British and French nuclear submarines collide in Atlantic', Telegraph, (16 February 2009), www.telegraph.co.uk/news/uknews/defence/4634582/British-and-French-nuclear-submarines-collide-in-Atlantic.html

Stanley Kubrick's *Dr Strangelove* (1964). It is also a distinct possibility that nuclear weapons could be stolen and used by terrorists or non-state actors – again a subject that is addressed in popular culture (see Appendix 3). Finally, a number of nuclear weapons have been lost in the past and remain unaccounted for.

The evidence suggests that as long as nuclear weapons exist, there will always be a chance of accidents or unauthorised use, and even the possibility of an accidental nuclear war. Indeed, as Scott Sagan has argued, 'the nuclear weapons safety problem is like walking on thin ice. The fact that the system has not caved in so far, does not mean than [sic] it will not in the future.'[17] As a result, the safety and security of nuclear weapons represent a key aspect of nuclear command and control, and a continuing challenge for the global nuclear order.

(ii) Safety and security

Given the potential for unwarranted use of a nuclear device, it is paramount that measures are taken to protect against the unauthorised use, theft or loss of nuclear weapons, and that these can only ever be armed and used by and with the correct authority. However, the safety and security of nuclear weapons has tended to be seen as a secondary priority throughout the nuclear age, partly because it could impinge on their usability, but also because incorporating the technology and systems to do so is difficult. As a result, many nuclear weapons will have only rather crude safety mechanisms to prevent accidental (or deliberate) explosions, and others are not as secure as they could be. A selection of these measures are examined below:

- *Permissive Action Links (PALs)* Bombs and nuclear devices are increasingly fitted with various safety mechanisms, often known as PALs, to ensure that they cannot be used without the correct authority, but these are by no means foolproof, and are not fitted to every nuclear device. An example of this type of safety measure is the use of launch and arming codes that will only be held by senior military and civilian personnel. As a result, many (but not all) nuclear weapons now include PALs and other safety measures which mean that they cannot be detonated without proper authorisation.[18] Bombs may also be fitted with Environmental Sensing Devices (ESDs) as well as other mechanisms to ensure that they can only detonate if the correct conditions are met.
- The *two-man rule* is the notion that at least two people should participate in every phase of the process of delivering a nuclear weapon from the laboratory to its final military use.[19] This is augmented by rigorous Personnel Reliability Programmes (PRPs) that focus on the training and screening of forces, in particular the military personnel responsible for all areas of the nuclear weapons complex. In the words of one expert, the PRP 'carefully monitors the physical, psychological, and financial health of all

military personnel involved with nuclear weapons'.[20] It is not clear that all nuclear-armed states follow this process.

- *One-point safe* This refers to a nuclear device that will not produce a nuclear yield if there is a single conventional explosion on the core. This is part of a broader set of *fail-safe mechanisms* which ensure that if something goes wrong with a weapon it fails safely rather than failing lethally (i.e. causes a nuclear detonation). According to Peter Feaver, 'In an abnormal environment such as a fire or a highly charged atmosphere, the weak links needed to detonate the weapon will fail before the strong links inhibiting the detonation, hence no nuclear explosion will occur'.[21]

A further method for ensuring nuclear weapons safety and security is to keep the warhead and the delivery vehicle separate (known as *de-mating*) and/or to ensure that the weapons have to be programmed before they can hit a target (known as *de-targeting*).

It is important to remember that the levels of security and safety will necessarily be different between nuclear-armed states. Indeed, it is likely that the 'more experienced' states will have better mechanisms in place while newer nuclear states will not. As Bruce Blair makes clear:

Prospective nuclear rivals with fewer resources to lavish on command and control systems indeed face even higher risks. Their safeguards are bound to be cruder and weaker and are likely to be tested more often. The volatile relations between many of these states have a large potential to erupt into a full-blown military confrontation, intensifying the trade-off between positive and negative control and creating more opportunities for weaknesses in safeguards to emerge.[22]

That said, all nuclear-armed states face significant nuclear weapons management challenges.

(iii) Balancing command and control

In an ideal world the safety and security of nuclear weapons would be the primary concern of all those involved in nuclear command and control. However, nuclear weapons must also be reliable and in extreme circumstances usable. This creates a strong tension at the core of the command and control system between keeping weapons safe and planning for their use. In the words of Peter Feaver:

At the heart of nuclear command and control lies the always/never dilemma. Leaders want a high assurance that the weapons will always work when directed and a similar assurance the weapons will never be used in the absence of authorized direction. Weapons must be reliable: unlikely to fail at the moment when leaders want to use them; safe: unlikely to detonate accidentally; and secure: resistant to efforts by unauthorized people to detonate them.[23]

Consequently, a third pressure on command and control is the credibility and reliability of nuclear forces should they ever need to be used.

From a purely military point of view, therefore, one of the biggest challenges in the nuclear age has been how to control nuclear forces to ensure they are always ready to be used if necessary, but that they are never used unless the decision is made to do so by the highest authorities. This balance has been made even more difficult by the reduced warning times that may be available to respond to a nuclear attack (this could be as little as a few minutes with ballistic missiles). Indeed, it has led to policies of launch on warning (i.e. before any nuclear weapons have been detonated), highly coordinated methods of nuclear use, such as the Single Integrated Operational Plan (SIOP) operated by the United States between 1961 and 2003, a possible pre-delegation of launch authority to military commanders in the field and a general feeling that in a time of heightened tensions you either use nuclear weapons or you lose them. Putting weapons on high alert, however, raises the risk of miscalculation, and this might mean that nuclear weapons are launched before the threat can be fully analysed. As Eric Schlosser points out with regard to the USA during the Cold War:

> The reliability of America's early warning system attained an existential importance. If the sensors failed to detect a Soviet attack, the order to launch might never be given. [However, on the other hand,] ... if they issue an attack warning erroneously, millions of people would be killed by mistake.[24]

Such concerns even led to the development of a semi-autonomous nuclear retaliation system in the Soviet Union – known as the 'Dead Hand' (and by others as 'the doomsday machine') – which would fire Russian nuclear missiles automatically if the country had been attacked and the leaders were killed.[25] The command and control balance is further complicated by *who* should control nuclear weapons: civilian authorities (the heads of government, elected officials, a national command centre), or the military (a central military command authority and/or commanders or officers in the field). Both have their advantages and disadvantages:

- *Civilian control* provides a level of political accountability and theoretically increases the threshold of nuclear use. However, civilian control could make a state slower to respond and therefore potentially vulnerable to a first strike or a 'bolt from the blue', particularly if the national civilian command infrastructure is destroyed.
- *Military control* increases the credibility and chance of a swift response, and the likelihood that nuclear forces can and will be used if necessary. However, military control raises the risk of unauthorised use by a rogue commander, particularly if authority has been pre-delegated, and could undermine any ability to control a nuclear exchange.

Broadly speaking, civilian control will tend towards the safe or 'never' side of the nuclear dichotomy, while military controllers will necessarily focus more on usability and the 'always' side.[26]

Given the many thousands of nuclear weapons that have been built since 1945, accidents are actually relatively rare. However, available records show that we have come very close to disaster on at least a couple of occasions. The command and control of nuclear forces is a delicate balance: too much control and a state's second-strike credibility – and therefore deterrent – may suffer, too little control and nuclear weapons may be used without any wish to do so. As Shaun Gregory points out, 'the requirement for military readiness will always mean that nuclear weapons will not be as safe as human ingenuity could make them'.[27]

(iv) The cyber challenge

The final set of challenges facing command and control involve the development of new military technologies that may augment or possibly supplant the role of nuclear weapons in international security. In particular, the growth and expansion of so-called cyber weapons – the use of computer programs for surveillance, theft or the destruction of enemy computer systems and networks – represents a new and growing challenge to nuclear strategy and command and control.

Cyber weapons can take many different forms and attack many different targets, and the true extent of their impact on global security has yet to fully be examined. In terms of nuclear weapons, their most obvious impact is on command and control and early warning systems, sensitive information relating to current and future nuclear-related weapons systems, and threat and risk assessment. As Stephen Cimbala points out:

> If the ultimate weapons of mass destruction – nuclear weapons – and the supreme weapons of soft power – information warfare – are commingled during a crisis, the product of the two may be an entirely unforeseen and unwelcome hybrid.[28]

Cyber attacks and cyber weapons cover a very broad spectrum of dynamics, from espionage and hacking, to interference with key systems, to direct attacks on civilian or military targets; these attacks can be carried out physically (i.e. by people) or logically (through computer networks), and may include a variety of different methods, ranging from logic bombs, hacking and malware to espionage, botnets and more traditional cyber-espionage.[29] Because of this, it has been difficult to establish a working definition of 'cyber warfare', or how cyber weapons might be used against nuclear facilities, nuclear command and control or how they will influence a crisis between nuclear-armed adversaries.

Various 'cyber weapons' and cyber techniques have already been used against nuclear weapons-related systems. Two examples of the new link between nuclear and cyber are indicative of this emerging trend.

- *Syrian air defence* The first was the use of use of cyber capabilities to undermine air-defence radars as part of an attack on suspected Syrian nuclear weapons facilities by Israel in 2007. While the exact details remain unclear, it seems that Syrian air-defence radars were fed erroneous images of a clear sky to allow Israeli fighter jets to pass by undetected as part of an electronic warfare package known as the 'Suter' airborne attack system.[30]
- *Stuxnet and Olympic Games* The second was the use of malware by the United States (and probably Israel) to attack Iranian uranium-enrichment facilities – the so-called Stuxnet virus. The Stuxnet computer virus was a piece of malware aimed at causing clandestine damage to Iran's uranium enrichment programme at Natanz. The virus operated for over a year until it was discovered in the summer of 2010. Stuxnet was just one part of a covert cyber campaign – known as Operation Olympic Games – against the Iranian nuclear programme, which also included the viruses Flame and Duqu. It remains unclear exactly how successful these cyber attacks were in retarding Iranian nuclear efforts, but the evidence suggests that these may have contributed to a significant reduction in enrichment during this period, potentially putting the timeline for a possible nuclear weapon back by a number of months.[31]

In addition to this, cyber industrial espionage, and in particular the theft of military and possibly nuclear-related secrets and industrial information, is becoming an ever-increasing concern.

In the future it is not inconceivable that various cyber weapons could be used in a variety of ways against nuclear weapons and related systems, and therefore provide a substantial challenge to the command and control of nuclear forces. Cyber weapons could equally be used by terrorists or non-state actors to cause unintended detonations and accidents (and to steal nuclear secrets), or by nation states to undermine the ability of certain actors to use these weapons, or at least to decrease their confidence that such weapons will work when required.

(3) The nuclear taboo and the norm of non-use

Perhaps the biggest mystery of the nuclear age, especially when compared with other major weapons developments, is why nuclear weapons have only been used twice (the two bombs dropped on Japan by the United States in August 1945). Even the most optimistic observers in the late 1940s couldn't have predicted that seven decades would pass without further nuclear use – be it deliberate or accidental – and notwithstanding the large number of nuclear tests that have taken place and weapons that have been built during this time. As Thomas Schelling pointed out in 2005:

> The most spectacular event of the past half-century is one that did not occur. We have enjoyed sixty years without nuclear weapons exploded in anger.[32]

This dynamic has held true on two different levels: first, between nuclear capable actors, and second, between nuclear capable and non-nuclear capable states. While the non-use of nuclear weapons between two nuclear-armed states can perhaps be understood through the condition of nuclear deterrence and mutual assured destruction or MAD (use against another nuclear-armed state would potentially be suicidal given the high likelihood of nuclear retaliation – see Chapter 4), the reasons why nuclear-armed states have chosen not to use them against non-nuclear states, and perhaps more interestingly states that do not possess nuclear weapons have initiated war against nuclear-armed states despite them having these weapons, appear to require further explanation. It is the aim of this section to introduce you to the idea of a nuclear taboo and the norm of nuclear non-use that is widely held to underpin these phenomena.

The reason why we have not seen nuclear weapons used since 1945 is probably the result of a number of factors, first among them being a good deal of luck (possibly even as opposed to judgement). Nevertheless, there is no question that a particular stigma has emerged surrounding 'the bomb' since the 1940s, which is based fundamentally on the notion that nuclear weapons are somehow different from all other weapons and simply should not be used. It is this belief that nuclear weapons should never be used by a civilised society that underpins the idea of a 'nuclear taboo'.

What is the nuclear taboo? The nuclear taboo is an expression popularised by political scientist Nina Tannenwald (although the idea has been around since the 1950s) referring to the widespread norm that has developed since the dawn of the nuclear age that nuclear weapons cannot be used again. Essentially, the taboo – something proscribed by society as unacceptable – refers to a belief that using nuclear weapons would be amoral given the vast destruction that such acts would cause, and because of the special status that nuclear weapons hold within international society. According to Tannenwald:

> A powerful taboo against the use of nuclear weapons has developed in the global system, which, although not (yet) a fully robust prohibition, has stigmatized nuclear weapons as unacceptable weapons – 'weapons of mass destruction'.[33]

Another aspect of the taboo is that there is something inherently different about nuclear weapons, thereby making their use unlike that of any other weapon developed by human beings (including chemical and biological weapons). In this sense, there is a taboo against nuclear use irrespective of the yield of the nuclear device or the potential causalities caused, and also irrespective of whether using a non-nuclear weapon – or indeed, lots of non-nuclear weapons – might have caused a similar amount of destruction or death.

This taboo is also more broadly part of the 'norm of non-use' – a slightly different idea associated with another political scientist, T.V. Paul. According to Paul:

This tradition has largely been shaped by two dominant factors: first, an appreciation of the material character of the weapon concerned (i.e., the horrendous short- and long-term impact its use would create), beginning with Hiroshima and Nagasaki, but more powerfully entrenched following the hydrogen bomb tests in the early 1950s; second, the negative reputational effects its use would generate, especially in terms of projecting poor images, signalling wrong intentions, and setting bad precedents.[34]

Taken together the taboo and norm of non-use present a powerful challenge to the utility and relevance of nuclear weapons in the modern world.

The taboo in action The greatest example of nuclear non-use is clearly seen during the bipolar Cold War between East and West that dominated international politics for nearly five decades (1945–1991), but this can perhaps best be explained alongside other more traditional factors, such as nuclear deterrence and MAD (see Chapter 4). However, such conventional explanations lack credibility in a much larger range of scenarios where only one protagonist had nuclear weapons and the other(s) did not. This in itself works in two ways: (1) a certain reluctance by nuclear-armed states to use nuclear weapons even when facing possible defeat against a weaker non-nuclear-armed adversary; and (2) the lack of concern shown by non-nuclear states about going to war with states that possess nuclear weapons. According to Paul:

> It seems that the apparent boldness of nonnuclear states in initiating war against a nuclear adversary has been partially influenced by the tradition of non-use that all nuclear states have thus far observed. Nonnuclear initiators seem to believe that the nuclear defender is self-deterred through the operation of the tradition and other possible political and strategic constraints.[35]

Table 27 provides some examples of when the so-called taboo or norm of non-use has played out in international relations – although these examples are by no means exhaustive. Nuclear weapons were not the only key factors in these conflicts, but the fact that there are so many examples of nuclear non-use is often used as evidence of the reality of the taboo.

Criticisms of the taboo While the notion of the nuclear taboo may be becoming increasingly persuasive, some scholars have questioned both its validity and its usefulness. As Colin Gray points out:

> Although the proposition of a nuclear taboo is both plausible and attractive, it is perilously flawed in a way that is likely to set damaging ambushes for those who have been imprudently optimistic.[36]

In a sense, thinkers such as Gray argue that the notion of a taboo is preventing the international community from really dealing with the central problems produced by nuclear weapons, and is a barrier to ensuring against their future

Table 27 Examples of (selective) nuclear non-use[i]

Scenario	Nuclear Actor/s	Non-Nuclear Actor/s	Description
Korean War (1950–1953)	USA	North Korea, China	The USA decided not to use nuclear weapons to end the stalemate
Vietnam War (1965–1973)	USA	North Vietnam	The USA rejected calls for widespread nuclear use against the Vietcong
Yom Kippur War (1973)	Israel	Egypt, Syria, Iraq, Jordan	The Arab allies launched a surprise attack on nuclear-armed Israel
Sino-Vietnamese War (1979)	China	Vietnam	Vietnam went to war with China despite a Chinese nuclear weapons capability
Afghan War (1979–1989)	Soviet Union	Afghanistan	The Soviet Union decided not to use nuclear weapons, despite suffering huge losses
Falklands War (1982)	The UK	Argentina	Argentina invaded the Falkland Islands despite the UK having nuclear weapons
Persian Gulf War (1990–1991)	The USA	Iraq	The USA chose not to use nuclear weapons against Iraq despite threats of chemical attack
Afghanistan (2001–)	The USA, UK	Afghanistan (Taliban)	The USA chose not to use tactical nuclear weapons against the Taliban/Al-Qaeda

[i] Table adapted from T.V. Paul, 'The tradition of non-use of nuclear weapons', (Stanford CA, Stanford University Press: 2009) pp.144–145

use. Herman Kahn was far less optimistic: 'my guess is that nuclear weapons will be used sometime in the next hundred years'.[37]

(4) Key points and guide to further reading and resources

This chapter has sought to provide you with an overview of the major dynamics and challenges facing the future of global nuclear politics and strategy. A summary of these key points is provided below:

- More and more countries are looking to nuclear power to meet their ever-increasing energy requirements and this creates three main challenges: the safety and security of nuclear reactors and reactor fuel; the prevention of weapons proliferation; and dealing with nuclear waste.
- There have been numerous nuclear weapons accidents since 1945, and it is highly likely that there have been many more that we do not know about. However, so far none has resulted in an accidental nuclear explosion. The threat of nuclear accidents (civilian or military) remains ever present.

(Continued)

(Continued)

- The issue of command and control of nuclear forces is complex and involves balancing the need for weapons to be reliable and ready to use against the need for safety, security and the insurance that they can only be used when authorised.
- The advent of cyber weapons and 'information warfare' presents a whole new spectrum of challenges for the safe and secure management of nuclear weapons and facilities.
- The nuclear taboo is the notion that nuclear weapons haven't been used because they are simply too destructive. Unlike with many other weapons a norm has developed over time against nuclear use. Whether this norm can continue indefinitely remains central to our nuclear future.
- The nuclear 'non-use norm' works in three main ways: between nuclear-armed actors; against nuclear-armed states engaging in conflict with non-nuclear-armed states; and for non-nuclear states engaging in conflict with nuclear-armed states.

Further reading and resources

On nuclear power see Charles Ferguson 'Nuclear energy' (2011); Maxwell Irvine 'Nuclear power' (2011); and for a good basic introduction to the nuclear fuel cycle P.D. Wilson 'The nuclear fuel cycle' (1997). On the vulnerabilities of civilian nuclear power plants see Bennet Ramberg 'Nuclear power plants as weapons for the enemy' (1992). William Alley and Rosemary Alley 'Too hot to handle' (2012) is a very good introduction to the problems of nuclear waste.

On the link between civilian power and weapons proliferation see Matthew Fuhrman 'Atomic assistance' (2012), 'Spreading temptation' (2009) and 'Splitting atoms' (2012); and on the Nuclear Suppliers Group see Ian Anthony et al. 'Reforming nuclear export controls' (2007), and the organisation's website at www.nuclearsuppliersgroup.org. On civilian nuclear accidents see J Samuel Walker 'Three Mile Island' (2006); Svetlana Alexievich and Keith Gesen 'Voices from Chernobyl' (2006); R.K. Mould 'Chernobyl record' (2000); and David Lochbaum et al. 'Fukushima' (2014). See also the film *The China Syndrome* which was released just weeks before the Three Mile Island incident.

On military nuclear accidents, command and control and near misses see Eric Schlosser 'Command and control' (2013); Shaun Gregory 'The hidden cost of deterrence' (1990); Scott Sagan 'The limits of safety' (1993);

Ashton Carter et al. 'Managing nuclear operations' (2001); Peter Feaver 'Guarding the guardians' (1992) and 'Command and control in emerging nuclear nations' (1992); and Bruce Blair 'The logic of accidental nuclear war' (1993). See also Randall Maydew and Julie Bush 'America's lost H-bomb' (1997); Joel Dobson 'The Goldsboro broken arrow' (2013); and Barabara Moran 'The day we lost the H bomb' (2009). The films *K-19: The Widowmaker* about the disasters that befell a Soviet nuclear submarine and *Fail Safe* about an accidental nuclear attack by the USA on the Soviet Union may also be of interest.

On the relationship between cyber and nuclear weapons see Stephen Cimbala 'Nuclear weapons in the information age' (2012) and 'Nuclear crisis management and "cyberwar"' (2011); and Joseph Nye 'From bombs to bytes' (2013). Jason Healey (ed.) 'A fierce domain' (2013) provides a good general introduction to the concept of cyber warfare, as does Richard Clarke and Robert Knake 'Cyber war' (2010).

The best books on why nuclear weapons have not been used since 1945 are T.V. Paul 'The tradition of non-use of nuclear weapons' (2009) and Nina Tannenwald 'The nuclear taboo' (2007). Colin Gray 'The second nuclear age' (1999) provides an interesting critique of the idea of the taboo, as does George Quester 'Nuclear first strike' (2005).

Notes

1. On this see Laura Arnold, 'Windscale 1957: anatomy of an accident', (Basingstoke, Palgrave Macmillan: 2007).
2. See J. Samuel Walker, 'Three Mile Island: a nuclear crisis in historical perspective', (Berkeley CA, University of California Press: 2006).
3. See R.F. Mould, 'Chernobyl record: the definitive history of the Chernobyl catastrophe', (London, Institute of Physics Publishing: 2000).
4. See David Lochbaum, Edwin Lyman and Susan Stranahan, 'Fukushima: the story of a disaster' (New York, New Press: 2014).
5. Charles Ferguson, 'Nuclear energy: what everyone needs to know', (Oxford, Oxford University Press: 2011) p.28.
6. Matthew Fuhrmann, 'Atomic assistance: how "atoms for peace" programs create nuclear insecurity', (London, Cornell University Press: 2010) p.2.
7. Matthew Fuhrmann, 'Spreading temptation: proliferation and peaceful nuclear cooperation agreements', International Security, 34:1 (2009) p.8.
8. Charles Ferguson, 'Nuclear energy: what everyone needs to know', (Oxford, Oxford University Press: 2011) pp.190–191.
9. Ibid, p.193.
10. For more on this see P.D. Wilson, 'The nuclear fuel cycle: from ore to waste', (Oxford, Oxford University Press: 1997).
11. Ibid.
12. On this see William Alley and Rosemarie Alley, 'Too hot to handle: the problem of high-level nuclear waste', (Cambridge, Cambridge University Press: 2012).

13. Ashton Carter, John Steinbruner and Charles Zraket, 'Introduction', in Ashton Carter, John Steinbruner and Charles Zraket (eds.), 'Managing nuclear operations', (Washington DC, The Brookings Institution Press: 1987) p.1.
14. See Shaun Gregory, 'The hidden cost of deterrence: nuclear weapons accidents', (London, Brassey's: 1990) pp.49–81.
15. Ibid, pp.10–11.
16. Eric Schlosser, 'Command and control', (London, Penguin Books Ltd: 2013) p.481.
17. Scott Sagan, 'The limits of safety: organizations, accidents and nuclear weapons', (Princeton NJ, Princeton University Press: 1993) p.267.
18. See Peter Stein and Peter Feaver, 'Assuring control of nuclear weapons: evolution of Permissive Action Links', (Washington DC, Rowman & Littlefield: 1987).
19. Peter Feaver, 'Guarding the guardians: civilian control of nuclear weapons in the United States', (London, Cornell University Press: 1992) p.14.
20. Ibid, p.17.
21. Ibid, p.14.
22. Bruce Blair, 'The logic of accidental nuclear war', (Washington DC, The Brookings Institution Press: 1993) pp.9–10.
23. Peter Feaver, 'Command and control in emerging nuclear nations', International Security, 17:3 (1992) p.163.
24. Eric Schlosser, 'Command and control', (London, Penguin Books Ltd: 2013) p.357.
25. See David Hoffman, 'The dead hand: Reagan, Gorbachev and the untold story of the Cold War arms race', (London, Icon Books Ltd: 2011) pp.421–423.
26. Peter Feaver, 'Guarding the guardians: civilian control of nuclear weapons in the United States', (London, Cornell University Press: 1992) pp.26–28.
27. Shaun Gregory, 'The hidden cost of deterrence: nuclear weapons accidents', (London, Brassey's: 1990) p.47.
28. Stephen Cimbala, 'Nuclear weapons in the information age', (London, Continuum International Publishing: 2012) p.45.
29. Good introductory guides to cyber weapons can be found in Jason Andress and Steve Winterfeld, 'Cyber warfare: techniques, tactics and tools for security practitioners', (London, Syngress: 2011), and Peter Singer and Allan Friedman, 'Cybersecurity and cyberwar: what everyone needs to know', (Oxford, Oxford University Press: 2014).
30. John Leyden, 'Israel suspected of "hacking" Syrian air defences', The Register, (4 October 2007), www.theregister.co.uk/2007/10/04/radar_hack_raid.
31. Chris Morton, 'Stuxnet, flame and duqu – the Olympic games', chapter in Jason Healy (ed.), 'A fierce domain: conflict in cyber space, 1986 to 2012', (USA, Cyber Conflict Studies Association: 2013) pp.212–231.
32. Thomas Schelling, 'The nuclear taboo', The Washington Post, (24 October 2005), http://online.wsj.com/news/articles/SB113010182444876942.
33. Nina Tannenwald, 'The nuclear taboo: the United States and the non-use of nuclear weapons since 1945', (Cambridge, Cambridge University Press: 2007) p.2.
34. T.V. Paul, 'The tradition of non-use of nuclear weapons', (Stanford CA, Stanford University Press: 2009) p.2.
35. Ibid, p.144.
36. Colin Gray, 'The second nuclear age', (Boulder CO, Lynne Rienner Publishers: 1999) p.103.
37. Herman Khan, 'Thinking about the unthinkable in the 1980s', (New York, Simon & Schuster: 1984) p.28.

CONCLUSION: SURVIVING OUR NUCLEAR FUTURE

This book has been written both as a reference guide to the subject of nuclear weapons, and as a direct contribution to what I perceive to be an important gap in public nuclear knowledge more generally. In this way, it is not meant as a scare tactic (although I hope it will help people realise the high stakes involved in the subject), but rather as a plea for a better understanding of the weapons that have dominated international life for nearly seven decades. It is very much the mantra of the book that the best way to survive further generations of the nuclear age is through a better knowledge, understanding and appreciation of the dynamics that we so often take for granted or are blissfully unaware of. Indeed, whatever our nuclear future – whether it be total abolition as some wish, or a better-managed nuclear status quo, or perhaps more likely somewhere in between – knowledge presents the power to mitigate against potential future nightmare nuclear scenarios.

The best way forward in our nuclear world is of course up to you to decide – I have tried consciously (and hopefully succeeded) to remain neutral throughout the book, so as to provide the information and tools for views and decisions rather than to indoctrinate and persuade towards my own beliefs (which continue to change). As I expressed in the introduction, there are no right and wrong answers when it comes to nuclear weapons, only ones that work (we will pay a very high price if we get it wrong). I would suggest that a culture of openness, discussion and different well-thought-out viewpoints can only be a positive contribution to the ongoing debate about nuclear weapons – too often subjects such as nuclear politics and nuclear strategy are not subjected to outside scrutiny and analysis, and this can only ever be to the broader detriment of what is a vital issue to us all. In this regard, any new views, suggestions and opinions regarding nuclear politics should always be welcomed, particularly from those outside the traditional nuclear hub.

That we have survived the nuclear era thus far is as much because of luck as judgement, and we must work hard to ensure that nuclear weapons are never used again. In this regard, we should not automatically assume that just because nuclear weapons have not been used since 1945 that they will not be used in the future – the spectre of accidental, unauthorised and even deliberate nuclear use remains with us today, and will do so as long as nuclear weapons exist. The likelihood of miscalculation and above all the security dilemma make it likely that any nuclear use will lead to an escalation and potentially unimaginable global consequences. Moreover, while we may well be living in an age of unprecedented global peace, the potential for this to change remains, and the implications of this should not be forgotten.

Perhaps the first thing for all of us to remember is that views on the role and importance of nuclear weapons are not homogeneous across the globe, and we must be wary of an ethnocentric analytical and personal bias. Put simply, and while national security is arguably the dominant variable across cases, states build and retain (and of course don't build) nuclear weapons for different reasons. These include internal political reasons, normative, cultural and social reasons, and technological reasons – nuclear weapons mean different things to different actors. It is clear for example that Russia, Britain, France and possibly India see nuclear weapons as a key part of their cultural identity and status. It is equally clear that Israel, Pakistan and North Korea see nuclear weapons as integral to their national security. Meanwhile the United States has made it clear that it will keep nuclear weapons as long as other states do the same – arguably for a mixture of both reasons – and China is unlikely to disarm while it is faced with both US and Russian nuclear weapons. In addition to this, we must also be cognizant of the various security environments across the globe and the perceived requirements that these produce: contemporary Western Europe or North America is not the same as the Middle East, South Asia or Northeast Asia, and any attempt to conflate these challenges is as disingenuous as it is complex.

Views on nuclear weapons are of course also split between the nuclear-weapon states (NWS), the non-nuclear-weapon states (NNWS), and states with nuclear weapons not recognised by the Non-Proliferation Treaty (NPT). It should not be a surprise therefore that each of these groups view nuclear weapons in a different light, and envisage a very different pattern towards a peaceful and stable nuclear future: the NWS argue that they are working in good faith towards disarmament under Article VI of the NPT, but that the current unpredictable nature of the contemporary global nuclear world order necessitates that they keep these arsenals for the time being; the NNWS charge that the NWS have avoided their legal commitment to disarm in good faith under the NPT, and have overly focused on non-proliferation instead; while the nuclear-armed states outside the treaty argue that the current international nuclear regime is biased against them and even based on a policy colloquially known as 'nuclear apartheid'. Within this of course we have the NNWS that are protected by extended nuclear deterrence guarantees – primarily by the United States – that view the nuclear weapons of others as central to their security, but nevertheless have no desire to acquire the bomb, and large parts of the globe that are already covered by nuclear-weapon-free zones (NWFZs). Addressing these divergent views and perceived strategic requirements remains a pressing challenge for the international community.

While the nuclear landscape may have changed in what has become popularly termed the second nuclear age, the main purpose of nuclear weapons remains deterrence – in all but the most extreme circumstances the actual use of nuclear weapons is difficult to envisage – and our nuclear world continues to be based on the theory – or as some would have it – a condition, of mutual assured destruction (MAD). As such, and although the debate may be split on the relative costs and benefits of nuclear proliferation, it is generally accepted that nuclear weapons are to deter and not to fight wars. As a result, and while MAD may not be perfect, it is arguably the best of a bad set of choices – essentially, the status quo isn't ideal but it could be a lot worse. That said, the threat of a conventional conflict escalating to the nuclear level remains a possibility, particularly in South Asia, the Middle East or Northeast Asia, or of course between the US/NATO and Russia, and MAD can do little to address the potential threat of nuclear use by a non-state actor. Consequently, the safety and security of nuclear weapons and related infrastructure remain of paramount importance to our nuclear future, and have rightly been placed at the top of the international agenda. Our past is littered with a number of close calls, and the threat of a catastrophic accident involving nuclear weapons or nuclear power facilities remains constant – as Fukushima in Japan demonstrated in 2011. Likewise, the importance of well-managed nuclear forces and secured fissile material can hardly be over-emphasised in an era dominated by the threat of transnational terrorism and following the revelation of the A.Q. Khan nuclear smuggling network. A crude nuclear bomb – which might be acquired illicitly, stolen, or in a worst-case scenario supplied by a state actor – could cause considerable damage if detonated in a large city, and even the detonation of a conventional dirty bomb would mean significant disruption, panic and probably death. Strong civilian command over nuclear forces, material and expertise is therefore a must; however, there are areas of the globe where it is deemed necessary to keep nuclear forces on alert for genuine national security reasons.

The grand bargain at the heart of the NPT between disarmament and non-proliferation therefore seems set to endure, although it will certainly be tested in the next few years. Indeed, it is unclear whether the regime could survive another setback – such as if Iran does go on to develop nuclear weapons, or if several leading NNWS left the treaty in protest – but we are currently devoid of any better international mechanism. Nuclear disarmament must therefore play a key role in non-proliferation, just as much as nuclear non-proliferation must play a key role in nuclear disarmament. Nevertheless, we must also be clear that despite the problems inherent in the NPT and the global non-proliferation regime, this nevertheless remains the best way to manage the contemporary global international order. Ultimately however, as long as some states decide that they need to keep their nuclear weapons, these weapons will appear attractive to others too, and it will be hard to stop a determined would-be proliferator – the recent experiences of Pakistan, North Korea and Iran are a case in point.

These challenges are compounded by the fact that the nuclear arms control process has appeared to reach something of a stalemate – fuelling the concerns of the NNWS – and this has not been assuaged by the recent P5 process initiative to seek a way forward. The deployment of ballistic missile defences – while increasingly technologically credible and viable – remains strategically problematic, and is arguably a major reason for the current roadblock in nuclear arms control, driving right to the heart of the contemporary security dilemma. Moreover, comprehensive civil defence against a nuclear attack remains a panacea, and has gradually become subsumed under broader efforts at disaster management, which treats nuclear attack as an outlier.

While the efficacy of nuclear weapons is increasingly being challenged on a number of levels – including but not limited to the normative, political, economic and military – this does not mean these weapons will disappear anytime soon. The spread of NWFZ, the growth in support for a Nuclear Weapons Convention, and the normalisation of the nuclear taboo and norm of non-use are all certainly steps in this direction. But the continued and increasing reliance on nuclear power (not to mention the nuclear weapons of the current nuclear-armed states), and indeed its spread globally, means that we are likely to be faced with the prospect of latent nuclear-weapon states again in the near future – notwithstanding what happens with Iran – and ultimately of course we cannot uninvent nuclear weapons and the knowledge needed to produce them.

While none of these nuclear issues are simple or straightforward, ignoring them will not make them go away. As such, we can do no worse than seek to understand what drives and shapes our contemporary nuclear world so that we can attempt to manage and control it – if not ultimately transform or change it entirely. Moreover, while it is true that we shouldn't base predictions that nuclear weapons will be not be used in the future just because they were not in the past, we should equally not necessarily feel constrained by the same axioms and dogma that characterised that past. Above all, a secure and safe nuclear future will not be easy to achieve, but it should not be impossible either.

APPENDICES

Appendix 1: Nuclear weapons timeline
Appendix 2: Glossary of key terms and acronyms
Appendix 3: Countries with civilian nuclear power
Appendix 4: Nuclear weapons in fiction, film and TV

Appendix 1
NUCLEAR WEAPONS TIMELINE

1905

September — Albert Einstein publishes his special theory of relativity ($E = mc^2$)

1938

December — Otto Hahn and Fritz Strassman discover fission in uranium

1939

1 October — A letter warning about nuclear weapons by Albert Einstein and Leo Szilard is delivered to US President Franklin Roosevelt

1941

9 October — President Roosevelt creates the US Atomic Project

1942

December — Enrico Fermi's 'nuclear pile' goes critical in Chicago

1945

16 July — The USA conducts the Trinity Test in the New Mexico desert

6 August — The USA drops the 'Little Boy' uranium bomb on Hiroshima

9 August — US drops the 'Fat Man' plutonium bomb on Nagasaki

1946

January — The UN forms the Atomic Energy Commission (AEC)

June — Bernard Baruch outlines a plan for international control of atomic weapons – the so-called 'Baruch Plan'

August — The US McMahon bill prohibits sharing any nuclear information with any other country

1949

4 April	The North Atlantic Treaty is signed creating NATO
29 August	The Soviet Union detonates its first nuclear device at Semipalatinsk in Kazakhstan

1950

June	The Korean War begins (1950–1953)

1952

3 October	The UK conducts its first nuclear test in the Montebello Islands, Australia
31 October	The USA explodes its first hydrogen bomb, codenamed 'Ivy Mike'

1953

12 August	The first Soviet hydrogen bomb test is conducted
8 December	The Atoms for Peace programme is launched by US President Dwight Eisenhower

1954

21 January	'Nautilus' – the first nuclear-powered submarine – is launched by the USA
June	The first nuclear power plant is opened in the Soviet Union

1954

March	The USA conducts 'Castle Bravo' tests in the Marshall Islands

1955

10 May	The USSR proposes an nuclear test ban
14 May	The Warsaw Treaty Organization (Warsaw Pact) is formed

1956

12 July	Indian proposal to end nuclear weapons tests

1957

15 May	The UK explodes its first hydrogen bomb
29 July	The International Atomic Energy Agency (IAEA) is established
26 August	The Soviet Union launches the Sputnik satellite into orbit
September	The Mayak nuclear incident in the Soviet Union
	Pugwash, SANE and CND are established

1958

July	The USA–UK Mutual Defense Agreement (MDA) is signed
10 October	The Windscale nuclear reactor catches fire in the United Kingdom

1959

February	The first Soviet intercontinental ballistic missiles (ICBMs) become operational
October	The first US ICBMs become operational

| December | The first US ballistic missile submarine becomes operational |
| | The Antarctic Treaty is signed |

1960

13 February	The first French nuclear test is conducted in the Algerian desert
March	The UN Conference on Disarmament (CD) is established in Geneva
November	The first Soviet ballistic missile submarine is launched

1961

| January | The Goldsboro nuclear accident in the USA |
| 30 October | The Soviet Union tests the Tsar Bomba nuclear device |

1962

June	The first Permissive Action Links (PALs) are fitted to nuclear weapons
16–28 October	The Cuban Missile Crisis brings the world to the edge of nuclear war
18 December	The Nassau or 'Polaris' agreement is signed between the USA and the UK

1963

| 5 August | The USA, Soviet Union and the UK sign the Limited Test Ban Treaty (LTBT) |

1964

| 21 July | The declaration of the denuclearisation of Africa |
| 16 October | China explodes its first nuclear device |

1966

| 17 January | A US bomber carrying four hydrogen bombs crashes at Palomares, Spain |

1967

| 27 January | The Outer Space Treaty is signed |
| 14 February | A Latin American nuclear-weapon-free zone (NWFZ) is established |

1968

| 1 July | The nuclear Non-Proliferation Treaty (NPT) opens for signature |

1969

| | A secret agreement is reached between the USA and Israel over the Israeli nuclear programme |

1971

| 11 February | The Seabed Treaty is signed |

1972

| 26 May | Richard Nixon and Leonid Brezhnev sign the Strategic Arms Limitation Treaty (SALT) I and Anti-Ballistic Missile (ABM) Treaty |

1974

18 May	India detonates a 'low-yield' nuclear device under the Rajasthan desert, codenamed 'Smiling Buddah'
3 July	The nuclear Threshold Test Ban Treaty (TTBT) is signed

1975

23 April	The Nuclear Suppliers Group (NSG) is created

1976

28 May	The Peaceful Nuclear Explosions Treaty is signed
July	A.Q. Khan establishes the Kahn Research Laboratories in Pakistan

1978

May	The first UN Conference on Disarmament is convened

1979

28 March	The Three Mile Island nuclear power plant in the USA suffers a partial meltdown
18 June	The SALT II agreement is signed by the USA and Soviet Union
22 September	A suspected South African–Israeli nuclear test takes place in the southern Indian Ocean

1980

October	The last atmospheric nuclear test is conducted (by China)

1981

7 June	Israel attacks and destroys the Osirak nuclear reactor in Iraq

1982

29 June	The START treaty negotiations begin between the USA and Soviet Union
December	The Greenham Common protests take place in the UK

1983

23 March	Ronald Reagan announces the Strategic Defense Initiative (SDI)
November	Able Archer 83 – a huge NATO nuclear exercise – is conducted

1985

6 August	The Treaty of Rarotonga creates the South Pacific NWFZ
5 October	*Sunday Times* publishes Mordachai Vanunu's revelations about the secret Israeli nuclear arsenal

1986

April	The Chernobyl nuclear reactor suffers a critical meltdown in the Ukraine
11–12 October	The Reykjavik summit between Ronald Reagan and Mikhail Gorbachev takes place

1987

8 December	The Intermediate-Range Nuclear Forces (INF) Treaty is signed by the United States and the Soviet Union

1991

31 July	George H.W. Bush and Mikhail Gorbachev sign the first START Treaty
27 November	The Nuclear Threat Reduction Act is passed by the US Congress
4 December	Cartagena Declaration creating a NWFZ in Latin America and the Caribbean
25 December	The Soviet Union dissolves

1992

20 January	A Joint Declaration on Denuclearisation of the Korean Peninsula is signed
17 July	The Conventional Forces in Europe (CFE) Treaty is signed by Russia and NATO
3 August	France signs the NPT
October	The United States announces a unilateral moratorium on nuclear testing

1993

3 January	The START II Treaty is signed by the USA and Russia
March	South Africa declares and then renounces nuclear weapons

1995

25 January	The Norwegian rocket incident takes place
23 March	Negotiations begin on a Fissile Material Cut-off Treaty (FMCT)
May	178 nations renew the NPT in New York
December	A NWFZ is established in Southeast Asia

1996

11 April	The Pelindaba Treaty is signed creating an African NWFZ
10 September	The Comprehensive Test Ban Treaty (CTBT) is adopted by the United Nations

1997

A.Q. Khan begins to transfer nuclear components to Libya

1998

13–15 May	India conducts five nuclear weapons tests
28–30 May	Pakistan conducts six nuclear weapons tests
31 August	North Korea launches the three-stage Taepo-dong ballistic missile over the Sea of Japan
December	Iraq expels United Nations Special Commission (UNSCOM) weapons inspectors

1999

May–June	The Kargil War between India and Pakistan takes place
13 October	The US Senate fails to ratify the CTBT

2001

11 September	Terrorists attack the World Trade Center and the Pentagon in the USA
13 December	President George W. Bush announces the US abrogation of the ABM Treaty

2002

24 May	The Strategic Offensive Reductions Treaty between USA and Russia is signed
14 August	The Iranian nuclear programme is publicly revealed

2003

10 January	North Korea announces its intention to leave the NPT
May	The Proliferation Security Initiative is launched
August	The six-party talks about North Korea's nuclear programme begin
19 December	Libya agrees to give up its weapons of mass destruction (WMD) programmes

2004

January	The A.Q. Khan nuclear smuggling network is revealed
28 April	UN Security Council Resolution 1540 is signed
June	A nuclear hotline between India and Pakistan is established

2005

May	The third NPT Review Conference is held in New York
18 July	The US–India Civil Nuclear Agreement is signed

2006

April	Iran announces that it has mastered uranium enrichment
8 October	North Korea tests its first nuclear device

2007

4 January	The 'four horsemen of the nuclear apocalypse' publish their first op-ed piece in *The Wall Street Journal*
6 September	Israel attacks a suspected Syrian nuclear weapons facility
	The International Campaign for the Abolition of Nuclear Weapons is established

2008

September	The Nuclear Suppliers Group grants India a waiver
December	The Global Zero campaign is launched

2009

February	UK and French ballistic missile submarine, collide in the Atlantic Ocean
5 April	US President Barack Obama makes a speech on nuclear disarmament in Prague, Czech Republic
July	An African NWFZ is announced

2010

8 April	The New START Treaty is signed by the USA and Russia
12 April	The first Nuclear Security Summit is held in Washington, DC
3–28 May	The fourth NPT Review conference takes place in New York
June	The Stuxnet computer virus is discovered in the Iranian nuclear programme

2011

11 March	The Fukushima nuclear disaster takes place in Japan
March	Germany announces that it will phase out nuclear energy by 2020

2012

26 March	The second Nuclear Security Summit is held in Seoul, South Korea

2013

12 February	North Korea conducts its third nuclear test
4–5 March	A Conference on the Humanitarian Effects of Nuclear Weapons is held in Oslo, Norway
28 November	A temporary deal is agreed between the P5+1 and Iran to temporarily freeze certain aspects of Iran's nuclear programme

2014

February	Second meeting on the Humanitarian Impacts of Nuclear Weapons takes place in Nayarit, Mexico
March	The third Nuclear Security Summit takes place in The Hague, Netherlands

Appendix 2
GLOSSARY OF KEY TERMS AND ACRONYMS

For an extensive overview of terms relating to nuclear weapons, readers should consult Rodney Carlisle's 'Encyclopaedia of the atomic age' (New York, Facts on Fact Inc: 2001) or Jeffrey Larsen and James Smith's 'Historical dictionary of arms control' (Oxford, The Scarecrow Press: 2005).

Able Archer 83 A NATO military exercise in October 1983 that significantly raised tensions between East and West in the Cold War.

Active defence Measures taken to lessen the impact of a nuclear attack before detonations (missile and air defence for example).

Additional Protocol (IAEA) Grants the IAEA legal authority for extra monitoring and verification of nuclear facilities.

Air burst A nuclear detonation above the intended target, designed to maximise the extent of blast damage.

Air-launched cruise missile (ALCM) A cruise missile delivered by an aircraft that can be nuclear armed.

Anti-Ballistic Missile (ABM) Treaty A treaty agreed in 1972 by the USA and USSR to prohibit the deployment of strategic ballistic missile defences. Abrogated by the United States in 2002.

A.Q. Khan network Nuclear smuggling network established by Pakistani scientist Abdul Qadeer Khan which provided nuclear technology to Pakistan and a number of aspiring nuclear states.

Atom bomb (A-bomb) A nuclear bomb that uses nuclear fission, such as those dropped on Japan in 1945.

Atoms for Peace US President Dwight Eisenhower's programme to supply civilian nuclear technology to the world in the 1950s.

Ballistic missile A missile that follows a ballistic trajectory before falling to earth to hit its target. Longer-range missiles travel into space.

Ballistic Missile Defence (BMD) Systems designed to intercept and destroy nuclear-armed missiles in various stages of their flight before they hit their intended target.

Baruch Plan A proposal by the United States in the late 1940s to create an international organisation to regulate all nuclear technology.

Bolt from the blue A nuclear strike without any warning.

Brinkmanship Pushing your opponent to the brink of disaster to test their resolve.

Broken arrow The term used to describe accidents involving nuclear-armed aircraft.

Campaign for Nuclear Disarmament (CND) An organisation that campaigns for the United Kingdom to unilaterally abolish its nuclear weapons.

Centrifuge The mechanism used to separate different isotopes of uranium in order to enrich it.

Chagai An area of Pakistan (in the Ras Koh Hills of Balochistan) that gives its name to the nuclear tests conducted there in May 1998.

Chain reaction The process whereby the release of neutrons from one atomic nuclear reaction begins a nuclear reaction in another atom, which then initiatives further atomic reactions.

Chernobyl A civilian nuclear disaster that occurred in the Ukraine in 1986.

Cold start The Indian military doctrine that would target Pakistani nuclear forces in the event of nuclear hostilities.

Cold test   (also Sub-critical test) Nuclear test without an explosion.

Cold War   Military and geopolitical stand-off between a Western bloc led by the United States and NATO against an Eastern bloc led by the Soviet Union and the Warsaw Pact, 1945–1991.

Comprehensive Test Ban Treaty (CTBT)   Treaty to eliminate all nuclear testing, which opened for signature in 1996.

Contamination   Radioactive particles deposited after a nuclear blast that remain harmful and lethal to humans.

Continuation of Government (CoG)   Plans to ensure the continuation of government following a nuclear strike – part of civil defence.

Continuous-at-sea Deterrence (CASD)   Policy adopted by the UK whereby one nuclear ballistic missile armed submarine is always at sea ready to fire its nuclear weapons.

Convention on Physical Protection of Nuclear Material and Nuclear Facilities   An international agreement that seeks to protect nuclear materials established in 1980 and updated in 2005.

Counter-force   Targeting strategy based on destroying the enemy's nuclear and military installations.

Counter-value   Targeting strategy based on destroying large population centres.

Critical mass   The necessary amount of fissile material required to sustain a nuclear fission reaction.

Cuban Missile Crisis   US–Soviet crisis over the placement of Soviet nuclear-capable missiles in Cuba in 1962. Regarded as the closest we have ever been to nuclear war.

Dead Hand   The name of the semi-autonomous Soviet nuclear response system. Also known as the Perimeter system.

De-alerting   The removal of nuclear forces from instant, hair-trigger alert, and from fire on warning.

Decommissioning   The process to remove nuclear weapons from active status in order to dismantle them.

Depleted uranium High-density material containing very low levels of U235 used for civilian purposes and armour plating and armour-piecing projectiles. Can be produced as a by-product of enrichment.

De-targeting Ensuring bombs/warheads have no fixed target before they have to be used.

Dirty bomb A weapon designed to maximise the distribution of radioactive material via a conventional explosion. Also known as a radiological dispersal device (RDD).

Doomsday Clock Indication of nuclear threat run by the *Bulletin of the Atomic Scientists*.

Dual-use technology Technology that can be used for both civilian and nuclear weapons purposes.

E = mc² Formula devised by Albert Einstein that paved the way for nuclear energy.

Electromagnetic pulse (EMP) A burst of energy from a nuclear explosion that is highly destructive to any electric-based equipment.

Enhanced radiation weapon (ERWs) Weapons designed to maximise radiation rather than blast to kill enemy forces but not destroy infrastructure. The neutron bomb was an example of an ERW.

Enola Gay Name of the B-29 aircraft that dropped the first atomic bomb on Hiroshima.

Extended nuclear deterrence The provision of a nuclear deterrent guarantee by a nuclear-armed state to another state that does not possess nuclear weapons.

Fat Man Name of the plutonium atomic bomb dropped on Nagasaki.

Fissile material A chemical element able to perform **fission** (be split).

Fissile Material Cut-off Treaty (FMCT) Treaty to ban the production of new fissile material (U235 and PU239).

Fission The process whereby a nucleus of an atom is split, emitting excess neutrons.

Force de dissuasion The name given to the French nuclear weapons force. Previously know as the *force de frappe*.

Four horsemen of the nuclear apocalypse Henry Kissinger, Sam Nunn, William Perry and George Schultz.

Fuel cycle The process from mining through to use (in a reaction or weapon) to the reprocessing and storage of nuclear fuel.

Fukushima Civilian nuclear disaster that occurred at the Fukushima–Daiichi plant in Japan in March 2011.

Fusion The process whereby atoms are fused together to create enormous heat and energy – used in a hydrogen bomb.

Geiger counter Instrument for measuring nuclear radiation.

Geneva Interim Agreement Temporary agreement reached by the P5+1 and Iran in November 2013 to halt parts of the nuclear programme in return for sanctions relief.

Global Zero Global movement seeking the abolition of nuclear weapons.

Gravity bomb Nuclear bomb dropped by aircraft that falls to earth to hit its intended target.

Highly enriched uranium (HEU) Uranium that has been enriched to very high levels of U235 (80 per cent +) for use in a nuclear bomb or warhead.

Horizontal proliferation The proliferation of nuclear weapons to new actors.

Hydrogen bomb (also known as the H-bomb, 'the super' or thermo-nuclear bomb) A nuclear bomb based on the process of nuclear fusion.

Intercontinental ballistic missile (ICBM) A missile able to strike targets anywhere in the world in a very short space of time. Normally armed with one or more nuclear warheads.

International Atomic Energy Agency (IAEA) International institution set up to promote and regulate the peaceful use of nuclear energy.

International fuel bank (also known as nuclear fuel bank) is a proposal to manage the supply of enriched uranium.

Isotope A variation of a chemical element with a different number of neutrons.

Joe 1 The name of the first Soviet atomic bomb exploded in 1949. Also known as RDS 1.

Kargil War   The only time two nuclear-armed states (India and Pakistan) have fought each other directly (in 1999).

Kiloton (Kt)   The unit of measurement equal to one thousand tonnes of conventional explosive.

Limited Test Ban Treaty (LTBT)   The 1963 treaty banning nuclear testing in the atmosphere, in space and under water. Also known as the Partial Test Ban Treaty (PTBT).

Little Boy   The name of the uranium bomb dropped on Hiroshima in August 1945.

Loose nukes   Nuclear weapons or material not accounted for after the collapse of the Soviet Union.

Low-enriched uranium (LEU)   Uranium enriched to low levels of U235 to be used in a nuclear reactor (typically around 5 per cent).

Manhattan Project   The name of the US-led programme to build the first atomic bombs.

Megaton (Mt)   Unit of measurement equal to one million tonnes of conventional explosive.

Meltdown   The consequence of a nuclear reactor overheating, where fissile products are released.

Minimum deterrence   Smallest number of weapons needed to retain a credible nuclear posture.

Mixed oxide fuel (MOX)   Mixture of reprocessed uranium and plutonium fuel that can be used in a nuclear reactor.

Multiple independently targetable re-entry vehicle (MIRV)   Missile with multiple nuclear warheads that can be targeted individually.

Mushroom cloud   Large distinctive cloud produced by a nuclear explosion.

Mutual assured destruction (MAD)   Condition whereby nuclear weapons will not be used against another nuclear-armed actor because to do so would be suicidal.

North Atlantic Treaty (NATO)   A multi-national military and defence organisation established in 1949.

Neutron bomb   A bomb designed to maximise radiation and effects on humans while minimising its effect on infrastructure.

New START Treaty   The treaty between the United States and Russia signed in 2010 limiting deployed strategic nuclear forces.

No first use (NFU)   A declared policy not to use nuclear weapons first in a conflict.

Non-Aligned Movement (NAM)   A large group of states not aligned to any major power block, critical of the lack of progress made towards disarmament by the NWS.

Non-nuclear-weapon state (NNWS)   A state signatory to the NPT that can never possess nuclear weapons under the treaty.

Norwegian Rocket Incident   A nuclear scare in 1995 after Russian leaders mistook a Norwegian rocket launch for a NATO nuclear missile strike.

Nuclear apartheid   The condition whereby under the NPT some states can legally have nuclear weapons while others cannot.

Nuclear deterrence   Using the threat of nuclear weapons to deter nuclear use by another actor.

Nuclear Non-Proliferation Treaty (NPT)   The treaty opened for signature in 1968 with three main pillars: (1) signatories must work towards nuclear disarmament; (2) all signatories have the right to civilian nuclear power; (3) states must not proliferate nuclear weapons or materials to others.

Nuclear opacity   The policy adopted by Israel of neither confirming nor denying its possession of nuclear weapons.

Nuclear Suppliers Group (NSG)   A multinational body that controls the manufacture and sale of nuclear-related material and technologies.

Nuclear taboo   A normative concept that has developed against any use of nuclear weapons.

Nuclear waste   The by-products of nuclear fission reactions that must be suitably disposed of.

Nuclear weapon   A weapon that derives its power from the nucleus of an atom of a particular chemical isotope.

Nuclear Weapons Convention (NWC) A proposed multilateral treaty to outlaw nuclear weapons.

Nuclear-weapon free zone (NWFZ) A geographical zone where the manufacture, testing, deployment and stockpiling of nuclear weapons is prohibited.

Nuclear-weapon state (NWS) One of the five states legally recognised as possessing nuclear weapons under the 1968 Non-Proliferation Treaty (the USA, Russia, the UK, France and China).

Nuclear winter The possible result of large-scale nuclear use leading to reduced sunlight and cold weather for a sustained period, which in turn could lead to death and environmental destruction.

Operation Plowshare The US programme to develop nuclear devices for peaceful construction and engineering purposes.

Osirak An Iraqi nuclear reactor attacked by Israel in 1981.

P5 The five permanent members of the UN Security Council. Also the five recognised nuclear weapons states under the NPT (the USA, Russia, the UK, France and China).

P5 process An initiative to facilitate steps towards nuclear disarmament by the P5 as warranted by the NPT.

Partial Test Ban Treaty (PTBT) See **Limited Test Ban Treaty (LTBT)**.

Passive defence Measures taken to lessen the impact of a nuclear attack once it has happen (bomb shelters, emergency response, etc.).

Peaceful nuclear explosions (PNEs) Nuclear detonations for non-military purposes.

Permissive Action Links (PALs) Various mechanisms to ensure nuclear weapons cannot be detonated without proper authorisation.

Petrochemical-3 The code name for the Iraqi nuclear weapons programme initiated in 1990.

Plutonium Predominantly man-made chemical element that can be used for atomic fission. Plutonium is separated from other products following a nuclear reaction of uranium.

Pokhran   Name given to the Indian nuclear tests – named after the test site in Rajasthan. Pokhran I refers to the 'peaceful test' of 1974 and Pokhran II to the overt weapons test of 1998.

Radiation   The particles released naturally by certain chemical isotopes and through nuclear reactions.

Radiation sickness   The severe health effects of high exposure to radiation that can lead to various illnesses and death. Also known as acute radiation syndrome (ARS).

Radioactive fallout   The radioactive particles of earth and other material scattered into the air as a result of a nuclear blast, many of which are highly dangerous for humans.

Reprocessing   The method used to transform spent nuclear fuel into either new MOX fuel for a reactor or to separate plutonium for a bomb.

Roentgen equivalent man (rem)   Unit used to measure ionising radiation.

Samson Option   The strategy of massive nuclear response purportedly to be adopted by the Israeli government if the existence of the state is threatened.

Ship submersible ballistic nuclear (SSBN)   A nuclear-powered submarine armed with nuclear-tipped ballistic missiles.

Six-party talks   The diplomatic effort to prevent and then curb North Korea's nuclear ambitions involving the USA, Russia, China, Japan, South Korea and North Korea (2006–).

Smiling Buddha   The name given to the 'peaceful' nuclear test conducted by India in 1974.

Solimoes Project   The name given to the secret Brazilian nuclear weapons programme.

Sputnik   The name of the first artificial earth orbiting satellite launched by the Soviet Union in 1957.

Strategic Defense Initiative (SDI)   A plan to build a shield against ballistic missile attack announced by US President Ronald Reagan.

Stuxnet   The computer virus discovered within the Iranian uranium-enrichment programme in 2010.

Submarine-launched ballistic missile (SLBM) A ballistic missile (which can be nuclear armed) launched from a submarine.

Submarine-launched cruise missile (SLCM) A cruise missile (which can be nuclear armed) launched from a submarine. An SLCM has a far shorter range than an SLBM.

Suitcase bomb A tactical nuclear weapons that is small enough to be carried by a single person in a backpack.

Technological determinism A theory that suggests that advances in technology drive social and political developments.

The Gadget The name given to the first nuclear bomb exploded as part of the Trinity Test in 1945.

Three Mile Island A civilian nuclear reactor meltdown in the United States in 1979.

Threshold nuclear weapons capability State with the necessary capabilities to build nuclear weapons in a relatively short space of time if it chose to but is not current considered as nuclear armed.

Threshold Test Ban Treaty (TTBT) Treaty signed in 1974 limiting underground nuclear tests to a maximum of 150kt yield.

Trinity Test The first test of a nuclear weapon in Alamogordo, in the New Mexico desert, USA, in July 1945.

Tsar Bomba The largest nuclear weapon ever tested – detonated by Russia in October 1961.

Tube Alloys The name of the secret British nuclear weapons research programme established in the early 1940s.

U233 A third possible source of fissile fuel for a nuclear reactor bred from thorium.

Ummah Tameer-e-Nau (UTM) A militant organisation based in Pakistan believed to have discussed supplying Al-Qaeda with nuclear material.

United Nations Security Council Resolution 1540 The UN resolution agreed in 2004, seeking to prevent the spread of nuclear and other WMD material to non-state actors.

Uranium A naturally occurring chemical element that can be enriched to be used in a nuclear reactor or a nuclear weapon. Only U235 can be used in a nuclear bomb.

Uranium enrichment The process to increase the concentration of the fissile isotope U235 in uranium so that it can be used in a reactor or bomb.

Uranverein Project The name of the nuclear weapons project conducted by Nazi Germany during the Second World War.

US–India Civil Nuclear Agreement The agreement signed in 2005 allowing India access to US civilian nuclear technology in return for placing Indian civilian nuclear facilities under IAEA safeguards. Also known as the 123 Agreement.

Vela Incident Suspected nuclear detonation carried out in the southern Indian Ocean in 1979, widely rumoured to have been a joint South African–Israeli nuclear test.

Vertical proliferation An increase in the numbers of nuclear weapons held by current nuclear-armed states.

Virtual nuclear-weapon state A state with latent a nuclear weapons capacity – i.e. it has the fissile material and weapons complex but has not built the bomb.

Vitrification Placing nuclear waste in a glass compound to ensure its security.

Weapons of mass destruction (WMD) Usually refers to nuclear, but also includes chemical, biological and radiological weapons. Anything designed to cause mass casualties and destruction.

Windscale The first major nuclear accident in the UK in 1957 after a civilian power reactor caught fire.

Yellowcake Material containing partially refined uranium oxide.

Yield Measurement of energy released in a nuclear explosion.

Appendix 3
COUNTRIES WITH CIVILIAN NUCLEAR POWER

	Nuclear Reactors	Total Capacity (MW)
USA	100	98,560
France	58	63,130
Japan	50	44,215
Russia	33	23,643
Republic of Korea	23	20,739
India	21	5,308
Canada	19	13,500
China	18	13,860
United Kingdom	16	9,231
Ukraine	15	13,107
Sweden	10	9,474
Germany[i]	9	12,608
Spain	8	7,567
Belgium	7	5,927
Czech Republic	6	3,804
Taiwan	6	5,028
Switzerland	5	3,308
Finland	4	2,752
Hungary	4	1,889
Slovakia	4	1,816
Pakistan	3	725
Argentina	2	935
Brazil	2	1,884

COUNTRIES WITH CIVILIAN NUCLEAR POWER

	Nuclear Reactors	Total Capacity (MW)
Bulgaria	2	1,906
Mexico	2	1,330
Romania	2	1,200
South Africa	2	1,860
Armenia	1	375
Iran	1	915
The Netherlands	1	482
Slovenia	1	688
United Arab Emirates	Under construction	

[i] Germany has recently declared its intention to close all of its nuclear power plants by 2022 – partly as a result of the Fukushima disaster in 2011. On this see, for example, Detlet Jahn and Sebastian Korolczuk, 'German exceptionalism: the end of nuclear energy in Germany!', *Environmental Politics*, 21:1 (2012) pp.159–164.

Source: See International Atomic Energy Agency, 'Power Reactor Information System', www.iaea.org/PRIS/World Statistics/OperationalReactorsByCountry.aspx.

Appendix 4

NUCLEAR WEAPONS IN FICTION, FILMS AND TV

Nuclear weapons have a rich history in popular culture, particularly in books, on TV and in film, and a selection of these – along with some non-fiction and official media – are included below. These lists are by no means exhaustive and you might also be interested in Scott Zeman and Michael Amundson (eds.) 'Atomic culture' (2004).

Fiction

'Arc light' (1994) A novel by Eric Harry about a limited global nuclear war.

Broken Arrow (1996) A Hollywood film about the theft of two nuclear weapons.

Countdown to Looking Glass (1984) A made-for-TV film depicting the lead-up to a limited nuclear war between the United States and the Soviet Union.

Crimson Tide (1995) A Hollywood film portraying the stand-off between the captain and the executive officer of a US nuclear-armed submarine following an incomplete nuclear launch order.

Dr Strangelove (1964) A black comedy film in which a US airforce officer orders a nuclear first strike on the Soviet Union.

'Fail safe' (1962) A fictional thriller by Eugene Burdick and Harvey Wheeler depicting an accidental nuclear attack by the United States on the Soviet Union as the result of a computer failure. The book was later made into a film (1964 and 2000).

Fat Man and Little Boy (1989) A Hollywood film telling the story and re-enacting the Manhattan Project during the Second World War. Released in the UK as *Shadow Makers*.

Hiroshima (1995) A film about the lead-up to the decision to drop the first atomic bomb in 1945.

K-19: The Widowmaker (2002) A Hollywood thriller about the disasters that befall a Soviet nuclear submarine.

'London after the bomb' (1982) A book by Owen Greene, Barry Rubin, Neil Turok, Philip Webber and Graeme Wilkinson about what London might look like after a nuclear attack.

Lucky Dragon No. 5 (1959) A Japanese film based on the shipping vessel that was hit by fallout following US nuclear testing in 1954.

Octopussy (1983) A James Bond film about a possible nuclear attack on NATO forces designed to force nuclear disarmament.

'On the beach' (1957) A novel written by Nevil Shute depicting people in Australia as they await the arrival of deadly radiation from a nuclear exchange in the northern hemisphere. The book was later made into a film (1959) and a TV movie (2000).

Special Bulletin (1983) A film based on the fictional live broadcasts of a terrorist plot to blackmail the US government by placing a nuclear bomb in Charleston harbour.

The China Syndrome (1979) Thriller about a fictional nuclear meltdown.

The Day After (1983) An American television film depicting the build-up to and the effects of a nuclear war between the USA and the Soviet Union on several groups of people living in Missouri.

'The fourth protocol' (1984) A novel by Frederick Forsyth about a Soviet plot to detonate a nuclear bomb in the United Kingdom weeks before a general election.

'The letter of last resort' (2012) A play by David Greig dealing the decisions taken by UK prime ministers on what to do in the event of nuclear war.

'The sum of all fears' (1991) A novel by Tom Clancy describing a terrorist plot to detonate a nuclear bomb at an American Super Bowl game. The book was later turned into a Hollywood film of the same name (2002).

The War Game (1965) A television docudrama depicting the effects of a nuclear war on the United Kingdom.

'The world set free' (1914) A novel by H.G. Wells predicting a future world dominated by nuclear weapons.

'Third world war' (1982) A novel written by John Hackett in the style of a historical account of a nuclear war between NATO and the Warsaw Pact countries set in 1985.

Thirteen Days (2000) A Hollywood portrayal of the 1962 Cuban Missile Crisis.

Threads (1984) A British television drama describing the effects of a nuclear attack on a number of different families in the British city of Sheffield.

'Trinity's child' (1983) A novel by William Prochnau depicting the events of a fictional Third World War between East and West. It was later turned into film called *By Dawn's Early Light* (1990).

Thunderball (1965) A James Bond film based around the theft of two NATO nuclear weapons.

'Warday' (1984) A novel by Whitely Strieber and James Kunetka providing a fictional account of a journey across America five years after a limited nuclear attack.

War Games (1983) A film about a computer hacker who accidentally begins to initiate a nuclear war by hacking into the Pentagon's supercomputer.

When the Wind Blows (1986) A graphic novel by Raymond Briggs that shows the effects of a nuclear attack on a retired couple in the United Kingdom. It was made into an animated film in 2005.

'Z for Zachariah' (1974) The story of a 16-year-old girl who survives a nuclear war, by Robert O'Brien. It is to be made into a film in 2015.

Non-fiction

America's Atomic Bomb Tests (2005) A documentary looking at early Cold War American nuclear testing.

Beating the Bomb (2010) A documentary charting the history of the British peace movement and their campaigns against nuclear weapons.

Blowing up Paradise (2006) Archival footage chronicling French nuclear weapons testing in the South Pacific between the 1960s and the 1990s.

Countdown to Zero (2010) A documentary film warning against the growing threat of nuclear weapons, particularly from nuclear terrorism.

Duck and Cover (1951) An American civil defence film geared towards children.

Nuclear Tipping Point (2010) A documentary film making the case for the elimination of nuclear weapons.

Protect and Survive (2010) A collection of secret films made by the UK government in the 1970s providing information on what to do in the event of a nuclear war.

The Atomic Bomb Movie (1995) A documentary film telling the story of the development and testing of nuclear weapons between 1945 and 1964.

The Atomic Café (1982) A documentary film based on archival footage of the early atomic era.

BIBLIOGRAPHY

James Acton, 'Deterrence during disarmament: deep nuclear reductions and international security', Adelphi Paper 417, (London, Routledge for the International Institute for Strategic Studies: 2011)

Samina Ahmed, 'Pakistan's nuclear weapons programme: turning points and choices', International Security, 23:4 (1999) pp.178–204

Muthiah Alagappa (ed.), 'The long shadow: nuclear weapon and security in 21st century Asia', (Stanford, Stanford University Press: 2008)

David Albright, 'Peddling peril: how the secret nuclear trade arms America's enemies', (London, The Free Press: 2010)

David Albright, Paul Brannan & Andrea Schell-Stricker, 'Detecting and disrupting illicit nuclear trade after A.Q. Khan', The Washington Quarterly, 33:2 (2010) pp.85–106

David Albright, Kathryn Buehler & Holly Higgins, 'Bin Laden and the bomb', Bulletin of the Atomic Scientists, 58:1 (2002) pp.23–24

David Albright & Corey Hinderstein, 'Algeria: a big deal in the desert?', Bulletin of the Atomic Scientists, 57:3 (2001) pp.45–52

David Albright & Corey Hinderstein, 'Unravelling A.Q. Khan and future proliferation networks', The Washington Quarterly, 28:2 (2005) pp.111–128

Brian Alexander and Alistair Miller (eds.), 'Tactical nuclear weapons: emergent threats in an evolving security environment', (Dulles VA, Potomac Books Inc: 2003)

Svetlana Alexievich & Keith Gesen, 'Voices from Chernobyl: the oral history of a nuclear disaster', (New York, St. Martin's Press: 2006)

William Alley & Rosemarie Alley, 'Too hot to handle: the problem of high-level nuclear waste', (Cambridge, Cambridge University Press: 2012)

Graham Allison, 'Nuclear terrorism: the ultimate preventable catastrophe', (New York, Times Books: 2009 [2004])

Graham Allison, 'How to stop nuclear terror', Foreign Affairs, 83:1 (2004) pp.64–74

Graham Allison, Owen Cote, Steven Miller & Richard Falkenrath, 'Avoiding nuclear anarchy: containing the threat of loose Russian nuclear weapons and fissile material', (Cambridge, MA, The MIT Press: 1996)

Graham Allison & Phillip Zelikow, 'Essence of decision: explain the Cuban Missile Crisis', (Boston, MA, Little, Brown & Company: 1999 [1971])

Jason Andress & Steve Winterfeld, 'Cyber warfare: techniques, tactics and tools for security practitioners', (London, Syngress: 2011)

Ian Anthony, Christer Ahlstrom & Vitaly Fedchenko, 'Reforming nuclear export controls: the future of the Nuclear Suppliers Group', (Oxford, Oxford University Press: 2007)

David Armstrong and Joseph Trento, 'America and the Islamic bomb: the deadly compromise', (Hanover NH, Steerforth Press: 2007)

Laura Arnold, 'Britain, Australia and the H-bomb', (Basingstoke, Palgrave Macmillan: 2001)

Laura Arnold, 'Windscale 1957: anatomy of an accident', (Basingstoke, Palgrave Macmillan: 2007)

Jim Baggot, 'Atomic: the first war of physics and the secret history of the Atom Bomb 1939–49', (London, Icon Books Ltd: 2009)

Desmond Ball, 'The MX basing decision', Survival, 22:2 (1980) pp.58–65

Desmond Ball, 'Can a nuclear war be controlled?', (London, International Institute for Strategic Studies: 1981)

Howard Ball, 'Justice downwind: America's atomic testing program in the 1950s' (Oxford, Oxford University Press: 1986)

Frank Barnaby, 'How to build a nuclear bomb and other weapons of mass destruction', (London, Granta Books: 2003)

Frank Barnaby & Douglas Holdstock (eds.), 'The British nuclear weapons programme, 1952–2002', (London, Routledge: 2003)

Claudia Baumgart & Harald Müller, 'A nuclear weapons free zone in the Middle East: a pie in the sky?', Washington Quarterly, 28:1 (2004) pp.45–58

Andrea Berger & Malcolm Chalmers, 'Great expectations: the P5 process and the Non-Proliferation Treaty', RUSI Whitehall Report 3–13, (August 2013), www.rusi.org/downloads/assets/WHR_3-13_Web.pdf

Frans Berkhout, Oleg Bukharin, Harold Feiveson & Marvin Miller, 'A cutoff in the production of fissile material', International Security, 19:3 (1994–1995) pp.167–202

Barton J. Bernstein, 'The perils and politics of surrender: ending the war with Japan and avoiding the third atomic bomb', Pacific Historical Review, 46:1 (1977) pp.1–27

Jeremy Bernstein, 'Hitler's uranium club: the secret recordings at Farm Hall', (New York, Copernicus Books: 2001)

Jeremy Bernstein, 'Nuclear weapons: what you need to know', (Cambridge, Cambridge University Press: 2008)

Ken Berry, Patricia Lewis, Benoît Pélopidas, Nikolai Sokov & Ward Wilson, 'Delegitimizing nuclear weapons', (Monterey, CA, Center for Nonproliferation Studies, the Monterey Institute of International Studies: 2010)

Pierre Billaud & Venance Journé, 'The real story behind the making of the French hydrogen bomb: chaotic, unsupported, but successful', The Nonproliferation Review, 15:2 (2008) pp.353–372

Kai Bird & Martin Sherwin, "American Prometheus: the triumph and tragedy of J. Robert Oppenheimer', (London, Atlantic Books: 2009)

David Blades & Joseph Siracusa, 'A history of nuclear testing and its influence on nuclear thought', (Washington DC, Rowman & Littlefield: 2014)

Bruce Blair, 'The logic of accidental nuclear war', (Washington DC, The Brookings Institution Press: 1993)

David Blair, 'Iran's nuclear programme "may spark Middle East" weapons race', Telegraph, (20 May 2008), www.telegraph.co.uk/news/worldnews/middleeast/iran/1994117/Irans-nuclear-programme-may-spark-Middle-East-weapons-race.html

Stephen Blank (ed.), 'Russian nuclear weapons: past, present and future', (Carlisle Barracks PA, Strategic Studies Institute, U.S. Army War College: 2012)

Barry Blechman, 'Crawling towards nuclear zero', The Nonproliferation Review, 19:3 (2011) pp.597–600

Hans Blix, 'Verification of nuclear proliferation: the case of Iraq', The Washington Quarterly, 15:4 (1992) pp.57–65

Hans Blix, 'Why nuclear disarmament matters', (Cambridge MA, The MIT Press: 2008)

Paul Bolt & Albert Willner (eds.), 'China's nuclear future', (Boulder CO, Lynne Reiner: 2005)

Ken Booth & Nicholas Wheeler, 'The security dilemma: fear, cooperation and trust in world politics', (Basingstoke, Palgrave Macmillan: 2008)

John Borrie, 'Humanitarian reframing of nuclear weapons and the logic of a ban', International Affairs, 90:3 (2014) pp.625–646

John Borrie & Tim Caughlet (eds.), 'Viewing nuclear weapons through a humanitarian lens', (Geneva, Switzerland, The United Nations Institute for Disarmament Research: 2013)

Olivia Bosch & Peter Van Ham, 'Global non-proliferation and counter-terrorism: the impact of UNSCR 1540', (Washington DC, Brookings Institution Press: 2007)

Wyn Bowen, 'Libya and nuclear proliferation: stepping back from the brink', (London, Routledge for the International Institute for Strategic Studies: 2006)

Wyn Bowen & Jonathan Brewer, 'Iran's nuclear challenge: nine years and counting', International Affairs, 87:4 (2011) pp.923–943

Wyn Bowen, Matthew Cottee & Christopher Hobbs, "Multilateral cooperation and the prevention of nuclear terrorism: pragmatism over idealism", International Affairs, 88:2 (2012) pp.349–368

Paul Bracken, 'The command and control of nuclear forces', (New Haven CT, Yale University Press: 1983)

Paul Bracken, 'The second nuclear age: strategy, danger and the new power politics', (New York, St. Martin's Press: 2013)

Victor Bragin, John Carlson & John Hill, 'Verifying a fissile material production cut-off treaty', The Nonproliferation Review, 6:1 (1998) pp.97–107

Tania Branigan, 'North and South Korean navies exchange fire', Guardian, (10 November 2009), www.theguardian.com/world/2009/nov/10/north-korea-south-navy-ships-exchange-fire

William Broad, '"Tellers' war": the top secret story behind the star wars deception', (New York, Simon & Schuster: 1992)

William Broad, 'Why they called it the Manhattan Project', New York Times, (30 October 2007), www.nytimes.com/2007/10/30/science/30manh.html?pagewanted=all&_r=0

William Broad, John Markoff & David Sanger, 'Israeli test on worm called crucial in Iran nuclear delay', New York Times, (15 January 2011), www.nytimes.com/2011/01/16/world/middleeast/16stuxnet.html?pagewanted=all&_r=0

Bernard Brodie, 'Nuclear weapons: strategic or tactical?', Foreign Affairs, 32:3 (1954) pp.217–229

Bernard Brodie, 'The anatomy of deterrence', The RUSI Journal, 104:613 (1959) pp.32–44

Bernard Brodie, 'Escalation and the nuclear option', (Princeton NJ, Princeton University Press: 1966)

Bernard Brodie, 'The development of nuclear strategy', International Security, 2:4 (1978) pp.65–83

Bernard Brodie, 'Strategy in the missile age', (Santa Monica CA, The RAND Corporation: 2008 [1959])

Bernard Brodie, Frederick Dunn, Arnold Wolfers, Percy Corbett & William Fox, 'The absolute weapon: atomic power and world order', (New York, Harcourt: 1946)

Harold Brown, 'The strategic defense initiative: defensive systems and the strategic debate', Survival, 27:2 (1985) pp.55–64

Kate Brown 'Plutopia: nuclear families, atomic cities, and the great Soviet and American plutonium disasters' (New York, Oxford University Press: 2013)

Michael Brown, Owen Cote, Sean Lynn-Jones & Steven Miller, 'Going nuclear: nuclear proliferation in the 21st century', (London, The MIT Press: 2010)

Hedley Bull, 'The control of the arms race', (Westport CT, Praeger: 1961)

Richard Dean Burns & Lester H. Brune, 'The quest for missile defenses, 1944–2003', (Claremont CA, Regina Books: 2003)

Richard Dean Burns & Joseph Siracusa, 'A global history of the nuclear arms race: weapons, strategy, and politics', (Santa Barbara CA, Praeger Security International: 2013)

Declan Butler, 'France seeks to clean up nuclear image', Nature, 380:6569 (1996)

Daniel Byman, 'Iran, terrorism and weapons of mass destruction', Studies in Conflict & Terrorism, 31:3 (2008) pp.169–181

Kurt Campbell, Robert Einhorn & Mitchell Reiss (eds.), 'The nuclear tipping point: why states reconsider their nuclear choices', (Washington DC, The Brookings Institution Press: 2004)

Julio Carasales, John Redick & Paulo Wrobel, 'Nuclear rapprochement: Argentina, Brazil, and the nonproliferation regime', The Washington Quarterly, 18:1 (1995) pp.107–122

Mario Carranza, 'An impossible game: stable nuclear deterrence after the Indian and Pakistani tests', The Nonproliferation Review 6:3 (1999) pp.11–24

Mario Carranza, 'From non-proliferation to post-proliferation: explaining the US–India nuclear deal', Contemporary Security Policy, 28.3 (2007) pp.464–493

Ashton Carter, John Steinbruner & Charles Zraket, 'Managing nuclear options', (Washington DC, The Brookings Institution Press: 2001)

Victor Cha, 'The second nuclear age: proliferation pessimism versus sober optimism in South Asia and East Asia', Journal of Strategic Studies, 24:2 (2001) pp.79–120

Bhumitra Chakma (ed.), 'The politics of nuclear weapons in South Asia', (Farnham, Ashgate: 2011)

Malcolm Chalmers, "Bombs away"? Britain and nuclear weapons under New Labour', Security Dialogue, 30:1 (1999) pp.61–74

Malcolm Chalmers, 'Towards the UK's nuclear century', The RUSI Journal, 158:6 (2013) pp.18–28

Malcolm Chalmers & William Walker, 'Unchartered waters: the UK, nuclear weapons and the Scottish question', (East Lothian, Tuckwell Press: 2001)

Malcolm Chalmers & William Walker, 'Will Scotland sink the United Kingdom's nuclear deterrent?', The Washington Quarterly, 36:3 (2013) pp.107–122

Glenn Alan Cheney, 'They never knew: the victims of nuclear testing', (Jacksonville FL, Franklin Watts: 1996)

Mike Chinoy, 'Meltdown: the inside story of the North Korean nuclear crisis', (New York, St. Martin's Press: 2009)

Jae Ho Chung & Myung-hae Choi, 'Uncertain allies or uncomfortable neighbors? Making sense of China–North Korea relations, 1949–2010', The Pacific Review, 26:3 (2013) pp.243–264

Shahram Chubin, 'Does Iran want nuclear weapons?', Survival, 37:1 (1995) pp.86–104

Stephen Cimbala, 'Shield of dreams: missile defense and US–Russian nuclear strategy', (Annapolis MD, Naval Institute Press: 2008)

Stephen Cimbala, 'New START or not? US–Russia nuclear arms reductions in perspective', Comparative Strategy, 29:3 (2010) pp.260–277

Stephen Cimbala, 'Nuclear crisis management and "cyberwar": phishing for trouble?', Strategic Studies Quarterly, Spring (2011) pp.117-131

Stephen Cimbala, 'Nuclear weapons in the information age', (London, Continuum International Publishing Group: 2012)

Joseph Cirincione, 'Bomb scare: the history and future of nuclear weapons', (New York, Columbia University Press: 2007)

Rodger Claire, 'Raid on the sun: inside Israel's secret campaign that denied Saddam the bomb', (Random House Digital, Inc: 2004)

Ian Clarke, 'Limited nuclear war: political theory and war conventions', (Princeton NJ, Princeton University Press: 1982)

Richard Clarke & Robert Knake, 'Cyber war: the next threat to national security and what to do about it', (New York, HarperCollins: 2010)

Daniel Clery, 'A piece of the sun: the quest for fusion energy', (London, Gerald Duckworth & Co. Ltd: 2013)

Andrew Cockburn & Leslie Cockburn, 'One point safe', (New York, Little, Brown & Company: 1997)

Anver Cohen, 'Israel and the bomb', (New York, Columbia University Press: 1998)

Anver Cohen, 'The worst kept secret: Israel's bargain with the bomb', (New York, Columbia University Press: 2010)

Anver Cohen & Joseph Pilat, 'Assessing virtual nuclear arsenals', Survival, 40:1 (1998) pp.129–144

Anver Cohen & Marvin Miller, 'Bringing Israel's bomb out of the basement: has nuclear ambiguity outlived its shelf life?', Foreign Affairs, 89:5 (2010) pp.30–44

Yoel Cohen, 'Whistleblowers and the bomb: Vanunu, Israel and nuclear secrecy', (London, Pluto Press: 2005)

Paul Cole, 'Atomic bombast: nuclear weapons decision making in Sweden 1946–72', The Washington Quarterly, 20:2 (1997) pp.233–251

Craig Collie, 'Nagasaki: the massacre of the innocent and unknowing', (London, Portobello Books: 2011)

Tom Collina & Daryl Kimball, 'Going back: 20 years since the last US nuclear test', The Arms Control Association Issue Brief, 3:14 (20 September 2012), http://armscontrol.org/issue-briefs/No-Going-Back-20-Years-Since-the-Last-US-Nuclear-Test

Jean Conant, '109 East Palace: Robert Oppenheimer and the secret city of Los Alamos', (New York, Simon & Schuster: 2005)

Gordon Corera, 'Shopping for bombs: nuclear proliferation, global insecurity and the rise and fall of the A.Q. Khan network', (London, Hurst & Company: 2006)

David Cortright & Raimo Vayrynen, 'Towards nuclear zero', Adelphi Paper 410, (London, Routledge for the International Institute for Strategic Studies: 2010)

Campbell Craig and Sergey Radchenko, 'The atomic bomb and the origins of the Cold War', (New Haven CT, Yale University Press: 2008)

Peter Crail, 'Implementing UN Security Council resolution 1540: a risk-based approach', Nonproliferation Review, 13:2 (2006) pp.355–399

Ivo Daalder & Jan Lodal, 'The logic of zero: toward a world without nuclear weapons', Foreign Affairs, 87:6 (2008) pp.80–95

Ola Dahlman, Svein Mykkwltveit & Hein Haak, 'Nuclear test ban: converting political visions into reality', (New York, Springer: 2009)

Tracey Davies, 'Stages of emergency: Cold War nuclear civil defense', (Durham NC, Duke University Press: 2007)

Lynn Davis, 'Lessons of the INF treaty', Foreign Affairs, 56:4 (1988) pp.720–734

Therese Delpech, 'Nuclear deterrence in the 21st century: lessons for a new era of strategic piracy', (Santa Monica CA, RAND Corporation: 2012)

Anatoli Diakov, Eugene Miasnikov & Timur Kadyshev, 'Nuclear reductions after New START: obstacles and opportunities', Arms Control Today, 41:4 (2011) pp.15–22

Jane Dibblin, 'Day of two suns: US nuclear testing and the pacific islanders', (New York, New Amsterdam Books: 1990)

Michael Dobbs, 'One minute to midnight: Kennedy, Khrushchev and Castro on the brink of nuclear war', (London, Arrow: 2009)

Joel Dobson, 'The Goldsboro broken arrow: the B52 crash of January 24, 1961, and its potential as a tipping point for nuclear war', (lulu.com: 2013)

The Economist, 'North Korea: bad or mad? Kim Jong Un is likely to realise his nuclear ambitions, but the two sides already face military stalemate', (26 October 2013), www.economist.com/news/special-report/21588196-kim-jong-un-likely-realise-his-nuclear-ambitions-two-sides-already-face

Eric Edelman, Andrew Krepinevich & Evan Braden Montgomery, 'The dangers of a nuclear Iran', Foreign Affairs, 90:1 (2011) pp.66–81

Rob Edwards, 'Swiss planned nuclear bomb', New Scientist, 2031, (25 May 1996)

Mohamed ElBaradei, 'The age of deception: nuclear diplomacy in treacherous times', (London, Bloomsbury: 2011)

David Fairhall, 'Common ground: the true story of Greenham', (London, I.B. Tauris & Co. Ltd: 2006)

Nazila Fathi, 'Iran's Ayatollah affirms peaceful nuclear plans', New York Times, (19 January 2006), www.nytimes.com/2006/01/19/international/middleeast/19iran.html

Peter Feaver, 'Guarding the guardians: civilian control of nuclear weapons in the United States', (London, Cornell University Press: 1992)

Peter Feaver, 'Command and control in emerging nuclear nations', International Security, 17:3 (1992) pp.160–189

Charles Ferguson, 'The long road to zero', Foreign Affairs, 89:4 (2010) pp.86–94

Charles Ferguson, 'Nuclear energy: what everyone needs to know', (Oxford, Oxford University Press: 2011)

Charles Ferguson & William Potter, 'The four faces of nuclear terrorism', (London, Routledge: 2005)

Mark Fitzpatrick, 'Can Iran's nuclear capability be kept latent?', Survival, 49:1 (2007) pp.33–58

Mark Fitzpatrick, Alexander Nikitin & Sergey Oznobischev, 'Nuclear doctrines and strategies', (London, IOS Press: 2008)

Christopher Ford, 'Debating disarmament: interpreting Article VI of the Treaty on the Non-Proliferation of Nuclear Weapons', The Nonproliferation Review, 14:3 (2007) pp.401–428

Philip Fradkin, 'Fallout: an American nuclear tragedy', (Boulder CO, Johnson Books: 2004)

Benjamin Frankel (ed.), 'Opaque nuclear proliferation: methodological and policy implications', (London, Frank Cass & Company Ltd: 1991)

M. Taylor Fravel & Evan Medeiros, 'China's search for assured retaliation: the evolution of Chinese nuclear strategy and force structure', International Security, 35:2 (2010) pp.48–87

Lawrence Freedman, 'The evolution and future of extended nuclear deterrence', Adelphi Papers, 29:236 (1989) pp.18–31

Lawrence Freedman, 'Prevention, not preemption', The Washington Quarterly, 26:2 (2003) pp.105–114

Lawrence Freedman, 'The evolution of nuclear strategy', (Basingstoke, Palgrave Macmillan: 2003)

Lawrence Freedman, 'Deterrence', (Cambridge, Polity Press: 2004)

Lawrence Freedman, 'Disarmament and other nuclear norms', The Washington Quarterly, 36:2 (2013) pp.93–108

Robin Frost, 'Nuclear terrorism after 9-11', Adelphi Paper 378, (Abingdon, Routledge for the International Institute for Strategic Studies: 2005)

Michael Fry & Patrick Keating (eds.), 'Nuclear non-proliferation and the non-proliferation treaty', (New York, Springer-Verlag: 1990)

Matthew Fuhrmann, 'Spreading temptation: proliferation and peaceful nuclear cooperation agreements', International Security, 34:1 (2009) pp.7–41

Matthew Fuhrman, 'Atomic assistance: how "Atoms for Peace" programs cause nuclear instability', (London, Cornell University Press: 2012)

Matthew Fuhrman, 'Splitting atoms: why do countries build nuclear power plants?', International Interactions, 38:1 (2012) pp.29–57

Matthew Fuhrmann & Bryan Early, 'Following START: risk acceptance and the 1991–1992 presidential nuclear initiatives', Foreign Policy Analysis, 4:1 (2008) pp.21–43

Matthew Fuhrmann & Todd Sechser, 'Signaling alliance commitments: hand-tying and sunk costs in extended nuclear deterrence', American Journal of Political Science, (2014)

Alexandr Fursenko & Timothy Naftali, 'One hell of a gamble: Khrushchev, Castro, and Kennedy, 1958–1964: the secret history of the Cuban Missile Crisis', (New York, W.W. Norton & Company: 2001 [1997])

Andrew Futter, 'Getting the balance right: US ballistic missile defense and nuclear nonproliferation', Comparative Strategy, 30:3 (2011) pp.254–267

Andrew Futter, 'Ballistic missile defence and US national security policy', (London, Routledge: 2013)

Andrew Futter & Benjamin Zala, 'Advanced US conventional weapons and nuclear disarmament', The Nonproliferation Review, 20:1 (2013) pp.107–122

Robert Gale, 'Radiation: what it is, what you need to know', (New York, Vintage Books: 2013)

Carole Gallagher, 'American ground zero: the secret nuclear war', (Cambridge MA, MIT Press: 1993)

Pierre Gallios, 'The balance of terror: strategy for the nuclear age', (Boston MA, Houghton Mifflin: 1961)

Sumit Ganguly & Devin Hagerty, 'Fearful symmetry: India–Pakistan crises in the shadow of nuclear weapons', (Seattle WA, University of Washington Press: 2005)

Samit Ganguly & S. Paul Kapur (eds.), 'Nuclear proliferation in South Asia: crisis behaviour and the Bomb', (Abingdon, Routledge: 2010)

Samit Ganguly & S. Paul Kapur, 'India, Pakistan and the bomb: debating nuclear stability in South Asia', (New York, Columbia University Press: 2012)

Dee Garrison, 'Bracing for Armageddon: why civil defense never worked', (New York, Oxford University Press: 2006)

Anne Gearan & Joby Warrick, 'Iran, world powers reach historic nuclear deal', The Washington Post, (23 November 2013), www.washingtonpost.com/world/national-security/kerry-in-geneva-raising-hopes-for-historic-nuclear-deal-with-iran/2013/11/23/53e7bfe6-5430-11e3-9fe0-fd2ca728e67c_story.html

Paul Gibson, 'Nuclear weapons of the United States: an illustrated history', (Atglen PA, Schiffer Publishing Ltd: 1996)

Samuel Glasstone & Philip Dolan, 'The effects of nuclear weapons', (United States Department of Defense: 1977)

Ami Gluska, 'The Israeli military and the origins of the 1967 war: government, armed forces and defence policy 1963–67', (Abingdon, Routledge: 2006)

Patrick Glynn, 'Closing Pandora's box: arms races, arms control, and the history of the Cold War', (New York, Basic Books: 1992)

Dore Gold, 'The rise of nuclear Iran: how Tehran defies the west', (Washington DC, Regnery Publishing Inc: 2009)

Jozef Goldblat, 'Nuclear free zones: a history and assessment', The Nonproliferation Review, 4:3 (1997) pp.18–32

Margaret Gowing, 'Britain and atomic energy 1939–1945', (London, Palgrave Macmillan: 1964)

Matthew Grant, 'After the bomb: civil defence and nuclear war in Britain, 1945–68', (Basingstoke, Palgrave Macmillan: 2010)

Colin Gray, 'Nuclear strategy: the case for a new theory of victory', International Security, 4:1 (1979) pp.54–87

Colin Gray, 'The second nuclear age', (Boulder CO, Lynne Rienner Publishers: 1999)

Colin Gray & Keith Payne, 'Victory is possible', Foreign Policy, 39 (1980) pp.14–27

Owen Greene, Barry Rubin Neil Turok, Philip Webber & Graeme Wilkinson, 'London after the bomb: what a nuclear attack really means', (New York: Oxford University Press, 1982)

Owen Greene, Ian Percival and Irene Ridge, 'Nuclear winter: the evidence and the risks', (Cambridge, Polity Press: 1985)

Shaun Gregory, 'The hidden cost of nuclear deterrence: nuclear weapons accidents', (London, Brassey's Ltd: 1990)

Shaun Gregory, 'The terrorist threat to nuclear weapons in Pakistan', European Leadership Network, (4 June 2013), www.europeanleadershipnetwork.org/the-terrorist-threat-to-nuclear-weapons-in-pakistan_613.html

Gerald de Groot, 'The bomb: a life', (London, Jonathan Cape: 2004)

Leslie Groves, 'Now it can be told: the story of the Manhattan Project', (Cambridge MA, Da Capo Press: 1983)

David Halberstam, 'The coldest winter: America and the Korean War', (London, Pan Macmillan Ltd: 2009)

Paul Ham, 'Hiroshima Nagasaki: the real story of the atomic bombings and their aftermath', (London, Transworld Publishers: 2013)

Michael Hamel-Green, 'Nuclear weapon-free zone initiatives: challenges and opportunities for regional cooperation on non-proliferation', The Nonproliferation Review, 21:3 (2009) pp.357–376

Susan Allen Hannah, 'The determinants of economic sanctions success and failure', International Interactions, 31:2 (2005) pp.117–138

Keith Hansen, 'The Comprehensive Test Ban Treaty: an insider's perspective', (Stanford, Stanford University Press: 2006)

Marianne Hanson, 'The future of the NPT 1', Australian Journal of International Affairs, 59:3 (2005) pp.301–316

Matthew Harries, 'Britain and France as nuclear partners', Survival, 54:1 (2012) pp.7–30

Mark Harwell, 'Nuclear winter: the human and environmental consequences of nuclear war', (New York, Springer-Verlag: 1984)

Jason Healy (ed.), 'A fierce domain: conflict in cyber space, 1986 to 2012', (USA, Cyber Conflict Studies Association: 2013)

Siegfried Hecker & William Lious, 'Dangerous dealings: North Korea's nuclear capabilities and the threat of export to Iran', Arms Control Today, 37:2 (March 2007)

Yoaz Hendel, 'Iran's nukes and Israel's dilemma', Middle East Quarterly, (Winter 2012) pp.31–38

Peter Hennessey, 'The hidden state: preparing for the worst 1945–2010', (London, Penguin Books Ltd: 2010)

Greg Herken, 'The brotherhood of the bomb: the tangled lives and loyalties of Robert Oppenheimer, Ernest Lawrence, and Edward Teller', (Basingstoke, Macmillan: 2003)

John Hersey, 'Hiroshima', (London, Penguin Books: 2001)

Seymour Hersh, 'The Samson option: Israel's nuclear arsenal and American foreign policy', (New York, Random House: 1991)

Seymour Hersh, 'A reporter at large: on the nuclear edge', The New Yorker, (29 March 1993) www.newyorker.com/archive/1993/03/29/1993_03_29_056_TNY_CARDS_000363214

Rudolph Herzog, 'A short history of nuclear folly', (London, Melville House: 2013)

Richard Hewlett & Jack Holl, 'Atoms for peace and war, 1945–1961', (Berkeley CA, University of California Press: 1992)

Mark Hibbs, 'Will South Korea go nuclear?', Foreign Policy, (15 March 2013), www.foreign-policy.com/articles/2013/03/15/will_south_korea_go_nuclear

Christopher Hill, 'The elusive vision of a non-nuclear North Korea', The Washington Quarterly, 36.2 (2013) pp.7–19

Theodore Hirsch, 'The IAEA Additional Protocol: what it is and why it matters', The Nonproliferation Review, 11:3 (2004) pp.140–166

HM Government, 'Trident Alternatives Review', (16 July 2013), www.gov.uk/government/uploads/system/uploads/attachment_data/file/212745/20130716_Trident_Alternatives_Study.pdf

Christopher Hobbs & Matthew Moran, 'Nuclear dominoes: exploring regional responses to a nuclear Iran', (Basingstoke, Palgrave Macmillan: 2013)

David Hoffman, 'Dead hand: Reagan, Gorbachev and the untold story of the Cold War arms race', (London, Icon Books Ltd: 2011)

Daniel Horner, 'South Korea, US at odds over nuclear pact', Arms Control Today, (September 2012), www.armscontrol.org/act/2012_09/Sout-Korea-US-at-Odds-Over-Nuclear-Pact

Michael Howard, 'On fighting a nuclear war', International Security, 5:4 (1981) pp.3–17

Roger Howard, 'Operation Damocles: Israel's secret war against Hitler's scientists, 1951–1967', (New York, Open Road Media: 2013)

Kate Hudson 'CND – now more than ever: the story of a peace movement' (London, Vision Paperbacks: 2005)

Jacques Hymans, 'The psychology of nuclear proliferation: identity, emotions and foreign policy', (Cambridge, Cambridge University Press: 2006)

Jacques Hymans, 'Theories of nuclear proliferation: the state of the field', The Nonproliferation Review, 13:3 (2006) pp.455–465

Jacques Hymans, 'When does a state become a nuclear weapon state? An exercise in measurement validation', The Nonproliferation Review, 17:1 (2010) pp.161–180

Jacques Hymans, 'Achieving nuclear ambitions: scientists, politicians and proliferation', (Cambridge, Cambridge University Press: 2012)

Fred Ikle, 'The coming of the second nuclear age', Foreign Affairs, 75:1 (1996) pp.119–128

Maxwell Irvine, 'Nuclear power: a very short introduction', (Oxford, Oxford University Press: 2011)

Igor Ivanov, 'The missile-defense mistake: undermining strategic stability and the ABM Treaty', Foreign Affairs, 79:5 (2000) pp.5–20

Alireza Jafarzadeh, 'The Iran threat: President Ahmadinejad and the coming nuclear crisis', (New York, Palgrave Macmillan: 2007)

Detlef Jahn & Sebastian Korolczuk, 'German exceptionalism: the end of nuclear energy in Germany!', Environmental Politics, 21:1 (2012) pp.159–164

Douglas Jehl, 'CIA nominee wary of budget cuts', New York Times, (3 February 1993), www.nytimes.com/1993/02/03/us/cia-nominee-wary-of-budget-cuts.html

Bruce Jentleson & Christopher Whytock, 'Who "won" Libya? The force-diplomacy debate and its implications for theory and policy', International Security, 30:3 (2005/06) pp.47–86

Robert Jervis, 'Perception and misperception in international politics' (Princeton NJ, Princeton University Press: 1976)

Robert Jervis, 'Cooperation under the security dilemma', World Politics, 30:2 (1978) pp.167–214

Robert Jervis, 'The meaning of the nuclear revolution: statecraft and the prospect of Armageddon', (Ithaca NY, Cornell University Press: 1989)

Shashank Joshi, 'The permanent crisis: Iran's nuclear trajectory', (Abingdon, Routledge for the Royal United Services Institute: 2012)

Shashank Joshi, 'Pakistan's tactical nuclear nightmare: déjà vu?', The Washington Quarterly, 36:3 (2013) pp.159–172

Daniel Joyner, 'Interpreting the Non-proliferation Treaty', (Oxford, Oxford University Press: 2011)

Colin Kahl & Kenneth Waltz, 'Iran and the bomb: would a nuclear Iran make the Middle East more secure?', Foreign Affairs, 91:5 (2012) pp.157–162

Chen Kane 'Detecting nuclear weapons: the IAEA and the politics of proliferation' (Basingstoke, Routledge: 2015)

S. Paul Kapur, 'India and Pakistan's unstable peace: why nuclear South Asia is not like Cold War Europe', International Security, 30:2 (2005) pp.127–152

David Karl, 'Proliferation pessimism and emerging nuclear powers', International Security, 21:3 (1996) pp.87–119

Michael Karpin, 'The bomb in the basement: how Israel went nuclear and what it means for the world', (London, Simon & Schuster: 2006)

Kerry Kartchner, 'Negotiating START: Strategic Arms Reduction Treaty and the Quest for Strategic Stability', (Piscataway NJ, Transaction Publishers, 1992)

Milton Katz, 'Ban the bomb: a history of SANE, the Committee for a Sane Nuclear Policy, 1957–1985', (Westport CT, Greenwood Press: 1986)

Scott Kaufman, 'Project Plowshare: the peaceful use of nuclear explosives in Cold War America', (New York, Cornell University Press: 2012)

Cynthia Kelly (ed.), 'The Manhattan Project: The birth of the atomic bomb in the words of its creators, eyewitnesses, and historians', (New York: Black Dog & Leventhal Publishers: 2007)

R. Scott Kemp, 'The nonproliferation emperor has no clothes: the gas centrifuge, supply-side controls, and the future of nuclear proliferation', International Security 38:4 (2014) pp.39–78

Ian Kenyon & John Simpson (eds.) 'Deterrence and the new global security environment', (Abingdon, Routledge: 2006)

Feroz Hassan Khan, 'Challenges to nuclear stability in South Asia', The Nonproliferation Review, 10:1 (2003) pp.59–74

Feroz Hassan Khan, 'Eating grass: the making of the Pakistani bomb', (Stanford, Stanford University Press: 2012)

Herman Khan, 'Thinking about the unthinkable in the 1980s', (New York, Simon & Schuster: 1984)

Herman Khan, 'On thermonuclear war', (Piscataway NJ, Transaction Publishers: 2007 [1960])

Saria Khan, 'Iran and nuclear weapons: protracted conflict and proliferation', (Abingdon, Routledge: 2010)

Zafar Khan, 'Cold Start doctrine: the conventional challenge to South Asian stability', Contemporary Security Policy, 33:3 (2012) pp.577–594

Scott Kirsch, 'Proving grounds: Project Plowshare and the unrealized dream of nuclear earthmoving', (Piscataway NJ, Rutgers University Press: 2005)

Henry Kissinger, 'Nuclear weapons and foreign policy', (New York, Harper & Brothers: 1957)

Jeffrey Knopf, 'Recasting the proliferation optimism-pessimism debate', Security Studies, 12:1 (2002) pp.41–96

Jeffrey Knopf, 'Nuclear disarmament and nonproliferation: examining the linkage argument', International Security, 37:3 (2012) pp.92–132

Dean Kohlhoff, 'Amchitka and the bomb: nuclear testing in Alaska', (Seattle WA, University of Washington Press: 2003)

Sarah Kreps & Matthew Fuhrmann, 'Attacking the atom: does bombing nuclear facilities affect proliferation?', The Journal of Strategic Studies, 34:2 (2011) pp.161–187

Hans Kristensen & Robert Norris, 'Indian nuclear forces, 2012', Bulletin of the Atomic Scientists, 68:4 (2012) pp.96–101

Matthew Kroenig, 'Exporting the bomb: technology transfer and the spread of nuclear weapons', (Ithaca NY, Cornell University Press: 2010)

A. Vinod Kumar, 'India and the nuclear non-proliferation regime: the perennial outlier', (Cambridge, Cambridge University Press: 2014)

William Langewiesche, 'The atomic bazaar: dispatches from the underground world of nuclear trafficking', (London, Penguin Books Ltd: 2007)

Jeffrey Larsen & James Smith, 'Historical dictionary of arms control', (Oxford, Scarecrow Press, Inc.: 2005)

Thomas Lehrman, 'Rethinking interdiction: the future of the proliferation security initiative', The Nonproliferation Review, 11:2 (2004) pp.1–45

Paul Lettow, 'Ronald Reagan and his quest to abolish nuclear weapons', (New York, Random House: 2005)

Paul Leventhal & Sharon Tanzer (eds.) 'Averting a Latin American nuclear arms race', (New York, St. Martin's Press: 1992)

Michael Levi, 'On nuclear terrorism', (New York, Council on Foreign Relations: 2007)

Michael Levi & Michael O'Hanlon, 'The future of arms control', (Washington DC, The Brookings Institution Press: 2005)

Jeffrey Lewis, 'The minimum means of reprisal China's search for security in the nuclear age', (Cambridge MA, The MIT Press: 2007)

Patricia Lewis, 'A Middle East free of nuclear weapons: possible, probable or pipe dream?', International Affairs, 89:2 (2013) pp.433–450

Peter Liberman, 'The rise and fall of the South African bomb', International Security, 26:1 (2006) pp.45–86

Kier Lieber & Daryl Press, 'Why states won't give the bomb to terrorists', International Security, 38:1 (2013) pp.80–104

Robert Lifton, 'Destroying the world to save it: Aum Shinrikyo, apocalyptic violence and the new global terrorism', (New York, Henry Holt & Company Inc.: 2000)

James Lindsay & Ray Takeyh, 'After Iran gets the bomb: containment and its complications', Foreign Affairs, 89:2 (2010) pp.33–50

Robert Litwak, 'Non-proliferation and the dilemmas of regime change', Survival 45:4 (2003) pp.7–32

David Lochbaum, Edwin Lyman & Susan Stranahan, 'Fukushima: the story of a disaster' (New York, New Press: 2014)

Sverre Lodgaard, 'Nuclear disarmament and non-proliferation: towards a nuclear-weapon-free world', (London, Routledge: 2011)

George Lopez & David Cortright, 'Containing Iraq: sanctions worked', Foreign Affairs, 84:3 (2004) pp.90–103

Kenneth Luongo, 'Loose nukes in new neighborhoods: the next generation of proliferation prevention', Arms Control Today, May 2009, www.armscontrol.org/act/2009_5/Luongo

Ewen MacAskill & Chris McGreal, 'Israel should be wiped off map, says Iran's president', The Guardian, (27 October 2005), www.theguardian.com/world/2005/oct/27/israel.iran

Richard Macey, 'Laser enrichment could cut cost of nuclear power', The Sydney Morning Herald, (27 May 2006), www.smh.com.au/news/national/laser-enrichment-could-cut-cost-of-nuclear-power/2006/05/26/1148524888448.html

Jenifer Mackby & Paul Cornish (eds.), 'US–UK nuclear cooperation after 50 years', (Washington DC, The CSIS Press: 2008)

Shane Maddock, 'Nuclear Apartheid: the quest for American atomic supremacy from World War II to the present', (Chapel Hill NC, University of North Carolina Press: 2010)

Morten Bremer Maerli & Sverre Lodgaard (eds.), 'Nuclear proliferation and international security', (London, Routledge: 2007)

Arnav Manchanda, 'When truth is stranger than fiction: the Able Archer incident', Cold War History, 9:1 (2009) pp.111–133

Michael Mandelbaum & Strobe Talbott, 'Reykjavik and beyond', Foreign Affairs, 65:2 (1986) pp.215–235

Oishi Matashichi, 'The day the sun rose in the west: Bikini, the Lucky Dragon, and I', (Honolulu HI, University of Hawaii Press: 2011)

Randall Maydew & Julie Bush, 'America's lost H-bomb: Palomares, Spain, 1966', (Manhattan KS, Sunflower University Press: 1997)

Michael Mazaar, 'Nuclear weapons in a transformed world: the challenge of virtual nuclear arsenals', (Basingstoke, Macmillan Press: 1997)

Catherine McArdle Kelleher & Judith Riply (eds.), 'Getting to zero: the path to nuclear disarmament', (Stanford CA, Stanford University Press: 2011)

David McDonough, 'Nuclear superiority: the "new triad" and the evolution of nuclear strategy', Adelphi Paper 383, (Abingdon, Routledge for the International Institute for Strategic Studies: 2006)

Raja Menon, 'A mismatch of nuclear doctrines', The Hindu, (22 January 2014), www.thehindu.com/opinion/op-ed/a-mismatch-of-nuclear-doctrines/article5602609.ece

David Meyer, 'A winter of discontent: the nuclear freeze and American politics', (New York, Praeger Publishers: 1990)

Zia Mian & A.H. Nayar, 'Playing the nuclear game: Pakistan and the Fissile Material Cut-off Treaty', Arms Control Today, (April 2010), www.armscontrol.org/act/2010_04/Mian

Richard Miller, 'Under the cloud: the decades of nuclear testing', (The Woodlands TX, Two Sixty Press: 1991)

Walter Miscamble, 'The most controversial decision: Truman, the atomic bombs and the defeat of Japan', (Cambridge, Cambridge University Press: 2011)

Zeev Maoz, 'The mixed blessing of Israel's nuclear policy', International Security, 28:2 (2003) pp.44–77

James Clay Moltz, 'Future nuclear proliferation scenarios in Northeast Asia', The Nonproliferation Review, 13:3 (2006) pp.591–604

James Clay Moltz and Alexander Mansourov (eds.) 'The North Korean nuclear program: security, strategy and new perspectives from Russia" (New York, Routledge: 2012)

Barabara Moran, 'The day we lost the H-bomb: Cold War, hot nukes and the worst nuclear weapons disaster in history', (New York, Random House: 2009)

Matthew Moran & Matthew Cottee, 'Bound by history? Exploring challenges to French nuclear disarmament', Defense & Security Analysis, 27:4 (2011) pp.341–357

RF Mould, 'Chernobyl record: the definitive history of the Chernobyl catastrophe', (London, Institute of Physics Publishing: 2000)

John Mueller, 'Atomic obsession: nuclear alarmism from Hiroshima to Al-Qaeda', (Oxford, Oxford University Press: 2010)

John Mueller & Karl Mueller, 'Sanctions of mass destruction', Foreign Affairs, 78:3 (1999) pp.43–53

Harald Müller, 'The future of nuclear weapons in an interdependent world', The Washington Quarterly, 31:2 (2008) pp.63–75

Harald Müller, 'The 2010 NPT review conference: some breathing space gained, but no breakthrough', The International Spectator, 45:3 (2010) pp.5–18

Harald Müller, 'A nuclear non-proliferation test: Obama's nuclear policy and the 2010 NPT Review Conference', The Nonproliferation Review, 18:1 (2011) pp.219–236

Harald Müller & Carmen Wunderlich, 'Norm dynamics in multilateral arms control' (Athens GA, University of Georgia Press: 2013)

Vipin Narang, 'Five myths about India's nuclear posture', The Washington Quarterly, 36:3 (2013) pp.143–157

John Newhouse, 'Cold dawn: The story of SALT', (New York, Holt, Rinehart & Winston: 1973)

John Newhouse, 'The nuclear age: from Hiroshima to Star Wars', (London, Michael Joseph: 1989)

Paul Nitze, 'The relationship of strategic and theatre nuclear forces', International Security, 2:2 (1977) pp.122–132

Olav Njolstad (ed.), 'Nuclear proliferation and international order: challenges to the Non-Proliferation Treaty', (Abingdon, Routledge: 2011)

Janne Nolan, 'Guardians of the arsenal', (New York, Basic Books Inc: 1989)

Polmar Norman & Robert Norris, 'The U.S. nuclear arsenal: a history of weapons and delivery systems since 1945', (Annapolis MD, Naval Institute Press: 2009)

Robert Norris & Hans Kristensen, 'Global nuclear weapons inventories, 1945–2010', Bulletin of the Atomic Scientists, 66:7 (July/August 2010) pp.77–83

Robert Norris & Hans Kristensen, 'US tactical nuclear weapons in Europe, 2011', Bulletin of the Atomic Scientists, 67:1 (2011) pp.64–73

Robert Norris & Hans Kristensen, 'The British nuclear stockpile 1953–2013', Bulletin of the Atomic Scientists, 69:4 (2013) pp.69–75

Joseph Nye, 'Nuclear ethics', (New York: The Free Press: 1986)

Joseph Nye, 'From bombs to bytes: can our nuclear history inform our cyber future?', Bulletin of the Atomic Scientists, 69:8 (2013) pp.8–14

Mahdi Obeidi & Kurt Pitzer, 'The bomb in my garden: the secrets of Saddam's nuclear mastermind', (Hoboken NJ, John Wiley & Sons: 2004)

Tanya Ogilvie-White, 'Is there a theory of nuclear proliferation: an analysis of the contemporary debate', The Nonproliferation Review, 4:1 (1996) pp.43–60

Michael O'Hanlon, 'A skeptic's case for nuclear disarmament', (Washington DC, Brookings Institution Press: 2010)

Harsh Pant, 'The US–India nuclear pact: policy, process, and great power politics', (New Delhi, Oxford University Press: 2011)

Jan Parawitz, 'Nuclear option to non-nuclear promotion: the Sweden case', (Stockholm, Swedish Institute for International Affairs: 1995)

Robert Paterson, 'Britain's strategic nuclear deterrent: from before the V-bomber to beyond Trident' (Abingdon, Routledge: 1997)

T.V. Paul, 'Power versus prudence: why nations forgo nuclear weapons', (Montreal, McGill-Queen's University Press: 2000)

T.V. Paul, 'The tradition of non-use of nuclear weapons', (Stanford, Stanford University Press: 2009)

Keith Payne, 'Deterrence in the second nuclear age', (Lexington KT, The University of Kentucky Press: 1996)

George Perkovich, 'India's nuclear bomb: the impact on global proliferation', (London, University of California Press: 2002)

George Perkovich & James Acton, 'Abolishing nuclear weapons', Adelphi Paper 396, (London, Routledge for the International Institute for Strategic Studies: 2008)

Charles Perrow, 'Normal accidents: living with high-risk technologies', (Princeton NJ, Princeton University Press: 1999)

Steven Pifer & Michael O'Hanlon, 'The opportunity: the next steps in reducing nuclear arms', (Washington DC, Brookings Institution Press: 2012)

Joseph Pilat & Robert Pendley, 'A new beginning for the NPT', (New York, Plenum Press: 1995)

Anna Pluta & Peter Zimmerman, 'Nuclear terrorism: a disheartening dissent', Survival, 48:2 (2006) pp.55–69

Jonathan Pollack, 'No exit: North Korea, nuclear weapons and international security', Adelphi Paper 418–419, (Abingdon, Routledge for the International Institute for Strategic Studies: 2011)

Kenneth Pollack, 'Unthinkable: Iran, the bomb and American strategy', (New York, Simon & Schuster: 2013)

William Potter & Gaukhar Mukhatzhanova, 'Divining nuclear intentions: a review essay', International Security, 33:1 (2008) pp.139–169

William Potter with Gaukhar Mukhatzhanova (eds.), 'Forecasting nuclear proliferation in the 21st century', Volumes 1 & 2, (Stanford, Stanford University Press: 2010)

William Potter & Gaukhar Mukhatzhanova (eds.), 'Nuclear politics and the Non-Aligned Movement: principles vs. pragmatism', Adelphi Paper 427, (Routledge for the International Institute for Strategic Studies: 2012)

William Potter & John Shields (eds.), 'Dismantling the Cold War: US and NIS perspectives on the Nunn–Lugar Cooperative Threat Reduction program', (London, The MIT Press: 1997)

Ronald Powaski, 'Return to Armageddon: the United States and the nuclear arms race 1981–1999', (Oxford, Oxford University Press: 2000)

Pavel Podvig (ed.), 'Russian strategic nuclear forces', (Cambridge MA, The MIT Press: 2004)

Kenneth Pollack, 'Unthinkable: Iran, the bomb, and American strategy', (New York, Simon & Schuster: 2013)

Larry Poole & Cheryl Poole (eds.), 'EMP survival: how to prepare now and survive when an electromagnetic pulse destroys our power', (CreateSpace Independent Publishing Platform: 2011)

Charles Pritchard, 'Failed diplomacy: the tragic story of how North Korea got the bomb', (Washington DC, The Brookings Institution Press: 2007)

Peter Pry, 'War scare: Russia and America on the nuclear brink', (Westport CT, Greenwood Publishing Group: 1999)

Helen Purkitt & Stephen Burgess, 'South Africa's weapons of mass destruction', (Bloomington IN, Indiana University Press: 2005)

George Quester, 'Nuclear first strike: consequences of a broken taboo', (Baltimore MA, Johns Hopkins University Press: 2005)

George Quester, 'Preemption, prevention and proliferation: the threat and use of weapons in history', (London, Transaction Publishers: 2009)

Michael Quinlan, "Thinking about nuclear weapons": principles, problems, prospects', (Oxford, Oxford University Press: 2009)

Bennet Ramberg, 'Nuclear power plants as weapons for the enemy: an unrecognised military peril" (London, University of California Press: 1992)

Alisa Rebane (ed.), 'The new START Treaty between the US and Russia', Hauppauge NY, Nova Science Publishers Inc: 2011)

John Redick, Julio Carasales & Paulo Wrobel, 'Nuclear rapprochement: Argentina, Brazil, and the nonproliferation regime', The Washington Quarterly, 18:1 (1995) pp.107–122

Thomas Reid & Danny Stillman, 'The nuclear express: a political history of the bomb and its proliferation', (Minneapolis MN, Zenith Press: 2009)

Mitchell Reiss, 'Bridled ambition: why countries constrain their nuclear capabilities', (Washington DC, The Woodrow Wilson Centre Press: 1995)

Richard Rhodes, 'The making of the atomic bomb', (London, Simon & Schuster: 1986)

Richard Rhodes, 'Dark sun: the making of the hydrogen bomb', (London, Simon & Schuster: 1995)

Richard Rhodes, 'Arsenals of folly: the making of the nuclear arms race', (London, Simon & Schuster: 2008)

Richard Rhodes, 'The twilight of the bombs', (New York, Vintage Books: 2011)

Wu Riang, 'China's anxiety about US missile defences: a solution', Survival, 55:5 (2013) pp.29–52

Jeffrey Richelson, 'Spying on the bomb: American nuclear intelligence from Nazi Germany to Iran and North Korea', (New York, W.W. Norton & Co.: 2007)

Nick Ritchie, 'A nuclear weapons-free world? Britain, Trident and the challenges ahead', (Basingstoke, Palgrave Macmillan: 2012)

Nick Ritchie, 'Valuing and devaluing nuclear weapons', Contemporary Security Policy, 34:1 (2013) pp.146–173

BIBLIOGRAPHY

Nick Ritchie, 'Pathways and purposes for P-5 nuclear dialogue', European Leadership Network Policy Brief, (September 2013), www.europeanleadershipnetwork.org/medialibrary/2013/09/03/ca6e5ece/Nick%20Ritchie%20Pathways%20and%20Purposes%20for%20P%205%20Nuclear%20Dialogue%20E LN%20Policy%20Brief%20September%202013.pdf

Alan Robock, Luke Oman & Georgiy Stenchikov, 'Nuclear winter revisited with a modern climate model and current nuclear arsenals: still catastrophic consequences', Journal of Geophysical Research: Atmospheres, (1984–2012), 112: D13 (2007)

Denny Roy, 'Parsing Pyongyang's strategy', Survival, 52:1 (2010) pp.111–136

Maria Rost Rublee, 'Taking stock of the nuclear nonproliferation regime: using social psychology to understand regime effectiveness', International Studies Review, 10:3 (2008) pp.420–450

Maria Rost Rublee, 'Nonproliferation norms: why states choose nuclear restraint', (Athens GA, University of Georgia Press: 2009)

Maria Rost Rublee, 'Nuclear threshold states', The Nonproliferation Review, 17:1 (2010) pp.49–70

Bertrand Russell, 'Common sense and nuclear weapons' (London, Routledge: 2001)

Jan Ruzicka, 'Reflections on the 2010 NPT review conference', Medicine, Conflict and Survival, 26:4 (2010) pp.259–267

Jan Ruzicka & Nicholas Wheeler, 'The puzzle of trusting relationships in the Nuclear Nonproliferation Treaty', International Affairs, 86:1 (2010) pp.69–85

Randy Rydell, 'Looking back: going for Baruch: the nuclear plan that refused to go away', Arms Control Today, (June 2006), www.armscontrol.org/print/2064

Lora Saalman, 'The China–India nuclear crossroads: China, India and the new paradigm', (Washington DC, The Carnegie Endowment: 2012)

Carl Sagan, 'Nuclear war and climatic catastrophe: some policy implications', Foreign Affairs, 62:2 (Winter 1983–4) pp.257–292

Carl Sagan, Richard Turco, George W. Rathjens, Ronald H. Siegel, Starley L. Thompson, & Stephen H. Schneider, 'The nuclear winter debate', Foreign Affairs 65:1 (1986) pp.163–178

Scott Sagan, 'The limits of safety: organizations, accidents and nuclear weapons", (Princeton NJ, Princeton University Press: 1993)

Scott Sagan, "The perils of proliferation: organization theory, deterrence theory, and the spread of nuclear weapons', International Security, 18:4 (1994) pp.66–107

Scott Sagan, 'Why do states build nuclear weapons? Three models in search of a bomb', International Security, 21:3 (1996–7) pp.54–86

Scott Sagan, 'How to keep the bomb from Iran', Foreign Affairs, (2006) pp.45–59

Scott Sagan (ed.), 'Inside nuclear South Asia', (Stanford, Stanford University Press: 2009)

Scott Sagan, 'The causes of nuclear weapons proliferation', Annual Review of Political Science, 14 (2011) pp.225–244

Scott Sagan & Jane Vaynman, 'Introduction: reviewing the Nuclear Posture Review', The Nonproliferation Review, 18:1 (2011) pp.17–37

Scott Sagan & Jane Vaynman, 'Conclusion: lessons learned from the 2010 Nuclear Posture Review', The Nonproliferation Review, 18:1 (2011) pp.237–262

Scott Sagan & Kenneth Waltz, 'The spread of nuclear weapons: a debate renewed', (London/New York, W.W. Norton & Company: [1995] 2003)

Jean-Loup Samaan & David Gompert, 'French nuclear weapons, Euro-deterrence, and NATO', Contemporary Security Policy, 30:3 (2009) pp.486–504

Choe Sang-Hun, 'South Korea publicly blames the North for ship's sinking', New York Times, (19 May 2010), www.nytimes.com/2010/05/20/world/asia/20korea.html?ref=global-home&_r=0

Tom Sauer & Bob Van Der Zwaan, 'US tactical nuclear weapons in Europe after NATO's Lisbon summit: why their withdrawal is desirable and feasible', International Relations, 26:1 (2012) pp.78–100

Robert Scheer, 'With enough shovels: Reagan, Bush and nuclear war', (New York, Vintage Books: 1983)

Jonathan Schell, 'The fate of the earth', (London, Jonathan Cape Ltd: 1982)

Thomas Schelling & Morton Halperin, 'Strategy and arms control', (New York, Twentieth Century Fund: 1961)

Thomas Schelling 'Arms and influence', (New Haven CT, Yale University Press: 1966)

Thomas Schelling, 'The strategy of conflict', (Cambridge MA, Harvard University: 1960)

Thomas Schelling, 'The nuclear taboo', The Washington Post, (24 October 2005), http://online.wsj.com/news/articles/SB113010182444876942

Eric Schlosser, 'Command and control', (London, Penguin Books Ltd: 2013)

Mark Schneider, 'The nuclear forces and doctrine of the Russian Federation', Comparative Strategy, 27:5 (2008) pp.397–425

Stephen Schwartz (ed.), 'Atomic audit: the costs and consequences of US nuclear weapons since 1940', (Washington DC, The Brookings Institution Press: 1998)

Andrew Selth, 'Myanmar's nuclear ambitions', Survival, 52:5 (2010) pp.5–12

Mohamed Shaker, 'The Nuclear Non-Proliferation Treaty: origin and implementation 1959–1979', (London, Oceana Publications, Inc.: 1980)

Fred Shaprio (ed.), 'The Yale book of quotations', (Newhaven CN, Yale University Press: 2007)

Michael Sheehan, 'Arms control: theory and practice', (Oxford, Basil Blackwell Ltd: 1988)

John Shields & William Potter (eds.), 'Dismantling the Cold War: US and NIS perspectives on the Nunn-Lugar Cooperative Threat Reduction program', (London, The MIT Press: 1997)

Marlise Simons, 'Soviet atom test used thousands as guinea pigs, archives show', New York Times, (7 November 1993), www.nytimes.com/1993/11/07/world/soviet-atom-test-used-thousands-as-guinea-pigs-archives-show.html

John Simpson, 'Nuclear non-proliferation in the post-Cold War era', International Affairs, 70:1 (1994) pp.17–39

John Simpson, 'The nuclear non-proliferation regime: back to the future?', Disarmament Forum, 1 (2004) pp.5–16

Peter Singer & Allan Friedman, 'Cybersecurity and cyberwar: what everyone needs to know', (Oxford, Oxford University Press: 2014)

Jaswant Singh, 'Against nuclear apartheid', Foreign Affairs, 77:5 (1998) pp.41–52

Joseph Siracusa, 'Nuclear weapons: a very short introduction', (Oxford, Oxford University Press: 2008)

Scott Snyder & See-Won Byun, 'Cheonan and Yeonpyeong: the Northeast Asian response to North Korea's provocations', The RUSI Journal, 156:2 (2011) pp.74–81

Nikolai Sokov, 'The origins of and prospects for Russian nuclear doctrine', The Nonproliferation Review, 14:2, (2007) pp.207–226

Etel Solingen, 'Sanctions, statecraft and nuclear proliferation' (Cambridge, Cambridge University Press: 2012)

Leonard Spector & Avner Cohen, 'Israel's airstrike on Syria's reactor: implications for the non-proliferation regime', Arms Control Today, 38:6 (2008) pp.15–21

Peter Stein & Peter Feaver, 'Assuring control of nuclear weapons: evolution of Permissive Action Links', (Washington DC, Rowman & Littlefield: 1987)

Hannes Steyn, Richard Van Der Walt & Jan Van Loggerenberg, 'Nuclear armament and disarmament: South Africa's nuclear experience', (Lincoln, iUniverse Inc: 2007)

Jeremy Stocker, 'The United Kingdom and nuclear deterrence', Adelphi Paper 386, (Abingdon, Routledge for the International Institute for Strategic Studies: 2007)

Ronald Takaki, 'Hiroshima: why America dropped the atomic bomb', (London, Little, Brown & Company: 1995)

Strobe Talbott, 'Endgame: The inside story of SALT II', (New York: Harper & Row: 1979)

Nina Tannenwald, 'The nuclear taboo: the United States and the normative basis of nuclear non-use', International Organization, 53:3 (1999) pp.433–468

Nina Tannenwald, 'The nuclear taboo: the United States and the non-use of nuclear weapons since 1945', (Cambridge, Cambridge University Press: 2007)

Philip Taubman, 'The partnership: five cold warriors and their quest to ban the bomb', (New York, HarperCollins Publishers: 2012)

Edward Teller, 'The constructive uses of nuclear explosives', (New York, McGraw-Hill Inc: 1968)

Bruno Tertrais, 'The last to disarm? The future of France's nuclear weapons', The Nonproliferation Review 14:2 (2007) pp.251–273

Bruno Tertrais, 'The illogic of zero', The Washington Quarterly, 33:2 (2010) pp.125–138

Ramesh Thakur (eds.), 'Nuclear-weapons free zones', (Basingstoke, Palgrave Macmillan: 1998)

Bradley Thayer, 'The causes of nuclear proliferation and the utility of the nuclear non-proliferation regime', Security Studies, 4:3 (1995) pp.463–519

Phillip Traubman, 'The partnership: five cold warriors and their quest to ban the bomb', (New York: HarperCollins: 2013)

Richard Turco, Owen Toon, Thomas Ackerman, James Pollack & Carl Sagan, 'Climate and smoke: an appraisal of nuclear winter', Science, 247:4939 (1990) pp.166–176

Mark Valencia, 'The Proliferation Security Initiative: making waves in Asia', Adelphi Paper 376, (Oxford, Routledge for the International Institute for Strategic Studies: 2005)

J.W. de Villiers, Roger Jardine & Mitchell Reiss, 'Why South Africa gave up the bomb', Foreign Affairs, 72:5 (1993) pp.98–109

J. Samuel Walker, 'Prompt and utter destruction: Truman and the use of atomic bombs against Japan', (London, University of North Carolina Press: 1997)

J. Samuel Walker, 'Recent literature on Truman's atomic bomb decision: a search for middle ground', Diplomatic History, 29:2 (2005) pp.311–334

J. Samuel Walker, 'Three Mile Island: a nuclear crisis in historical perspective', (Berkeley CA, University of California Press: 2006)

Mark Walker, 'Nazi science: myth, truth, and the German atomic bomb', (New York, Basic Books, 2001)

William Walker, 'Nuclear weapons and the former Soviet republics', International Affairs, 68:2 (1992) pp.255–277

William Walker, 'A perpetual menace: nuclear weapons and international order', (London, Routledge: 2011)

William Walker, 'International affairs in the nuclear age, 1946–2013', International Affairs, 90:1 (2014) pp.107–123

Nick Paton Walsh, 'Russian nuclear theft alarms US', Guardian, (19 July 2002), www.theguardian.com/world/2002/jul/19/chechnya.nickpatonwalsh Kenneth Waltz, 'Why Iran should get the bomb', Foreign Affairs, 91:4 (2012) pp.2–5

Aiden Warren, 'The promises of Prague versus nuclear realities: from Bush to Obama', Contemporary Security Policy, 32:2 (2011) pp.432–547

Aidan Warren, 'The Obama administration's nuclear weapons strategy: the promises of Prague', (Abingdon, Routledge: 2014)

Eileen Welsome, 'The plutonium files: America's secret medical experiments in the Cold War', (New York, Dial Press: 1999)

Michael Wesley, 'It's time to scrap the NPT', Australian Journal of International Affairs, 59:3 (2005) pp.283–299

Robert Wilcox, 'Japan's secret war: Japan's race against time to build its own atomic bomb', (New York, Marlowe & Co.: 1995)

Dean Wilkening, 'Ballistic-missile defence and strategic stability', Adelphi Paper 334, (Oxford, Oxford University Press for the International Institute for Strategic Studies: 2000)

Clay Wilson, 'High Altitude Electromagnetic Pulse (HEMP) and high power microwave (HPM) devices: threat assessments', Congressional Research Service, (21 July 2008), www.fas.org/sgp/crs/natsec/RL32544.pdf

P.D. Wilson, 'The nuclear fuel cycle: from ore to waste' (Oxford, Oxford University Press: 1997)

Ward Wilson, 'Five myths about nuclear weapons', (New York, Houghton Mifflin Harcourt: 2013)

Christine Wing & Fiona Simpson, 'Detect dismantle, disarm: IAEA verification 1992–2005', (Washington DC, United States Institute of Peace Press: 2013)

Andrew Winner, 'The proliferation security initiative: the new face of interdiction', Washington Quarterly, 28:2 (2005) pp.129–143

James Wirtz and Peter Lavoy (eds.), 'Over the horizon proliferation threats', (Stanford CA, Stanford University Press: 2012)

Joel Wit, Daniel Poneman and Robert Gallucci, 'Going critical: the first North Korean nuclear crisis', (Washington DC, The Brookings Institution Press: 2004)

Lawrence Wittner, 'The struggle against the bomb: one world or none: a history of the world nuclear disarmament movement through 1953', (Stanford CA, Stanford University Press: 1993)

Lawrence Wittner, 'The struggle against the bomb: resisting the bomb: a history of the world nuclear disarmament movement, 1954–1970', (Stanford CA, Stanford University Press: 1995)

Lawrence Wittner, 'Towards nuclear abolition a history of the world nuclear disarmament movement: 1971–present', (Stanford CA, Stanford University Press: 2003)

Lawrence Wittner, 'Confronting the bomb: a short history of the nuclear disarmament movement', (Stanford CA, Stanford University Press: 2009)

Amy Woolf, 'Nunn–Lugar Cooperative Threat Reduction Programs: issues for Congress', Congressional Research Service, (23 March 2001), www.au.af.mil/au/awc/awcgate/crs/97-1027.pdf

Amy Woolf, 'Nuclear arms control: the Strategic Offensive Reductions Treaty', Congressional Research Service, (7 February 2011), www.fas.org/sgp/crs/nuke/RL31448.pdf

Amy Woolf, 'Non-strategic nuclear weapons', Congressional Research Service, (3 January 2014), http://fas.org/sgp/crs/nuke/RL32572.pdf

Amy Woolf, 'The New START Treaty: central limits and key provisions', Congressional Research Service, (8 January 2014), www.fas.org/sgp/crs/nuke/R41219.pdf

Toshi Yoshihra & James Holmes, 'Strategy in the second nuclear age: power, ambition and the ultimate weapons' (Washington DC, Georgetown University Press: 2012)

David Yost, 'France's new nuclear doctrine', International Affairs, 82:4 (2006) pp.701–721

David Yost, 'France's evolving nuclear strategy', Survival, 47:3 (2005) pp.117–146

David Yost, 'The US and extended deterrence in Europe', Adelphi Paper 326, (Oxford, Oxford University Press for the International Institute for Strategic Studies: 1999)

David Yost, 'Assurance and US extended deterrence in NATO', International Affairs 85:4 (2009) pp.755–780

Stephen Younger, 'The bomb: a new history', (New York, HarperCollins Publishers: 2009)

Steven Zaloga, 'The Kremlin's nuclear sword: the rise and fall of Russia's strategic nuclear forces, 1945–2000', (Washington DC, Smithsonian Institution Press: 2002)

Scott Zeman & Michael Amundson, 'Atomic culture: how we learned to stop worrying and love the bomb', (Boulder CO, University Press of Colorado: 2004)

Micah Zenko & Michael Cohen, 'Clear and present safety: the United States is more secure than Washington thinks', Foreign Affairs, 91:2 (2012) pp.79–93

Baohui Zhang, 'US missile defence and China's nuclear posture: changing dynamics of an offence–defence arms race', International Affairs, 87:3 (2011) pp.555–569

Hui Zhang, 'China's perspective on a nuclear-free world', The Washington Quarterly, 33:2 (2010) pp.139–155

INDEX

Able Archer 83 (1983), 84–85, 223
accidents. *See* nuclear accidents
Acheson, Dean, 174
active defence, 146–148, 223
Additional Protocol (IAEA), 194, 223
Afghan War (1979–1989), **207**
Afghanistan, **207**
Agni V (intercontinental ballistic
    missile), 43
Ahmadinejad, Mahmoud, 125, 127
air-launched cruise missiles (ALCMs), 39–40,
    43, 223
airburst, 78, 223
Al Qaeda, 154–155, 160, 161–162
Albright, David, 156, 161
Alexander, Danny, 99
Algeria, 33, 37, 180
Allison, Graham, 164
Antarctic Treaty (1961), **182**
Anthony, Ian, 98–99, 166–167
Anti Ballistic Missile (ABM) Treaty (1972),
    74, **137**, 147, 223
apocalyptic groups, 160
AQ Khan network
    Al Qaeda and, 161
    catalysts for, 117
    Libya and, 157, 158, 180
    North Korea and, 157, 158, 163
    overview, 155, 157–158, 224
    Pakistan and, 119, 157–158, 163
    threat of, 213
Arbatov, Alexei, 97
Argentina, 2, 179, **234**
Armenia, **235**
atom bomb (A-bomb), 22, 224
Atomic Weapons Establishment (AWE), 175
Atoms for Peace, 125, 194, 224
Aum Shinrikyo, 160
Australia, 15, 34, 36

Ball, Desmond, 82
ballistic missile defences (BMD), 103, 139,
    146–147, 224

ballistic missiles, 38, 40, 224. *See also*
    intercontinental ballistic missiles
    (ICBMs); submarine launched ballistic
    missiles (SLBMs)
Bangkok, Treaty of (1997), **182**
Barnaby, Frank, 35
Baruch, Bernard, 174
Baruch Plan, 174, 224
battlefield nuclear weapons, 38–39, **38**
Belarus, 2, 141–142, 179
Belgium, 3, 180, **234**
Berger, Andrea, 91, 93
Bhutto, Zulfikar Ali, 116, 158
Bikini Atoll. *See* 'Ivy Mike' test
bin Laden, Osama, 160, 161–162
Blair, Bruce, 201
Blank, Stephen, 96
Bockscar (aircraft), 20
bolt from the blue, 75, 224
bomb shelters, 148. *See also* passive defence
bombers, 38, 39–40, 42
Booth, Ken, 72
Bowen, Wyn, 125–126
Bracken, Paul, 57, 116
Brazil, 2, 64, 179, **234**
Brewer, Jonathan, 125–126
brinkmanship, 32, **82**, 224
Broken Arrow, 224
Bulgaria, **235**
Bull, Hedley, 135
Bulletin of the Atomic Scientists of Chicago
    (later *Bulletin of the Atomic Scientists*),
    174
Bush, George H. W., 137–138
Bush, George W., 167

Caesium-137, 35
Campaign for Nuclear Disarmament (CND),
    175, 176, **177**, 224
Canada, 17, **234**
Carter, Ashton, 197
Castle Bravo nuclear test (1954), 36
centrifuges, 15, 158, 196, 224

Cha, Victor, 57
Chagai I (underground nuclear tests), 118, 224
Chagai II (underground nuclear tests), 118, 224
chain reaction, 14–15, 17, 22, 224
Chalmers, Malcolm, 91, 93
Chechen rebels, 160
Chernobyl nuclear disaster (Ukraine, 1986), 4, 192, 193, 224
China
 AQ Khan network and, 158
 civilian nuclear power and, **234**
 Comprehensive Test Ban Treaty and, 33
 current nuclear forces of, 43
 hydrogen bombs and, 23
 India and, 116
 nuclear deterrence and, 73, 78, 102–104
 nuclear disarmament and, 102–104
 nuclear testing and, **3**, 33, **33**
 nuclear weapons stockpiles in, 2, 3, **3**, 54–55
 Partial Test Ban Treaty and, 31–32
 role of nuclear weapons in, 212
 South Asian nuclear balance and, 119–120
 triad of nuclear forces and, 42
 United States and, 95
Cimbala, Stephen, 203
civil defense, 148–149
civilian nuclear power, 4, 15–16, 163, 192–196, **234–235**. *See also* nuclear accidents; nuclear latency
Clinton, Bill, 121
cobalt bombs, 35
Cohen, Avner, 61, 113, 115
Cohen, Michael, 165
Cold Start doctrine, 119, 224
cold tests (sub-critical tests), 117, 225
Cold War, 2, 73, 79, 137, 225. *See also* Cuban Missile Crisis (1962)
Comprehensive Safeguards Agreement, 144
Comprehensive Test Ban Treaty (CTBT) (1996), 4, 30, 31–33, 136, 178, 225
contamination, 34–37, 225
continuation of government (CoG), 225
Continuous At Sea Deterrence (CASD), 43, 99–100, 225
Convention on Physical Protection of Nuclear Material and Nuclear Facilities, 165, 225
Cooperative Threat Reduction (CTR) programme, 164–165
Cottee, Matthew, 101
counter-force, **79**, 225
counter-proliferation, 166–167
counter-value, 76, **79**, 225
critical mass, 14, 16, 18, 20, 225
cruise missiles, 40, 42

CTBT Organisation (CTBTO), 32–33
Cuban Missile Crisis (1962), 5, 84, 175, 225
cyber weapons, 203–204
Czech Republic, **234**

Daghlian, Harry, 36
Dahlman, Ola, 32
Davy Crocket recoilless gun, 42
de-alerting, 225
De Klerk, F. W., 179
de-mating, 201
de-targeting, 201, 226
Dead Hand, 202, 225
decommissioning, 54, 225
Democratic People's Republic of Korea (DPRK). *See* North Korea
depleted uranium, 226
Diakov, Anatoli, 139
Dibblin, Jane, 36
Ding, Arthur, 63–64
dirty bombs, 163, 226
domestic politics model, 52, **53**
Doomsday Clock, 174, 226
doomsday machine, 202
Dr Strangelove (film), 198–200
dual-use technology, 156, 226
Duqu (virus), 204
Dvokin, Vladimir, 96–97

The Economist (newspaper), 123
Edelman, Eric, 127
Egypt, 2, 114
Einstein, Albert, 16, 17, 174–175
Einstein-Szilard letter, 17
Eisenhower, Dwight, 194
ElBaradei, Mohammed, 62
Electromagnetic Pulse (EMP) waves, 35, 226
$E=MC^2$, 16, 226
enhanced radiation weapons (ERW), 35, 226
Enola Gay (aircraft), 20, 226
escalation, 81–85, **82**
ETA (Spain), 160
European Nuclear Disarmament (END) group, 176, **177**
extended nuclear deterrence, 79–80, 226

Falklands War (1982), **207**
Fat Man (nuclear bomb dropped on Nagasaki, 1945), 19, 20–22, **20**, 24–25, **24**, 226
Feaver, Peter, 201
Federation of American Scientists (FAS), 174
Ferguson, Charles, 160, 195
fighter aircraft, 39–40
films, 198–200, 236–238
Finland, **234**
fissile material, 14–16, 157, 164, 226

Fissile Material Cut-Off Treaty (FMCT), 136, 166, 195, 226
fission, 14–16, 22, 226
Flame (virus), 204
force de dissuasion, 43, 101–102, 226
force de frappe, 101, 226
four horseman of the nuclear apocalypse, 173, 182–183, 227
France
  civilian nuclear power and, 193–194, **234**
  Cold War and, 80
  Comprehensive Test Ban Treaty and, 31–32, 33
  current nuclear forces of, 43
  force de dissuasion and, 43, 101–102, 226
  hydrogen bombs and, 23
  Israel and, 112
  nuclear deterrence and, 78
  nuclear disarmament and, 101–102, 138–139
  nuclear testing and, **3**, 33, **33**, 37
  nuclear weapons stockpiles in, 2, 3, **3**, 54–55
  Partial Test Ban Treaty and, 31–32
  role of nuclear weapons in, 212
Fravel, Taylor, 103–104
Freedman, Lawrence, 74
Frisch, Otto, 18
fuel cycle, 195–196, 227
Fuhrmann, Matthew, 195
Fukushima nuclear disaster (Japan, 2011), 4, 193, 213, 227
fusion, 22–23, 227

Gaddafi, Muammar, 180
the gadget, 18–19, 232
Gandhi, Indira, 117
Garrison, Dee, 148–149
geiger counter, 227
Geneva Interim Agreement (2013), 125, 227
Germany, 3, 17, 34, 180, **234**
Global Initiative to Combat Nuclear Terrorism (GICNT), 167
Global Zero agenda, 102, 172, 182–186, 227
Goldblat, Jozef, 181
Gorbachev, Mikhail, 137–138, 173, 176–177
gravity bombs, 42, 227
Gray, Colin, 82, 206
Greenpeace, 34, 175, **177**
ground burst detonations, 78
Groves, Leslie, 17–18

Hahn, Otto, 16–17
Halperin, Morton, 135
Hanson, Marianne, 143
hard targets, 78
Herzog, Rudolph, 5, 32

Hezbollah, 127, 160
highly enriched uranium (HEU), 15, 16, 227
Hiroshima, atomic bombing of (1945), 20–22, **20**, 24–25, **24**, 228
Hollande, Francois, 101
horizontal proliferation
  definition of, 227
  India and, 116–120
  Iran and, 124–128
  Israel and, 111–115, **115**
  North Korea and, 120–124
  overview, 54–56, **54–55**, **56**
  Pakistan and, 116–120
  threat of, 110–111
Howard, Michael, 83
Humanitarian Initiative to Prohibit Nuclear Weapons, 24, 183, 185
Hungary, **234**
Hussein, Saddam, 158, 179–180
hydrogen bombs (H-bombs, thermo-nuclear bombs), 22–23, 36, 227. *See also* neutron bombs
Hymans, Jacques, 51, 52

Ikle, Fred, 58–59
illicit nuclear trade, 155–157, 162–163. *See also* AQ Khan network
India
  civilian nuclear power and, 193–194, **234**
  Cold Start doctrine and, 119
  Comprehensive Test Ban Treaty and, 33
  current nuclear forces of, 43
  Kargil War and, 5, 85, 118, 228
  Maoist guerrillas in, 160
  nuclear deterrence and, 73
  Nuclear Non-Proliferation Treaty and, 2, 141, 143
  nuclear testing and, **3**, 32, 33, **33**, 34
  nuclear weapons stockpiles in, 2, 3, **3**
  role of nuclear weapons in, 212
  triad of nuclear forces and, 42
Inter-Service Intelligence (ISI), 118
intercontinental ballistic missiles (ICBMs), 38, 40, 42, 138, 227
interdiction, 166–167. *See also* counter-proliferation
Intermediate Nuclear Forces Treaty (INF) (1987), **137**
intermediate range ballistic missiles (IRBMs), 38, 40
International Atomic Development Authority (IADA), 174
International Atomic Energy Agency (IAEA), 62–63, 121–122, 136, 140, 144, 194, 227
International Campaign Against Nuclear Weapons (ICAN), 183–184
International Campaign to Abolish Nuclear Weapons (ICAN), **177**, 178

International Fuel Bank (Nuclear Fuel
    Bank), 227
International Nuclear Event Scale, 193
International Physicians for the Prevention
    of Nuclear War (IPPNW), 176, **177**, 178
Iodine-131, 35
ionising radiation, 34–35
Iran
    AQ Khan network and, 157, 158
    civilian nuclear power and, 193–194, **235**
    Comprehensive Test Ban Treaty and, 33
    Middle East Nuclear Weapons Free Zone
        and, 181–182
    nuclear deterrence and, 73
    nuclear latency and, 64
    Nuclear Non-Proliferation Treaty and, 2–3
    as nuclear outlier, 124–128
    Stuxnet and, 204
Iraq, 2, 114, 157, 179–180
Irish Republican Army (IRA), 160
irradiated fuel, 195–196
isotopes, 14–16, 227
Israel
    civilian nuclear power and, 193–194
    Comprehensive Test Ban Treaty and, 33
    current nuclear forces of, 43–44
    Iran and, 127
    Middle East Nuclear Weapons Free Zone
        and, 181–182
    Nuclear Non-Proliferation Treaty and,
        141, 143
    nuclear opacity and, 111–115, **115**
    nuclear testing and, **3**, 33
    nuclear weapons stockpiles in, 2, 3, **3**
    role of nuclear weapons in, 212
    Stuxnet and, 204
    Syrian air defence and, 204
Israeli Atomic Energy Commission
    (IAEC), 112
Italy, 3, 180
'Ivy Mike' test (1952), 23, **24**

Jafarzadeh, Alireza, 125
Jamaat al Islamiya (Indonesia), 160
Japan
    atomic bombing of Hiroshima and
        Nagasaki, 19, 20–22, **20**, 24–25, **24**
    Aum Shinrikyo and, 160
    civilian nuclear power and, **234**
    nuclear deterrence and, 73
    nuclear latency and, 63
    World War II and, 17
Joe 1 (Russian nuclear bomb), 19, 227
Journe, Venance, 102

Kahn, Herman, 207
Kargil War (1999), 5, 85, 118, 228
Kazakhstan, 2, 141–142, 179

Kennedy, John F., 49, 175
Khamenei, Ali, 126
Khan, Abdul Qadeer (AQ), 117, 157–158.
    See also AQ Khan network
Khan, Feroz Hassan, 118
Khan, Herman, 83
Khan Research Laboratories (KRL), 158
Kiloton (Kt), 228
Kim Il-Jung, 121–122
Kim Il-Sung, 121
Kim Jong-Il, 123
Kim Jong-Un, 122, 123
Kirana I nuclear test (), 117
Kissinger, Henry, 182–183
Korean War (1950–1953), **207**
Kosygin, Alexei, 146
Kubrick, Stanley, 198–200

Larson, Jeffrey, 135
Libya, 2, 157, 158, 180
Lilienthal, David, 174
limited nuclear deterrence, 77–78, **77**
Limited Test Ban Treaty (LTBT). *See* Partial
    Test Ban Treaty (PTBT) (1963)
Little Boy (nuclear bomb dropped on
    Hiroshima, 1945), 20–22, **20**, 24–25,
    24, 228
Lodgaard, Sverre, 91
long-range strategic bombers, 38, 39–40, 42
loose nukes, 163, 164–165, 228
low enriched uranium (LEU), 15, 195, 228
Lucky Dragon (Japanese fishing boat), 36
Lugar, Richard, 164–165

Mahmood, Bashiruddin, 161
Manhattan Project, 17–22, 36, 174, 228
Mao Tse Tung, 84
Maoist guerrillas, 160
Marshall Islands. *See* Castle Bravo nuclear
    test (1954)
maximum nuclear deterrence, 77–78, **77**
McDonough, David, 95
Medeiros, Evan, 103–104
medium-range ballistic missiles (MRBMs),
    38, 40
Megaton (Mt), 228
Meir, Golda, 112–113
meltdown, 163, 192–193, 228
Mexico, **235**
Middle East Nuclear Weapons Free Zone
    (MENWFZ), 181–182
Miller, Marvin, 115
Miller, Steven, 91
minimum nuclear deterrence, 76, **77**, 78,
    98–100, 102–104, 228
Minuteman I warheads, 24
Minuteman III Intercontinental Ballistic
    Missiles, 42

mixed oxide fuel (MOX), 195–196, 228
Mongolian Nuclear Weapons Free Zone, **182**
Moran, Matthew, 101
Morin, Herve, 37
Mueller, John, 145, 160–161
Mueller, Karl, 145
multiple independently targetable re-entry
    vehicles (MIRV), 138, 228
mushroom cloud, 19, 32, 228
Mutual Assured Destruction (MAD), 4–5,
    73–76, 205, 213, 228
Mutual Defence Agreement (MDA), 98
Myanmar (Burma), 158, 180

Nader, Alireza, 145
Nagasaki, atomic bombing of (1945), 19,
    20–22, **20**, 24–25, **24**, 226
National Committee for a Sane Nuclear
    Policy (SANE), **177**
national missile defences (NMD), 147
national security, 50–52, **53**, 96–98, 212
nationalist groups, 160
Nazi Germany, 17
Nehru, Jawaharlal, 174–175
neo-Nazi parties, 160
Netherlands, 3, 180, **235**
neutron bombs, 35, 228
New Strategic Arms Reduction Treaty
    (New START Treaty) (2010), 4, 94, **138**,
    186, 229
new triad of strategic forces, 94
Newhouse, John, 21, 176–177
Nikita, Khrushchev, 83
Nixon, Richard, 112–113
No-First Use (NFU) policy, 76, 78, 96,
    103, 229
Non-Aligned Movement (NAM),
    92, 229
Non-Nuclear Weapons States (NNWS), 2,
    90–92, **92**, 140–141, 212–213, 229
non-proliferation, 166–167, 213–214. *See
    also* Nuclear Non-Proliferation Treaty
    (NPT) (1968)
non-strategic nuclear weapons, 38–39, **38**
norm of non-use, 82, 205–206, **207**. *See also*
    nuclear taboo
norms model, 52, **53**
North Atlantic Treaty Organisation (NATO),
    3, 80
North Korea
    AQ Khan network and, 157, 158, 163
    civilian nuclear power and, 193–194
    Comprehensive Test Ban Treaty and, 33
    current nuclear forces of, 43
    nuclear deterrence and, 73
    Nuclear Non-Proliferation Treaty and,
        2, 141, 143
    as nuclear outlier, 120–124, **124**

North Korea *cont.*
    nuclear testing and, **3**, **24**, 31, 32, 33,
        33, 122
    nuclear weapons stockpiles in, 2, 3, **3**
    Partial Test Ban Treaty and, 31–32
    role of nuclear weapons in, 212
North Korean Nuclear Crisis (1993–1994),
    121–122
North Korean Nuclear Crisis (2002–2006),
    122
Norwegian Rocket Incident (1995), 85, 229
NPT Review Conferences (RevCons), 92,
    178, 181, 182
nuclear accidents
    civilian nuclear power and, 4, 192–193, 213
    nuclear weapons and, 198–200, **199**
nuclear apartheid, 212, 229
nuclear arms control, 134–140
nuclear deterrence
    definition of, 229
    extended nuclear deterrence, 79–80
    MAD and, 4–5, 205, 213
    nuclear posture, 76–78, **77**
    security dilemma and, 71–73
nuclear disarmament
    China and, 102–104
    France and, 101–102, 138–139
    Global Zero agenda and, 102, 172,
        182–186, 227
    history of, 172–178
    nuclear arms control and, 135
    Nuclear Non-Proliferation Treaty and,
        89–93, **92**
    Nuclear Weapons Free Zones and, 172,
        181–182, **182**, 213, 214, 230
    role of, 213–214
    Russia and, 96–98
    South Africa and, 2, 136, 179
    successes of, 178–181
    United Kingdom and, 98–100, **100**, 136,
        138–139
    United States and, 93–96
Nuclear Freeze movement, 176
nuclear latency, 60–65
Nuclear Non-Proliferation Treaty (NPT)
    (1968)
    Brazil and, 64
    civilian nuclear power and, 4, 62,
        194–195
    Iran and, 64
    Japan and, 63
    North Korea and, 121–122
    nuclear disarmament and, 89–93, **92**
    overview, 140–143, **142**, 229
    signatories of, 2
    See also NPT Review Conferences
        (RevCons)
nuclear opacity, 229

nuclear outliers
  India as, 116–120
  Iran as, 124–128
  Israel as, 111–115, **115**
  North Korea as, 120–124, **124**
  Pakistan as, 116–120
  threat of, 110–111
nuclear posture, 76–78, **77**
nuclear proliferation
  civilian nuclear power and, 193–194
  debate on, 56–60, **58**, **60**
  nuclear latency and, 60–65
  reasons for, 50–52, **53**
  See also horizontal proliferation; vertical
    proliferation
nuclear security, 164–166
Nuclear Security Summits, 165–166, 186
nuclear strategy
  escalation and, 81–85, **82**
  extended nuclear deterrence and, 79–80
  MAD and, 4–5, 73–76, 205, 213, 228
  nuclear posture and, 76–78, **77**
  security dilemma and, 71–73
  targeting strategy and, 78–79, **79**
Nuclear Suppliers Group (NSG), 119, 167,
  194–195, 229
nuclear taboo, 82, 94–95, 204–206, **207**,
  214, 229
nuclear terrorism, 127, 154–155, 159–167,
  161, 213
nuclear testing
  cold tests and, 117, 225
  Comprehensive Test Ban Treaty and, 4,
    30, 31–33, 136, 178, 225
  effects of, 4, 30–31, 35–37
  North Korea and, 122
  overview, **3**, 31–34, 117–118
  Partial Test Ban Treaty and, 30, 31–32,
    175, 228, 230
  Peaceful Nuclear Explosions and, 33–34,
    116–117, 175, 230
  Threshold Test Ban Treaty and, 32, 232
  See also Vela Incident (1979)
nuclear war, 1–2, 81–85
nuclear waste, 194, 195–196, 229
nuclear weapons
  command and control of, 197–204, **197**, **199**
  current nuclear forces by state, 42–44
  current stockpiles of, 2–4, **3**, 54–55, **54–55**
  definition of, 229
  delivery of, 39–42, **41**
  effects of, 23–25, **24**
  future of, 211–214
  genesis of, 16–19
  key ingredients of, 14–16
  in popular culture, 198–200, 236–238
  timeline, 216–222
  types of, 37–39, **38**

Nuclear Weapons Convention (NWC),
  92, 136, 229
Nuclear Weapons Free Zones (NWFZ)
  definition of, 230
  Middle East and, 114–115, 181–182
  overview, 172, 181–182, **182**
  spread of, 214
  view of nuclear weapons in, 213
Nuclear Weapons States (NWS)
  nuclear disarmament and, 89–93, **92**
  overview, 2, 140–141, 230
  role of nuclear weapons in, 212
nuclear winter, 1, 23–24, 230
Nunn, Sam, 164–165, 182–183
Nunn-Lugar nuclear threat reduction
  programme, 164–165
Nye, Joseph, 1

Obama, Barack
  Israel and, 112
  nuclear disarmament and, 93–94, 102,
    172, 173, 183, 184–185
  Nuclear Security Summits and, 165–166
  on nuclear terrorism, 159
O'Hanlon, Michael, 139–140
one-point safe, 201
Operation Olympic Games, 204
Operation Plowshare, 33–34, 230
Oppenheimer, J. Robert, 17–18, 19
Osirak nuclear reactor (Iraq), 114, 230
Outer Space Treaty (1967), **182**

P5, 89, 230. *See also* Nuclear Weapons
  States (NWS)
P5 process, 93, 214, 230
Pakistan
  AQ Khan network and, 157–158, 163
  civilian nuclear power and, 193–194, **234**
  Comprehensive Test Ban Treaty and, 33
  current nuclear forces of, 43
  Kargil War and, 5, 85, 118, 228
  NPT and, 2
  nuclear deterrence and, 73
  Nuclear Non-Proliferation Treaty and,
    141, 143
  nuclear testing by, **3**, 32, 33, **33**
  nuclear weapons stockpiles in, 3, **3**
  role of nuclear weapons in, 212
Pakistan Atomic Energy Committee
  (PAEC), 117
Partial Test Ban Treaty (PTBT) (1963), 30,
  31–32, 175, 228, 230
passive defence, 148–149, 230
Paul, T. V., 205–206
Peace Action, 175
Peaceful Nuclear Explosions (PNEs), 33–34,
  116–117, 175, 230
Peierls, Rudolf, 18

Pelindaba, Treaty of (2009), **182**
Permissive Action Links (PALs), 200, 230
Perry, William, 182–183
Persian Gulf War (1990–1991), **207**
Personnel Reliability Programmes (PRP), 200–201
Petrochemical-3 (Iraqi nuclear weapons programme), 179, 230
Pifer, Stephen, 139–140
Pilat, Joseph, 61
plutonium, 14–16, 18–19, 230
plutonium separation, 15
point defence, 147
Pokhran I (Smiling Buddha nuclear test) (1974), 34, 116–117, 230, 231
Pokhran II nuclear test (1998), 117, 230
politico-religious groups, 160
Pollack, Jonathan, 63, 120, 122
Pollack, Kenneth, 126
population defence, 147
Potsdam Declaration, 19–20
Potter, William, 160
Presidential Nuclear Initiatives (PNI), 136, 137–138
Proliferation Security Initiative (PSI), 167
Pugwash Conferences on Science and World Affairs (Canada), 175, **177**
Putin, Vladimir, 167

Quester, George, 145
Quinlan, Michael, 81

radiation, 34–37, 231
radiation sickness, 34–35, 231
radioactive fallout, 34–35, 231
radioactivity, 34–37
radiological dispersal devices (RDD, dirty bombs), 163, 226
Rarotonga, Treaty of (1986), **182**
RDS 1. See Joe 1 (Russian nuclear bomb)
Reagan, Ronald, 149, 173, 176–177
Reiss, Mitchell, 63
reprocessing, 194–196, 231
Republic of Korea (ROK). See South Korea
RevCons. See NPT Review Conferences (RevCons)
Rhodes, Richard, 19
Ritchie, Nick, 93, 98
Robock, Alan, 24
Roentgen Equivalent in Man (REM), 231
Romania, **235**
Roosevelt, Franklin, 17
Rosenburg, Julius and Ethel, 19
Rotblat, Joseph, 89–90
Roy, Denny, 123–124
Rublee, Maria Rost, 63
Russell, Bertrand, 174–175
Russell, James, 64

Russell-Einstein Manifesto (1955), 175
Russia
  bilateral agreements and, 136–137
  Chechen rebels and, 160
  civilian nuclear power and, **234**
  Comprehensive Test Ban Treaty and, 33
  current nuclear forces of, 42–43
  national security and, 96–98
  New START Treaty and, 4
  nuclear deterrence and, 78
  nuclear disarmament and, 96–98
  nuclear testing by, **3**, 33, **33**
  nuclear weapons stockpiles in, 2, 3, **3**, 54–55
  role of nuclear weapons in, 212
  triad of nuclear forces and, 42
  United States and, 95–96
Rutherford, Ernest, 16

Saalman, Lora, 104
Sagan, Carl, 24
Sagan, Scott, 51–52, 59–60, 200
Samson Option, 113, 231
Sane Nuclear Policy (SANE), 175, 176
Sarkozy, Nicolas, 101, 102
Saudi Arabia, 64
Schelling, Thomas, 135, 204
Schlosser, Eric, 198, 202
Scotland, 100
Scottish National Party (SNP), 100
Seabed Treaty (1972), **182**
second nuclear age, 57–60, **58**
security dilemma, 71–73
security model, 51–52. See also national security
Semei, Treaty of (2009), **182**
separatist groups, 160
ship submersible ballistic nuclear (SSBN), 41, 75, 99–100, 231
ships, 40–41
short-range ballistic missiles (SRBM), 40
short-range nuclear attack missiles (SRAM II), 138
Shoumikhin, Andrei, 98
Shultz, George, 182–183
Single Integrated Operational Plan (SIOP), 202
single-issue terrorists, 160
Sino-Vietnamese War (1979), **207**
Six-Day War (1967), 112
Six Party talks, 122, 231
Slotin, Louis, 36
Slovakia, **234**
Slovenia, **235**
Smiling Buddha nuclear test (1974), 34, 116–117, 230, 231
Smith, James, 135
soft targets, 78

Sokov, Nikolai, 97
Solimoes Project, 179, 231
Solingen, Etel, 144–145
South Africa
 civilian nuclear power and, 193–194, **235**
 Comprehensive Test Ban Treaty and, 33
 nuclear disarmament and, 2, 136, 179
 Nuclear Non-Proliferation Treaty and, 141–142
 nuclear testing and, 113
 nuclear testing by, 33
South Korea
 civilian nuclear power and, 63, **234**
 North Korea and, 73, 121, 122–123
 nuclear programme and, 2, 63, 180
Soviet Union
 bilateral agreements and, 136–137, **137–138**
 Cold War and, 73, 80
 Dead Hand and, 202
 hydrogen bombs and, 23
 Joe 1 and, 19, 227
 loose nukes and, 163, 164–165
 nuclear deterrence and, 80
 nuclear espionage and, 19
 nuclear testing and, 23, **24**, 32, 33–34, **33**, 36
 Peaceful Nuclear Explosions and, 33–34
 Potsdam Declaration and, 19
Spain, **234**
spent fuel, 195–196
Sputnik satellite, 231
Stalin, Joseph, 19
Strassman, Fritz, 16–17
Strategic Arms Limitation Treaty (SALT) (1972), **137**
Strategic Arms Limitation Treaty (SALT II) (1979), **137**
Strategic Arms Reduction Treaty II (START II) (1993), 138, **138**
Strategic Arms Reductions Treaty I (START I) (1991), 138, **138**
strategic battlefield nuclear weapons, 38–39, **38**
Strategic Defence Review (SDR), 99
Strategic Defense Initiative (SDI) (1983), 84–85, 147, 177, 231
Strategic Offensive Reductions Treaty (SORT/ Moscow Treaty) (2002), **138**
Strontium-90, 35
Stuxnet (virus), 204, 231
sub-critical tests (cold tests), 117, 225
submarine launched ballistic missiles (SLBMs), 38, 42, 43, 231
submarine launched cruise missiles (SLCMs), 41, 232
submarines, 40–41, 43. *See also* ship submersible ballistic nuclear (SSBN)

suitcase bombs, 42, 232
Sweden, 2, 180, **234**
Sweeney, Charles, 20
Switzerland, 2, 180, **234**
Syria, 2, 114, 157, 158, 180, 204
Szilard, Leo, 17

Taiwan, 2, 63–64, 73, 180, **234**
Tamil Tigers (Sri Lanka), 160
Tannenwald, Nina, 205
targeting strategy, 78–79, **79**
Taubman, Philip, 183
technological determinism, 52, 53, 232
Teller, Edward, 22
terrorism. *See* nuclear terrorism
Tertrais, Bruno, 101
theatre missile defences (TMD), 147
thermo-nuclear bombs (hydrogen bombs), 22–23, 36, 227. *See also* neutron bombs
Three Mile Island (USA) (1979), 4, 192–193, 232
threshold nuclear weapons capability, 232
threshold nuclear weapons states, 61
Threshold Test Ban Treaty (TTBT) (1974), 32, 232
Tibbets, Paul, 20
Tlatelolco, Treaty of (1969), **182**
transmutation, 17
triad of nuclear forces, 41–42
Trinity Test (1945), 18–19, 232
Truman, Harry, 19
Tsar Bomba, **24**, 32, 232
Tube Alloys, 17, 232
Turkey, 3, 180
two-man rule, 200–201

Ukraine, 2, 141–142, 179, **234**
Ummah Tameer-e-Nau (UTN) network, 161, 232
UN Security Council, 89, 121–122, 232
United Arab Emirates, **235**
United Kingdom
 anti-nuclear demonstrations in, 176
 civilian nuclear power and, **234**
 Cold War and, 80
 Comprehensive Test Ban Treaty and, 33
 current nuclear forces of, 43
 hydrogen bombs and, 23
 Manhattan Project and, 17
 nuclear deterrence and, 78, 98–100
 nuclear disarmament and, 98–100, **100**, 136, 138–139
 nuclear testing by, **3**, 33, **33**, 36
 nuclear weapons stockpiles in, 2, 3, **3**, 54–55
 role of nuclear weapons in, 212
 Trident replacement and, 98–100
 Tube Alloys and, 17

United Nations (UN), 89, 121–122, 136, 144, 165, 174, 232
United Nations Office of Disarmament Affairs (UNODA), 174
United States
  bilateral agreements and, 136–137, **137–138**
  civilian nuclear power and, **234**
  Cold War and, 73
  Comprehensive Test Ban Treaty and, 178
  current nuclear forces of, 42
  hydrogen bombs and, 23
  Israel and, 112–113
  Manhattan Project and, 17–22, 36, 174, 228
  New START Treaty and, 4
  new triad and, 93–96
  nuclear deterrence and, 78, 80
  nuclear disarmament and, 93–96
  nuclear testing and, **3**, 18–19, **24**, 32, 33–34, **33**, 36, 175, 232
  nuclear weapons stockpiles in, 2, 3, **3**, 54–55
  Peaceful Nuclear Explosions and, 33–34, 175
  Presidential Nuclear Initiatives and, 136, 137–138
  role of nuclear weapons in, 212
  Stuxnet and, 204
  triad of nuclear forces and, 42
  See also Obama, Barack
unwarranted nuclear use, **197**, 198–200
uranium, 14–16, 15, 18, 232
uranium enrichment, 15, 233
Uranverein Project, 17, 233
URENCO, 157–158
US–India Civil Nuclear Agreement, 118, 233
used fuel, 195–196

Vanunu, Mordachai, 112
Vela Incident (1979), 33, 113, 179, 233

vertical proliferation
  commitment to nuclear disarmament and, 89–93, **92**
  definition of, 233
  overview, 54–56, **54–55**, **56**
Vietnam War (1965–1973), **207**
virtual nuclear weapon states, 61, 233
vitrification, 233

W-76 warhead, **24**
Walker, J. Samuel, 22
The Wall Street Journal, 182–183
Waltz, Kenneth, 59–60, 127–128
weapons of mass destruction (WMD), 114, 165, 233
Wells, HG, 173
West Germany, 180
Westley, Michael, 143
Wheeler, Nicholas, 72
White Sands Proving Ground nuclear testing (Trinity Test, 1945), 18–19, 232
Wigner, Eugene, 17
Wilson, Clay, 35
Windscale nuclear accident (1957), 192, 233
Wittner, Lawrence, 173
Woolsey, James, 110–111
The world set free (Wells), 173
World War II
  atomic bombing of Hiroshima and Nagasaki, 19, 20–22, **20**, 24–25, **24**
  Manhattan Project and, 17
  Potsdam Declaration and, 19

yellowcake, 157, 233
Yeltsin, Boris, 85, 138
yield, 233
Yom Kippur War (1973), 112, **207**

Zala, Benjamin, 95
Zenko, Micah, 165
Zhang, Hui, 103
Zia-ul-Haq, Mohammad, 117